Moving On

From the Memoirs of the Late Sir Rupert Grayson

Bob Scholfield

Matador
9 Priory Business Park
Kibworth Beauchamp
Leicestershire LE8 0RX, UK
Tel: (+44) 116 279 2299
Fax: (+44) 116 279 2277
Email: books@troubador.co.uk
Web: www.troubador.co.uk/matador

ISBN 978 1783060 108

British Library Cataloguing in Publication Data.
A catalogue record for this book is available from the British Library.

Typeset in 11pt Aldine401 BT Roman by Troubador Publishing Ltd, Leicester, UK

Matador is an imprint of Troubador Publishing Ltd

For Bob

NOTE:

The "VOICE" throughout the script is that of the "present" Rupert Grayson looking back on the events portrayed.

FOREWORD

Born into the wealthy Liverpool shipbuilding family of Sir Henry Grayson, Sir Rupert Grayson, leaving Harrow, joined the Irish Guards and was wounded in World War I by the shell that killed Rudyard Kipling's son, John. Rupert roamed the world as a seafarer, talent scout, writer, King's Messenger, eccentric, romantic, epicure, wit, and friend of the colourful, gifted and famous. He married twice, but only briefly.

He was made a Knight of the Holy Sepulchre by the Pope and dodged death from a drugged-up army officer on the Moscow-Leningrad Express. He jumped ship as a seaman in New York, suspected of murdering the captain, travelled the world carrying secret documents to British Embassies, and encountered the traitor-spy Kim Philby. He devised a cocktail with Scott Fitzgerald in Paris one boozy night and discovered then-unpublished verses by Noel Coward in a remote guesthouse in Peru. His life, oiled by charm, threads through a string of enchanting interludes. He claimed to have dedicated himself "unselfishly and wholeheartedly to extracting as much pleasure from life as it has to offer" – a pleasure to be shared. Many of these adventures and much more are to be found in MOVING ON.

Bob met Rupert when both were living in Denia, Spain, in the 1970s. Both were writers and as Rupert grew older, he increasingly relied on Bob to help him with publishing some of his work, giving him written authority to edit and market this. I had the privilege of meeting Rupert several times myself towards the end of his life, when he had returned to the UK.

Rupert had published sixteen crime novels in the 1930s and, in 1969 and 1971, two volumes of memoirs. Bob was a freelance journalist.

In the late 1980s Bob had custody of most of Rupert's writing. Using everything that he had, Bob produced a Book at Bedtime script in six episodes, which was read on Radio Four in 1990. It was well received.

When Rupert died in 1991 at the age of 94, Bob put Rupert's memoirs together and, since the life described was so full of incident and adventure, saw it in a visual context – hence the film script. He completed this in the last year of his life, passing away in 2000.

I was bequeathed everything and so I started trying to contact film producers, television companies and publishers. I had much interest and positive feedback, but nothing definite became of it. I gained the interest of a literary agent, who suggested a biography would be better.

I then found three published writers who would possibly co-author such a book with me, but again, these all fell by the wayside for various reasons. After a while, I decided to try to rewrite the script into biographical form myself and completed several chapters. However, I realised the enormity of the task and had to abandon it due to various life changes.

I finally decided to go back to basics – that is, to take the script exactly as Bob wrote it and self-publish. It would make a wonderful film or documentary, but in any case, I believe Rupert's story is worth telling to a wider public.

Helen Scholfield

Helen and Bob, from their old friend Rupert. Florida 1989

*Continental departure platform at Charing Cross Station on a cold winter's night in 1909. Fog swirls around the gas lamps. A tall man (**Sir Henry Grayson**) and a boy (**Rupert Grayson**) of twelve, both well and warmly dressed, stand together by the door of a first-class carriage of the Paris boat train, about to board it. **A Porter** steps from train door to platform, touches his cap and smiles as **Sir Henry** hands him a sovereign, which he pockets.*

PORTER: Thankin' you, Sir Henry, the footwarmers are in your compartment. A safe and comfortable journey to you both.

SIR HENRY: Thank you, Jeffries.

*Farther along the platform, the **Guard**, red flag in hand, glances now and then from his silver watch to the station clock. The last hampers are loaded from trolleys to restaurant car. Steam billows from the giant engine, ready to go. A whistle shrills and a voice shouts "All aboard". The last passengers bustle on to the train, which bears the livery of the London, Chatham and Dover Railway.*

★ ★ ★ ★ ★

*CUT TO – Entrance to platform. The figure of a man materialises as it enters the light from the shadows beyond. At the same time, the **Stationmaster** emerges from his office, doffs his silk top hat to the newcomer and walks ahead to the door of his carriage, which he opens, and pauses by it. **Two Porters**, one carrying a travelling rug and the other pulling a trolley on which rest a suitcase and a large green and white-striped bag, follow. The **Gentleman** saunters down the platform with no sign of urgency, drawing on a cigar as he goes. The **Porters** enter the compartment with the **Gentleman's** belongings, followed by their owner, as the **Stationmaster**, with hat raised, bids him goodnight. The **Porters** leave the compartment and blinds are drawn down from within.*

★ ★ ★ ★ ★

CUT TO – *Close-up of* **Rupert** *looking up at* **Sir Henry's** *face, wonderingly.*

BOY: Who is that, Father?

SIR HENRY *[putting arm around son]*: That is the King's Messenger, travelling the world charged with the safety and security of secret dispatches.

Rupert *looks back at the window of the compartment the* **Gentleman** *has entered and keeps staring at it as a* **Porter** *begins to ring the departure bell.*

SIR HENRY: Come on or we'll miss it.

The pair walk towards their compartment, **Rupert** *dawdling thoughtfully while* **Sir Henry** *waits at the door for him to get aboard.*
★ ★ ★ ★ ★

CUT TO – *Inside compartment, where they dispose themselves comfortably.* **Rupert** *moving dreamily, preoccupied.*

SIR HENRY *[quizzically]*: Penny for your thoughts.

RUPERT *[after hesitating, in mock-solemn declaration]*: Well, Father, God willing, I, Rupert Stanley Harrington Grayson, will become the King's Messenger, travelling the world charged with the safety and security of secret despatches.

SIR HENRY: We'll see.
★ ★ ★ ★ ★

CUT TO – *In a train, forty years later.* **Rupert**, *middle-aged, is speeding through countryside in a compartment to himself. Close-up of label on his suitcase on the rack, which says "Johnson", then of a page of the notebook in which he is writing. Under the heading "Gratuities", alongside the date June 1949, he writes: "Porter, Victoria, £2". Through the window are hop fields, oasthouses, orchards and white cricketers* *on a village green – typical Kent on a late summer's evening with long shadows. In the distance, a farmer on a tractor hauls a trailer-load of hay homewards across a field. Cows and sheep are dotted about.*

VOICE: *[Rupert soliloquy, now cultivated, languid, reflective]* I made an excellent start in life, for I was born into a wealthy and loving family; and if the spoon in my mouth was not pure silver, it was surely richly plated. I had eleven brothers and sisters, and we had the best of everything: toys, tears, love and laughter. The summers were long and hot; the winters short, with ice and snow. It was always someone's birthday and however tall we grew, the Christmas tree grew taller, the decorations more exciting, the presents packed in bigger boxes.

Rupert *smiles wistfully as the scene fades to another of long ago.*

★ ★ ★ ★ ★

CUT TO – The boy **Rupert** *is in a winter setting of snow and bare trees at the lodge-gate that bears the name of the house beyond: Aberduna Hall. Although it is daytime, lights come from many of its windows.* **Rupert** *saunters up the drive, kicking snow as he goes, and turns back once to wave to the* **Lodge-Keeper**, *who waves back. At the house he approaches the biggest and brightest window and looks into a large room where his* **Brothers** *and* **Sisters** *are chattering and joking around a Christmas tree, which almost touches the ceiling and is elaborately decorated and heavy with presents. Excitement, laughter, teasing. A uniformed* **Nanny** *tries to keep control, pulling apart two boys who squabble over a parcel, turning to shush others. A* **Butler** *glances into the room, looks pained, shakes his head and retreats.*

★ ★ ★ ★ ★

CUT TO – **Rupert** *enters the room containing his siblings, the Christmas tree and a* **Nanny** *battling unruliness, yelling vainly in her native French. Most of them look at* **Rupert** *as he enters and the pandemonium moderates.*

SEVERAL BROTHERS AND SISTERS *[in chorus, almost]*: Where have you been?

3

A SISTER *[answering for him]*: Wandering again.

ANOTHER SISTER*[triumphantly]*: Half your presents have wandered, too.

A BROTHER *[looking around, feigning concern]*: Where's the new bicycle? Who took Rupe's bike? Oh, well *[shrugs]*, maybe he didn't want it.

TWIN BROTHERS *[in unison]*: Or need it.

ANOTHER BROTHER: … if he walks everywhere…

A SISTER: … and it's snowing.

ONE TWIN: He walks so much; maybe Father Christmas left him some shoes.

OTHER TWIN: Father Christmas or Father?

ANOTHER BROTHER *[wagging finger]*: Shush; Rupe's a believer!

A SISTER: Let's all look for Rupert's shoes.

They converge on the tree, parting the branches, peering into it and beginning to wreck it as the **Nanny** *tries to pull them away.*

RUPERT: *[good-naturedly]* You're really all very amusing, but the fact is that I changed my order to a horse, and I've just been down to the stables to see it. You are not allowed to ride it, of course, but whoever is lucky enough to own a camera may take a photograph of me on it, going where no bicycle could go.

VOICE: Our nannies were French, and they came and went like the seasons. Mother was always looking for replacements as Jeanne or Marie or Yvonne packed her bags and returned to the land where the name of Grayson must surely have been dreaded. Father was strong, though…

★ ★ ★ ★ ★

CUT TO – Corridor leading to the Christmas-tree room, where **Sir Henry** *strides imposingly towards the door and opens it, releasing the din within. A* **Sister** *is trying to jump on the* **Nanny's** *back while a* **Brother** *pulls her by the apron strap.*

BROTHER [*pulling Nanny*]: Anyone for a ride on Rupert's horse? Half-price today.

Sir Henry *enters and claps his hands, at which the noise stops and the* **Nanny** *is freed. The girls stifle giggles while the boys stroll about awkwardly, with glances at* **Sir Henry.**

★ ★ ★ ★ ★

CUT TO – Train compartment in Kent.

VOICE: He was a kind man, and he stood a lot from us children – except for one thing: illness.

★ ★ ★ ★ ★

FADE TO: Stable yard at Aberduna, where **Farm Worker (Roberts)** *is tossing bedclothes and pyjamas on a fire. Young* **Rupert** *approaches around the corner of a building and sums the situation up.*

RUPERT: What's happening, Roberts? The plague?

ROBERTS [*straightening up*]: Sir Henry's orders, Master Rupert. Brian is poorly and his clothes and linen must be burned.

RUPERT: I'd like new clothes. What disease do you recommend, Roberts?

ROBERTS [*grinning deferentially*]: They do say scarlet fever's giving lots of people a fright, Master Rupert.

5

RUPERT *[somewhat anxiously]*: Are you sure that's not what my brother's got?

ROBERTS *[with small laugh]*: Not likely, Master Rupert. Bit of a sniffle is all, I should think. Leastwise, that's how it looked when I saw him and your brother Tristram down by the stables half an hour ago.

RUPERT *[eyes narrowing]*: What were they doing?

ROBERTS *[airily, looking sideways at Rupert]*: Well, Master Rupert, Brian was walking away with a leather lead in his hand.

RUPERT *[stiffening]*: Why was he doing that?

ROBERTS *[poking the fire with a stick]*: It could have been, Master Rupert, because the lead had a bridle on the other end of it

RUPERT *[catching on]*: And did the bridle have anything in it?

ROBERTS: So far as I recall, Master Rupert, it contained the head of a horse, with, of course, the rest of the horse attached to it – a fine-looking animal I had not seen before. Oh, and astride the horse was Master Tristram, but how long he would stay there I could not guess because he was laughing fit to fall off.

Rupert *turns and runs towards the stables.*
★ ★ ★ ★ ★
CUT TO – Train compartment in Kent again, more summer evening views.

VOICE: Father's aversion to illness was total and we travelled so often by ship that seasickness was no exception. It didn't matter how bad the weather was, we were absolutely forbidden to be sick. Any of us showing the slightest tinge of green would be made to run around the decks until he could do nothing but drop down exhausted. I am not sure Father didn't have the cure for many of today's illnesses.

His eyes open wide, but less for looking than remembering.

VOICE: It was not only at sea that the weather influenced events. Our house faced Moel Vindick.

★ ★ ★ ★ ★

CUT TO – Moel Vindick, with sun on it.

VOICE: When Vindick smiled, we knew the picnic baskets could be packed, but when Moel Vindick frowned, we were warned not to go beyond the garden. *[pause]* Not that we had to go far to find danger…

★ ★ ★ ★ ★

FADE TO – beyond house and orchard to undergrowth, zooming in on old railway sleepers lying across entrance to mine-shaft. **Rupert** *is stretched along one sleeper, his elder brother* **Brian** *along another.*

BRIAN *[face puckering in distaste]*: To think some people make soup out of them!

RUPERT *[reaching precariously for a stone]*: Out of what?

Rupert *drops the stone, cocks his head to one side and hears it glancing off the old shaft before splashing into water far below.*

Close-ups of brothers in turn as each speaks.

BRIAN: Those stinking nettles.

RUPERT: They pong, don't they, but there are worse things to think about.

7

BRIAN: I'm sure you're right, even if you are only quoting Father. Did you have anything in mind?

RUPERT: Oh, nothing much. I just wondered whether you had inspected that sleeper before lying on it. It's rotten and you haven't lost any weight. From here I can see right through it and the stone I just dropped tells me it's fifty feet to the water. Some dive!

Brian *releases the stones in his hand and they clatter down the shaft as he wriggles back off the sleeper. A grimace suggests he is trying desperately not to be heavy.* **Rupert** *follows in retreat, but less urgently – his sleeper being sounder.*

★ ★ ★ ★ ★

CUT TO – Train going through Kent.

VOICE: But the moment we loved was when Father returned home in the evening after his day at the shipyards, founded on the Mersey by his family in 1697. The horse-drawn gig would meet him at the station and bring him up the last eight miles of hill. We knew he had walked the decks of many ships, seen a hundred foreign flags in a city of tall masts and smoking funnels, and a riverside of docks and cranes with the clang of rivets and whine of winches. However, he still had time for the bedtime stories we loved.

As we gathered around, he told us of strange and mysterious happenings with all the details. It was not enough that the hero had dined. We must know which food he ate and which wine he drank – though we children had to mix our wine with water, which was never done by d' Artagnan or any other gentleman of France riding up from the sunny south on the road to Paris and adventure. He illuminated life for us. Only when listening to his bedtime stories were we all quiet. But sometimes illumination came from elsewhere, and not always through the ears. I was beginning to notice what the eyes, and especially the eyes of our nannies, could tell someone of the opposite sex. I was becoming alert for signs.

Sometimes, we visited the village. The path we preferred was one that led ultimately to the sweet shop, but on the way a call was usually made at a small cement works where Mr Radley was the manager. He was one of our childhood heroes.

★ ★ ★ ★ ★

*FADE TO – Gate of cement works. A **Nanny**, pretty and uniformed in blue tunic, white shoulder straps and big bow at the back, ushers four younger children – two sisters and two brothers, one of them* Rupert *– towards the office, from which emerges* **Radley**, *who is large and rotund and oozes a welcome, mainly to the nanny.*

RADLEY *[Beaming ingratiatingly]*: Ah, good morning, children, and *bonjour, M'mselle.* To use the telephone again, *oui? [waggling hands continentally]*

NANNY *[smiling, small curtsy]*: If *Monsieur* would not mind, it would be a great favour.

RADLEY *[words tumbling out]*: Rather, not at all, please do come in, er, but first… *[turns and bellows towards the office]*… Jenkins!

At the office door appears the figure of a young man – thin, pale, bespectacled **Jenkins.**

JENKINS *[whose buck teeth show when he speaks]*: Yes, Mr Radley sir?

RADLEY: Be a good chap, Jenkins, and take these young folk to get some of the nicest sweeties you can while *Mademoiselle* is using the office telephone. The farthest shop, if you please, Jenkins; the quality is better there.

JENKINS *[querulous yet eager]*: The first shop is good, though, Mr Radley. My Aunt Myfanwy is behind the counter there and it is excellent value.

RADLEY *[sternly]*: Jenkins, you heard: the farthest shop. Take a shilling from petty cash and don't let the children stray.

★ ★ ★ ★ ★

CUT TO – *Inside office as* **Jenkins** *withdraws to it, muttering.*

JENKINS *[annoyed, to himself]*: Not so much sweeties galore as *Folies Bergères*, Mr Radley, if you ask me.

★ ★ ★ ★ ★

CUT TO – *Outside in yard, where* **Radley** *has returned to smiling winsomely at the* **Nanny**.

RADLEY: Come, my dear. The telephone is waiting. Clothilde, is it not?

NANNY: *Oui*, Meester Radley. You'ave a good memoree.

RADLEY *[looking as strong and capable as he can]*: In this business, Clothilde *[tapping corner of eye as Frenchmen do to suggest shrewdness]*, forgetfulness is a luxury.

Radley *returns to normal and addresses the children as* **Jenkins** *joins them.*

RADLEY: Ask Jenkins for whatever you want, children, and mind the puddles.

Radley *leads* **Nanny** *into the office and closes the door, while* **Jenkins** *and his band head for the village. As* **Jenkins** *strides off indignantly, his four charges lag behind and soon he is far enough ahead for them to gossip without his hearing.*

Close-up of the four.

FIRST SISTER: Mother said Clothilde might use the telephone in the house. Why do you think she prefers to ask favours of that humpty-dumpty?

SECOND SISTER: It beats me. What do you think, Rupe?

RUPERT: Perhaps she's an impressionist and is secretly painting him. There cannot be many shaped like him in France.

FIRST SISTER: On the contrary, most Frenchmen look like pears. Those of the clerical class, anyway. They are always sitting, doing accounts. But that black moustache curled like ram's horns, there's a dash of Spanish there, and the eyes…

BROTHER [interrupting]: More likely Laing told her not to use the phone at home. You know what a bore he is, even with Mother. You wouldn't think he was only her secretary, the respect she gives him.

SECOND SISTER: Or perhaps it's simply more private. She might have special things to say to a special person. Don't you think, Rupe?

RUPERT: Possible. But I seem to remember that last time she used the phone in Radley's office, she came out looking extraordinarily pleased and out of breath, as though she had run a hundred yards. Being pleased I might understand, but [raising eyebrows] I didn't think a telephone conversation could be strenuous.

FIRST SISTER: Let's catch Jenkins or he'll think we're talking behind his back.

SECOND SISTER: Well, aren't we?

★ ★ ★ ★ ★

CUT TO – Close-up of **Rupert** looking thoughtful, turning away, eyes narrowed, as though he has realised something.

★ ★ ★ ★ ★

CUT TO – **Jenkins** and the four children return to the yard of the cement factory as the door opens and **Nanny** and **Radley** emerge.

Close-up of **Brother** and **Rupert**.

11

BROTHER [*whispering*]: Do you think my watch is fast?

RUPERT: Why?

BROTHER [*whispering*]: If it is telling the truth, the phone call has lasted forty minutes.

RUPERT [*whispering mischievously*]: Perhaps it was not all phone call.

BROTHER [*whispering*]: Not one that was *très jolie*, at any rate. Why do you think her eyes are red?

RUPERT [*affecting concern*]: She does seem upset, doesn't she, and I'm sure it's not because she's had no sweeties.

★ ★ ★ ★ ★

CUT TO – Path back to Aberduna Hall. **Nanny's** *four charges follow her. They arrive in time to see* **Aunt Clara**, *who has been visiting from London, saying her farewells to* **Brian** *and* **Lady Grayson** *at the front of the house. She puts a shiny gold half-sovereign into* **Brian's** *hand, clasps it shut on the coin and kisses his forehead.*

AUNT CLARA: Goodbye. You've been such a good little boy.

BRIAN: Yes, and I haven't once mentioned your moustache.

★ ★ ★ ★ ★

FADE TO – Train in Kent; now dark outside, lights flitting past in place of countryside.

VOICE: Mother never handled money. Anything that called for instant payment was settled by one of the servants, who were thus well paid. Cheques to dressmakers, florists and furriers were issued monthly by secretaries who followed each other in succession like prime ministers: Mr Aspinall, Mr Kelly, Miss Nichols, Mr Laing, Mr Taylor. Mr Aspinall, who died in our service, loved fun. He used to drive me around the Welsh villages and the horse would know just where to pull in. The final stages of the homeward journey…

★ ★ ★ ★ ★

FADE TO – Narrow country lane with young **Rupert** *sitting in the gig beside* **Aspinall** *in top hat and horse galloping furiously. There is a jangling of glass in the back of the gig.* **Bystanders** *staring in alarm dive to safety as* **Aspinall***, laughing and singing, almost runs them down.*

VOICE: … were as exciting as any boy could wish, with the gig pitching and swinging to the music of the bottles and the locals leaping into the ditches at our approach.

★ ★ ★ ★ ★

FADE TO – Train in Kent.

VOICE: When it became his turn to serve, Mr Laing was very much part of the family. He was probably one of the last of the great private secretaries, a character in his own right, with his own private income. He had lived his entire life with wealthy people who accepted him for what he was: a man cultured in literature, music and good living, and skilled in the art of making his employer's life more comfortable.

*Aerial view of Warwickshire countryside: smaller, neater, tidier, greener, hedgier, tamer, less mountainous, more populous than north Wales. Zoom to Bilton prep school, whose architecture is a Victorian-Tudor mix: crude stained-glass windows, tall and heavily mullioned, corridors wandering in search of rooms "with low ceilings and frowning windows". Narrow stairs occur unexpectedly. In a quadrangle **a few boys**, including **Rupert**, exchange holiday chat, which subsides as the headmaster comes into view on his way to the Old House in which he lives. He is thin, middle-aged, in mortarboard and black gown "draped to his body like a sullen crow". He passes with a cursory nod and disappears.*

FIRST BOY *[to all]*: Hands up those who hate being back.

Boys look at each other but no one puts hand up.

RUPERT *[slowly raising hand]*: Last term, there was an occasion when I was the only one who was dishonest. So now I shall be the only one who is honest.

SECOND BOY: Why, Grayson? Is it because home is so good or here so bad?

*They look at **Rupert**, but, before he can answer, other boys speak.*

THIRD BOY: What makes you think we hate being back?

FOURTH BOY: How were you dishonest last term?

RUPERT *[smiling disarmingly]*: You have just seen Dracula over there. That ought to have reminded you.

FIRST BOY: Oh, yes. Dracula sneaked up and whacked us all for pillow-fighting in the dorm, but you escaped because you didn't own up.

A chorus of affirmatives are variously expressed as eyes train on **Rupert**.

SECOND BOY: Just saying you hate it is not going to make up for that. I could hardly sit down for a week. Anyway, you haven't said why.

RUPERT: Why what?

SECOND BOY: Why you hate being back – or say you do.

THIRD BOY *[catching on]*: Yes, if you only say you do, how do we know it's true?

SECOND BOY: Even if it is true, it doesn't make up for my sore bum.

Chortles.

FIRST BOY: Or mine.

ALL BOYS *[in chorus]*: Or mine.

THIRD BOY: To make up properly, you would have to go to Dracula and confess you deceived him and request a whacking.

RUPERT: Too late for that. Anyway, my bottom was punished in another way during the hols, and I'm sure it was worse than your whacks.

Raised eyebrows, questioning murmurs.

FIRST BOY *[exaggeratedly supercilious]*: And, pray, can you tell us what dire torture your bottom underwent?

RUPERT [*with stoicism, dignity*]: Yes, and I hope you are sensitive enough to appreciate what torture it was – compared with a dab from scrawny old Dracula who can barely lift a spoon. I had my new horse stolen and my bottom was therefore deprived of the saddle in which it had hoped to spend days on end, as it were. So, don't boast of having suffered more than your share of punishment.

VOICE: My imagination had begun its journey.

RUPERT: Another thing [*faint mischievous smile*], you lose face when you are caned by someone as dishonourable as our head. If you were in Japan, you would have to fall on your swords for having anything to do with him.

FIRST BOY: Dishonourable, why?

RUPERT: You know which school Dracula went to?

FIRST BOY: Marlborough, wasn't it?

RUPERT: Yes, and do you know where he persuades parents to send their sons when they finish here?

SECOND BOY: Tell us.

RUPERT: Rugby, of course. So does he not strike you as a traitor?

Collective, non-committal murmur from the others as they want to respond, but don't quite know how.

FIRST BOY [*eventually*]: "Traitor" is a bit strong, Grayson, for someone who might be only disloyal.

THIRD BOY: And being loyal to his old school could mean being disloyal to the parents who pay our fees, if he thinks Rugby is better.

SECOND BOY: You haven't thought it through, Grayson.

FOURTH BOY: No. It could well be a privilege to be whacked by old Drac, because he's got your interest at heart and knows what's good for you.

FIRST BOY: Make an appointment with him now, Grayson.

RUPERT: Perhaps you're right – better have the bottom numbed by Dracula than the brain numbed by you lot.

At which **Rupert** *drifts away, tossing a brief smile over his shoulder to show he is joking.*
★ ★ ★ ★ ★
CUT TO – Quadrangle with several masters coming and going; the old ones trying to look young, the young ones looking old without trying. As **Voice** *reminisces, the view slowly closes on the master,* **Henshall,** *to which its reflections now narrow.*

VOICE: School was bearable only because I treated it as an adventure. Life was divided into two camps, as in Father's stories of the Houses of York and of Lancaster, with their white roses and red. It was for me to choose which colour to wear. I enjoyed my friendships and chose my enemies with care. I was impatient for life's journey. *[pause]* There was one master, Mr Henshall, who used to lean over our desks to correct our work. At the same time, he would try to rub his rough face against one's cheek.
★ ★ ★ ★ ★
CUT TO – **Henshall** *in classroom strolling about and bending down as described.* **Rupert,** *when his turn comes, tilting his face away to avoid the master's.*

VOICE: Fortunately, he so reeked of eau-de-cologne that we were

17

warned of his approach. He soon learned which boys liked his mannerism or were prepared to tolerate it. Those who did were invited to his study for extra tuition. He was probably no more than a kindly "old auntie" who would have been equally happy teaching at a girls' school. I was pleased when Father, at my request, asked him to stay with us on his way to Ireland, where he was to spend the holidays. I was resolved to keep the poor man's weakness secret. Instinctively, I must have realised Father was so essentially heterosexual that he would not have believed any other attitude was possible, let alone permissible, among those he met socially.

★ ★ ★ ★ ★

CUT TO – *Bedroom, in which* **Lady Grayson** *and a* **Maid** *are fussing to make sure the room is just right, adjusting this, patting that, standing back to inspect.* **Laing** *stands in the doorway, viewing the proceedings loftily.*

LADY GRAYSON *[To Maid]*: Another spare blanket, Martha, I think. We don't want the poor man to be cold and take it out on his pupil, who must already be in disfavour to have invited him.

MAID *[stroking the folded blanket she has placed at the end of the bed, before leaving the room]*: Of course, Lady Grayson. About the blanket, I mean; not Master Rupert.

LAING: I know it's your son's first grown-up guest here, your ladyship, but do you not think that flowers on the dressing-table are a trifle, er…?

LADY GRAYSON *[defiantly]*: Excessive, Mr Laing?

LAING: Something along those lines, perhaps, Lady Grayson.

LADY GRAYSON: No, I do not. Let the poor boarding-school creature think we are trying to maintain life as he knows it. We must show him *[she adds, in one of her questionable metaphors, uttered all the more emphatically because she is unsure about it]* that we do not distinguish between the sheep and the goats.

★ ★ ★ ★ ★

CUT TO – **Lady Grayson,** *who has turned to and is peering down through the window.*

LADY GRAYSON: Speaking of which, I do believe our guest is arriving at this very moment. Behold, Laing, what the cab from the village has disgorged.

★ ★ ★ ★ ★

CUT TO – **Laing** *sauntering from doorway to window to share her observation.*

LAING *[head and eyes down, eyebrows up]*: A rufus, to be sure, and wild-looking at that. Ah, and there's Master Rupert greeting him. Lucky he saw him arrive.

★ ★ ★ ★ ★

CUT TO – View from above: **Rupert** *skipping down the front steps on to the gravel drive to meet* **Henshall.**

LADY GRAYSON: Lucky, my foot. He's been waiting at the window for an hour.

LAING *[still eyeing newcomer]*: He's probably a stentor, too. Those red-headed characters usually are. Had he gone into municipal duties rather than education, he could well have been, in an earlier age, a town crier. Not much above the mouth, but plenty behind it.

LADY GRAYSON *[turning from the window to study Laing]*: Sometimes, Mr Laing, I think you become unhinged at the end of the month, like those wild things on the moor. Except that, in your case, it's the zeros in the accounts rather than full moons that seem to do the damage.

LAING *[with small bow and wintry smile]*: If you say so, your ladyship.

19

★ ★ ★ ★ ★

FADE TO – Drawing room, in which family members are taking coffee. **Sir Henry Grayson** *proffers a box of cigars to the red-haired, sideburned* **Henshall,** *who is in the centre of things.*

SIR HENRY: Cigar, Mr Henshall? Cuban.

HENSHALL: Exquisite, I'm sure, but no thank you, Sir Henry. *[Into Henshall's radiant smile enters a shadow of concern]* It's my voice, you know. I don't know whether he's told you, but young Rupert and his classmates are my *protégés* for not only the sterner discipline of arithmetic but also the more decorative fulfilment of song. And, of course, I lead them with what poor voice I have. I fear, therefore, that even the kindest of Cuban leaf could impair any vocal gift God gave me.

SIR HENRY *[grave, puzzled, withdrawing the box]* Quite so.

★ ★ ★ ★ ★

CUT TO – Elder brother **Brian,** *seated on other side of* **Henshall.**

BRIAN: Perhaps Mr Henshall would oblige us with a song, if it is not too soon after his dinner?

★ ★ ★ ★ ★

CUT TO – The **Twins,** *who are sitting farther away among their sisters. One mutters to the other, trying, like a ventriloquist, to seem not to be speaking and at the same time looking warily around lest he attract the attention of* **Sir Henry** *or* **Lady Grayson.**

TWIN: Yes, but too soon and we might hear a Puccini-flavoured burp.

OTHER TWIN: Or flatulence-flavoured Fauré.

★ ★ ★ ★ ★

CUT TO – **Rupert's** *face, grimly studying the twins, whose mischief he has perceived. They, in turn, feel* **Rupert's** *scrutiny and adopt an innocence bordering on the giggles.*

★ ★ ★ ★ ★

CUT TO – **Henshall** *close-up, smiling coyly.*

HENSHALL: Do you really mean it?

SIR HENRY: Of course, Rupert has often spoken of your music, and here is our chance for a taste of the real thing, Please … [*Sir Henry waves forth a hand, indicating the way to the piano.*]

★ ★ ★ ★ ★

CUT TO – **Rupert**, *who looks uneasily from the* **Twins** *making fun, to* **Sir Henry** *and* **Brian** *concocting a deeper kind of embarrassment.*

★ ★ ★ ★ ★

CUT TO – **Brian**, *who clicks his fingers to catch sister* **Ailsa's** *attention and speaks to her.*

BRIAN: Mr Henshall is going to play and sing… [*waggles his fingers and points to the Bechstein in a corner of the room.*]

★ ★ ★ ★ ★

CUT TO – **Ailsa**, *who brightens attentively.*

AILSA: Oh, Splendid.

Ailsa *gets up, walks to the piano, lifts the lid and pulls the stool out.* **Henshall** *approaches the piano and adjusts himself on the stool while the babble in the room subsides.* **Rupert** *looks grimly at* **Henshall**, *with defensive glances now and then to* **Sir Henry**, **Brian** *and the others, and swallows anxiously.* **Henshall**, *as he shoots one cuff and then the other, wriggles a little on the stool and looks around, ready to begin. He launches into "Little Old Lady" with such gusto that* **Rupert** *glances at the chandelier.* **Lady Grayson** *now sits beside* **Sir Henry**, *to whose ear she leans and whispers.*

LADY GRAYSON: I do hope he is not referring to me. [*Then murmurs to herself, away from Sir Henry's ear*] A stentor indeed. Mr Laing can pick 'em; I wonder whether he is so clever with the horses.

21

Henshall, *as song ends, is flushed and pleased with applause; relief on* **Rupert's** *face; bravos from his siblings, whose eyes twinkle as they glance at each other.*

★ ★ ★ ★ ★

FADE TO – Corridor [next day] with **Rupert** *running along it and almost colliding with* **Francis** *the footman.*

Close-up of **Francis'** *face.*

FRANCIS *[in some alarm]*: Tut, tut, Master Rupert; is there a fire?

Rupert *pauses to explain.*

RUPERT *[puffing]*: Sorry… Francis… Mr Henshall's leaving… I don't want to miss him.

FRANCIS *[gently shaking head]*: I don't know what kind of school you go to, Master Rupert, but at mine a master wouldn't have had holes in his shoes.

★ ★ ★ ★ ★

CUT TO – Schoolroom scene; boys listening to master, whose voice – but not image – fades as **Voice** *takes over.*

VOICE: There was one master, Granville Earle, to whom I shall always feel grateful, for he recounted history rather than taught it. He paraded it before my dreaming eyes like a pageant – the kings of the period, their manners, pursuits, battles, mistresses. Later, under another historian, George Townsend Warner, I was to rummage in similar dust-heaps. Thus, I learned to distinguish between the different ages, their arts and arms, their loyalties, passions and treacheries.

★ ★ ★ ★ ★

CUT TO – Pan around library, its books enclosed behind wire.

VOICE: Although our library was not good, the books were kept on shelves behind latticed wire, like wild animals, and the cages were opened

22

only once a day. It was here I discovered Dumas and was carried to heaven. He may have taken liberties with history, but his books taught me to be interested in the story of France. I counted spiders with the mad Louis XI, rode to Paris with Henry of Navarre, threw a glove in Richelieu's face, kissed the hand of Louise de la Vallière and wandered down the pages of French history.

★ ★ ★ ★ ★

FADE TO – Pastoral scene with three boys fooling about on the grass among the trees, idly throwing things, joking and enjoying summer.

VOICE: I made two close friends at Bilton and imagined they would remain so for life. It was not to be. Freddie Selous was the son of a great African hunter. Even then, he was a naturalist and man of the woods. The other, George Robinson, came from Somerset. For me, whose imagination dwelt in palaces, castles and the dim-lit alleys of medieval cities, they acted as a corrective. When the time came to move on, George accompanied me to Harrow, but Freddie went to nearby Rugby. A few years later, a bullet from an enemy plane sent him hurtling to his death.

In the 1914-18 war, George moved on the right squares, bent his body and leaned his head where the air was empty, and survived unscathed. A few weeks after the war, out shooting, he climbed a stile with a loaded gun under his arm. The ghost of a thwarted enemy must have seized its chance and squeezed the trigger when George was in the way.

At Bilton, however, we did not know that timber for the myriad crosses was ready for the felling. We worked and played as though God would be kind.

★ ★ ★ ★ ★

FADE TO – View from rear of inside school chapel, looking across a congregation of mostly boys towards a priest delivering a sermon from the pulpit. The organ is playing background music, which hints that the sermon is concluding. Close in to **Rupert** *and the boy beside him, who is busy doing something beneath the pew in front.*

VOICE: Sometimes, the sermons at chapel were long and I envied a certain master his well-camouflaged periodical, *Sporting and Dramatic*. I used to sit next to Freddie…

CLOSE TO – **Rupert's** *face showing repugnance, then move to see* **Freddie** *skinning a rabbit.*

VOICE: … until he started skinning dead rabbits during the service.

Priest, *as the sermon ends, straightens up, squares shoulders and gazes out across the rows of young boys to affirm the message, at the same time slapping shut the Bible and raising his voice to save the peroration from drowning in the crescendo with which the organist is having his own last say. As the* **Priest** *steps down from the pulpit and flaps his way along the aisle to the door of the church to farewell the congregation, the organ plays some jauntier departure music.*

VOICE: I liked the music and believe I was, what the English call, "musical". I had reason to be, with family blood that included Irish and Hungarian on Mother's side and at the least the din of shipyards on Father's, which perhaps inclined me towards Stravinsky. Our headmaster's talents, I'm afraid, lay elsewhere.

Front of chapel as participants emerge slowly into the day and **Freddie** *slips away, hunched to hide the bulge under his jacket.* **Headmaster** *beams here and there as benevolently as his features allow, boys catching each other's attention and rolling their eyes to acknowledge that the* **Headmaster** *is not in everyday mode. A* **Father** *approaches the* **Headmaster** *and, after felicitations, becomes more businesslike.*

FATHER: Tell me, Mr Earle, why did your organist give us "Rule, Britannia" this year?

HEADMASTER: Well, Mr Simmonds, it is Empire Day.

FATHER: Yes, but at the opening we normally have "God Save the King".

HEADMASTER *[taken aback, pausing thoughtfully]*: You're right. Why, indeed? I'll look into it. Er, laddie *[putting hand on shoulder of boy who happens to be passing]*, send Mr Lucas to me like a good chap if you will.

★ ★ ★ ★ ★

CUT TO – *Those who have attended the service saying their goodbyes and sauntering off.*

Lucas, *the organist, tall and shadowy, approaches the* **Headmaster**, *who is still talking to the* **Father**.

HEADMASTER *[turning to LUCAS]*: Ah, Lucas, tell me: why did we have "Rule, Britannia" instead of "God Save the King" this year?

LUCAS *[lugubriously]*: The organ-blower blew "Rule, Britannia", Headmaster, so there was nothing I could do but play it.

HEADMASTER: Of course, I quite understand, and thank you, Lucas, for explaining.

Father, *bewildered, opens and closes mouth soundlessly.*

FATHER *[managing a smile, looking at watch]*: Thank you, Mr Earle. I hadn't realised. I'll be off now.

Father *walks away, turning once to look back, puzzled, at* **Headmaster**.

★ ★ ★ ★ ★

CUT TO – *Room with upright piano and pictures of classical composers around the walls. At the piano sits* **Rupert** *on one stool and a woman (**Miss Sadd**) on another beside him. From behind it can be seen that her bottom spreads over the whole of her stool, while* **Rupert's** *occupies only half of his.*

View from half front of pair at piano: **Miss Sadd** *plump and plain, while* **Rupert's** *expression mixes effort and resignation as he struggles to play (badly).*

VOICE: Although I have always enjoyed music, I'm afraid my understanding of it was little better than the headmaster's. I took piano lessons from Miss Sadd, who had been many years at the school.

MISS SADD [*sighing, as Rupert's fingers make discords*]: How long is it, Rupert, since I began teaching you pianoforte?

RUPERT [*guiltily*]: You have been trying to teach me for more than a year, Miss.

MISS SADD: We don't seem to be making much progress, do we?

RUPERT: No, Miss. Not more, I suppose, than if I were trying to teach you Chinese.

MISS SADD [*brusquely*]: I don't think that analogy quite fits, Rupert, since you do not, to my knowledge, know Chinese, whereas I do know something about music. Could the fault be, perhaps, with the learning rather than the teaching?

RUPERT: Probably, Miss. I do enjoy it when you play Debussy, Ravel and Scriabin for me, and I shall love it forever, but what you teach about making the sounds for myself does not go from my ears to my fingers.

MISS SADD: I'm not sure that it even goes from your ears to your brain, Rupert. Perhaps you ought to be learning Chinese, because if you don't get your hair cut soon, you will have enough for a pigtail. Anyway, that's all for today.

They both stand, **Miss Sadd** *gathering up her sheets of music and* **Rupert** *escaping from the room.*

★ ★ ★ ★ ★

CUT TO – **Rupert** *at a window of the Bursar's office, where he is handed a letter by a girl.*

RUPERT: Thank you, Miss Thomas

He walks off slowly, opening it and reading the contents as he creeps along.

VOICE: Mother's letters came regularly, full of news and sometimes accompanied by chocolate, a flower or a silk handkerchief. Her letters followed me all my life to many corners of the world. When I was in France during the First World War, she wrote daily, though the letters were not delivered at that frequency and sometimes arrived in great batches. She never lost faith in me: cheering, comforting and overflowing with love and sympathy. Even now an old letter is lying somewhere near me, and I feel her presence close and her cool hands stroking my head.

★ ★ ★ ★ ★

CUT TO – Exterior of Main Street in the village of Dunchurch, closing on the Dun Cow, an old coaching inn. Inside sits **Lady Grayson** *at a table by the window, alternately writing and pausing for inspiration. Through the window, she sees people going to and fro.*

VOICE: Often, Mother would visit Dunchurch, the nearby village, for weekends – unbeknown to the school authorities. Sometimes, she spent a whole day there waiting to see me for perhaps no more than an hour.

★ ★ ★ ★ ★

CUT TO – Bilton school quadrangle as **Sir Henry Grayson** *approaches: tall, tanned, immaculate; greeted by boys and masters, among whom he pauses now and then to joke and chat.*

VOICE: Father used to come at half-term, a soldierly figure among the shambling masters. He would tip those who could make life pleasanter for me and never forgot to look after old Bailey, who was organ blower, gardener and keeper of the lodge gates. Bailey would make straight for the

27

Green Man and stay there until the money was gone. The lodge gates were thus never closed to me and I knew well the villages around, for I was already acquiring a taste for travel and looking towards the horizon.

Additional food was served to sons whose parents could pay for it. On birthdays, boys would laboriously list those invited to take a portion of their cake, which was handed round by the totties, or footmen. On my birthday, however, no list was necessary because Mother sent enough cakes, strawberries and cream for the whole school, including the totties. I was therefore spared the ordeal of selection.

★ ★ ★ ★ ★

CUT TO – Rustic room at the Dun Cow, full of boys and food of all descriptions, like a small Fortnums: hams, chickens, tongues, pate, strawberries, peaches, apples, bananas, cakes, pies, chocolates, sweets, marrons glaces, great jugs of cream fresh from the farm…

VOICE: My friends loved Father. They knew he could drive a cricket ball out of any ground and had broken a pavilion window at Lord's; that he smoked delicious-smelling cigars, built ships and knew Greek and Latin better than our classics master. However, Father had his own disappointments. One was when my brother Denys, the dreamer, always delicate and rheumatic, was told by doctors that Winchester lay too low for his health and Eton was in the damp Thames Valley. So, it had to be Harrow. Father's Wykehamist attitude to the others, however splendid, was "Eton we know and Harrow we know, but who are ye?" I was delighted when I learned Denys was going there and longed for my turn to come. I had already delved into Byron, Trollope and Sheridan, and wanted to climb the hill to the school for poets, writers and adventurers.

★ ★ ★ ★ ★

CUT TO – Swimming pool, with boys cheering on competitors. The race ends in victory for **Rupert,** *who is helped, exhausted but jubilant, from the water to have back slapped and hand shaken.*

VOICE: When term followed term at Bilton, it became more difficult to sustain my chameleon-like existence. When I won the swimming championship, I had to appear for the presentation of the cup…

★ ★ ★ ★ ★

CUT TO – Speech night, with **Headmaster** *in full regalia on stage, flanked by* **Senior Masters, School Governors** *and other* **Dignitaries***, seen over sea of boys' heads in auditorium.*

HEADMASTER: The championship this year has been won by a boy called Grayson, but the really interesting thing is that it has been won in the slowest time in the annals of the school.

★ ★ ★ ★ ★

CUT TO – Aberduna, with **Rupert** *stepping from an old-fashioned car in front of the house and a pack of dogs running to greet him.*

VOICE: The holidays between terms were growing more interesting. Father had become enthusiastic about motoring.

★ ★ ★ ★ ★

CUT TO – Two men in overalls enter the yard with three garages. The more authoritative of them, **Davis***, opens the doors one by one. Inside each, a car of different make can be seen.* **Davis** *motions to the other man [who knows the routine and needs no explanation], who pushes out the cars one after another while* **Davis** *helps a little by steering with one hand as he walks.* **Davis** *and his helper fuss about, lifting bonnets, tinkering, cleaning, checking tyres and performing general inspection and maintenance. Nearby, workmen are preparing the site for a fourth garage.*

VOICE: Those were the days when we wore white linen coats and goggles for motoring, which was often used as the excuse for a picnic in a Manet setting.

★ ★ ★ ★ ★

FADE TO – A "Manet setting" among trees by a river. Two cars are parked at the edge of a clearing. **Davis***, in white linen coat and goggles perched in the hair above his forehead, is attending to the cars, one of which is giving off some steam, while another man in servant's attire prepares tables and accoutrements for dining al fresco.*

Mother and sisters are wearing veils over their straw hats, knotted beneath the chin. Rupert and two of his brothers lark by the river.

VOICE: I can still see their lips smiling and eyes dancing as we set off for an afternoon in the sunshine. We had a chauffeur, a keen-eyed, ex-navy man called Davis, who drove fast and seldom used his brakes, which in those days were in any case less effective than brakes are today.

★ ★ ★ ★ ★

CUT TO – Village street with a Grayson car whooshing along it, as chickens and pigs and even people scatter to right and left. As it recedes in the distance, the people resume their activities, the chickens ruffle their feathers and settle down again and the pigs stop squealing, but a few of the more agitated humans shake their fists at the car as it shrinks and disappears.

VOICE: People had not yet learned to keep their chickens behind wire, and this was a strain on the brakes unless you enjoyed roast poultry every night. Davis persuaded Father to buy one car after another, which was interesting for us and profitable for Davis, who doubtless had an arrangement with the suppliers. It also delighted Father because it gave him an excuse to build yet another garage.

★ ★ ★ ★ ★

*CUT TO – **Sir Henry's** office at Mersyside shipyard, as glimpsed from outside through a window. **Sir Henry** sits at a large desk, addressing executives.*

*Pan to the shipyard itself: a panorama of cranes, girders, cables, steel sheets, men going ant-like in all directions and others occupied where they are, doing things to the accompaniment of clangs and bangs of metal on metal. Into sight in the distance, beyond earshot, comes **Rupert** the boy being shown around by a **Young Man**. **Rupert** points to two ships that are half-built.*

VOICE: Seeing new cars keep arriving was exciting. It did not occur to us to wonder where the money came from to buy them, or where it came from for ponies, roller-skates, hammocks, steam-engines or anything else we wanted. We only knew that Father built and repaired ships. Life was running smoothly. Everything in the garden, as they say, was lovely.

CLOSE TO – **Rupert** and the **Young Man** in the shipyard.

YOUNG MAN: The nearer one is a cargo vessel that will travel to wherever in the world its owners require. The other is destined for the American run – at least at first, so far as I know. At this stage [smiles] they look like the carcasses of turkeys on Boxing Day, don't you think? And after they have left the slip, a score or more will follow them. Coal, steel and the invention of steam-power – that's where the wealth is.

Rupert looks up thoughtfully at **Young Man's** face and then even more thoughtfully to the ships under construction.

★ ★ ★ ★ ★

CUT TO – Harrow school. Pan around buildings, classrooms, chapel, playing fields and the activities they represent.

VOICE: Had we been more experienced, we might have sensed the lull before the storm. Something was about to happen that would alter the current of our lives. For the moment, however, we could still pretend.

★ ★ ★ ★ ★

CUT TO – Harrow theatre or auditorium, with a handful of boys preparing for and rehearsing a production. One boy appears to be in charge, ordering the others about with authority. It is **Denys**: the brother too frail for the dampness of Winchester or Eton.

VOICE: Denys, now at Harrow, discovered Shakespeare. He also decided his destiny was to produce plays. His most sinister discovery, however, was that he had a whole company of actors and actresses to hand: his brothers and sisters.

★ ★ ★ ★ ★

31

CUT TO – Bursar's office, where **Rupert** *takes a letter, thanks* **Miss Thomas** *and walks slowly away, opening it.*

MISS THOMAS *[calling out]*: Wait, Master Grayson. There's another for you – rather large, and with a Harrow postmark.

★ ★ ★ ★ ★

CUT TO – **Rupert**, *turning on his heel and taking the second letter.*

RUPERT *[a trifle irritably]*: Thank you, Miss Thomas. Now I shall not need to read the postmark myself.

★ ★ ★ ★ ★

CUT TO – **Miss Thomas**, *who reddens and flusters at the beginnings of an apology.*

MISS THOMAS: Forgive me, Master Rupert, but…

RUPERT *[seeing her discomfort]*: On the contrary, Miss Thomas, forgive me … but I know what's in it *[waving the envelope]*: a lot of work from my tyrant of a brother, who I think has gone mad.

MISS THOMAS *[hands up, eyes wide]*: Oh, Master Rupert, I do hope …

RUPERT *[with short laugh]*: No, don't worry. It's temporary and does not run in the family.

Rupert *strolls back to his room, reading his mother's letter – the Harrow one tucked under his arm.*

VOICE: From Harrow, he sent me my part underlined in red and I spent hours beneath the bedclothes with a torch learning it. Henceforth, no holiday was complete without the production of at least one Shakespeare play. *[Adopt stage voice]* Methought I heard a voice cry, *Sleep no more! Denys does murder sleep.*

★ ★ ★ ★ ★

CUT TO – An outbuilding being converted by workmen into a theatre, the outlines of stage and seating beginning to take shape.

VOICE: Father was not one to miss the opportunity to build something. The coach-house of an old stable was converted into a theatre, complete with stage and trapdoor and a magnificent proscenium with red velvet curtains drawing up into the corners – just as at His Majesty's in the Haymarket. The auditorium seated a hundred.

★ ★ ★ ★ ★

FADE TO – Interior of the finished article, all seats filled and a few rustics standing at the back, with the more presentable of the audience in front. Backstage, brother **Brian** *approaches sixteen-year-old* **Denys** *in some agitation, though* **Denys** *speaks first.*

DENYS *[glancing at wristwatch, before tucking the anachronism well back under the frilled sleeve of his costume]*: Five minutes to go. Something the matter?

BRIAN: No… that is… how does a second murderer brush his hair?

★ ★ ★ ★ ★

FADE TO – Carpenter's shop at Bilton, boys in aprons working away with planes, saws, chisels and mallets, and the instructor trying to speak to **Rupert**, *who cannot understand, however, because the mouthful of nails protruding from between the speaker's lips are marring his pronunciation.*

VOICE: All I wanted was to make a cedar lining for one of Mother's hanging cupboards, but it was not to be. The outcome of months of hard work was a breadboard – not quite circular, splintered and almost flat. It eventually proved ideal for skimming across the duckpond at Aberduna. I cannot think why, but carpentry spread from school as a duty to Aberduna as an enthusiasm. Father built a shop fitted with a bench and full complement of tools that none of us, including him, knew how to use.

★ ★ ★ ★ ★

CUT TO – Brand new carpentry shop at Aberduna. **Rupert** *works away at a lump of wood, first with a chisel, then putting it in a vice to plane it, then applying a fret-saw and sandpaper, all with much clumsiness.* **Laing** *(***Lady Grayson's** *secretary) enters and looks fastidiously, even distastefully, around at the artisan ambience. He approaches* **Rupert** *from behind and taps him on the shoulder, at which* **Rupert** *stops work and swings around.*

RUPERT *[alarm turning to relief]*: Oh, it's you, Laing. I should be careful here if I were you. Don't come too close when we're working and don't frighten anyone. Do you know that D'Artagnan could draw his sword in his sleep if he were suddenly disturbed?

LAING *[stiffly]*: I don't know about that, Master Rupert, but your mother would like to know what you're up to. Is it a pair of bookends, perhaps, that we are making for her? Or, er *[twiddles fingers and looks airily around the ceiling]* reproduction Chippendale?

RUPERT *[trying to match LAING's condescension]*: If you must know, what I am working on at the moment is a set of wooden false teeth for Sarah Macphillips. As you might have noticed, her present ones are not up to much.

LAING *[amused]*: As your mother's seamstress for a dozen years, Sarah would probably thank you more for a new set of eyes, but I don't know whether *[flicking a speck of sawdust from his sleeve]* you are up to eyes yet – even though you may be up to your eyes.

★ ★ ★ ★ ★

CUT TO – A long, low passage at the end of which is a small room with a little old woman peering closely at the garment she is working on, surrounded by fabrics, threads, sewing machine and other paraphernalia.

VOICE: Sarah's room smelled of cotton, silks, alpaca and the whiff of an oil she used for the machine. She was never happier than when telling stories about former husbands, who numbered five. To us she was a cross between Bluebeard and Henry VIII, as five husbands took some accounting for.

CLOSE TO – **Sarah Macphillips**, *her face puckered and lips working as she concentrates on needle and thread.*

VOICE: Husband number three had been an embalmer and she could describe gruesomely the details of a body laid out ready to "pass over". We loved her description of a funeral cortege: the beautiful black hearse with its shining silver fittings, the horses' tails sweeping the ground, the escort of sad, silk-hatted mutes. Our favourite song from her old lips was "The Mistletoe Bough", about a young bride who, during a game of hide and seek at her wedding party, hid herself in an old oak chest. Too late she realised that the lid was too heavy for her to lift from inside and her bridegroom, who must have been stupid indeed, failed to find her. Centuries later, her skeleton was discovered, gowned in her wedding dress, which in some curious way was still white and beautiful. I have never heard it since, but I believe not even Callas could have surpassed the pathos of Sarah's rendering.

★ ★ ★ ★ ★

FADE TO – *Same scene except that* **Rupert** *is now sitting beside* **Sarah Macphillips**.

VOICE: Sarah taught me to sew. I made dresses of striped print, blue and pink, for Miss Catchpole, who had been summoned as usual, rather optimistically, to improve my mathematics during the holidays. I learned later that Sarah substituted her own neat stitches for mine at night, but Miss Catchpole must have been pleased with my summer gift, for the ruler lay idle in her long white hands for the rest of the holidays.

★ ★ ★ ★ ★

CUT TO – *Scene from bridge of ship forging through the ocean.*

35

VOICE: Father had followed the sea, felt the hearts of many ships and moved to their pulsing; laughed and wept with them, known them from stem to stern. He had watched masts drawing their circle about the sun or pitching a line against a windy sky and following sea – or at night, motionless like dreaming spires pointed to the stars. He wanted to introduce us to the joys of living – his sorrows were strictly his own – so he took us off the nursery slopes earlier than we should have left them.

The advice Father used to give me from time to time, though probably not original, was memorable: never chase two hares at the same time; be wary of men who walk silently; never drink against a teetotaller; never start something you can't finish; stretch your legs according to the length of the blanket; never have an affair with a woman and discuss it afterwards; always pee when you get the opportunity; and never leave the red ball over the pocket.

We sailed the Norwegian fjords as far north as the midnight sun, explored the Greek islands, travelled the smooth waters of the Nile up to the second cataract. We sailed the turbulence from Ushant to Finisterre and south to Madeira. *[Pause]* But we were not always at sea. The corridors of the Ritz-Carltons, the Grands, the Beaux-Sites, the Palaces, the Metropoles and Hermitages became our playgrounds. We learned how to skim a beer-pad from our hotel window almost up to the very feet of Napoleon, standing so scornfully on the top of his column in the Place Vendôme. The valets, hall porters, *maitres d'hôtel, femmes de chambres* and *chasseurs* were our friends ashore; at sea, the bosuns, the deckhands and the firemen.

★ ★ ★ ★ ★

FADE TO – Aberduna and **Sir Henry's** *study, on the door of which* **Rupert,** *holding a book in one hand, knocks. Inside the study,* **Sir Henry** *swings round in his chair to face* **Rupert.**

SIR HENRY *[affably]*: Hello, son. *[Sees book]* More Shakespeare?

RUPERT: No, Father; the antidote to him, really. *[Holds the book up] The life of General Wolfe.*

36

SIR HENRY [brightening]: Ah, yes, let me see…

Sir Henry *gets up and walks to a shelf from which he takes a map, which he unfolds on a table as* **Rupert** *joins him to look at it.*

SIR HENRY: This is not just a map of eastern Canada, but of the actual campaign, tracing Wolfe's route up the St Lawrence as he moved against Montcalm… scaling the Heights of Abraham… fascinating.

RUPERT: Will you take me to Canada, Father?

SIR HENRY: How old are you, Rupert?

RUPERT: Fifteen.

SIR HENRY: I'll take you there when you're sixteen.

RUPERT [aglow]: That's wonderful, because I'm sixteen tomorrow. Shall I pack my bag?

★ ★ ★ ★ ★

CUT TO – Quayside bustle of passengers and stores boarding a liner at Liverpool.

VOICE: When he said something, he meant it, and he liked sudden departures. We sailed on the *Empress of Ireland* with ten trunks, though there would have been twenty had Mother been with us. She had too many bazaars and charity concerts to leave home, but my sisters Ailsa and Nancy, the fair and the dark, accompanied us.

★ ★ ★ ★ ★

CUT TO – At sea. **Sir Henry** *in shipboard garb ascends stairs from lounge, in one corner of which are the two good-looking sisters,* **Ailsa** *and* **Nancy,** *with male acquaintances, while in another is* **Rupert** *with a pretty little girl sucking from a bottle with a straw.*

VOICE: Father spent most of his time with the captain on the bridge, while Ailsa and Nancy made slaves of two men they had already known and met again by chance. It was not long before I found a little girlfriend of my own and because she liked soft-drinks and liqueur chocolates, I had to go to Father for the first time – though, not the last – for money. I hired her a costume for the fancy-dress and bought her a yard of blue ribbon to encircle her waist. Among her accomplishments…

★ ★ ★ ★ ★

CUT TO – Promenade deck, with **Rupert** *and new girlfriend on deckchairs not far from the rail, over which the girl, after filling her lungs with air and swirling the ammunition in her mouth, expels an arc of saliva.* **Rupert** *arches his eyebrows and makes an "O" of admiration with his mouth.*

VOICE: …was that of being able to spit from her deckchair over the promenade-deck rail, though her knowledge, despite being Canadian-born, did not extend to General Wolfe or Montcalm. Was it possible that these two gallant gentlemen were less important than I had imagined? I parted from her regretfully at Quebec, for her parents were taking her directly to Toronto.

★ ★ ★ ★ ★

CUT TO – Convoy of three cars carrying the four Graysons and their luggage approaching Château Frontenac, and the bustle of their arrival at the entrance.

Foyer of hotel, **Rupert** *and sisters looking around as* **Sir Henry** *at reception checks them in.*

Rupert's *room, he and his father surveying it.*

SIR HENRY *[jerking thumb towards one side of the room]*: I'm next door there, and *[jerking other thumb towards other side of room]* the girls are next door there. So you're well protected.

RUPERT: Sandwiched, you might say.

SIR HENRY: You might, except that you'd have to be rather larger than you are to be the filling in a Canadian sandwich. We shall try one, later, but while you and the girls unpack and hang things up, I'm going out. When I return, we'll try the dining room. Are you hungry?

RUPERT: Famished. How long will you be, Father?

SIR HENRY: An hour or so. Can you wait?

RUPERT: Not really, but I guess there's no choice.

SIR HENRY [probingly]: What's this "I guess"? You seem to have picked up Canadian when you've scarcely been here five minutes.

RUPERT [blushing]: Perhaps I had some practice on the boat, Father. But you're changing the subject.

SIR HENRY: Not "boat", "ship". Perhaps you could study that [pointing to a framed plan of hotel features on wall of hotel, followed by close-up of wall plan] and know where the dining room is, so that we'll lose no time searching.

RUPERT: Yes, but by then I'll be able to smell my way to the dining room blindfolded.

Sir Henry, *with a grunt, leaves the room and closes the door while* **Rupert** *nonetheless walks to the wall plan and examines it.*

VOICE: Father was never fond of personally conducted tours. On arrival in a strange place, he would leave us to settle in and go off alone to spy out the land. Later, he would take us to anything that had interested him. We saw many of the musts – museums, art galleries, historic buildings – that every traveller sees, but he was an expert in collecting *vignettes:* a house, a view, a café or a square that most of the world passed by. He pointed out things that still live in my memory. One day, we were taken down the river on a yacht by the owner of a shipyard, who – he had heard on the grapevine – wanted Father to buy it.

★ ★ ★ ★ ★

FADE TO Arrival and tying up at wharf, **Owner**, *effusive, and skipper helping first* **Ailsa** *and* **Nancy**, *then* **Sir Henry** *and* **Rupert** *along the gangway to the yard, with gantries, jib cranes, railway lines, trolleys, steel plates, girders and dozens of men walking here and there and noisily doing things.*

★ ★ ★ ★ ★

CUT TO Large office in shipyard. Guests and **Owner** *are seated in easy chairs arranged around, the* **Owner** *having left his desk to sit with them. Refreshments on a table nearby have been offered by a junior shipyard employee, but the guests have had their fill and are beginning to wave them away. They are sitting forward on their chairs as though about to make a move.* **Sir Henry** *consults his watch and rises, as do the others.*

SIR HENRY: Time to go, Tom. These youngsters don't let an old man stay put for long. Thank you; most impressive.

OWNER: Think it over, Henry. It could be the piece of the jigsaw you need. And remember *[big man-to-man laugh]*: other wolves are pricking up their ears.

SIR HENRY *[With more moderate English laugh]*: Yes, Rom, but this wolf wants to be sure there's some meat on the bone. Thanks again; we'll be in touch.

Owner *shakes hands with* **Sir Henry**, **Rupert** *and his sisters.*

OWNER: Jason will take you back to town. Enjoy your stay, *au revoir*.

CLOSE TO – **Owner**, *whose expression is a little less buoyant than when the*

40

party arrived, having sensed that the meeting with **Sir Henry** *did not proceed so promisingly as he had hoped.*

★ ★ ★ ★ ★

CUT TO – View from some distance away [out of earshot] of launch heading back to city, **Sir Henry** *pointing out sights to* **Rupert**, *the sisters chatting to each other.*

★ ★ ★ ★ ★

CUT TO – Hotel dining room, the four at table. Waiter attending them scribbles on pad, bows, thanks them for the orders and departs.

NANCY: I couldn't do justice to it, Father. Your Canadian ruined my appetite.

AILSA: Same here. Those sandwiches were like barges, don't you think, Father?

SIR HENRY: I warned you. You must nibble in Canada, my dear. Everything's twice the size.

RUPERT: Including our host. I should not like to be a beetle if he walked on me. His salesmanship was not all that wizened, either. Will you buy the yard, Father?

SIR HENRY No. *[Puts a lump of bread roll in his mouth, chews it slowly and keeps looking at Rupert without saying more.]*

RUPERT *[taken aback]*: Why, Father? Why so definite? Are you not at least thinking about it?

SIR HENRY *[after swallowing the bread]*: No.

RUPERT: It looked busy and successful.

SIR HENRY: That's the trouble. When I came by yesterday, *reconnoitring,* there was nothing much happening at all. Even today, if you looked hard, you could tell they weren't really making or repairing anything.

RUPERT: Do you mean that today it was rigged?

SIR HENRY [eyebrows raised]: Let's say "stage-managed" – like Shakespeare.

RUPERT [marvelling]: I must tell Denys.

★ ★ ★ ★ ★

CUT TO – On board ship in the St Lawrence.

VOICE: We took a steamer up the river, visited the Heights of Abraham and explored the battlefield. [Pause] I was impatient to reach the Ritz Carlton in Montreal, where I hoped a letter might await me. I was not disappointed. It was my first love letter and one to treasure, but I never replied. Life was beginning to move too fast for letters.

★ ★ ★ ★ ★

CUT TO – Scenes of Montreal, including the Ritz Carlton and the Graysons installed there.

VOICE: We had been a fortnight in Montreal when Father became restless to return to Ravenspoint, the new house he was building on a wild piece of the Anglesey coastline. He must live on an island and have the sea at his door and mountains in the distance. He wanted rock for the house and river-sand for the mortar, the sea to fill the baths and the sun to flood the windows. Father's pet architect stayed in Holyhead, ready to alter his designs at a moment's notice. Mother visited the headland to supervise the kitchen arrangements, servants' quarters, linen cupboards. A stone-flagged courtyard had spread itself before the front door and beyond it a terrace stretched like the promenade deck of a liner. The house, which overlooked the Irish Sea, sprawled away in a jumble of roofs and windows. Cottages for guests were going up, a garage for ten cars, an open fives-court. Great stone walls had begun to reach out over the cliffs, twisting and turning, climbing and falling with the contours of the headland. All this, Father was beginning to miss.

★ ★ ★ ★ ★

CUT TO – *Hotel lounge, where* **Rupert** *sits with a dark young Mexican,* **Juan,** *taking coffee.*

JUAN: It does not matter if it is your last night in Canada, Rupert. You must pay us the courtesy of visiting our suite this evening. Otherwise, I shall ask my father, who is a minister in the government of Mexico, to declare war on England.

RUPERT *[amused]*: What would you use for ammunition? Tacos?

JUAN: For your frail English stomachs, that would probably suffice. But we could call up reinforcements in the shape of tequila.

RUPERT *[in mock resignation]*: Then I see no alternative. What is your room number?

★ ★ ★ ★ ★

CUT TO – *Sitting room of suite, to which* **Rupert** *has just been admitted by* **Juan,** *who introduces two girls: one fair, the other dark like himself.*

JUAN *[to the girls, with a sweep]*: This is Rupert, from England. His father builds ships for the British Empire.*[To Rupert]* This *[indicating the fair girl]* is Lucille, who is Canadian, and this *[indicating the dark one]* is Loreta, my *paisana.*

Lucille *is sitting in an armchair, but* **Loreta,** *the Mexican, is curled up cat-like on a pink damask chair with her legs tucked under her playing a mouth organ. She stops playing, lowers the instrument and looks* **Rupert** *straight in the eyes, without smiling. As the eyes lazily survey him, he blushes. Inspection over, she looks no more at him and it is his turn to sum her up surreptitiously.* **Juan** *hands* **Rupert**

43

a glass filled to the brim and **Rupert** *drinks.* **Rupert** *flinches as the drink hits him. His eyes water and he turns away to hide the shock. When he looks back,* **Loreta's** *chair is empty.*

★ ★ ★ ★ ★

PAN TO – Closed door of bedroom, through which the mouth organ music comes distantly. CUT TO – **Juan**, *whose smile is studied rather than casual.*

JUAN *[gently, suavely]*: The music could be a summons, Rupert.

RUPERT *[emboldened by the drink, grinning]*: A call to arms, perhaps?

JUAN Yes. There are arms of more than one kind.

Rupert *goes to bedroom door, enters and closes it behind him as* **Juan** *and* **Lucille** *exchange glances.*

★ ★ ★ ★ ★

CUT TO – Inside bedroom. **Loreta** *lies naked on the bed, her body brown against the white sheets. Despite the drink,* **Rupert** *is nonplussed, thinking he may have taken her by surprise. He averts his gaze, walks to the window and looks down on to the hotel patio, where people are seated at supper under red and white-striped umbrellas sprouting from tables. He sees an orchestra playing but cannot hear it because of* **Loreta's** *mouth organ. She stops playing and* **Rupert** *turns from the window, by now realising he has not caught her unawares. Her face for the first time smiles and shows interest. She resumes playing the mouth organ but with her free hand beckons him to her. He recognises the music as the Mexican national anthem. It ends with a discord, the instrument falls to the floor and both her arms entwine his neck holding him tight while her lips consume him and their breathing quickens.*

★ ★ ★ ★ ★

CUT TO – The living room, where **Juan** *and* **Lucille** *jostle to look through the keyhole into the bedroom.*

★ ★ ★ ★ ★

CUT TO **Rupert's** *room in the hotel, where the clock says 5.30 a.m. Tousled, he sits on the bed and speaks into the telephone.*

RUPERT: That's right. Dark red. Two dozen. To Room 513 this morning. No name or message. Charge them to the account of Sir Henry Grayson, Room 410. Thank you.

Rupert *slams the phone down, kicks the wastepaper basket, which sails through the open window, throws clothes around the room and flings himself on the bed, smiling in disbelief.*

VOICE: Though I knew nothing of her but the ecstasy of her skilled embrace, I was never to forget this first experience of animal love and my initiation into its mysteries by a nameless, lovely, garlic-scented Mexican. Many years later, when I was drinking tequila with a bunch of bums in Mexico City, I learned that Juan, at the time I met him in Montreal, was already a well-known *voyeur*. Yet even the knowledge that I was only providing entertainment for him has done nothing to dim the glory of that first of all first nights.

Montage of scenes: farewelling Bilton, train journey to London and on to Harrow, presented during narration by **Voice**.

VOICE: I had gone to Harrow after leaving Bilton, but, strangely, few memories of the years there stir my mind. I remember hardly any masters and only a few boys, including Francis Queensberry, L.P. Hartley and Gulbenkian. Nubar, even at that age, was a character. Years later, when we were dining at the Ritz with his second wife, he told me how the master of his hunt remarked that he had never seen a man following hounds so unconventionally dressed, even to an orchid; to which Nubar replied: "To me, sir, it is obvious that you have never before seen an Armenian Jew in the hunting field."

My brothers were to excel there at work and play. I was the pedestrian among the runners. Father did little to encourage me to work. He paid scant attention to school reports and was interested in only that final item that came under the forbidding heading of "General conduct". Mother, for all her Irish casualness, took a much more practical view of our studies and it was she who helped me to move in. She had my room repapered, carpeted and furnished to her usual good taste. Father sent me to his tailor to be fitted and my school blazer, worn in the afternoons, was made in the High Street. Thus conventionally coated and comfortably housed, I began my undistinguished career as a Harrovian.

With the hours, I found nothing unreasonable. They allowed me ample time for reading. I found my way to the Vaughan Library, which became my hideaway. The first friend I made was William Sigismund Alexander. We knew him as Alex, but in the years ahead, in the Irish Guards, he was called "Baby" because he had an elder brother, Harold, later the distinguished field-marshal. Alex had a delightful sense of the ridiculous and a sharp wit. Our mutual friend was a boy called Masterman, who effortlessly became Head of the school. The only bullying I ever noticed was the persecution of certain masters, in particular those who were inexperienced and short-sighted. One boy regularly brought two bricks into form with him…

★ ★ ★ ★ ★

FADE TO – Rear of classroom across backs of about twenty boys to **Master** *on dais, gowned and wearing thick spectacles and mortarboard, who is explaining the difference between active and passive voice.*

MASTER: … so, to sum up *[turns his back to the class, steps to the blackboard, writes "ACTIVE" and "PASSIVE" on the board, and is about to add more]*, we speak in the active voice when we say…

★ ★ ★ ★ ★

CUT TO – Close-up of boy suddenly throwing a stone that smashes one of the room's windows and almost simultaneously throws another at the **Master's** *desk, causing the* **Master** *to drop his chalk, spin round and look in alarm – first at the desk and then at the smashed window, which he approaches warily from the solid part of the wall, as though fearing a second missile. Pandemonium, meanwhile, breaks out among the boys, some rushing to the window to see who has thrown the stone from outside, others racing from the room vowing to catch the culprit, while the* **Master** *flaps about trying to restore order.*

★ ★ ★ ★ ★

FADE TO – Another, similar classroom, but with a quite different master: **Prior**, *dark, bearded, fluent, dominant.*

VOICE: For French, on the other hand, we had *Monsieur* Prior, who was not only an excellent French teacher, but even looked and smelled like one. As the scent of garlic clung to him, so did his teaching cling to me. Nor did he mind the odd laugh.

★ ★ ★ ★ ★

CUT TO – Close-up of **Prior**.

PRIOR *[chin raised, addressing boy with hand up]* : What is it, Smithton?

SMITHTON *[earnestly]*: I'm quite prepared to pronounce these French words as you suggest I should, Monsieur, but it all sounds very affected to me.

PRIOR *[looks at wall clock, shuts book as form's mirth subsides]*: That's all for now. *[Looks at Rupert, lowers voice]* Please wait, Grayson.

The other boys gather up their things and go. **Prior** *points to a front desk near the master's table and* **Rupert** *sits at it.*

PRIOR: You know of Dumas *père*?

RUPERT *[pleased but apprehensive]*: My favourite author, sir.

PRIOR *[a French side-to-side tilting of the head to suggest such a preference is normal]*: Once, Grayson, a young American girl studying under him, overwhelmed by his stature as a writer, started adoringly to say: *"Monsieur Dumas, votre nom bril…"* – but she was not yet fluent and hesitated. "Young lady," said Dumas, "do not go into ecstasies over something you have never seen." The poor girl was going to say *"nom brillant." "Nombril"* is "navel", or, as I think you call it, "belly button". If you are stuck in French expression as you were today, make sure you stick where it is not embarrassing.

Prior *smiles kindly and waves* **Rupert** *away.*

★ ★ ★ ★ ★

CUT TO – Door of **Headmaster's** *office with sign on it to that effect. Pan to adjoining door, which indicates that it is the* **Headmaster's** *waiting room. Inside it sits* **Rupert**, *glumly staring at the floor. He looks up as the door opens to admit the* **Headmaster's** *two small boys.* **Rupert's** *frown gives way to a smile and he pats their heads as they approach and speak to him.*

★ ★ ★ ★ ★

CUT TO – Inside **Headmaster's** *office, where, gowned and austere at his desk, the incumbent is sifting papers, thinking, scribbling, consulting books, signing. Cocks his head and glances at the waiting room, having heard young voices there that are excited and laughing. He leaves the desk, goes to the dividing door and opens it.* **Rupert** *is on all fours, one of the boys riding him like a horse and the other impatient to get on.*

VOICE: One day, through carelessness, I was caught cribbing to make a Latin test easier and was duly sent up to the headmaster, Lionel Ford. His two sons, aged six and seven, joined me in the annexe to his study, making a welcome distraction at a time that was not at all pleasant. Many years later, Ford confessed that, on opening the door to call me in, the preview of my bottom, excellent cricketer and racquets player though he was, so put him off his stroke that he could not remember having thrashed anyone with less enthusiasm.

★ ★ ★ ★ ★

CUT TO – **Rupert's** *rooms, so nicely done-out by his mother.* **Alex**, **Masterman** *and* **Rupert** *are sitting around;* **Rupert** *on the table dangling his legs, the other two in armchairs. The discussion is serious.*

MASTERMAN: I agree, Rupe. The teamwork is right – you, local news, Alex the witty stuff and I editorials, and the formula has proved itself: we're sold out every issue. And there is nothing wrong with *A la Carte* as the title. Yet, I see clouds.

RUPERT *[gloomily]*: I, too.

ALEX: It's *The Harrovian* that's the trouble. If it attacks us as the official school magazine, then the Pharisees who run the place can hardly not take up its tune.

MASTERMAN: Especially when we're making money out of it, even at

49

sixpence a copy. There's jealousy about, don't you think?

RUPERT: Not much doubt about that. And they don't like it being sold alongside reputable textbooks in bookshops and stationers.

MASTERMAN: That story of yours in the second-last issue, Rupe, about the Frog's nocturnal rooftop visit to the pastrycook's daughter – maybe we took a risk there… good name of the school and all that.

ALEX: Not so much that as your editorial, Masterman, declaring that being French saved him from punishment.

RUPERT: We are successful, but there's too much against us in this very sanctimonious age. Let's stop the diagnostics now. On Monday, after our salvo against the public schools' system in Friday's issue, it could be a post-mortem we are conducting.

★ ★ ★ ★ ★

CUT TO – **Headmaster's** *office again, the three standing before him.*

HEADMASTER You were warned. You are not yet perhaps of an age to take respect and dignity as seriously as you will have to one day, but, even allowing for immaturity, you have gone too far. Last Friday's issue of your… your… rag was a disgrace and I'm afraid I can no longer resist the demands being made on me to close it down. In effect, you are telling your parents, and all the other parents, that they are wasting their money paying for boys to come here. You are lucky to escape punishment as well as closure. Now, go.

Wordlessly, the three turn and leave the office; the **Headmaster's** *gaze, once the door has closed, following them with a suggestion of amusement.*

VOICE: And so my first publishing venture ended in ignominy and it was not the last to do so, for life had hardly begun.

★ ★ ★ ★ ★

CUT TO – *The three walking sheepishly along the corridor away from* **Headmaster's** *study, saying nothing until* **Alex** *speaks.*

ALEX: Perhaps it's just as well, because we can now proceed with our education – though, mind you, I still think they are more interested in schooling than in teaching.

RUPERT: And it saves us from spoiling the fun at Lord's tomorrow by having to report it.

★ ★ ★ ★ ★

CUT TO – *Lord's, pre-1914, the Eton-Harrow cricket match, one of the great London social events and the last of the London Season. Players in white are batting, bowling and shouting on the green. At the garden party that encircles it, well-dressed young men in top hats mingle with gorgeous girls under wide-brimmed straw hats, decorated with shimmering satin bows, and wearing muslin frocks with pink, blue or mauve sashes round their waists, and long white gloves. The young men sport cornflower buttonholes for Harrow, carnations for Eton.* **Rupert** *and school friend* **(Andy Wilson)** *saunter towards a coach and two tables – one for drinks, the other for food – around which there is a buzz of cornflowers, carnations and elders.*

RUPERT: We are approaching the Grayson colony.

WILSON *[impressed]*: The coach and the tables?

RUPERT: Yes. It's Father's annual contribution to the jolliity.

WILSON *[eyeing a rotund figure in morning dress]*: That's not the famous Turner, is it?

RUPERT: None other, my dear Watson.

WILSON: I say, what a splash! And those two dapper chappies he is ordering about – they are part of the shebang?

RUPERT: Two of our footmen, Pinkerton and Perkins. Pinky and Perky, we call them. Father says they fuss around Turner like acolytes attending on a bishop.

A **Large Woman** *with goblet in hand swerves towards them unsteadily and waves it in the direction of the field, some of the contents splashing on to* **Rupert***, who leaps aside.*

LARGE WOMAN *[with American voice]*: Excuse me, but what are the little boys in white doing on the grass?

RUPERT *[irritated, wiping jacket with handkerchief]*: Selling ice creams, madam.

At which she looks again at the players, seems mystified and moves on. The two arrive at the drinks and food tables and partake.

WILSON: I hope the school catering manager takes note of all this.

RUPERT: He'd be too bashful to show his face. Mind you, it's the time of year for this sort of thing. The salmon, lobster, strawberries and raspberries – all at their prime.

WILSON: Perhaps he's here in disguise. I suppose you know everyone – at least, those at your table?

RUPERT: Come to mention it *[tilting his head in the direction of the table]*, there is one I can't place: the dapper old codger next to Denys. But he's not the catering manager.

Lady Grayson *approaches.*

RUPERT: Here's Mother. Let's ask.

She smiles, about to pass them en route to somewhere else. **Rupert** *intercepts her.*

RUPERT: Mother, you've met Andy Wilson, have you not?

LADY GRAYSON: Indeed I have. Hello, Andy, you look well.

WILSON *[raising hat]*: Good day, Lady Grayson. Thank you. You likewise, if I may say so.

At which **Lady Grayson** *goes to move on, but* **Rupert** *detains her.*

RUPERT: A moment, Mother. *[With his back to the table, in a near-whisper]* Who is the silver-haired cove sitting next to Denys?

LADY GRAYSON *[glancing at the man, puzzled, then at Rupert]*: It's odd, but no one seems to know him, and he is so presentable and friendly and at home that asking him who he is, to his face, doesn't seem, somehow…

RUPERT *[teasing]*: Even for you, Mother?

LADY GRAYSON: I don't know what you mean, my boy, but I'll tell you something: *[lowers voice to a whisper that almost excludes Wilson or at least lets him know that what she is saying is confidential]* Turner could find no initials on the lining of his hat.

RUPERT *[more openly, to re-admit Wilson to the conversation]*: Good God! – That almost makes him a vagrant. But if Turner doesn't know, who does?

LADY GRAYSON *[ignoring the rhetorical question]*: Although it lacks a name, the dossier is not entirely blank.

RUPERT: Oh?

LADY GRAYSON: It's nothing much, but according to my informant…

RUPERT *[interrupting]*: Turner?

LADY GRAYSON: Not Turner.

RUPERT: Go on, Mother

LADY GRAYSON: As I was saying, it seems that our stranger had a dream about a woman he had met only casually, but his dream was so delightful and vivid that next morning he knew he was in love with her. That very day he chanced to meet her, proposed, was accepted, and they lived happily thereafter.

RUPERT: He did not bring her with him?

LADY GRAYSON: It seems not. Perhaps it was no longer possible.

RUPERT: Oh. Perhaps.

LADY GRAYSON: You must excuse me. Enjoy yourselves.

Lady Grayson *smiles and departs.* **Rupert** *and* **Wilson** *drift to the drinks table and take champagne.*

WILSON: Enchanting.

RUPERT: Mother?

WILSON: No. I mean, yes *[flustered]*, of course she is, but I meant the story she told.

RUPERT: Ah, yes. Mother, you see, is not only Irish but grew up in South America, where romance breeds like… [hesitates]

WILSON [*venturing inquiringly*]: Yeast? Rabbits? Flies?

RUPERT [*with friendly sarcasm*]: I was going to say porterhouse steak, but you're so damned quick off the mark.

A pretty, dark-eyed girl, **Amanda,** *strolls up to them, twirling her parasol.* **Rupert** *gazes intently and admiringly at her. The two raise their hats.*

RUPERT [*indicating the food table*]: Will you join us, Amanda?

AMANDA: Thank you, but I'm looking for Giles. Have you seen him?

RUPERT: No, but I do hope you find him. I'm sure it's careless of a brother to leave such a sister unattended.

She smiles coyly and goes on her way.

WILSON: You're rather quick off the mark yourself, don't you think?

★ ★ ★ ★ ★

CUT TO – *Four gentlemen getting to their feet in the grandstand. They are dominated physically and conversationally by* **Sir Henry Grayson.**

SIR HENRY [*scanning and addressing his three companions*]: So nice to have seen you, but I'm off before [*smile*] they start the rough stuff.

FIRST MAN [*nodding towards the concourse below*]: I think you're too late, Henry.

On the concourse in front of the stand has begun the annual ritual of the friendly fight between Harrow and Eton supporters, who try to bash each other's top hats with sticks tasselled in the respective teams' colours.

SIR HENRY [*scanning the goings-on*]: You're right. Well, this is one time when I hope I look my age.

SECOND MAN [*ironically*]: I'm sure, Henry, you look quite as advanced in years as your repair bills do in pounds.

FIRST MAN [*to SIR HENRY*]: How's your brood? I saw Rupert down there earlier, ogling a pretty girl. Brings back memories, eh?

SIR HENRY [*with a smile and sideways look*]: One or two... I say, look at that. Age is no protection, after all.

* * * * *

CUT TO – The object of their attention: two ancient gentlemen on the outskirts of the headbashers who have taken to each other with umbrellas, but, despite all their efforts, are getting nowhere because the handles have become interlocked like the horns of fighting rams, and the two geriatrics are purple with frustration.

SECOND MAN: You could say they are making no headway, I suppose.

The four laugh and disperse.

* * * * *

CUT TO – A montage of sequences in the West End that night, showing streets, restaurants, foyers and bars frequented by revellers in white ties, tail-coats and white kid gloves, sporting the cornflowers and carnations, singing and dancing, shouting school war-cries. Scene closes with **Rupert** *and school chums singing and laughing bawdily and drunkenly. The clock shows three in the morning as four of them climb awkwardly into a hansom cab, falling back into the street on to horse manure, wiping it roughly off and trying again before successfully entering the vehicle.*

* * * * *

CUT TO – Inside cab. **Rupert** *lies on floor as it lurches along. The* **Cabbie** *opens his roof at the top of the passenger compartment, his face showing anxiety.*

CABBIE: Everything satisfactory dahn there, Master Grayson? You don't want to stop, loik, for a breath of fresh hair?

RUPERT [*looking up, woozy, seeing the hole*]: No, but if you don't close that hole in the floor, I'll fall out willy-nilly and then there'll be no one to pay your fare. My friends here haven't got a bean.

ALEX *[less inebriated]*: What he's asking, Rupe, is whether you want to be sick. And, if you do, don't use the hole in the floor because it's actually in the roof and that means gravity is not on your side.

★ ★ ★ ★ ★

CUT TO – Next day in **Rupert's** *study.* **Alex** *opens the window and a breeze blows the curtain in.* **Rupert** *sits in a chair with his head in his hands.*

RUPERT: Wider, Alex, if you want to save my life.

Alex *pushes the window higher still and the curtain flaps about wildly and* **Rupert** *groans.* **Masterman** *knocks, enters and looks enquiringly at* **Rupert**.

ALEX *[nodding at Rupert, still clutching his head]*: He's had an unforgettable experience.

MASTERMAN *[frowns with concern]*: What do you mean? *[pointing to Rupert, whispering]* Shock?

ALEX: Not exactly. Last night he was drunk for the first time, and you never forget the first of anything.

Linger on **Rupert**, *receding.*

★ ★ ★ ★ ★

CUT TO – Playing field with game in progress, **Rupert** *excelling first in the scrum and then running and passing and finally winning through to a try.*

VOICE: I disliked football, particularly of the Harrow variety, played with a ball that appeared to be almost square. I hated the sweating nearness of other players. Yet, in life's contrary way, I excelled at this most disagreeable game and after having demonstrated proficiency at it was able to withdraw from playing – which did nothing, I'm afraid, to increase my popularity with either boys or masters. My weakness was that I never wished to excel. Yet there was much about Harrow that I loved and I shall always be grateful to Father for sending me there.

CUT TO – A steep lane leading to the churchyard that crowns the hill, closing to an inscription on an old wall that reads: NEAR THIS SPOT ANTHONY ASHLEY COOPER, AFTERWARDS SEVENTH EARL OF SHAFTESBURY, WHILE YET A BOY IN HARROW SCHOOL, SAW, WITH SHAME AND INDIGNATION, A PAUPER'S FUNERAL, WHICH HELPED TO AWAKEN HIS LIFELONG DEVOTION TO THE SERVICE OF THE POOR AND THE OPPRESSED.

VOICE: There were many things to be learned at Harrow that were not taught at lessons, chapel or even in the Vaughan Library, and the first of them was that kindness and consideration to those less fortunate than oneself must be guiding principles in a civilised life. I had many friends among the townsfolk on the hill: Willie Chatham the bootmaker, Mr Shepherd of Thomas Smith the tailors and his assistant Mr Fewtral, and Mr Guppy of the music shop – with all of whom I had accounts. There were two dear old ladies, the Armstrongs, and when one of the sisters died, the other described her death to Brian: "And just before her passing she raised her little hand as if to say 'Cheerio'."

★ ★ ★ ★ ★

CUT TO – The peak of the hill, with its parish church dominating the surrounding lands.

VOICE: It was in the church's old graveyard that Byron, my admired and noncoeval schoolfellow – whose tastes, but not, alas, talents, I was so enthusiastically to share – had wished that he might be buried. During his schooldays, it was said that he would often lie on the old gravestone carved with the name of one "Peachy", long-deceased, and known to subsequent generations of Harrovians as "The Peachy Stone".

★ ★ ★ ★ ★

58

CUT TO – The fields where Byron played cricket, Thames, Windsor Castle.

VOICE: Beyond the green of the meadow lies the Thames and, through summer haze, an occasional glimpse of Windsor Castle.

★ ★ ★ ★ ★

CUT TO – **Rupert** *lying on The Peachy Stone.*

VOICE: Lying stretched on his stone, I could feel some of Byron's romantic spirit rub off on me and strove to see with his romantic eyes the selfsame scene that he had looked upon. But his flesh must have been tougher than mine, for the stone had a most unromantic lack of comfort.

★ ★ ★ ★ ★

CUT TO – Interior of Covent Garden during Wagner's 'Parsifal'.

VOICE: Father's interest in music was confined mostly to Neapolitan and Sicilian songs, but that of Mother, who, like most of her generation, played the piano, was more classical. It was typical of Father that he should have allowed me to join the select few who were taken up to London by Percy Buck, the music master, to the operas at Covent Garden.

★ ★ ★ ★ ★

FADE TO – Dining room at Waldorf Hotel, **Rupert**, **Alex** *and another companion,* **Dynes**, *sharing a table to take food and drink in the long interval.*

DYNES *[snapping out of reverie]*: What? What? What?

RUPERT *[palms of both hands held up]*: Nothing, Dynes. I merely asked for the salt. Were you hypnotising yourself?

ALEX *[leaning towards Dynes, clapping once loudly]*: Quick, Dynes, what's my name?

DYNES: Oh, shut up, Alex. Wagner meant you to think and that's what I was doing. Offenbach is for people like you – all crutch and no cranium. I suppose you had thought *Parsifal* was a tropical fruit.

Alex *opens his mouth to speak but* **Rupert** *speaks first.*

RUPERT *[conciliating]*: Come, chaps. No discord. Dynes was just reflecting on how much Wagner had on his plate, weren't you, Dynes – what with Liszt forcing ideas on him, Liszt's daughter Cosima forcing herself on him, King Ludwig forcing money on him and French hooligans forcing *Tannhäuser* to close in Paris. Alex, you boned up on Wagner and his involvements before coming to be enchanted by him tonight, did you not?

ALEX: Of course. But it's quite gone from my head.

RUPERT: Oh, let Dynes explain it when he's back on earth. The politics are beyond me. I'm content to bathe in the sound. It's my first opera, you know, but it will certainly not be my last.

DYNES *[condescendingly]*: All I need say, I think, is that had we known Wagner personally, it would probably have poisoned us against his music unless we separated it from him as he separated it from his creditors.

RUPERT: Well, Alex, unless you wish to table an amendment to that, I think we should declare business closed and repair to the auditorium. All in favour?

★ ★ ★ ★ ★

CUT TO – Covent Garden as it recedes to Wagnerian music.

VOICE: And so we played, learned and grew up. We were young in a world that was gently sliding into the abyss, where the standard of comfort for the privileged few within the citadel had never in the history of the universe been surpassed; served and waited on by a further select few of the hordes who stood outside the gates. We wore life as a suit of clothes, which, once donned, could be forgotten. I knew nothing of poverty, frustration and famine, and was aware of only the hot sweet smell of the flowers in the window boxes as I arrived at our London house that night and handed my white kid gloves and top hat to one of the sleepy footmen.

Close slowly on Liverpool from Mersey to docks, or what used to be, and Grayson Street, focusing on its street sign.

VOICE: According to Liverpool legend, the first Grayson started making ships 300 years ago at a wharf now built over and known as Grayson Street. At seventeen, Father's mother had left him a thousand pounds a year. He was thus agreeably independent from early on, and this was probably why throughout his life he preferred the more selfish role of host to the more exacting one of guest. For all his experience, he was no judge of people, except when he married my mother. Those he backed in business invariably failed. It was strange that he himself had been able to expand the family firm so successfully. He sympathised with, rather than understood, those he employed. He was more amused than annoyed when, on reprimanding a secretary for continually being half an hour late, the man replied: "Yes, sir, but you forget that I always leave half an hour early."

None of my ancestors through whom the business passed down interested me much, except my great-great-grandfather Edward, who in 1804 became perhaps the last man in England to be killed in a duel. On my mother's side was Daniel Harrington, who served with Nelson on *Victory*. Nelson once said to him: "Mr Harrington, you're getting very bald." Daniel, who was not Irish for nothing, replied: "Is that to be wondered at, my Lord, considering all the men who have passed over me." *[Pause]* Father pretended to be angry when, in August 1914, I terminated my undistinguished career at Harrow and enlisted.

Sir Henry *at desk in his study at Aberduna Hall. The door opens and* **Rupert** *enters, looking sheepish.*

RUPERT: Evening, Father.

SIR HENRY: What's this I hear from your mother?

RUPERT [*trying to make light of it*]: I can only guess, Father, that she has told you I heeded the call to arms.

SIR HENRY [*crossly*]: Your guess is better than your judgment. What do you think you're playing at? You're not even of age. And by whose authority did you decide to chuck school and then join the service by the tradesmen's entrance?

RUPERT: I'm sorry, Father, if my feeling for King and Country upsets you, but do you think His Majesty would approve your disapproval?

SIR HENRY: I shall disregard those words, because immaturity is rash, but you seem to have forgotten the traditions of this family – one of which is that members of it who serve in the armed forces do so not in the ranks but as officers and gentlemen. No doubt someone has to peel potatoes, but not, if we can help it, a Grayson.

RUPERT: Potatoes are not what I had in mind, Father, so much as guns. There will surely be more triggers to pull than potatoes to peel.

Sir Henry *looks steadily at* **Rupert** *for ten seconds, then gazes around the walls of the study where, among others, are pictures of family forbears. His eyes return to* **Rupert**.

SIR HENRY: Can you shoot straight?

RUPERT: If my effect on Scotland's grouse population means anything, the answer must be no. But if I were to go to war through the front door, I should command others to do that.

SIR HENRY [*gruffly*]: Sit tight. Do nothing. Leave it to me.

At which **Sir Henry** *swivels around in his chair to face the desk again, so dismissing* **Rupert**, *who quietly leaves the room.*

★ ★ ★ ★ ★

CUT TO – Burlington House, in which several candidates are emerging from a hall after having sat an examination for, as a notice board indicates, entry into Sandhurst Royal Military Academy. **Rupert's** *face lights up on recognising, in the lobby, a fellow candidate,* **Pingo** *Langrishe, who looks equally delighted. They shake hands heartily.* **Pingo** *is good-looking and no less charming than* **Rupert**.

RUPERT: Pingo, what are you doing here? Don't tell me you've chucked Eton?

PINGO: Yes, and not a moment too soon. The food had become unbearable. I didn't expect to see you alive again after the last Lord's match.

RUPERT: A near thing, I admit. But come and tell me your story.

They cross the street to the Burlington Bar. **Rupert** *jerks his thumb back towards where they have come from.*

RUPERT: What about that?

PINGO: Oh, a formality. Name on the paper, that's all. I'm not one for exams, y'know. Could barely read the questions, let alone answer them.

RUPERT: Same here, I'm afraid. Mathematics always baffled me. Geography's more in my line now: first stop, France.

PINGO: Quite. Even if I could borrow Isaac Newton's brain for the morning, I had no interest in that stuff. Anyway, Sandhurst is for peacetime.

RUPERT: Of course it is. I was already halfway to France, y'know, because I joined up at the local recruiting office, but Father put his foot down and sent me to this military crammer in Tunbridge Wells. He boasted that none of his boys had ever failed to get into Sandhurst. *[Ruefully]* He can't say that any more.

PINGO: Your old man must have meant business. Did you learn nothing whatsoever from the crammer?

RUPERT: Not quite. His youngest daughter taught me to smoke a pipe.

PINGO: Huh! More useful than mathematics. You can't make smokescreens with algebra. I hope you taught her something in return.

But **Rupert's** *thoughts have moved on.*

RUPERT: Where to from here?

PINGO: I have a feeling I'm going to end up in the Irish Guards as a puppet on the end of family strings. And you?

Rupert *grins broadly.*

RUPERT: That's fantastic, because it's my destination, too. There's no other place for me. The Irish Guards are as much part of the Graysons as I am myself. Father had hoped to do it the tidy way, with Sandhurst as well as the Bible in my kitbag, but he has a line to the lieutenant colonel of the Brigade, and so… *[shows the palms of his hands]*.

PINGO: Then let's drink to it. But *[tapping upper lip with finger],* you know what it means, don't you?

RUPERT: What?

PINGO: We must grow moustaches. In the Guards, they are as important as trousers, I'm told.

★ ★ ★ ★ ★

CUT TO – Warley Barracks, home of the Irish Guards. A door bears the name of **Captain** *the Hon.* **Thomas Vesey,** *Adjutant. Inside,* **Rupert's** *interview with the adjutant is ending. As they stand,* **Captain Vesey** *speaks.*

CAPTAIN VESEY: Good luck, Grayson, and regards to Sir Henry. By the way, I note that you're clean-shaven. You're aware of the moustache tradition, are you not?

RUPERT: Yes, sir, I am.

CAPTAIN VESEY: Thought you would be. Thorough man, your father. I presume he told you it must be a proper moustache and not a Charlie Chaplin?

RUPERT: Yes, but what colour would you like it, sir?

CAPTAIN VESEY *[flushing, but settling for sarcasm]*: You know the regimental colours, Grayson: navy-blue trimmed with scarlet.

★ ★ ★ ★ ★

CUT TO – Troop train, ship, France.

VOICE: It was by no means the last I saw of Tom Vesey. The battlefields for which we were so eager came all too soon. Once, after an engagement more bloody than usual, in which we lost three officers and twenty-four other ranks, his first remark, on seeing me return alive, was "Christ! It had to be you". Yet there was an almost affectionate intonation in his voice. Years later, I used to meet him now and then in London after he become something in the City. He had mellowed, so that I wondered how he ever forced his harshness on my comrades and me. They had admired, feared and hated him, but my attitude towards him must have sprung from emotional laziness, for I realised then that I had no talent for hating, and I have failed to acquire it since – except towards obviously loathsome things like ventriloquists, pottery figures of animals, playing musical instruments and people who insist on recounting their dreams. Before we had tasted the real thing, those of us who were young regarded those first months of the war as a time of high adventure. For us who knew him, this prelude was enlivened by the wit and eccentricities of Pingo Langrishe.

★ ★ ★ ★ ★

CUT TO – Dinner at **Pingo's** *Knightsbridge house. As the* **Guests** *arrive, they are offered cigars, port, coffee and nuts.*

GUEST *[enters room, rubs eyes, turns to* **Rupert***]*: I know I had a few earlier, but have I arrived when it is all over?

RUPERT *[laughing]*: No, it's only Pingo being Irish with one of his back-to-front dinners. Your first time here?

GUEST: Yes. I'm a stranger to London now. Kenya's my beat. But *[looking round, trying to comprehend]*…

RUPERT *[expansively explicit]*: Don't nibble too many nuts or it will spoil the sweets – and after that the main course, *entrée*, fish, soup and *hors d'oeuvre* in that order, with wines to match; after which, to complete the Fenian fantasy, you might reverse out of the entrance into the cab that brought you here.

GUEST *[raising eyebrows, resigned]*: Well, I suppose it is all bound for the same destination, so what the hell!
RUPERT: That's the spirit. Speaking of destinations, do you return to Kenya soon?

GUEST: Eventually rather than soon, I think. I'm here to join up. *[Lowers voice]* Pingo's parents asked him to be nice to me. He is supposed to be putting me next to someone who knows which door to knock on.

RUPERT: Splendid. He and I took the plunge together some time ago and are waiting to become soldiers, in fact as well as name. I suspect that soon, in retrospect, even one of our host's upside-down meals will be ambrosia.

At which, **Pingo** *approaches.*

PINGO: I'm stealing him, Rupert.

★ ★ ★ ★ ★

FADE TO – Later. As the large clock says, it is midnight and the guests have moved into the drawing room for dry martinis. **Rupert** *sidles up to* **Pingo**.

RUPERT *[discreetly]*: Some of us are proceeding, as they say in the services, to a *debutante* do around the comer in Park Lane. Will you join us?

PINGO: Not invited, old boy. Are you suggesting I gatecrash?

RUPERT: Why not? I'll sponsor you. We'll be doing some serious gatecrashing soon. Might as well rehearse.

★ ★ ★ ★ ★

CUT TO – Lively dance amid splendour, young revellers joking, squealing, pranking. In an adjacent smoke room, **Pingo** *is lighting a long thin Havana. He finds a middle-aged* **Man** *helping himself to a large whisky.* **Pingo** *does the same and addresses the* **Man**.

PINGO: Perhaps this will improve it.

MAN: Improve what?

PINGO *[irritably]*: The occasion, the evening, the morning, whatever it is. It's quite the most boring dance I've attended in a long time.

MAN [*nodding vigorously*]: I'm afraid you're right. I could not have tried harder to dissuade my wife from giving it.

As the **Man's** *meaning dawns on the bleary* **Pingo**, *he freezes mid-sip, hiding behind the glass, while his eyes, looking over it, slowly turn to the* **Man** *and scrutinise him. Gradually, they smile wryly at each other.*

★ ★ ★ ★ ★

CUT TO – The ballroom, where **Pingo** *joins* **Rupert** *as he moves away from a couple of debs he has been amusing.*

RUPERT: Thought you'd gone home.

PINGO: No, just roaming around polishing my skills as a diplomat.

Pingo *gazes about him and quickly back again to* **Rupert**.

PINGO: Don't look now, but I've just spotted a fish out of water: that dreadful Gillett.

RUPERT: You mean the distinguished president of the fashionable Bachelors' Club? I think he's coming our way, so mind your manners.

Gillett *joins them. He is pompous and condescending, his smile false.*

GILLETT: Evening Grayson, Langrishe.

Rupert *mumbles an acknowledgement, but* **Pingo's** *is more explicit.*

PINGO: Good evening, Gillett. Are you here to protect your members against the latest swarm of butterflies?

GILLETT: I'd be more inclined to find some sort of answer to your question if you pronounced my name correctly, Langrishe. Kindly remember that the G is soft, as in "gentleman".

PINGO: Oh, I'm sorry; I thought it was hard, as in "bugger".

At which, **Gillett** *turns and, head held high and nostrils flared, walks away.*

RUPERT: I can see you did not polish your diplomacy in vain. It is so bright that poor Gillett couldn't stand the glare.

PINGO: I thought his interest in humanity was so confined to the aristocracy that he was dazzle-proof. It's amazing how far up the stairs an *arriviste* can climb so soon. Two steps a year, would you say?

RUPERT *[with chuckle]*: He is certainly a recommendation for haberdashery. That club he founded has a rather large turnover though, does it not?

PINGO: He reminds me more than anyone else of that verse by Robert Burns:

> *No more of your titled acquaintances boast,*
> *Nor in what – lordly company you've been.*
> *An insect is but an insect at most,*
> *Though it crawl on the head of a Queen.*

Rupert *smiles and nods silently several times.*

★ ★ ★ ★ ★

FADE TO – Pall Mall, moving through St James's Square to Jermyn Street in the company of two Irish Guards officers.

VOICE: Morning coat and top hat were worn in London when the king and queen were at Buck House. We never shook hands with each other, and, perhaps surprisingly in those more formal days, used first names only. We bought our clothes from the regimental tailor, spoke of "London" and never "town", and did not say "weekend". We were forbidden to travel on buses and to carry parcels, and must smoke only Turkish or Egyptian cigarettes. In the evening, we wore blue mess-kit with an inch of broad scarlet braid down the trouser-leg. Our greatcoats were steel-grey with scarlet linings. It was a rule in the brigade, even in the first years of the war, that an officer could wear a black tie and dinner jacket in a grille room, but in a restaurant, proper white tie and tailcoat were *de rigueur*.

★ ★ ★ ★ ★

CUT TO – Entrance to Savoy, then interior.

VOICE: I was about to dine in the Savoy one night when I detected the swift expression of invitation in the eyes of a girl passing through the foyer to the restaurant.

The eyes of **Rupert** *in dinner jacket and beautiful* **Girl** *crossing foyer connect, with a smile on the face of each.* **Rupert's** *attention suddenly skips to another part of the foyer where a man* [**Jackie Aird**] *in white tie and tailcoat is headed for the restaurant. As the* **Girl** *disappears,* **Rupert** *accosts* **Aird**, *whose figure, tall and graceful, contrasts with* **Rupert's** *dumpier one.*

RUPERT: So glad I spotted you, Jackie. Forgive my abruptness when there is so much else to talk about, but I find myself in a pickle and wonder whether you might help out.

AIRD: Well, I'll be blowed. I'd heard you were bound for the front to hound the Hun.

RUPERT: Yes, but there are preliminaries to attend to, and one of them is right here and now. The short of it is: might I briefly swap my dinner jacket for your tailcoat, old man? Without such dress I cannot enter the restaurant, and the need to do so has become irresistible. There is someone with whom I must have just one dance.

AIRD [*perplexed*]: I must say you're never short of the odd surprise, even when one is not craving for it. But anything for an old friend, I suppose,

71

and especially with such sisters. As a matter of fact, I was on the way to the restaurant myself, not yet having partaken, so don't be long.

RUPERT: Bless you. No, not that way *[as Aird, resigned to changing, begins to head for the men's room from which he has just come]*. There's a cubbyhole around the corner that Father uses now and then. Let me speak to Alf in the cloakroom.

★ ★ ★ ★ ★

FADE TO – The two returning together to the foyer, both looking ridiculous, **Aird's** *outfit too small and* **Rupert's** *too long. As* **Rupert** *makes for the restaurant,* **Aird** *heads for the American Bar, where, as his appearance is noticed and the denizens, with nudges and whispers, become aware of his outlandishness, the laughter becomes so uproarious that the scarecrow is forced to retreat from the bar to the men's room, where he miserably awaits the return of* **Rupert**, *having on the way whispered appropriate instructions to a waiter.* **Rupert**, *meanwhile, prompts amusement as he enters the restaurant and makes for the* **Girl**, *whom he has spotted at a table with a group of people. More laughter in the restaurant as* **Rupert** *the scarecrow is observed, albeit less raucous than in the American Bar. Already the strain of* **Rupert's** *broader chest and back has taken its toll on the tail coat, which has burst at the seams, allowing the lining to spill out, and the diamond and onyx buttons of the waistcoat, yielding to pressure, no longer holds the two sides together. The coat-tails hang almost to his ankles. The* **Girl** *and her companions all laugh as he arrives at their table. As he addresses them, he is handed a goblet of champagne and chairs are shuffled to make room for him at the table.*

RUPERT *[to girl]*: When I saw you in the foyer, I thought you were perhaps lost, but on more mature consideration – which is to say, a few seconds later – I realise that it was I who was lost. Please forgive my garb, but it was rather off-the-peg, I'm afraid. I see now *[beaming amiably at the other occupants of the table]* that there was no need for me to don any rescue gear at all. You are in wonderful hands. Would you oblige me, though, by also being in my arms for a dance.

At which, the interloper leads her on to the floor and, sartorial deficiency notwithstanding, whirls her around in a waltz she seems to enjoy.

★ ★ ★ ★ ★

FADE TO – Men's room an hour later, where **Rupert** *calls* **Jackie's** *name and sees him emerge from a cubicle.*

AIRD [*grumpishly good-natured*]: That was a hell of a long dance and I don't think my valet will applaud the depreciation my clothes appear to have sustained.

RUPERT [*beckoning him from the men's room and re-entering the cubby-hole*]: Sorry, Jackie, and thank you so much. I had not realised you dress so humorously.

Rupert *fishes in the jacket* **Aird** *returns to him, pulls out his wallet and takes from it a card, which he hands to* **Aird**.

RUPERT: There's the address of my tailor. Be a good chap and see him for a replacement. And don't say no – Father pays the bills.

AIRD: That's civil of you, Rupert. Perhaps I shall. We must keep the home fires burning, as the song says, and tailors must not starve just because their best customers are away. Did you achieve your purpose?

RUPERT [*smiling, looking at and through Jackie, musing*]: In a way, I suppose.

★ ★ ★ ★ ★

CUT TO – Warley Barracks, bustling with preparation.

VOICE: Neither Jackie nor I realised that the long dance I had enjoyed with the dreamy girl was to be the last of its kind. From now on, it was to be the *danse macabre* for us and thousands more. A few days later, I was posted to the second battalion, in command of a platoon. Field Marshall Lord Kitchener of Khartoum, who began his military career as a sapper, was appointed Colonel of the Irish Guards and in this capacity he inspected the battalion. After introductions and drinking port in the mess, we were grouped outside with him for the customary photograph. As one of the junior ensigns, I was standing next to John Kipling, the son of Rudyard Kipling, on a form in the back row.

★ ★ ★ ★ ★

CUT TO – The battalion set for its photograph, **John Kipling** *standing next to* **Rupert**. *In the silence just before the photograph is taken, and as his eyes pick out a grease spot on the field marshal's cap, Kipling's voice booms out.*

JOHN KIPLING: I told you, Rupert, that Kitchener would never make a guardsman.

Rupert's *face goes taut with alarm. He pulls his head down between his shoulders as though he is trying to disappear. Photo taken, the group dissolves,* **Rupert** *looking apprehensive and then relieved as he sees the old* **Kipling** *Rolls Royce at the edge of the parade-ground waiting to take them to Bateman's, the family home.*

★ ★ ★ ★ ★

CUT TO – The door of their quarters, from which **John Kipling** *and* **Rupert** *emerge and carry their bags to the Rolls.*

RUPERT: I thought you had us on a charge that time, John. Your eyesight is too good for war.

JOHN KIPLING: Better if you don't mention it to Father. It would take him an effort to see the funny side of it.

The car threads through the lanes of Sussex towards Burwash and Bateman's. In the village, it passes a farm cart with the wording on the side: R. Kipling, Bateman's, Burwash.

RUPERT *[nodding towards the cart]*: Not far from home, I see.

JOHN KIPLING: Ah, yes. Father is even more concerned about his agricultural than his literary identity. He would love to be considered a Sussex Man, but I'm afraid Man of Sussex is all he is around here. The neighbours are respectful but distant.

At which, the car rolls up the drive and has hardly stopped before the house when **Rudyard Kipling** *emerges to greet them: short, straight, wiry, neat.*

VOICE: The battalion was now under embarkation orders, so this was the last opportunity any of us had to go home. That evening, the old house stood so peacefully in its valley that it was as though the news of war in Europe had never reached it. I made my farewells to these people who had been so kind to me. Then the Rolls took me back to London to say even more poignant farewells to my own family. Father was at Waterloo to see us off to Southampton, for the boat that took us to France and the train to the Front. Mother had already fussed, scolded and cried over me at Warley Barracks.

★ ★ ★ ★ ★

CUT TO – Waterloo Station buffet, into which steps **Sir Henry** *Grayson, who approaches* **Rupert** *and* **John Kipling** *as they sit at a table sipping tea.*

RUPERT: Hello, Father. Tea?

SIR HENRY: Can't we find something a little stronger? I mean…

RUPERT: Good point, Father, but have you forgotten the licensing hours introduced recently by your chums in parliament to make sure your workers don't stay in bed all day or build your ships back to front?

At which, **Sir Henry** *goes to the bar and addresses the* **Barmaid**.

SIR HENRY: Three rather large tots of your best whisky, if you please, my girl.

BARMAID [with Irish voice]: Sorry, sir. Not allowed. Out of drinking hours.

SIR HENRY: Oh, come. These young officers [waving at them] are on their way to save you and others from Kaiser Bill. And I should not expect you to have such a crime on your conscience without some recompense to make it easier to bear.

Sir Henry *pulls a large white £5 note from his wallet and adds it to the coins he had already put on the counter.*

BARMAID: That's uncommon generous of you, sir, to be sure, but if I'm caught breaking the law, it could cost me my job.

SIR HENRY: But the law's brand new and I'm sure it takes time to remember the hours, even for such a pretty head as you have on your shoulders.

He adds another £5 note to the one on the counter, causing her to look around to see whether she is being watched.

BARMAID: Such generosity and charm are hard for a girl to refuse, sir, especially with a family to feed and prices so high. But glasses of whisky are as easy for inspectors to see as the hands of the clock.

SIR HENRY: Then don't refuse. And if you put it into a teacup for three of us who take no milk, the inspector will not know the difference unless he sticks his nose into the cups and sniffs.

BARMAID: You are not only generous, sir, but highly persuasive. Are you a lawyer, perhaps?

SIR HENRY: No, just a patriot who does not want to send young men off to war on an empty stomach, as it were.

BARMAID: If you'll be sitting over there with your soldier friends, sir, I'll see what I can bring over to you. And thank you, sir.

Whereupon, with her back to the counter, the **Barmaid** *attends to three thick railway cups and carries them, in* **Sir Henry's** *wake, to the table.*

RUPERT *[after bending down and sniffing his cup]*: What did I tell you, John? You owe me one pound.

★ ★ ★ ★ ★

CUT TO – Train at platform, with men in uniform leaning out of every window. One window frames the head, shoulders and arms of **Rupert** *and* **John Kipling**. *As the train draws out, they wave to* **Sir Henry**, *standing tall and erect on the platform, head and shoulders above the crowd. A close-up of him shows his lips moving as the two fade from view.*

SIR HENRY *[muttering to himself]*: Just eighteen!

Views of London as train passes through it heading south-west, the two ensigns looking out the window silently at what they might not see for a long time, if at all.

VOICE: For almost a year at Warley I had "prepared for war", but it was a war fought in storybooks rather than the realities of the high-explosives, poison gas and barbed wire that were awaiting us. Equipping for the storybook conflict had been pleasant and exciting. Among other essentials, I had acquired a folding canvas bed with blankets, a canvas washbasin on a wooden tripod, a canvas bath and bucket, and a canvas folding chair. The canvas was of the stoutest, the timber the weightiest and most durable. Transporting it to the scene of conflict would have needed a mule-train. There were also the more personal items said to be necessary for the destruction of the "Hun" – most of them, being expensive, obtainable at Asprey's or Finnegan's in Bond Street. They included field-glasses to bring the enemy under close observation before joining battle; a highly intricate compass, together with maps of Belgium and northern France, all contained in luxuriously smelling leather with my initials stamped on it; a felt-wrapped water-bottle carried by a shoulder-strap and so shaped that it would not unduly bruise the buttocks when on the march. My revolver and holster were supplied by the Ordnance Corps, but my Sam Browne belt, so lovingly polished by my servant, I bought myself. Apart from what was hung or attached to it on my back and shoulders, this ingenious piece of equipment also took the weight of the frog that secured my sword, which came from Wilkinson of Pall Mall.

★ ★ ★ ★ ★

CUT TO – The sword being bought at Wilkinson of Pall Mall. **Rupert** *weighs a sword on the palm of his hand while the salesman looks on with dignity.* **Rupert's** *eyes wander to a lighter sword, which, after handing the heavier one to the* *apprehensive salesman, he picks up and weighs.* **Rupert's** *expression shows that he prefers it.*

RUPERT *[brandishing it as though in swordplay]*: I say, this one's fun; I like it rather better.

SALESMAN *[deeply shocked]*: Oh, no, sir, this is the regulation sword. That is a dress sword – a court sword.

RUPERT *[after a few more flourishes]*: No, I have made up my mind, rightly or wrongly. Please have one forged for me just like this, and with the date and my initials engraved on the blade.

★ ★ ★ ★ ★

FADE TO – Train compartment en route to Southampton as dusk descends.

VOICE: This shocking breach of regulations escaped even the blue sea-bird eye of Tom Vesey, who must sometimes have lain awake wondering why I, of all the ensigns the most unlikely, displayed such dexterity in sheathing and unsheathing the flashing blade. Johns & Pegg made my khaki uniform. Cater's supplied me with caps. I used the field-glasses once only before they were blasted off me. I can only hope they were later found and proved their worth at Ascot. Before being parted from me, they gave me one glimpse of the wire bristling around the Hohenzollern redoubt at Loos, draped with the bodies of the gallant Highland Division, their kilts caught high in the barbs, their buttocks black and buzzing with flies. The compass I lost in a card game a few days after landing in France. The revolver I somehow retained, but never fired; it had a trigger that would have taxed the combined strengths of Alexander and Hercules, Hector and Lysander and such great men as these, let alone a stripling of eighteen. What happened to the map case, I have no idea. In any event, it would have been useless, as was most of the equipment dreamed up, I suppose, by some dear old boy in the War Office. We had no strong feelings about what the politicians called "the rape of little Belgium". We were afraid of one

79

thing only: not being there to see the fun, believing that any day it might be over.

The youth of Germany had much the same attitude. The German Crown Prince, "Little Willie", drank to *"ein fischer, frolicher Kreig"* – a brisk and merry war. I had nothing against the Germans, apart from their alleged addiction to raping nuns, which was anyway the traditional habit of brutal continental soldiery on the march. With their love of brass bands and drums, it was not surprising that they were warlike. I had been told that Kaiser Bill had come over for Queen Victoria's funeral, a gallant sorrowing grandson with the tears streaming down his face, and that it was in his arms that she had died. His moustache was too long and too upturned, and obviously he was no more than every other inch a gentleman, but surely the decent English side of his character would eventually prevail. Alas, it did not. In my lifetime, Kaiser Bill, with his fierce moustache and, twenty years later, Hitler, with his little one, were both to represent that strangest German mixture; the ridiculous and the sinister.

★ ★ ★ ★ ★

CUT TO – Deck of the ship carrying them across to Le Havre, **Rupert** *and* **John Kipling** *leaning on the rail, yarning, while not far below their faces is the water of the Channel swishing by in the dark.*

JOHN KIPLING: I don't know about you, Rupe, but I'm rather looking forward to being plied with some decently-priced superior wine instead of that iodine we have to drink at home.

RUPERT: I don't know about you, John, but I'm rather looking forward to sharing a haystack with one or two of those French girls that are even more delectable than peaches.

JOHN KIPLING: Do you think our tuition in Clarges Street has been equal to that? *Boudoirs*, yes, but haystacks?

VOICE: It was in Clarges Street, Mayfair, that a charming Irishwoman known as Mrs Fitz ran an establishment whose hospitality the Brigade enjoyed. The England of 1915 was not the sexually permissive society it has since become. To sleep with a girl of one's own age and class was then unthinkable; it would have "ruined her for marriage". So, the needs of the licentious soldiery had to be met elsewhere, with discretion, or what might be called a decent hypocrisy. Mrs Fitz's academy for military gratification was furnished, like herself, in Edwardian opulence and conducted with great etiquette and strict regard for rank and privilege. A field officer would be shown by a hatchet-faced parlourmaid to the upstairs drawing room, a mere lieutenant or ensign to a room on the ground floor. Wherever it was, it would have a well-stuffed sofa and gilt chairs with antimacassars facing a fireplace above which hung a "Stag at Bay" or "Charge of the Light Brigade". Here, one would be introduced to young ladies whose attitudes to life and love differed vastly from those found at deb-dances. Mrs Fitz kept open house from 6 pm to 3 am except on Sundays, certain feast-days, royal nuptials and bereavements, and the 4th June, when she visited her son at Eton. *[Pause]*

But the life of an ensign in the Guards was only one per cent pleasure; the rest was hell. Far from carrying privileges, holding a commission meant we were bullied, bawled at, hounded and humiliated by sergeant-major, drill-sergeant and officer – in front of our men – in a way that would never have been tolerated by the quick-tempered Irish in the ranks. But it was an ancient rite, handed down from generation to generation, that somehow turned us into guardsmen. Our soldiers felt sorry for us but admired the way we stuck it, and tried to temper our misery with loyalty. A compensation was that we were magnificently fit. It was with the comforts of Mrs Fitz's education and the discomforts of the Guards' initiation behind us, that we disembarked in high spirits at Le Havre and made for "the line". The only transport considered fit for infantry was one pair of hobnailed boots per man. We sang bawdily as we marched day after day. At the end of each day's slog of twenty-five miles, I could have dropped exhausted and slept forever. But I had to see that my men were fed and inspect their feet – it was our pride that no man should fall out – and install them in whatever shelter was available. Suddenly, the news would pass like fire through the batallion...

From being strewn about sleeping like logs where they had stopped, the soldiers begin to stir, removing hats that were covering their faces, sitting up, showing signs of excitement.

A FIRST SOLDIER *[waking bleerily, rubbing eyes]*: What's happening? [looks at watch] Not morning already?

SECOND SOLDIER: No, mate. It's the C.O., Alex – he's going to dance.

THIRD SOLDIER: How does he do it? Talk about iron man. Do you think he got a lift?

SECOND SOLDIER: Don't be nasty. He walked the whole way. But maybe they issued him with officers' legs.

FOURTH SOLDIER: Or maybe had them massaged by that *madamoiselle* he bought food from this morning.

A platform has been improvised on one of the mule-carts whose load has been removed for the occasion.

VOICE: The dancer was Harold Alexander, the future field marshal and Earl Alexander of Tunis, elder brother of Alex my schoolmate. When the moment came, the entire batallion would be seated around the platform, albeit with the weariness of men who had trudged from dawn to dusk. A man they loved, their commander, who had matched them step for step, pain for pain, the whole day through, was ready to ask still more of his feet, dancing for their delight.

As ALEX mounts the "stage"; the audience is electrified. He wears a hat with the upper part elevated and pressed back Russian-style, and beneath it his fair moustache and a bearing that could have been that of a Tsar.

VOICE: It might have been that we were about to see a Polovtsian dance to the music of Borodin amid the resin of pine trees, but it was only with the wail of the squeeze-box and the cries of the men that one realised the dance was the nostalgic jig, the music of the defiant Gael. There, Alex would be "steppin", head erect, arms and body rigid, feet tapping and lifting and leaping and crossing and clicking, like objects with a life of their own, as the lads of rural Ireland would jig at the crossroads after Mass on Sundays. The men stand enthralled, weariness cast off, stamping feet that Alex's performance has healed, uttering wild Gaelic yells and battle cries.

VOICE: Alex was charming, courageous, highly-strung, sensitive and luminously intelligent. Although steeped in the squalor of war from the outset, he rose above it more than most men could. Those he commanded worshipped him, though he kept the strictest discipline, morally rather than blindly. To be Alex's orderly, a man had to be adventurous, courageous and tough in more ways than one.

★ ★ ★ ★ ★

FADE TO – Night at the Front, flashes in the distance, **Alex's** *orderly, a* **Sergeant**, *reports to him in a trench.*

SERGEANT: Ready, sir.

ALEX: OK. Off we go.

They climb from the trench and melt into the dark, keeping low. After a time, **Alex** *taps the sergeant and points. With a spurt and a flying tackle, the* **Sergeant** *launches himself at a figure whose square-ish helmet identifies him as a* **German**, *who, after a struggle, is handcuffed.*

ALEX: Stay here and keep him quiet. I'll be back.

*Alex works his way towards the flashes of artillery. Soon, the sergeant joins him, hissing as he approaches lest **Alex** mistake him for the enemy.*

ALEX: I thought... where is he?

SERGEANT: 'e was gettin' troublesome, sir, so I finished 'im off with my pull-through *[putting his fists together, then jerking them apart]*.

ALEX: In that case, you're on a disobedience charge, Sergeant. See me in the morning.

SERGEANT: Yes, sir.

VOICE: Normally, however, obedience was absolute, as I once saw picturesquely demonstrated away from the distraction of the enemy.

★ ★ ★ ★ ★

CUT TO – *A parade of officers and men, the **C.O**, on his horse, giving the order Present Arms.*

C.O *[screams]*: Bat-talion... Pre-sent...

The formation stands frozen, waiting for the executive word of command, "Arms", when suddenly the horse whinnies, "Whee-ee-ee", and, as one man, in perfect unison, hands smack against rifle-stocks, swords and bayonets flash, and the battalion comes to the "Present".

★ ★ ★ ★ ★

CUT TO – *Soldiers resting beside road during a break in the march.*

VOICE: We marched on. During a pause, Tom Vesey, who missed little, noticed a canvas bag in the transport wagon. He ordered it to be ripped open, disclosing my pigskin suitcase containing shirts, dressing gown, bedroom slippers, ivory brushes, a bottle of Hill's hair-oil, two boxes of Roget *et* Gallet's soap, *David Copperfield* and Voltaire's *Candide* – in short, all those things that represented my last contact with another world, symbols of a civilised life.

Vesey looks with contempt at **Rupert's** *belongings, spots him lurking away from the transport wagon, beckons him over and points to the display of luxury.*

VESEY *[sadly]*: You haven't the makings of a soldier, Rupert.

RUPERT *[muttering to himself]*: Perhaps not, but I'll make a better civilian than you.

★ ★ ★ ★ ★

CUT TO – Back on the road, marching.

VOICE: Vesey ordered one of the men to throw my treasures into a ditch by the road and that was the last I saw of them. By now, we knew we were going straight to the Battle of Loos. For most of us, it was our "Baptism of Fire".

Approaching the battle, with shells landing near, horses taking fright.

VOICE: At first it was shrapnel kicking up earth and speaking the *pavé*, but as we moved forward, heavy shells started landing with alarming precision and regularity. I believe I would have been even more afraid than I was had the noise and roar not seemed to deafen my fear.

A shell lands on them.

VOICE: Suddenly, a blinding flash lit up my entire world. Stars exploded in my eyes and a mighty wind, charged with the acrid stench of high-explosive, channelled me through a vaulted cavern. I was riding the night, driving into a mirage of the past, present and future, then flung into total darkness. Kipling, in his *The Irish Guards in the Great War*, wrote: "Captain and the Adjutant the Hon. T. E. Vesey… and second lieutenants Sasoon and Grayson were wounded, the last being blown up by a shell". Tom was returned to England with me. Some strange rhythm seemed to govern our lives, so that although we were always marching together, we were rarely in step. In France, the regiment was still burying its dead, when on the grapevine I heard the news that froze my heart: John Kipling was reported missing.

VOICE: As I lay in hospital and closed my eyes, I could see Rudyard Kipling – short, wiry, alert, steely-blue eyes peering through his spectacles under bushy eyebrows and bald head, firm chin poked forward. His glasses were part of him as headlights are part of a car. At school, he was known as "gigs" after the lamps on each side of a gig. His wife, Carrie, chose his clothes, ties, shirts and shoes as she chose his publishers, agents and bankers; and it was whispered that she chose his friends as carefully. She was everything to him: mother of his children, wife, secretary, banker and literary adviser, from the time they were married at All Souls, Langham Place – which he called "the pepperpot" – until his death. I was more fortunate than I deserved in being honoured with his friendship. Any charm of manner I might have had could hardly have made up for my instability. He liked the old if they were interesting, but the young he liked because they were young. It was not long before **Lady** Edward **Cecil**, a great friend of the Kiplings, came to visit me in hospital.

★ ★ ★ ★ ★

CUT TO – Hospital ward. Lady Cecil is escorted by a nurse to **Rupert's** *bedside.*

NURSE: Lady Cecil to see you, Captain Grayson.

RUPERT: Thank you, nurse. *[To the visitor]* Hello, Lady Cecil. How nice to see you and be reminded of the pleasant times we knew at Bateman's. It seems long ago, but it's not.

LADY CECIL: Not so much long ago as far away, for it was a different world. Nothing will ever be the same, though I hope that does not apply to you, for I liked you as you were. On the mend, are we?

RUPERT *[dismissively]*: Oh, yes. Such wonderful people here. I'll soon be annoying you all again.

LADY CECIL: *[hesitantly]*: Is there anything you can tell me, Rupert, about John?

RUPERT *[bleakly]*: Not really. We were together when it happened, and might even have shared the shell that knocked me out. No one knows what "missing" means, but I fear the worst.

LADY CECIL: Bateman's is not what it was.

RUPERT: No. The sorrow is deep and wide.

VOICE: She rattled off some chit-chat, which we both knew was flat and empty, and left. Next day, Kipling himself came to see me. It was solely out of friendship and loyalty to John. He already knew I had nothing to tell him. He was holding himself under control, but the light had gone from his eyes. John had moved to God and history.

Scene: the mud of Flanders, desolation of battle.

VOICE: By October 1917, I was back in France and the regiment was in action again. In the lull that followed an attack during which we gained a few hundred yards of sodden, useless ground, I knelt before our Chaplain, Father du Moulin Browne, made my confession and was received into the Roman Catholic Church. Like many Irish Guards officers, Protestant or otherwise, I always went in command of my men to their church parade and attended their Mass. I never failed to be moved by the simple devotion of these hard-bitten Irish soldiers to their ancient faith. Accoutred for war, they knelt bare-headed in sun, wind or rain before their priest at his improvised altar and told their beads the whisper of the battle that awaited them, echoing their own muttered "Our Fathers" and "Hail Marys".

Scene: a tour of European cathedrals.

VOICE: The seeds of my own late-ripening faith had already been sown in the great cathedrals of France and Italy. I had slowly fallen in love with the Church as some men fall in love with women, though my love was secret, for Father was usually with me, and he believed in an English Protestant god whom I thought of as being rather like himself: majestic and powerful, but not quite so indulgent towards his children. The Church's discipline I was prepared to accept. After the Brigade, that would not be difficult. The Articles of Faith pointed without shortcuts the way that led to God, and it was a way I wished to follow; but it was the mystical romance of the liturgy, the fragrant reek of the incense eddying heavenwards with my prayers and the all pervading ambience of worship, faith and beauty that held me to my secret purpose. I received no formal instruction. In the battlefields of France and Flanders, death was too busy to allow God's minions much time to spare for others than its most immediate candidates...

Rupert *approaching, entering, kneeling inside and leaving tent with cross at apex, as guns thunder.*

VOICE: ... So, my secret resolve was accomplished kneeling in the peaceful twilight of a priest's tent to the distant and interminable rumble of the guns.

★ ★ ★ ★ ★

FADE TO – Same location at night, with flashes far and near. A shell bursts in a nearby crater and a piece of shrapnel zings towards **Rupert** *and stops in his leg.*

A Soldier *nearby hurries to his side.*

SOLDIER *[Beckoning with arm]*: Here, stretcher.

Bearers *load* **Rupert** *on to the canvas sheet between the stretcher arms, cover him with a blanket and set off along duckboards slippery with mud.*

VOICE: They negotiated me for six hours over planks, which, had the bearers slipped, could have become a diving-board to death by choking in the slimy sea of mud all around us.

The stretcher arrives at the dressing-station, a larger tent with another kind of cross atop it: this one red against a white background.

BEARER: We're here, sir.

RUPERT: Thank you, and bless you and your mates. What a trek you've had.

BEARER: Keeps us out of mischief, sir. We'll do another journey before night's out.

A doctor arrives, examines the shattered leg and straightens up, savouring the pause before going on to the next case.

DOCTOR: I hope you're good at choices, Lieutenant. Yours is between having the leg off above the knee or risking gangrene if you don't.

RUPERT: What do you think, doctor?

DOCTOR: There are many factors, but this is not Harley Street – we have no time to weigh them all.

RUPERT: I rather fancy myself as a gambler, so let me take the risk.

DOCTOR: Right. We'll clean the wound as best we can and put tubes in to drain it, before sending you on a third-class train ride to hospital – which should suit you as a gambler, because it is in the casino at Le Touquet and is sponsored by the Duchess of Westminster.

★ ★ ★ ★ ★

FADE TO – Le Touquet, where medical staff and other officers say goodbye as he departs for London.

AN OFFICER: Make the most of it. They'll have you back here in no time, if you give them the chance.

DOCTOR: The wounds are only ten days old, but I think that with any luck you'll keep the leg. No rugger, though.

Murmurs of goodbye as **Rupert** *leaves on a stretcher, medical details on a label tied to his pyjamas.*

★ ★ ★ ★ ★

FADE TO: Arrival at railway station and departure of train. Intermittent glimpes of **Rupert** *on the journey, carriages filled with other wounded, many groggy from injections administered on the way. Then, being loaded on a ship to cross the Channel and be put on a final, English train.*

NURSE *[before sticking needle in]*: This should smooth the jolts to Charing Cross, Lieutenant. Then, a spot of *terra firma* for you. The American Women's Hospital in Bayswater, I think.

★ ★ ★ ★ ★

CUT TO – Arrival at the AWH in a ward full of other wounded. As **Rupert** *is manoeuvred onto his bed, an officer in the bed next to his greets him.*

OFFICER: Welcome home.

RUPERT: Thank you. It's good to be here, especially since it is home for me: my family lives next door.

Lady Grayson *enters the ward and, after gently embracing him and exchanging endearments, sits on the very end of* **Rupert's** *bed, careful not to shake him.*

LADY GRAYSON: I have wanted to see you, Rupert, after all these months, but not like this. You realise, of course, where you are, don't you?

RUPERT: Yes, Mother. The army teaches you to know the whereabouts of enemies and friends. I've just told my companion here *[nods at officer in next bed]* what good neighbours we have.

LADY GRAYSON: I shall speak to one of your father's builders about knocking a hole in the wall, so you can be wheeled straight in to us when you are well enough to visit.

A nurse arrives with a trolley and draws a screen around **Rupert**, *addressing* **Lady Grayson** *as she does so.*

NURSE: Sorry, madam, but I must interrupt. Perhaps you could wait in the lobby for ten minutes.

LADY GRAYSON: Yes, very well. *[To Rupert]* Later, anyway; maybe this afternoon. You'll want to sleep, I imagine.

RUPERT: Perhaps, Mother. There'll be time to talk. I can't see them wanting me in France for a while, if ever.

They look at each other and smile. She gets up and leaves without further ado, and the nurse starts to get busy on **Rupert***.*

★ ★ ★ ★ ★

CUT TO – St James's Club some weeks later. **Rupert** *mounts the steps with a limp, enters and makes his way to the desk. After speaking to him, the attendant comes from behind the desk and leads* **Rupert** *to an anti-room where his host,* **Sir Courteney** *Forbes, is waiting.*

SIR COURTENEY: Ah, Grayson. Hungry?

RUPERT: Yes, and curious.

SIR COURTENEY: Then come with me and feed both appetites.

Rupert *accompanies his host to the dining room; on the way, they talk.*

SIR COURTENEY: We have not met for some time but I gather you've been busy.

RUPERT: On the contrary, sir, I've been waited on hand and foot these past weeks at the American Women's Hospital in Bayswater Road.

SIR COURTENEY: Speaking of "foot", I understand one of yours has been living dangerously?

RUPERT: More so than I liked, but it can now keep up with its mate and is ready for the world.

They sit at a table, to which they have been shown in a discreet corner, and order lunch.

SIR COURTENEY: A few words have been uttered at the top on your behalf, I'm glad to say, and the upshot is that I have the pleasure of confirming that you are being appointed as a temporary King's Messenger to carry a diplomatic bag to Rome. May I take it that you're agreeable?

RUPERT: Most decidedly, sir.

SIR COURTENEY: Good. Call me Courteney, if you will. It's better for our digestion.

RUPERT: Thank you, Courteney. It does sound less military, and that is a skin I have shed.

SIR COURTENEY: Yes, indeed. I hope you won't mind if I tell you something about the history of the organisation you'll be serving. *[Pause]* Since the time of Charles II, when the Corps of King's and Queen's Foreign Service Messengers was formed, the messengers have been charged, quote, with carrying out their sacred duties to preserve, secure and inviolate, to the utmost of their power, under every circumstance and every emergency, the dispatches entrusted to their care, unquote. *[Pause for a sip]* When Charles was in exile on the Continent, he instituted a regular service of messengers to convey his letters to England from Holland and back. Mostly, the messengers were skippers of Dutch fishing smacks. As few of them could speak English, they had to be given a means of ensuring safe delivery. Charles had with him at the time a silver dish, on the lid of which were embossed four greyhounds. These he cut off, giving two to his Dutch messenger and two to his English contact, so that on meeting at a certain tavern in Dover, they could prove their identity to each other. When Charles regained the throne, he decreed that the silver greyhound should be worn with the blue ribbon of the Order of the Garter. From then on, this became the official badge of the Corps. The number of messengers has varied with the exigencies of the time. Each must be prepared…

★ ★ ★ ★ ★

FADE TO – A tour of the everyday London outside, the skyline, rooftops, Burlington Arcade, Piccadilly, other landmarks, then back to their table.

SIR COURTENEY: … In short, you will be as much at home in an *auberge* in Provence as you are at an ambassador's table. In the Foreign Office, you will see hanging on the wall a motto adopted by the Corps, a quotation from Herodotus: "Neither snow nor rain nor heat nor gloom of night shall stay these couriers in the swift completion of their appointed rounds."

After the older man has stopped, they are silent for a moment.

SIR COURTENEY *[pulling out a gold watch and examining it]*: I allowed half an hour for indoctrination. Unavoidable, I'm afraid. Let's wash it down with a glass of Cockburn's '97, eh?

RUPERT: Thank you, Courteney, but I'd like to wash it up into the brain rather than down. The opportunity, I mean.

VOICE: To describe my feelings as elated would be an understatement. Even if I were to do only this one journey as King's Messenger before re-joining the regiment, I was making my first contact with the Corps. That night, when I left the St James's Club, I floated down Piccadilly. It was my first experience of levitation. I believe I am one of a privileged few to have enjoyed this most delightful form of movement several times in the course of life. I know of nothing comparable. You are never divorced from the earth, as when travelling in an aircraft. You are still part of the procession of life. But you have the wonderful bird-like advantage of watching, from above, the movements of mere mortals below. I levelled off somewhere near Hyde Park Barracks, coming to earth at Rutland Gate, where I completed the short journey home on foot.

Scene: Rome in hot summer 1918. **Rupert** *arrives by cab at the British Embassy, where he reports at reception.*

CLERK: Sir, may I be of help?

RUPERT *[smiling affably]*: My name is Grayson. May I speak to the archivist, please?

CLERK: I'm afraid he's elsewhere today, sir. Would Captain Whitton, the military *attaché*, do?

RUPERT: Nicely, I should think, thank you.

At which, the **Clerk** *picks up a* baroque *Italian phone, presses a button, rotates a handle, speaks and puts the phone down.*

CLERK: He's coming, sir. Please take a seat.

Before **Rupert** *can sit, from an inner door emerges the military* **Attache***: handsome, intelligent, soldierly, with hand outstretched.* **Rupert** *takes and shakes it.*

ATTACHE: Welcome. MacGregor Whitton. And you're Captain Grayson, seconded from the Brigade of Irish Guards.

RUPERT: Thank you. Yes. What a relief to be here. I have never *[with a twinkle]* seen so many knaves masquerading as ordinary decent people.

ATTACHE: I know, and all with designs on the bag. Didn't spot Moriarty among them, did you?

RUPERT [with a chuckle]: Yes, but shook him off.

ATTACHE: You're expected to dine at the embassy, but not until nine. I'll take you. Sir Henry is in Rome, you know.

★ ★ ★ ★ ★

CUT TO – The foyer of the Grand Hotel.

VOICE: At that time, Father was Director of Ship Repairs and, as such, often visited Rome, staying at the Excelsior. I booked at the Grand, not to avoid him, but in a desire to explore Rome on my own. I wanted to see the Eternal City through my eyes rather than his. To be truthful, what I wanted was a dark-eyed Roman girl with eyelids painted green, who would lead me to a flower-shop and thence to a cafe where we would spend the day drinking ice-cold wine, and in the evening, after visiting Keats's grave, who knows? I therefore had to keep out of Father's way.

★ ★ ★ ★ ★

CUT TO – Embassy drawing room, **Rupert** showing dismay as, having been introduced to the **Ambassador** on entry, he scans the people in the room and sees among them, tall and conspicuous, **Sir Henry**.

VOICE: But I had yet to learn that life is rarely so simple as one would wish, and it came as a blow when I found him among the guests in the embassy drawing room. Sir James Rennell Rodd, the ambassador, was a man of immense charm and erudition. It was said that even his dreams were in Latin and Greek. He was one of the old school of cultured diplomats and probably knew Rome better than the Romans. He was loved by the Italians, but in Roman society, Lady Rodd could be outspoken. Thus, they were called "Sir Rennell Rodd and Lady Rude". At dinner that evening, he told us he never walked in Rome without seeing something beautiful he had not previously observed. As he spoke, I caught Father's eye and knew he was already planning where he would take me next day, and that would be the end of my dark-eyed Roman girl. Father's tentacles were in fact already out, for on my return to the Grand that night I found a member of his staff waiting for me.

★ ★ ★ ★ ★

CUT TO – Lobby of Grand Hotel. As **Rupert** *enters, the receptionist exchanges glances with and nods slightly to a slim dark man* **(Giuseppe)** *seated in a corner and looking over the newspaper he is holding. The man stands and walks to* **Rupert,** *catching him before he reaches the desk.*

GIUSEPPE: Excuse me, sir. You are Captain Grayson, I believe. I am Giuseppe Modena. I help to run your father's office in Rome. It would give me great pleasure to show you a little of our nightlife.

RUPERT: How very kind! May I call you Giuseppe? I'm Rupert. Have you been waiting long? *[Laughs]* I feel ambushed.

GIUSEPPE: Ah, we all wait, Rupert, but what for? That is the question. I knew I was waiting for someone who has served his country bravely, so it was a privilege.

RUPERT: You sound like a philosopher. My father tells me you're a first-class negotiator without whom his life would be far more difficult.

GIUSEPPE: I am lucky, Rupert, but shall we walk as we talk? The evening is pleasant, and if you are not too tired…?

RUPERT: Not at all, please lead the way.

They walk together out of the hotel into the street, which is busy with pedestrians, carriages, bicycles and a few cars. **Giuseppe** *carries a Malacca cane with a round ivory knob exquisitely carved in the shape of a lion's head.*

GIUSEPPE: As I said, I am lucky. Some people are lucky with money, others with women. I am lucky with languages. They come to me like iron-filings to a magnet. So, I can talk to your father's clients in whatever voice is required – in terms of not only language, but also dialect, accent and nuance.

RUPERT: Marvellous. Which language do you prefer?

GIUSEPPE: I have no preference. I am like an actor who is so professional that he is always anybody but himself. His own persona has been wiped out by his work. If there is a preference, it is decided by the interlocutor. I adapt to whatever is his language, even to his region or class. If I am useful to Sir Henry, it is my linguistic flexibility – perhaps, one might say, promiscuity – that makes me so. Let me give you a small demonstration.

As they reach an intersection, with the word Scusi **Giuseppe** *gets the attention of two gorgeously attired policeman. Speaking in Italian, he tells them he and* **Rupert** *are lost and asks the way to the main railway station, at which, both speaking together and waving arms with the sort of gestures used for traffic, they tell* **Giuseppe** *the way to go. As he thanks them and moves off, they continue to look at* **Giuseppe** *and* **Rupert**, *and* **Giuseppe** *hears one make a remark to the other.*

GIUSEPPE: Did you hear that? The one with the larger feathers in his hat said: "These damned English – spend their holidays lost and think they can speak Italian".

RUPERT: Most impressive, but you'll be getting the English a bad name.

Giuseppe *hails a horse-drawn cab and they board it.*

VOICE: And so we visited several bars; each, it seemed, more entertaining than the last – though that could have been because of the drinks Giuseppe kept adding to an expense account that would no doubt finish on Father's desk. By around four in the morning, we had seen enough Roman brunettes to satisfy my eyes, if nothing else, and Giuseppe had left a trail of quasi-linguists baffled as to his nationality after he had treated them to Italian with a German accent, German with a Swedish accent and Polish with a Greek one.

★ ★ ★ ★ ★

CUT TO – A bar where a singer blasts forth the Italian version of an American jazz number and the two look at each other blearily.

RUPERT: Giuseppe, I'm not a spoilsport, but if the king is going to trust me to be his postman again, I must heed the call of the cot.

GIUSEPPE: Yes, I think we see eye-to-eye – or what passes for seeing at this hour – for I also have obligations tomorrow to Sir Henry.

RUPERT *[slyly, pointing a finger at his companion]*: Ah, are you sure you don't mean today, old chap? If I'm not mistaken, we have already made inroads into tomorrow.

GIUSEPPE *[pausing a moment to think]*: Absolutely right, Rupert. As students of the calendar, you English are tops. No wonder time begins at Greenwich. What do you say to walking back? I'll show you to your hotel on my way home.

RUPERT: S'fine by me. Should we take one or two of these young ladies with us?

GIUSEPPE: Too late, Rupert. We should have started sooner; in fact, yesterday.

They stand and prepare to leave.

RUPERT: Don't forget your cane. A very handy accessory for this sort of evening, I must say.

GIUSEPPE: It is, indeed, but perhaps not in the sense you intend. Maybe, I'll show you.

★ ★ ★ ★ ★

CUT TO – An alleyway down which they walk as dawn begins to appear. **Giuseppe**, *with a gesture and a shush, bids* **Rupert** *stand still while he stalks a cat that has sped across in front of them and now crouches in a shadow. The cane flashes and there is a sharp crack. The cat's skull slowly opens and the brains blossom from it.* **Rupert's** *face shows repugnance and the movement of his body suggests for an instant that he is going to attack* **Giuseppe**, *but abandons the impulse because he is in no condition to implement it.*

VOICE: Because of my wound, if nothing else, I was still too weak to assail him physically, and mentally I feared that his logic would outmatch mine. Had I told Father of the use to which that cane was put, he would consider **Giuseppe** to have blood on his hands and transfer him. My own attitude to the cat-hater was one of disgust – weakened, as usual, by indecision. I tried to persuade myself that it was the duty of every cat to exercise its self-protective instinct at the approach of danger. For I cannot think that anything so decisive as death is not preceded by some hitherto unclassified smell that animals, with their sharp premonitory instincts, should be the first to recognise. If I informed on the cat-hunter, Father would lose a first-class negotiator. Was it for me to weigh in the balance the importance of the work he was doing against the lives of a few stray cats? We were living in times when death had ceased to surprise, though it could still shock. Judged in the light of those days, Giuseppe might have been better employed in extinguishing Germans, to which no stigma was attached. He might, indeed, have used his distasteful talent more profitably in the Ypres salient, which I had only recently left – but killing cats was still considered inhuman and ungentlemanly.

They round a corner and **Giuseppe** *points the cane at a portico, which* **Rupert** *recognises as that of the Grand.*

RUPERT: Oh, yes, my digs. Goodnight, Giuseppe, and thank you so much for the evening – but I do not speak for the cat.

★ ★ ★ ★ ★

FADE TO – Next day, St Peter's Square, the crowds, the birds, the steps they climb. Then, from church to church.

VOICE: I had the opportunity to convey those thanks more directly next morning, when Father collected me from the Grand and took me on a tour of at least ten of the Eternal City's 600 churches, each seeming more beautiful and moving than the one before. In the musty darkness of the catacombs, to which, with my unconfessed hangover, I had been reluctantly drawn, we held our tapers surrounded by a group of camphor-smelling nuns.

★ ★ ★ ★ ★

CUT TO – Spanish steps, restaurant with awning, fountains. A stroll in the Borghese Gardens.

SIR HENRY: Rome is like drinking a good wine. So far you've had only a sip of it.

On and on: palaces, pictures, tapestries, painted ceilings.

RUPERT: All the obelisks, Father – how do you think they got them up?

SIR HENRY: With ropes and pulleys and the sweat of slaves, watched by a silent populace. There was only one penalty for making a sound or disturbing the air when they were raising an obelisk, and that was death.

RUPERT: As well they're not putting them up today. What a place, though, to forget the war.

SIR HENRY: Hm.

★ ★ ★ ★ ★

*CUT TO – **Rupert** and his father riding in a cab through the city, arriving at **Sir Henry's** hotel.*

VOICE: We drove back to the Excelsior as dusk fell. I drank a cocktail while he changed. We were not dining together. He had other arrangements. For all I knew, he and not I was dining with the dark-eyed Roman girl, with her eyelids painted green, and they would drink ice-cold wine in the flower-shop and never give a thought to poor Keats.

***Sir Henry** joins **Rupert** at the bar before going off for the evening.*

SIR HENRY: So, what's the next item on your programme, young man?

RUPERT: Rest and reflection. I'll just hover this evening.

SIR HENRY: Your career, though, the next step?

RUPERT: Who knows, Father? My mission is over. I report to the regiment.

SIR HENRY *[quizzically]*: And then? When I'm uncertain where I'm going, I invariably have my bags packed ready for Paris and usually find I unpack them at the Crillon.

***Rupert** remains tight-lipped.*

SIR HENRY: People tell me nothing *[Pause]* unless they're in trouble.

★ ★ ★ ★ ★

*FADE TO – Rome's main railway station. Train departs and **Rupert**, having just boarded it, settles into the compartment.*

VOICE: He was right in guessing I would unpack my bag in Paris. But I was not going there directly. I had already booked a *wagon-lit* compartment

103

on the train to Monte Carlo. Everyone has a place of dreams to which he must go or to which he wishes to return, but as we grow older it is to what we remember that we wish to return. Alas, nothing can ever be as we remember it, and we too have changed. I had been in Monte Carlo only as a boy, with my mother and father. Now, I was to return alone as a man.

The **Attendant** *visits* **Rupert's** *compartment to make up his bed for the night.*

ATTENDANT *[handing Rupert a basket containing a bottle to which a message is tied; speaking English with French accent]*: Good evening, Captain Grayson. I have been instructed to deliver this to you with Sir Henry's compliments. It is, of course, chilled.

RUPERT *[handing over a tip in exchange]*: Thank you, but how on earth…? *[Murmurs the contents of the note to himself.]*

RUPERT *[blushing]*: Bon voyage. I'll be at the Crillon in a few days' time.

ATTENDANT: Anything else, sir? Window closed, perhaps?

RUPERT: Thank you, no. Leave it open. I like the smell, you know: eucalyptus, pine, cedar… Good night.

Before the **Attendant** *has closed the door,* **Rupert** *becomes alert and calls him back.*

RUPERT: There is one thing: please put my bag off at Monte Carlo. I'm getting off at the station before.

ATTENDANT: Certainly, sir. Good night.

★ ★ ★ ★ ★

CUT TO – Alighting from train at penultimate stop, **Rupert** *walks through station to road and sets off on foot for Monte Carlo.*

104

VOICE: The colour and shape of flowers have never ceased to amaze me, but unfortunately I can name very few. Old James was our grandparents' coachman. When Grandfather died, Father inherited him along with the house and stables. With the coming of the motor car, horses and carriages went out, and there was no job for the old man. Although he knew nothing about flowers or gardens, Father appointed him head gardener, remarking, "He'll soon learn"; which was optimistic, since Old James was then about eighty. Wearing a large sombrero, he wandered about, prodding anything that looked like a weed and chatting as he lit and relit his pipe. I would walk with him because he loved children and his long white beard fascinated me. It was under his instruction that I learned the names of flowers. Rather than show his ignorance, he taught me names born of his imagination, and I have been ignorant of the correct ones ever since, except for orchids, carnations, roses and the other flowers one sends to girls. I believe James enjoyed my childish company because I was receptive to his invective against the motor car, which he hated fiercely. Though the under-gardeners must have realised how little he knew, they were too overawed by his patriarchal figure to argue with him. What wonderful names he could have invented for the vivid flowers of Monaco.

Scene: distant view of white towers of casino and curved facade of Hotel de Paris, and, lower down, the oriental domes of the Cafe de Paris. Bougainvillea cascades purple, pink and deep-red over walls of villas and hotels. Shops are just opening, and **Rupert** *finds himself walking in the shade of striped awnings. He enters a shop and makes a purchase.*

VOICE: I bought a box of Roger *et* Gallet carnation soap, the loveliest of soaps whose fragrance ranks with the great smells of the world: Havana tobacco, mimosa and well-cured leather.

★ ★ ★ ★ ★

CUT TO – Approaching and arriving at lobby at hotel, which is empty and gloomy, though immaculate.

The season at Monte Carlo was from February to the end of April, though the Hotel de Paris and Casino were open all year round. I had been given a letter to Monsieur Fleurie, the hotel's director. This exquisitely groomed and bearded man must have assumed that because I was visiting Monte Carlo in July, I was either mad or a poet; and as madmen and poets walked with kings and princes, he gave me a royal suite for the price of a double bedroom.

★ ★ ★ ★ ★

CUT TO – That evening in the casino; a tour of its splendours.

VOICE: The casino engaged the world's leading opera singers. It was here as a small boy that I heard Caruso and Melba as Rodolfo and Mimi. Caruso's tenor was probably too powerful for the little theatre, as also was the smell of garlic that pervaded it, making me wonder how Melba could sing so gloriously throughout a performance without being gassed. Subversive sounds were less pervasive, though, for Caruso enjoyed whispering dirty stories to "Mimi" during her death scene.

★ ★ ★ ★ ★

CUT TO – Yard with elegantly-attired rider who has just dismounted from horse, handing reins to groom to lead it away. Rider and manservant repair to a pavilion adjoining the stable, where the rider **(Von Sparlein)** *sits on a bench while the man* **(Antoine)** *prepares to remove the rider's top-boots.*

VOICE: It was in Monte Carlo that I sometimes met an Austrian friend called Von Sparlein, who had a manservant he had recruited from a Romanian circus where Sparlien was pursuing a beautiful trapeze-artist. The man, Antoine, was most impressive in removing his master's top-boots when he had been out riding. Sparlien would seat himself while Antoine turned his backside to him and, bending astride the outstretched leg, took a firm grip on the heel of the boot. Then came the precisely calculated tug. To help him, Sparlien would put his other foot on the man's buttock and thrust. This, of course, is a routine method of getting extracted from a top-boot; it was Antoine's embellishment that made the whole thing spectacular. As he tugged and Sparlien pushed, the boot was released and, at the moment of separation, Antoine leapt into the air, doing a double-somersault that landed him in exactly the position to remove the second boot. It called for split-second timing between man and master, and only once did I see the routine come unstuck, with the result that Antoine shot forward too fast and banged his head against the wall. But that was because he had failed to get opera seats for his master and Sparlien was in no mood to co-operate. [Pause] The bond between master and man had to be instinctive, each knowing when to give and when to take. But the relationship is disappearing from a world where there are no longer masters and men, only management and men.

Scene: Epsom racecourse during a stylish spring event.

VOICE: The war had ended, and many years would pass before I resumed my travels with the bags and their secrets. I was a man of leisure. I ate well, drank deep and played most of the kissing games, both indoor and outdoor, in hotels, flats and country houses, on trains, yachts and, on one occasion, I must confess, on a tombstone in the graveyard of a thirteenth-century church in Bangor. I still called on the services of Turner when they were available, for Turner was more than a second father; he was a major-domo, a friend and, most conveniently, a banker. He seemed always to carry on his person an amount of money as ample as himself. I was down at Epsom one day and happened to be in the paddock, where, I am convinced, the horses decide among themselves which of them is to win.

CUT TO – **Rupert** *with* **Pretty Girl** *on his arm. He sees a filly called Pretty Girl dancing around and acts on the inspiration.*

PRETTY GIRL *[at Ladbroke's, to which Rupert has steered her]*: What are you doing, Rupert?

RUPERT: Acknowledging you. See the board with the odds?

PRETTY GIRL: Yes.

RUPERT: Well, tell me the name of the one with "35-to-one" against it.

PRETTY GIRL *[blushing as she spots the name]*: "Pretty girl". Do you suggest you are on to a winner with me?

RUPERT: Don't know yet, but I'm wagering £20 to find out.

Pretty Girl, *the outsider, wins by a head.*

PRETTY GIRL: Do you always use that formula?

RUPERT: No, but I shall buy you dinner for inspiring it.

★ ★ ★ ★ ★

CUT TO – Consultation next day with Turner, who is more portly than ever.

VOICE: There was enough of the win left over to provide another inspiration: I would go to Paris and see what was happening over there. But to do so without financial anxiety required a supplement – and for this, Turner was my man. I had scarcely mentioned Paris when he whisked £500 from his pocket. There was almost no situation to which he was not equal.

★ ★ ★ ★ ★

CUT TO – Restaurant where **Rupert** *and five* **Friends**, *including* **Pretty Girl**, *are dining.* **Turner** *pours the first glass of wine before handing over to the sommelier.*

VOICE: I had acquired a habit, which my friends appreciated, of having wine sent from Father's cellar to the restaurant where we were to dine, for his cellar was excellent and it amused the guests to see Turner attending us with majestic indifference to the restaurant staff. There was probably a heavy price in corkage charged to my account, but in those days credit flowed as freely as the wine. My expenditure was far in excess of the generous allowance Father made me, but my credit was good. For a start, my tailors could always be relied on for a few hundred when I was pressed. My heaviest accounts were a string of bars, cabarets and flower shops in London and Paris; and Ladbroke's, with whom I had a running account. It was a way of life that might have continued had I not lavished money on a series of young apprentice mistresses from whom I obtained little satisfaction apart from having been fleetingly loved. *[Pause]*

Turner met me off the boat at Dover with a suitcase one grey Monday. On the preceding Saturday evening, I had been on my way to a supper party. *En route*, I stopped at Victoria Station to see friends off on the night train to Paris. I had drunk no more than usual, but my friends were in hilarious form.

★ ★ ★ ★ ★

FADE TO – Victoria Station. A cab draws up and lets **Rupert** *off. He walks to where the Continental trains depart and joins a group of* **Merrymakers,** *who, good-naturedly scornful of the top hat, white tie and tail coat in which he is attired, bundle him on to the train. One of them,* **Eddie,** *speaks to* **Rupert** *as the train gathers too much speed to get off.*

EDDIE: It looks as though you were intending to keep an appointment, Rupert, but surely not in Paris.

RUPERT: To be honest, I had been going to Paris, though not quite so soon and not in these togs. This is a surprise, but if you have some champagne available it need not be unpleasant.

EDDIE *[to another* **Merrymaker***]*: Joannie, a drink for Rupert immediately. He has had a nasty shock at the hands of kidnappers.

JOANNIE: No sooner said than… Here we are. Enjoy being kidnapped, Rupert.

With its contents spilling on the way, a goblet is passed to **Rupert***. It is the first of many. As the train draws into Folkestone,* **Rupert** *makes a speech of thanks.*

RUPERT: When I got up this morning and, indeed, until, I think… *[looks at watch]* …less than two hours ago, I had no idea my life would take the turn it has, but I must say that had it been designed, I could hardly have ordered it better. That, anyway, is the short-sighted view. In the longer-term, embarrassment awaits me, for I have no more clothing with me than what you see. But thank you all the same. I know you mean well: it is just that, being ignorant, you do not understand these things.

Both cheers and cries of "shame, shame".

CUT TO – Arrival of the train at Gare St-Lazare, Paris. As he steps into a world of sober morning commuters, **Rupert,** *in white tie and tails no longer so immaculate as when he started out, is stared and laughed at. Outside the station, he calls a cab and asks for the rue de Passy. On the way, he asks to stop at a flower stall and buys carnations. At the destination, he knocks on a door, which is opened by a woman who greets him with surprise and an embrace.*

VOICE: Fortunately, I already had shirts and socks in Paris, because I used to send my laundry to Madame Blandier, a *blanchisseuse*, who would return it to London the following week exquisitely washed and smelling faintly of chestnuts. I knew that I was not only feeling the worse for wear, but also looking it after my overnight journey, so I had bought as many carnations as I could carry, making them do double duty by screening my wilting shirt and delighting the old lady. She had not yet despatched my fresh linen to London, so after I changed into a clean shirt, tie and waistcoat, we went to the corner cafe, where she drank a Vermouth to every glass of water I swigged. I spent a delightful weekend, remaining in bed at the Daunou during the day and being called only in time to go out at night, hostage to my wardrobe.

CUT TO – Hotel Daunou, having panned from the opera to the rue Daunou off the Boulevard des Italiens.

VOICE: The Hotel Daunou was at that time a delightful *garonniere*, immediately above Ciro's, and contained about thirty rooms, each with a bathroom and occupied by such people as had no objection to the noise from the dance-band below, which played into the early hours of each morning. Its British proprietor had been acquitted of murder in Scotland.

111

CUT TO – Hotel Meurice, the lobby, the lift.

VOICE: My own brush with the law in Paris occurred about this time. I was visiting friends at the Meurice, that aristocrat of hotels. I stepped into the lift, minding my own business, when I was confronted by the only other occupant: a *gendarme* in uniform, wearing, of all things, an eyeglass. Believing he was a guest attending a fancy-dress party, I at once congratulated him on the excellence of his get-up. To my amazement he became indignant and demanded an apology. Seeing him feel for his notebook in an unmistakably official manner, I was not slow to express my regrets and we parted amicably after he had had a drink in my friends' suite.

★ ★ ★ ★ ★

CUT TO – Front of Hotel Daunou as **Rupert** *saunters in the evening to Harry's New York Bar directly across the street.*

VOICE: In the early Twenties, Harry's New York Bar in Paris was a *rendezvous* for foreign correspondents and expatriate Americans. I used to look in there frequently, despite the stench of Harry's black cigars. One evening, I saw Scott Fitzgerald's pale face peering at me through the reek. It looked as though he had been there some time, upholding his reputation as a high-calibre drinker.

Rupert *goes up to* **Scott***, who is sitting on a stool at the bar.*

SCOTT: Come join me, buddy. Long time no see.

On the other side of the bar, **Harry MacLehone** *is writing in a notebook, frowning and looking now and then at the rows of bottles on the shelf behind him.*

RUPERT: Hello, Harry. Stocktaking?

HARRY: Hi, Rupe. In a sense, yes: taking stock of what we lack.

SCOTT: Harry's got a problem. He's compiling a book of cocktails and their ingredients, and is short of recipes. Maybe we, as scholars, could help.

HARRY: Please do, and make full use of the bar – on the house.

RUPERT: I don't know about scholar in my case, but I'm not against research.

SCOTT: I've done some basic work already. I'm writing down the ingredients.

RUPERT: But, of course; you're a writer.

From the forest of bottles **Harry** *puts on the bar for them to use, they keep pouring, mixing and drinking* **Scott** *jotting as they go.*

SCOTT: Trouble is, there's no plot and no past. It's becoming too hard to remember the taste of the one before. It might be better for the memory if, instead of drinking, we simply sipped. Rupert, may I ask you a personal question?

RUPERT: By all means, but you might not get an answer. Fire away.

SCOTT *[by now quite drunk]*: Do you find it hard to say "simply sipped" without dribbling?

RUPERT: It's not a phrase I've come across, but if I do I'll let you know.

SCOTT: Thank you, Rupert. For a Limey, you're exceptionally dependable.

RUPERT: May I ask you a personal question?

SCOTT: Fire away.

RUPERT: Can you read your own writing?

Scott *squints at the paper, turns it this way and that, puts it down and shakes his head.*

RUPERT: For a Yank, you're not all that dependable.

★ ★ ★ ★ ★

FADE TO – Much later, both by now far gone, swaying on their stools, dawn seeping in the front door. **Harry** *approaches from the other end of the bar. They are the only customers still there.*

HARRY: Well, gentlemen of the jury, have you made your decision?

RUPERT: We are umanimous *[sic]*. The fruits of our work, distilled into beauty, are in this sample *[bangs a glass on the counter and some of the contents bounce out]* and the raw materials for it are here – these bottles we have put to one side, segregated. We have even given it a name for your book.

SCOTT*[slurring badly]*: And for the patents attorneys.

HARRY: What have you called it?

SCOTT: "The Desert Healer" – what else?

HARRY Can you say what's in it – for the book?

SCOTT: Just call it the most eclectic cocktail of all. It contains something of everything and its taste is brave and unapologetic. Hold it up to the light and see how it warns in rainbow colours; swallow it and feel the breath of a bunsen burner, sparked off with a dash of dynamite...

RUPERT *[to Harry]*: Had he not been a writer, he would have been a professional flame swallower.

SCOTT: That's as may be, but please excuse me.

Scott *dismounts clumsily from his stool, which he unintentionally sends flying with his hand, and tacks his way to the telephone booth.*

VOICE: A few weeks later, or so it seemed, I saw him returning. He was sailing out of the mist into a headwind, veering to port, swinging to starboard, then gybing until he almost came about before coming alongside. Although he was leaning close and speaking confidently, it was as though his voice came from a great distance.

CUT TO – **Scott** *speaking into* **Rupert's** *ear, lurching and butting his face from time to time.*

SCOTT: I'm glad I telephoned, because it's not whisky Zelda wants, it's rum and vodka. But she doesn't want it after all, because she still has some left in the bottle from last night, when I was supposed to have brought back vodka and gin and I took back a bottle of Scotch.

VOICE: By this time, I had lost all coherence. It was as if I had put on a stranger's reading glasses, for Scott, my unspeakable friend, seemed to advance towards me and then recede, as in a minuet, with solemn, measured tread.

Harry *returns from the front door and addresses the pair.*

HARRY: Your taxi, gentlemen. Goodnight, and thanks for your work.

They help each other to the door, mumbling goodnights on the way to customers no longer there. As the driver holds the car door open, **Scott** *gets in first, then* **Rupert**. **Scott** *sits down, but* **Rupert**, *hunched, keeps walking, opens the door on the other side of the car, steps out and continues to the hotel entrance straight ahead.* **Scott** *addresses a remark to* **Rupert** *and, getting no reply, looks confusedly in all directions to see where he has gone, but, of course, does not, and utters a cry of puzzlement.*

VOICE: Behind me, I heard Scott utter a startled cry. It was the last sound I ever heard him make. Months later, I happened to see an advance copy of Harry's book of cocktails and in it, boldly listed and fully acknowledged, was our "Desert Healer".

★ ★ ★ ★ ★

CUT TO – Kensington Gardens, London, across from Lancaster Gate.

VOICE: While I was in London, an important event happened in my life. Gertrude Lawrence, who was appearing at the Vaudeville Theatre, introduced me to her cousin, Victoria Banks, who had taken the stage name of Ruby Lorraine. Ruby was famous at the time as the model for Raphael Kirschner's pin-ups. Her face was as lovely as an Eastern dawn; her personality, irresistible. And I knew she was not indifferent to me, for I had pursued my courtship with ardour and some skill. At that time, I probably believed anything a woman told me so long as I wanted to hear it. I spoiled women in small ways. When I dined with a girl, I would have the waiter wear a huge carnation, the orchestra play her favourite tunes and the chef bring the dishes to the table, with each course on the menu named after her. The head-waiter served the *omelette surprise* and the *sommelier* did a minuet around the table with the champagne, the coffee, the liqueurs and the special Abdulla rose-tipped cigarettes. By the time we left the table, she was prepared to believe I had created the world. To avoid family interference, Ruby and I met in secret and arranged a trysting-place beneath a rather drab little tree in Kensington Gardens, near our home at Lancaster Gate.

From across Bayswater Road comes a footman carrying a large basket of crimson roses and a reel of silver wire. One by one, he attaches the blooms to the branches.

VOICE: Here, I would ask her to marry me. I told a footman to adorn the tree with crimson roses and they blazed in it as symbols of my passion. She accepted me, though the engagement remained, as had been the proposal, *sub rosa.* Two months later, we were married – against the advice of my parents and those friends who had forgotten how foolish it is to be young.

★ ★ ★ ★ ★

CUT TO – Ravenspoint. **Sir Henry** *emerges from his study and moves to the living room, where* **Lady Grayson** *is attending to papers at her desk. She draws his attention to a large parcel on a side table, addressed to him.*

SIR HENRY: French postmark. From Rupert, perhaps.

Sir Henry *laboriously opens the parcel and draws out a huge chocolate Easter egg, lavishly decorated with the fleur-de-lis design. After admiring it and untying the satin ribbon that encircles it, he prises the egg apart to find it stuffed with papers. His expostulation causes* **Lady Grayson** *to swing around enquiringly.*

LADY GRAYSON: What is it?

SIR HENRY: I was right about the sender, but the motive is not quite in the spirit of the occasion, except, perhaps, in hinting, blasphemously, that I was born yesterday.

LADY GRAYSON: What are you talking about, Henry?

Sir Henry *picks the papers one by one from the half of the egg in which they rest, as though in a boat, and unfolds them.*

SIR HENRY: Only mentioning, my dear, that your son has chosen to celebrate the birth of the Christ-child by using him as a postman to send me all his unpaid bills. I wonder that he found an egg large enough for them. It will be, I'm afraid, the very last time.

Lady Grayson, *with her indifference to financial matters, turns back with barely a comment to what she is doing.*

LADY GRAYSON: I agree; it does rather border on the tasteless, but he's your son, too, Henry.

★ ★ ★ ★ ★

CUT TO – Paris, where **Rupert** *and* **Ruby** *are completing their honeymoon. The post has arrived and* **Rupert** *slits open a letter, which he reads with eyebrows raised and face serious, as though it contains a proposal about which he has serious doubts.*

RUBY: What is it, Rupert? The old school begging for a donation?

RUPERT: No, my dear. It would know better than to waste paper on that. It's from Father. This time, I think he has me cornered. It must have been the Easter egg that did it.

RUBY: Cornered? How?

RUPERT: He's been stepping up his efforts to push me into a career. Push has now turned to pull. He is willing to finance me into something, but not just the pursuit of happiness.

RUBY: Do you mean business?

RUPERT: Ghastly as the prospect is, I see no alternative.

RUBY: Well, at least you've got an umbrella.

CUT TO – **Sir Henry's** *study at Ravenspoint. He is behind his desk,* **Rupert** *is in the visitor's chair.*

SIR HENRY: As I said, Eveleigh Nash is an old friend, well read and astute, and the company is sound, but he's got an idea for doing cheap reprints and needs an infusion of cash to grab the market before someone else gets the same idea. I'm prepared to invest £8000 with him. That would secure you a directorship and a salary of £1000.

RUPERT: Most generous, Father. Thank you. I must say I have always loved the smell of books.

SIR HENRY: You loved the smell of stables, too, as I recall. Nash has one of the finest stables of writers in London.

★ ★ ★ ★ ★

CUT TO – *Eveleigh,* **Nash's** *publishing house, as* **Rupert** *is introduced to the firm's operations by* **Nash** *himself.*

NASH: As to authors, among others we are printing William Le Queux, Cunninghame Graham, Robert Hitchens, John Collier, Edgar Lee Masters, Wyndham Lewis…

Nash *pauses as though to catch his breath.*

NASH: But we need new blood, Rupert, and here I believe your social grapevine could help.

RUPERT *[reflectively, almost to himself]*: Yes, there must be a few tales among all those heads. *[Speaking directly to Nash]* Father mentioned your plan for tapping into old blood, too, with reprints.

NASH: Yes, we've already got a list for that: Hardy, Conrad, Stevenson and others. Your father's investment will bring it to life.

Rupert *stands up to go.*

RUPERT: I'll leave you now, Eveleigh, and start a list of my own.

CUT TO – **Rupert's** *office along the corridor. View of London from window, then to Ennismore Street, Knightsbridge, showing the street sign and finding the house* **Sir Henry** *has built there for the newlyweds.*

VOICE: The house Father had built Ruby and me in Ennismore Street was one of the first non-basement houses in Knightsbridge, strategically situated between a pub on the corner of the mews and a French convent on the other side of the street.

Tour the house. Her bedroom: grey sycamore furniture inlaid with ivory. Drawing room: rosewood piano, floral design, pink, green and white. Dining room: white and gold table with oval mahogany top and chairs of matching design shipped from Paris, together with marble chimney-pieces.

VOICE: To reassemble the fireplaces, I had to employ Italians from Clerkenwell. They spent much of the day teaching us bawdy Neapolitan songs in the kitchen, eating macaroni and drinking *chianti*, which we bought from Soho. On my bedroom floor, I had a Khiva rug, which in damp weather came to life under my bare feet with the smell of the goats from whose hair it had been woven. Father had bought the chandeliers and many of the wall lights in Venice and had them shipped to London. In the drawing room, Charles Buchel had painted a *trompe-l'oeil* of an open french window leading on to a lawn with a distant view of bright flowerbeds. One could almost smell the garden. One day…

★ ★ ★ ★ ★

FADE TO – Drawing room, where **Rupert** *and* **Ruby** *suspend their conversation as a manservant* **[Edward]** *enters, bearing a tray of decanters and glasses, crosses the room and heads for the trompe-l'oeil. Alarmed,* **Rupert** *calls out.*

RUPERT: Where are you going, Edward?

EDWARD *[stopping and turning]*: It is such a beautiful day, sir, that I thought you might like to have your drinks served in the garden.

RUBY [*sotto voce*]: Oh, poor chap.

RUPERT: It's only a painting, Edward. Eyes a bit weak, eh?

EDWARD: 'fraid so, sir; they wouldn't take me in the army.

RUPERT: Well, don't regret it, Edward. You're alive, even if it does mean banging into the odd wall.

Edward *comes to where they are sitting and places the tray on a coffee table.*

RUBY: You do have a knack of looking on the bright side, Rupe.

RUPERT: I only hope my new masters do. We are trotting about rather a lot, don't you think? Monte Carlo in winter, Deauville in August, Biarritz in September…

RUBY: Not in vain, surely. You are squeezing the odd book out of people, are you not? And that means hunting them in their natural habitat.

RUPERT *[unenthusiastically, with a sigh]*: I suppose you are right. You usually are.

★ ★ ★ ★ ★

CUT TO – *Victoria Station, Continental Departures, the signboard for train to Vienna, people bustling aboard with their luggage, travelling rugs, newspapers, waving and kissing goodbye.*

VOICE: It was not long before I realised publishing was not quite what I wanted; rather like a suit that looks good, but does not fit. I resigned from the firm and my younger brother Brian, who was reading for the Bar, agreed to take my place. His qualities were such that I suspect Eveleigh Nash was only too delighted with the arrangement.

Eveleigh **Nash's** *office.* **Rupert** *in visitor's chair.*

NASH: You have rolled the ball a bit further for us, Rupert, and with Brian taking it over, I'm sure the Grayson name will always be remembered as part of the team.

Montage of the countries and towns through which passes the Orient Express on the way to its destination. Tour Vienna, homing in on the Kärtnering and Sacher's Hotel.

VOICE: After the interlude in publishing, I made one or two other abortive ventures into business, including several from a visit to Vienna – a city I had always longed to see, not least because it was the source of such colourful legends. I was after the eggs to make the omelette. In Vienna, having booked in at the Grand, on the advice of the Countess Larisch, whom I had met with Eveleigh Nash, I took a box of Laranagas Coronas I had bought at Trumper's in Curzon Street and presented them to Madame Sacher. She had been for two generations to Sacher's what Rosa Lewis was to the Cavendish in London. She was the confidente of grand dukes and an old friend of Emperor Franz Joseph himself. Her hotel was in many ways more musty and moth-eaten than the Cavendish, but it had prestige and a kind of rarity value.

★ ★ ★ ★ ★

CUT TO – MADAME SACHER sitting at her table in the hall, smoking the cigars RUPERT has given her. An ensemble in the foyer plays the city's favourite music.

VOICE: The old lady sat in the hall, watching her guests come and go as she chain-smoked the best cigars obtainable in Europe. She was delighted with my present and enquired about Countess Larisch. She had acted as a go-between in the ill-fated love affair of Marie Vetsera and Prince Rudolf, known in legend as Mayerling, where their suicide pact was enacted. This secured me a table in the smaller restaurant, which corresponded to being on the courtyard side of the Savoy Grill in London. I was not a table snob, but was in Vienna to pick up business propositions because the rate of exchange so heavily favoured the pound, and could do with such build-up. For my room and bathroom, I was paying less than five shillings a night. For several days, I enjoyed the income of a millionaire and spent it as money should be spent. I had the glorious opportunity of giving away hundreds of pounds that meant nothing to me.

*CUT TO – Glimpses of **Rupert** traipsing the streets and entering one business premises after another, corresponding with samples he is procuring as the foundation for his business career.*

VOICE: Before prices rose, I bought cigarette cases and specimens of Vienna's fabulous enamel-work. Popular at the time was a charming waltz song, *"Nur eine Nacht"*, the English performing rights of which I gained for a hundred pounds. A wonderful new violin had just reached the Austrian market with the strangely inappropriate name of Tim. I bought the agency for it.

★ ★ ★ ★ ★

*CUT TO – London's top shops in Jermyn and Bond Street, where **Rupert** is taken beyond the front counters to back rooms where he unloads the goods from Vienna.*

124

VOICE: On returning to London, I multiplied my investment many times on all the items I had bought, except the violin, but gave much of my haul away as presents and kept several objects for myself – including a cigarette case plaited in three colours of gold with a cabachon emerald opening-catch.

★ ★ ★ ★ ★

CUT TO – *A London building. In a corridor,* **Rupert**, *somewhat lost, stops an* **Office Girl** *and asks for directions.*

RUPERT: Can you tell me, please, where to find the Keith Prowse agency?

OFFICE GIRL: Yes, sir, next floor up, directly above where we are now. Stairs are at the end of this corridor *[and points]*.

RUPERT Thank you, dear.

★ ★ ★ ★ ★

CUT TO – *Corridor above,* **Rupert** *appearing at the end of it, having mounted the stairs, and arriving at a door with a signboard "Musical rights". He enters and asks for Mr* **Saunders**, *who is summoned to the desk.*

SAUNDERS: Ah, yes, Mr Grayson. You telephoned. If you leave your copy of the work, we'll give you a receipt and get our musical people to assess it. You said you have legal confirmation of the English rights?

Rupert *opens briefcase and brings forth the sheet of music and the envelope containing the letter.* **Saunders** *inspects the letter and hands it back to* **Rupert**, *but keeps the manuscript.*

SAUNDERS: I really don't know where we'd be without the Austrians and the Germans to supply us with sounds to make. Or, rather, with the recipes for making them. I expect that if your *"Nur Eine Nacht"* is as good as all the other stuff we get from that quarter, we'll make you an offer for it.

125

RUPERT: Yes, we do rather depend on foreigners – musically, anyway. The English are shy when it comes to baring the soul.

SAUNDERS: What about our poets: Wordsworth, Tennyson, Shelley… were they shy?

RUPERT *[rubbing chin]*: You have a point. What do you put it down to?

SAUNDERS: Embarrassment, sir. Starts in childhood. Continentals are uninhibited because there is a lot of the savage in them.

RUPERT *[consulting watch]*: Perhaps you're right. I'll think about it. And you'll think about the offer, eh?

SAUNDERS: We'll be in touch, sir, and I'm sure it will be to your advantage.

RUPERT: Thank you, goodbye for now.

★ ★ ★ ★ ★

CUT TO – **Rupert's** *departure from the building.*

VOICE: They paid me 200 pounds for *"Nur Eine Nacht"*. It was introduced into a musical comedy at the Gaiety Theatre and afterwards became a regular number in programmes around the world. I believe it earned at least 50,000 pounds in royalties.

★ ★ ★ ★ ★

CUT TO – **Rupert** *walking to his St James's club, settling into an armchair with a drink and The Times.*

VOICE: I saw that Fritz Kreisler was in London and knew he would be at the Hyde Park Hotel. I telephoned his secretary, asking whether he would pass judgment on the newest violin made in Vienna. I was not surprised when an appointment was confirmed for the next day. Kreisler would not refuse to try out an instrument that had come direct from his beloved city.

★ ★ ★ ★ ★

CUT TO – **Rupert** *walking the short distance from Ennismore Street to the Hyde Park Hotel, where he consults the desk and takes the lift, steps out and is greeted by* **Kreisler.**

VOICE: Next afternoon I had the extraordinary experience of hearing Kreisler play for me alone. He asked what I would like to hear and I asked for his *"Liebeslied"*. Of course, once he had the violin in his hands, he went on from one composition to another. He thought the violin excellent. The encounter should have spurred me to go ahead with the marketing of it, but possibly the effort of selling the cigarette cases and so on had been too much for me, for I did nothing about it. Months later, I had a letter from port officials in Southampton informing me that a hundred violins, addressed to me, were waiting to be cleared through customs. For all I know, they are still there.

★ ★ ★ ★ ★

CUT TO – The bustle of St James's Street.

VOICE: By now, it was clear that business was not my *metier* – yet, with three friends, I started another business in St James's Street. We acquired a huge machine for stamping out rubber heels. The machine was installed at enormous expense, including that of reinforcing the building and widening the front door, but it never went into production, thanks to a rise in the price of rubber or maybe a slump in heels – I forget which. Leslie Childers spent two months of masterly inactivity as managing director, while Jasper Plowden and I passed the time at the nearby Maclean Galleries looking at the latest importations of Manet, Renoir and Sisley. Eventually, we were able to dispose of the machine to someone who wanted it for an entirely different purpose.

★ ★ ★ ★ ★

CUT TO – Inside the Guards' Club in Brook Street, Mayfair. **Rupert** *is talking*

127

with his friend Tim **Nugent** *when they hear* **Someone** *apparently pleading with the club secretary's* **Assistant** *nearby.*

VOICE: We often met at the Guards' Club. The secretary's assistant was a charming man, but he liked to look upon the wine when it was redder than it should have been. We had all been asked not to encourage him. So we were surprised to hear someone inviting him to have a drink in one of the alcoves along the passage that led to the dining room.

Rupert *and his friend* **Nugent** *look at each other questioningly and listen.*

SOMEONE: Come on, you must have another whisky.

ASSISTANT: No, thank you.

SOMEONE: I insist.

ASSISTANT: Well, if you insist, I suppose…

SOMEONE: And a large one, too…

ASSISTANT: Well, if you insist…

A moment later, a waiter enters the alcove with two large whiskies. After he has gone, **Rupert** *gets up and peers round the corner of the alcove to see that the* **Assistant** *secretary is quite alone with the two large whiskies before him.*

★ ★ ★ ★ ★

FADE TO – Another day at the club.

VOICE: Many things in those days were not what they seemed. One day, Leslie Childers met me in a state of jubilation. An uncle of whom he had great expectations had died and Leslie received from his solicitors a letter saying he had been mentioned in the will. They wished to check on

Leslie's address before communicating the contents. That night, Leslie organised a magnificent dinner at Claridges to which he invited twenty-one of his friends. We duly saw him off on the night train to Scotland. It was a chastened Leslie I saw a few days later, when he told me that all the uncle had left him was a set of ivory chessmen. He did not play chess, he said, and was too old to learn. Some time later, he dug the chessmen out of the attic and gave them away as a wedding present. Soon, he was astonished to receive a letter of thanks more profuse than he had ever received before. "We cannot thank you enough for your most generous present," wrote the happy pair. "Neither of us plays chess, but we have learned that the set you gave us is valued at 1000 pounds." Leslie was nevertheless an optimist, prepared to gamble on anything. It was reported that he once backed a man who had invented an eiderdown, which, when it slipped off the bed, automatically sprang back. He was also thorough. It was said that when he was on a diet, he insisted that Robert Jackson supply him with *Gruyère* possessing king-sized holes.

Scene: Autumn forests and towns on the road from Paris to Berlin, followed by views of the German capital, narrowing to establishments in Friedrichstrasse: playground of sex perverts and deviants.

VOICE: In the years after the first war, I often visited Berlin. I had many friends there and when not travelling by Ostend, I would drive from Paris, sometimes through the golden autumn forests, a journey I never tired of. After Paris, the life of Berlin – or "the village", as the diplomats called it – was hard and brash, though the days could be lovely at Wannsee in the lakeside restaurants, and with friends I would burn the nights away. Berlin nightlife had sunk to a level of depravity unequalled in any other European capital, with every imaginable fantasy catered for. I made a friend in the police who showed me bars used by criminals, tolerated for their usefulness in keeping the police in touch with their clients. The German military collapse of 1918 was attended by widespread moral breakdown. Women of the now impoverished middle and professional classes were selling themselves for bars of chocolate, cakes or soap – and thereby antagonising regular working prostitutes.

★ ★ ★ ★ ★

CUT TO – A seedy café off the Friedrichstrasse, where Pat **Kirwan** *sits at a marble-topped table on which his folded arms pillow his head. A glass of brandy is by his elbow.*

VOICE: In the early Twenties of the ill-fated Weimar Republic, I came across my friend Patrick Kirwan. He shared my fascination with this bizarre underworld. Pat, like myself, had served in Flanders while still in his teens, and had twice been wounded, but, though he came of a long line of Irish professional soldiers, was so appalled by the slaughter of the

130

trenches and disgusted by the philistinism of the capitalist society that awaited the warriors' return, that he turned communist and revolutionary. He was working on clandestine publications under the direction of the brilliant but unwashed Russian conspirator and journalist, Karl Radek. Unlike myself, who had gained a faith in the war, Pat had lost one. But when the death of Lenin and the decline of Trotsky were followed by the seizure of power by Stalin, he realised he had taken to his heart not the fair genius of *liberté*, *egalité* and *fraternité*, but famine, tyranny and spiritual death. This swift and second loss of faith drove him to spend his days in a squalid café, cooling his elbows on a marble-topped table and consuming a throat-burning procession of brandies. Together, we drank our way out of our private grief.

Kirwan *suddenly comes to life, raises clenched fist and shouts.*

KIRWAN: Too long have I been the anvil.

Kirwan's *head slumps back to where it was until the next drink arrives, whereupon he straightens up, eyes flashing and fist raised, his voice booming throughout the café.*

KIRWAN: Now, I will be the hammer.

VOICE: His words, being a quotation from Goethe, were heard with respectful attention. Sometimes I could persuade him to sing the lovely, sad song of the Irish Famine in his clear baritone, with his fine head thrown back and his dark eyes flashing.

As **Kirwan** *begins to sing, the café becomes silent, waiters standing motionless, conversation dying to whispers.*

KIRWAN:
> *Oh the praties they are small,*
> *Over here, over here,*

Oh, the praties they are small,
And we dug them in the fall,
And we ate them coats and all full of fear.

I wish that we were geese,
Night till morn, night till morn,
I wish that we were geese,
For they spend their days in peace,
To the hour of their decease
Eating corn, eating corn.

We're down into the dust
Over here, over here,
We're down into the dust,
But with faith in God we trust,
He'll feed us with a crust,
Over here, over here.

VOICE: By the time he had reached the last verse, there was hardly a dry eye among the sentimental Germans, for even those who did not understand could divine the sincerity and mourning in the old lament.

★ ★ ★ ★ ★

CUT TO – The Tiergarten, with people strolling, a band playing. In a droschke, **Kirwan** *and an American* **Comrade** *are riding along an avenue.*

Close-up of the pair in conversation.

KIRWAN: Apart from sharing the mellowness of autumn together, Hartley, why have you got me here?

COMRADE: I am the bearer of tidings, Kirwan, and they are confidential and to your advantage. You are being posted to Moscow to work in the Comintern.

The **Comrade** *leans forward and taps the driver of the droschke on the shoulder, signalling him to stop. Inexplicably, he hands* **Kirwan** *an apple.*

KIRWAN: Thank you. Is this, perhaps, the Garden of Eden?

Kirwan *raises the apple to his nostrils, but as he lowers it, his face shows apprehension.*

COMRADE: I'm not a serpent, if that's what you mean?

★ ★ ★ ★ ★

CUT TO – The droschke stopping at **Kirwan's** *hotel and letting him out. He throws the apple core in a bin as though ridding himself of something unpleasant.*

VOICE: To Pat, the apple evoked no memories of girls laughing in sunlit orchards. It smelled of death. That night he headed not for Moscow, but, by a circuitous route, for London.

★ ★ ★ ★ ★

CUT TO – **Kirwan** *packing and tortuously picking his way out of Berlin, with an assortment of cabs and trains to Ostend and thence by fishing trawler to Grimsby and train to London.*

VOICE: In London, a party sympathiser let slip that Pat had been too open in his denunciation of Stalin. It was feared he might defect and tell what he knew. He need not have worried. Pat had a fine contempt for the shabby brigade of ex-communists. He had said to me: "When you have loved a woman, you don't write dirt about her – even if she was a bitch."

★ ★ ★ ★ ★

CUT TO – **Rupert** *and* **Kirwan** *dining together in a grand London hotel.*

VOICE: There was the other side of Pat, which loved to be with me under the chandeliers of the great international restaurants or living a life of ease and reading in the green twilight of tapestry-hung rooms. Life to him was a triptych of mirrors in which he could study the reflection from every angle. He could mix sadness with a zest for enjoyment, accompanied by a first-class mind and the gift of being able to break down a problem so that it became already half-solved. He was the only man I have known who could not only sum up a person correctly, but also see him as he appeared to himself. Thus, he was an ideal companion for someone of my temperament. Years later, I was best man at his marriage to Celia, one of the Paget twins, who were the toast of fashionable London. He had given up novels and *belles-lettres* and, with some amusement, was writing films for Korda and wartime *Evening Standard* leaders for Lord Beaverbrook. As we dined at the Connaught after the wedding reception at Claridges, it was almost impossible to realise that this was the same man who had been a down-at-heel *habitué* of seedy revolutionary hangouts, with a murderous committee awaiting him in Moscow.

★ ★ ★ ★ ★

CUT TO – **Rupert** *leaving Berlin's Hotel Adlon and walking to Magnus Hirschfeld's Museum.*

VOICE: One day, I visited Magnus Hirschfeld's Museum. Doctor Hirschfeld was the leading authority on all offbeat sexual matters. He had a library with the most Catholic collection of erotica in the world. I had a letter of introduction. I was given a guide to show me everything of interest that could be seen in one afternoon.

★ ★ ★ ★ ★

CUT TO – **Young Man** *escorting* **Rupert** *around the museum, directing him here and there to see this or that priority item of perversion, erotica or sadism. At the end of the tour, the* **Young Man** *takes* **Rupert's** *hand and guides it around his face. As they say goodbye, he kisses the same hand too long, causing* **Rupert** *to snatch it away.*

VOICE: He behaved politely throughout my visit, but as we were leaving took my hand and ran it over his cheeks and chin to demonstrate, he said, how all the hair had been electrically removed. I suppose that was reasonable enough, but I was taken by surprise when I felt the imprint of

134

his lips on my hand before he released it. Nor did I realise the difficulty I would have in scrubbing the lipstick off on my return to the Adlon. I learned later from Oswald Hafenrichter, who edited the film *The Third Man*, that the poor devil was well-known as a transvestite and committed suicide when Hitler decreed that all Germans should be "normal like himself".

★ ★ ★ ★ ★

*CUT TO – **Rupert** dressing for the evening at the Adlon, the hotel valet fussing about, laying out his clothes, arranging a tray of hors d'oeuvres and a dry Martini, drawing the bath, placing evening-studs next to gleaming silver brushes, and putting a Venetian-red carnation in a glass just wide enough to take a flower.*

VOICE: In the hotel bar, there was the usual bunch, drinking and gossiping. I knew most of them. After a while, I made my escape, for in their company the drinks were too cold, too strong and too frequent, and I was feeling tolerant enough to endure my own company that evening. After dining well in the restaurant, I remembered a cabaret, the Kazbec, that Bodker of Reuter had recommended if I wanted to be alone without being lonely.

★ ★ ★ ★ ★

*CUT TO – **Rupert** walking to the Kazbec. The door swings open and he enters. Around the dance floor, and lighting the room, are glittering globes with mirrored facets that catch and reflect the light as they revolve. The decor includes small fountains of water tinted green, blue and red. On each table is a telephone bearing an illuminated number.*

VOICE: I was assailed by the reek of stale cigar smoke, cheap perfume and perspiring bodies – when I should have recognised the stench of murder. There were girls galore and the whole operation was clearly intended to induce a friendly mood.

***Rupert** finds a table in a corner away from the dance floor. He has not been seated long when the table's telephone rings and a **Girl's** voice speaks.*

GIRL: Hello, do you like to dance?

VOICE: There was invitation in the voice, which was that of a very young girl.

RUPERT: You seem to have danced yourself away from school.

GIRL: Possibly…

From the orchestra come the strains of "The Blue Danube".

GIRL: You are English? Only an Englishman could come here dressed so. Your countrymen will go to Paradise wearing their black ties.

RUPERT: But supposing this is Paradise. Paradise is only where you find happiness… and angels.

VOICE: There was a pause before the low, sweet voice continued.

GIRL: If there are angels here, we have left our haloes at home…

RUPERT: With your dolls?

GIRL *[a gurgle of laughter, then a note of bitterness in the words]*: You cannot judge age from my voice. It is my thoughts you must read.

RUPERT: I was taught that it was rude to read people's thoughts.

GIRL: Then perhaps I shall enjoy talking to you. You should ask me whether I come here often. Oh yes, that is always the first question.

RUPERT: I'm certain you haven't been coming here very long.

VOICE: What was she like, the possessor of this lovely voice? I was only faintly interested in what she was saying. It was like listening to a beautiful voice singing in an unknown language. All I wanted to do was listen.

GIRL *[in a whisper]*: Not long; not long. Because *[hesitates]* Father forbade me to come here.

RUPERT: And your mother?

GIRL: My mother died during the war. She was sick and we were poor, if you understand the meaning of the word. Father was a soldier; then, later, a porter at a foreign embassy.

VOICE: Her voice was dark and warm, if a voice can be so described; though it was fresh and youthful, it was at the same time fully composed. It contained cadences I had heard before in no other human voice. I sat spellbound, allowing its caressing intonations to flow over and completely through me.

GIRL: He was afraid of pleasure. He was afraid of everything when it concerned me. And to be afraid of pleasure... *[a drawing-in of breath]* it is dangerous to be afraid of pleasure.

VOICE: The voice was not only melodious but compulsively interesting, with its ever-changing tones. Yet underlying it, there was a note of sadness. Then, I was conscious of something sinister. There were things she told me tenderly with the words hardly above a whisper – childhood stories; and a short childhood it must have been. She told me things that gave her pleasure; yet in the shadowed background, there stalked, limping, the angry figure of her father, remote and inflexible with his artificial leg, ill-fitting and irritating – a frustrated non-commissioned officer with no soldiers to bully.

CUT TO – A ghost picture: beside the Spree Canal, with barges passing.

GIRL: For other girls, there were the movies, parties, swimming and dancing; for me, nothing, except… those sad walks beside the Spree Canal alone with him, talking of the Kaiser and pre-war Germany and his exploits on the Somme, shouting his stories to the bargemen until he drove them below decks. Every day we would take our walk, and always I would see the men escaping below when they saw us approaching the quayside. Sometimes they would loosen the warps and steer midstream to avoid us, but my father would tempt them back with tobacco and cigars. It seemed that he spoke always of what others wanted to forget.

VOICE: It was difficult to know whether she was telling the truth. To make truth sound true, it is often necessary to embroider it with fiction – as if to magnify its gleam.

GIRL: It was not often that I was out of his sight, but there were times when his leg was too painful and I had to go alone to buy our provisions.

CUT TO – Back at the cabaret, the white tablecloth and the slender black bottle of hock in its ice bucket.

GIRL: Why am I telling you all this?

RUPERT: Because you know I am interested.

GIRL: Because your voice is gentle or because you're a stranger who'll forget, or because I feel that you understand things, good and bad. *[Whisper]* This is a cabaret confessional.

Rupert *waits wordlessly for the voice to resume.*

GIRL: One evening, because things happen to lonely people, a girl-friend

138

stopped me in the street and told me there was a man who wanted to know me.

RUPERT: You met him?

GIRL: Yes, and why not? It was the first time anyone had wanted to know me. So that very evening, as it was getting dark, I slipped away from Father. He shouted to me from the quayside, and tried to catch me, but with his artificial leg... you understand? He wasn't quick enough.

RUPERT: And the man?

GIRL: Oh, the man, he was old but he was kind.

VOICE: She paused and the silence was like a sigh.

GIRL: When I returned home, my father beat me.

VOICE: I seemed to detect a note of bravado as she went on.

GIRL: Of course, I was used to that, but please believe me *[pleadingly]* before that there had been no occasion to beat me.

RUPERT: And the next time?

GIRL: I escaped again and met the man, and later at the hotel he gave me money, much money. Had I not suffered to please him? He knew, because he'd seen the scars on my body. He showed me how to hide the money in the top of my stocking. That night, my father thrashed me again. This time, I felt the buckle-end of his belt. After that, I was a prisoner. All day he stayed with me, watching me, and when we walked the riverbank in the twilight, his hand clutched mine in his iron grip, but when he descended the steps to the water's edge, it was I who always had to hold him because the steps were slippery.

★ ★ ★ ★ ★

CUT TO – The riverbank, ominous in the twilight.

VOICE: When she spoke again, it was in a whisper, though every word was distinct. And it was to be the last time I was to hear the deathly beauty of that voice.

GIRL: Last night, Father slipped... and with his artificial leg... poor Father! No one could expect him to swim.

VOICE: I could hear her breathing, frightened, because she knew she had spoken. The need to confess had been too strong. Gently, I hung up the receiver and reached for my bill. Outside, morning was mantling the skies over the Kurfurstendamm; broad red spirals, swept by the winds, were fading in the light of the approaching day and the warm smell of fresh bread was beginning to spread through the city.

Scene: Moscow railway station. People on platform are boarding the Red Arrow for Leningrad. **Rupert** *appears among them, peering at numbers on carriages, looking at his ticket, directing the porter handling his luggage, avoiding being run down by trolleys.*

VOICE: The urge to travel farther afield was beginning to possess me. I realised I was too selfish to adjust to the mutual give-and-take of married life and the discipline of office-hours. The long honeymoon was over. The flood of happy-sad memories was overlaid with a dread of economic servitude and spiritual death. I decided that only manual work or constant travel could bring me a sense of freedom. I had grown to manhood in time of war, and to experience war is to lose all sense of reality. As I look back over the years, this hunger for reality, which unconsciously I must have been obeying, is the only justification I can see for my selfish escapism. I went to meet Sir Godfrey Thomas at the Foreign Office, but the Corps was already up to strength – besides which, it appeared that, although I had made one journey already as a King's Messenger, I was still too young even to go on the waiting list. Whatever decision I finally took, I had to visit Russia. It might be my first lesson in how the other half lived. Soon I was on the broad-gauge Red Arrow, returning to Leningrad after visiting Moscow. That evening, with two foreign correspondents, I had watched a dress rehearsal of *Prince Igor* at the Bolshoi Theatre. Never shall I forget the first part of that evening for its beauty – or the second for its ugliness.

★ ★ ★ ★ ★

CUT TO – Interior of train compartment with two bunks. **Rupert** *has just climbed into his, the upper, when the door opens and a Russian* **Officer** *enters to claim the other. He is smoking mahorka cigarettes, with the smoke of which the compartment soon fills.* **Rupert** *leans over and opens the window. The* **Officer** *closes it.* **Rupert**

141

opens it again. Wordlessly, the **Officer** *watches* **Rupert** *with expressionless, oriental eyes, slowly takes his revolver out and puts it on the mirror-shelf beyond* **Rupert's** *reach. Again the* **Officer** *closes the window, through which the lights outside become faster and fewer until there is only blackness. The* **Officer** *continues to stand by the window. The train slows and stops at a country station. Through the window can be seen horses with high wooden collars harnessed to farm carts. Tall bearded men, clearly visible in the moonlight, gaze up vacantly at the train. As the train moves off again, the* **Officer** *removes his uniform jacket and rolls up a shirtsleeve. From his case he takes a hypodermic needle and fills it from an ampoule. He holds the needle up to the light and, satisfied with what he sees, drives it into the antecubital vein that runs in a blue streak down his forearm.* **Rupert** *watches the procedure with fascination and revulsion. As the needle goes in he climbs down from the bunk, his back to the* **Officer***, puts on dressing-gown and slippers, stuffs his belongings into a suitcase and leaves the compartment. With his hand resting on the revolver, the* **Officer** *smirks as* **Rupert** *opens the door and leaves. In the corridor* **Rupert** *finds a car-attendant, and in a mixture of English, French and mime explains what has happened. The attendant locks the* **Officer** *in the compartment and installs* **Rupert** *in another. Next morning, as the train reaches Leningrad,* **Rupert** *is met on the platform by* **Tanya***, who has attached herself to him as a guide. He tells her what has happened.*

TANYA *[grey-eyed, level gaze]*: That is bad. *[Pause]* That is bad.

RUPERT: Bad for whom?

Down the platform, they see a military escort march the **Officer** *away.*

TANYA *[face taut]*: When it is proved against him, he will be punished as an enemy of the state.

VOICE: There was no future for an enemy of the state. I realised that I had brought death, or worse, to a man, for no better reason than he smoked *mahorka* cigarettes and sought forgetfulness in dreams. *[Pause]* I remember my first meeting with Tanya.

★ ★ ★ ★ ★

FADE TO – Leningrad's Hotel Astoria, the Torgsin store off the central hall. **Rupert** *is running his hand over a small Persian rug that has taken his fancy. He realises someone is standing just beside him, and turns to see* **Tanya**.

TANYA: You like Persian rugs?

RUPERT: It isn't often one sees two beautiful things at the same moment.

TANYA [*severely*]: I'm a guide.

RUPERT: Are there any more like you where you come from?

VOICE: She was the first well-groomed girl I had seen in Russia. She was beautiful in a European way, and looked capable of kissing her jewellery or being angry at having left her hand-mirror at home.

TANYA: I don't come from anywhere.

RUPERT: Where are you going to, then?

TANYA: Nowhere in particular.

RUPERT: That's where I was going, so we might as well go there together.

★ ★ ★ ★ ★

CUT TO – They traipse around Leningrad: streets, squares, parks, churches, Winter Palace, Hermitage, museums, university. **Rupert** *follows* **Tanya** *like a dog, drawing level and walking beside her when he can. She shoos away urchins who approach, trying to change money or sell black-market goods.*

VOICE: From then on, she was with me almost constantly, taking me to places I did not want to visit and showing me things I had no wish to see. I was not so foolish as to think that this first meeting beside the little

143

Persian rug had been by chance. She had, of course, been detailed to be my guide. There were times when I even believed I was reasonably in love with her, for under the hard shell of the Komsomol there existed a woman searching instinctively for the silks and satins of life. Yet she loved Russia, and had she suspected me of being an enemy, I believe she would have killed me – even with a kiss. She was quite prepared to liquidate the bourgeoisie single-handed, and although I was an ordinary man with an unquenchable thirst for the good things in life, to her I represented independence – something she secretly craved for. I believe that in the short time I knew her, she elevated me to a mystical state of, quote, independent man, unquote, merely because I had seen the sun rise and fall beyond her prison-world. To her, I represented life over the horizon; a future she was never likely to share with anyone, even someone she might one day love. I was a glimpse into a life that could never be more than part of her dreams.

★ ★ ★ ★ ★

CUT TO – Gorky Park, warm in spring sunshine, new leaves on the trees.

TANYA: There are sixteen pavilions here, each representing a province of the Soviet Union and showing the excellence of our industry, agriculture, research, art… it makes me proud.

RUPERT: Yes, Tanya, but what about the stars, the moon and laughter? And love? Do you not believe that some kind of love is necessary for a particular period of everyone's life?

TANYA: Love of country comes first. Otherwise it is froth, *bourgeois* emotion, a luxury not paid for.

★ ★ ★ ★ ★

CUT TO – **Rupert's** *hotel room.* **Tanya** *is lying on his bed with the sheets pushed down to her feet. She is wearing a pair of his silk pyjamas, which are so big on her that the jacket has slipped away from one shoulder. The other arm is raised to her head so that the hand is hidden in a dark cluster of curls.*

144

VOICE: It seemed to me, in my European way, unreasonable that I should not be allowed to love, at least temporarily, a girl whose company I enjoyed so much. There was a moment in my hotel when I surprised her lying on my bed wearing a pair of my pyjamas. An important part of her training was that she could pretend anything, and now she was pretending to be asleep. But I knew she was watching me under her lashes because I could see the narrow gleam of metallic grey that betrayed her.

RUPERT: You evade nothing by pretending.

Tanya *opens her eyes and looks at* **Rupert** *steadily.*

VOICE: She opened her eyes wide and gave me that level gaze she could assume when she wished to mislead me.

TANYA: You're watching me, *tovaric*, when it is I who should be watching you.

Tanya *puts her hands on her breasts and closes her eyes, and soon appears to be really asleep.*

VOICE: She moved each hand sleepily over her breasts in a circular movement and closed her eyes. A little while later she was genuinely asleep, breathing evenly like a child, dreaming her dreams of blast furnaces, sawmills, tractors and cement mixers, or whatever a Russian girl dreams about. There was nothing for it but to retire to the bar. If her training had been complete, she would know where to find me.

★ ★ ★ ★ ★

CUT TO – *Hotel lobby, enquiry desk.* **Rupert** *bends over a map of Leningrad under a sheet of plate glass, with all its streets in English lettering.*

VOICE: One evening, because what I had to do was none of her business, I gave her the slip. Many years before, my Uncle Maurice had married

145

Princess Natasha Gregoriev, but only after the greatest difficulty because the authorities had asked him to prove he was not already married. This was impossible to do. Even in those days, Russia was obsessed with the importance of papers and strangled in red-tape. Eventually they accepted Maurice's word that he was a bachelor, but only because Aunt Natasha's uncle was Governor of Kronstadt and stood guarantor. Before I left London, where she now lived, Natasha had made me promise to try to contact her sisters, who, she believed, might still be living in their old town house in the Avenue Garde de Cheval. But how to find my way there without making enquiries? Fortunately, at the hotel desk was a complete map of the city, and by chance my eyes immediately fell on the name of the avenue – probably because, as I should have guessed, the words were in French. Leningrad was uncomfortable for foreigners, for one was conscious of being observed from the moment of leaving the privacy of the bedroom. It was a city of watchers and listeners.

★ ★ ★ ★ ★

CUT TO – **Rupert** *walking street after street, now and then hesitating, looking at shadows of poles and trees for an idea of direction, receiving strange glances from other pedestrians and at last triumphantly spotting the sign of the avenue he wants. Not far along it, he finds the house. He enters a gate in a wall and walks to a door on which he knocks.*

★ ★ ★ ★ ★

CUT TO – Opening of door by a **First** *elderly* **Woman,** *a* **Second** *elderly* **Woman** *peering out over the first's shoulder.*

RUPERT *[winsome, tentative smile]*: Hello. Do you speak English?

Both women look anxiously beyond **Rupert** *to the street gate and the first one beckons him inside, standing aside as he enters.*

FIRST WOMAN *[more relaxed with the door shut]*: Please forgive us, but life here has changed. Has Natasha sent you?

RUPERT: Yes. I am Rupert Grayson, nephew of Maurice. You are Natasha's sister?

FIRST WOMAN: Yes, we are her two sisters.

Rupert *proffers his card but she declines it, turns and leads him to a room. The* **Second Woman** *calls a young girl and speaks to her in Russian, as a result of which the child posts herself on guard outside the door, which closes on the* **Sisters** *and* **Rupert.**

★ ★ ★ ★ ★

CUT TO – Inside the room. **Rupert** *takes letters from his inner pocket and hands them to the* **First Woman.**

FIRST WOMAN: From Natasha, of course.

RUPERT: Yes, her news. She would like to be in my shoes today, speaking to you with her tongue rather than her pen.

FIRST WOMAN: We, too, should like her to be here, but for her sake it is better that she is not. I think you can imagine.

RUPERT [*nodding*]: I hope I have not compromised you by coming.

FIRST WOMAN: No, Rupert. You limp a little; you were in the war?

RUPERT: Yes, but I was lucky. I live; many do not.

SECOND WOMAN: You came alone, from your hotel?

RUPERT: Yes. I have a shadow, a girl, but I managed to lose her today. I walked far before getting here. I'm sure I was not followed. For the next two days I am at the Hotel Astoria, should you have a reply for Natasha.

FIRST WOMAN: Just give her our love. A reply would be dangerous –
for you as well as for us. Natasha was lucky, too. She lives, does she not?
We cannot quite say that here.

★ ★ ★ ★ ★

*CUT TO – Hallway and front door of house. The girl is sent out to make sure the
coast is clear for* **Rupert's** *departure. They all embrace and he quietly leaves, hugging
the shadow of the walls as he makes his way up the avenue.*

VOICE: I was relieved when I got clear of the avenue and the dark
doorways that seemed to harbour waiting figures. I found my way to the
Yussupoff Palace, which, though it was not on official sightseeing tours, I
was determined to see.

Rupert *leans over a parapet and gazes into the canal, whose water stretches
like a silver ribbon reflecting the swift-moving clouds on its surface. Behind him
stand the heavy pillars that front the long, low Yussupoff Palace. Moonbeams
glint on the iron bars facing the windows of the cellar.* **Rupert** *moves up the
canal beyond the bridge and looks around as though to reconstruct the scene in
his mind.*

VOICE: It was here that Rasputin, an enemy of his country in 1916, was
assassinated in the name of Holy Russia by Prince Felix Yussupoff. The
side door showed black and forbidding. It was through it that the monk's
poisoned, bullet-ridden body was dragged. The executioners dumped it
in the canal higher up beyond the bridge, so that no suspicion would fall
on the palace. They broke the ice and pushed the body under, and even
after it was submerged, the hands of the half dead man kept clawing at the
ice until they were stamped under.

★ ★ ★ ★ ★

CUT TO – Back at the hotel, where Rupert climbs on to a stool next to an
American *man.*

AMERICAN: Evening, friend. Been having a look around? Tell me, what makes them tick? Here, they treat every individual child as a physical personality, not as a biological organism.

RUPERT: Are their methods pedagogical or merely prophylactic?

AMERICAN: Psycho-neurological, I'd say.

RUPERT: Well, well. In that case, I'll have a vodka, a large one, and another one on the side, please.

A barmaid – smiling, personable, inviting conversation – approaches, hears the order and executes it.

VOICE: If these hotel girls were employed as agents, *espionage* was taking a turn for the better. The Russian authorities were no fools: smiles like theirs, and laughing eyes so full of meaning, could learn far more than the rat-hole spies and clumsy shadows of the old *regime*. The American and I had nothing to impart, however, except what drinks we wished her to serve. We foreigners soon learned to keep our thoughts to ourselves.

★ ★ ★ ★ ★

CUT TO – Hotel dining room at breakfast, a smattering of guests, including **Rupert***, deal with their toast and coffee.* **Tanya** *joins him at the table.*

RUPERT: Good morning, Tanya. You're not letting me escape this morning, I see. A cup of coffee before starting our day as Siamese twins?

TANYA: It is not funny, Mr Grayson, when metaphor is at the expense of unfortunates.

RUPERT: Quite right, Tanya. Please accept my apologies. If you show me where, I'll put a *kopeck* in the poor-box.

TANYA: No, I already have punishment planned for you today, and you know, anyway, that there are no longer any poor in Soviet society. We are going to Tsarskoe Selo, a former imperial palace preserved as a museum – and as a reminder.

★ ★ ★ ★ ★

CUT TO – Tsarskoe Selo, **Rupert** *following* **Tanya** *about on their tour of the former royal apartments.*

VOICE: Everything was as the imperial family had left it on the night it departed on the journey to death. Even children's toys were scattered about the floor as though their owners would be back to clear up. In the Tsar's bedroom, I saw his suits and uniforms hanging up and his brushes on the dressing table. A book was open beside the bed. I could not resist the temptation to step over the cord stretched as a barrier across the room. Without touching the book, I saw that it was *Pools of Silence* by de Vere Stacpoole. On my return to England, I wrote to him, informing him that probably the last book on earth to be read by the Tsar was his story of the Belgian atrocities in the Congo. In due course, I received an invitation to visit him in Somerset.

★ ★ ★ ★ ★

CUT TO – Back at the hotel bar, where the tourists wait like sheep for their shepherdesses.

VOICE: Most of the tourists I saw were enthusiastic about everything that was shown to them. I was not much interested in the political significance of what was taking place, or concerned about the success or failure of the Five Year Plan. In my lazy way, I was interested only in the people and their reactions to what they were doing and what was being done to them. I was somehow excited by the strangeness of this new world, through which I was being so adroitly guided by Tanya with few chances of escape.

★ ★ ★ ★ ★

CUT TO – Next day, **Rupert** *and* **Tanya** *inspecting more factories and new workers' flats along with groups of other tourists.*

VOICE: That evening, I was anxious to look over the wharf from which my ship was due to leave next morning. Taking the roundabout route to throw off trackers had become habitual; I was becoming expert at it, except that one could never be sure that the man thrown off had not been replaced by another.

★ ★ ★ ★ ★

CUT TO – *Next morning.* **Rupert's** *hotel bedroom. After looking round to make sure nothing is left, he tips the hotel valet, an old man, who falls to his knees and kisses* **Rupert's** *hand.*

★ ★ ★ ★ ★

FADE TO – *The Torgsin shop, with* **Rupert** *and* **Tanya** *near where they had first met.*

VOICE: I said a final goodbye to Tanya in the Torgsin shop in the hotel, beside the same little prayer rug where she had first spoken to me.

TANYA: You think I am not going to cry; that I'm concerned only with a pattern of silly ideologies. A girl can dream in Russia as well as anywhere else.

Tanya *strikes her clenched fist on the palm of her hand.*

TANYA: Better, in fact, because here we deal in realities. You think I have enjoyed your lying silence.

Tanya *laughs, a little bitterly, and looks directly at him.*

VOICE: She lifted her eyes in that candid gaze I had come to like so much and was seeing for the last time.

TANYA: You forgot too often that I was your official guide.

RUPERT: You mean I didn't ask enough questions.

TANYA: You asked no questions… or none that I wanted to answer… and now it is too late.

VOICE: I was learning that in most things I was to be too early or too late. The next moment, she was gone. It was not easy to dismiss the thought of her from my mind. I was still young enough for a farewell to make me die a thousand deaths, but now there were other things to be considered.

★ ★ ★ ★ ★

CUT TO – **Rupert** *on the wharf, making his way through the channel of officialdom to the gangway, up which he and the porter bearing his belongings walk.*

★ ★ ★ ★ ★

FADE TO – A few days later, the ship, Smolny, enters the Thames and moors near Tower Bridge. **Rupert** *comes down the gangway and goes to a telephone box, returns to the ship and soon comes ashore again – this time carrying suitcase and bags.*

VOICE: There were no customs working that night and we were not supposed to leave the ship, but when I explained that I wanted to use the telephone, I was allowed to go ashore. I could see the dock gate was ajar, so, wasting no time, I collected my things, walked out, and took a taxi home.

★ ★ ★ ★ ★

CUT TO – Taxi arriving at the house in Ennismore Street. **Rupert** *alights and pays the driver, but asks him to wait. Through the window of the front room, he sees that his wife is entertaining a crowd of guests.*

VOICE: I don't know whether it was because I had been spending so much time with serious people or those oppressed and searching in vain for the truth, but I was suddenly filled with revulsion for the world of pleasure in which my wife and I moved and in which I had been so much at home.

Rupert *opens the front door angrily, flings the expensive sable coat he has bought* **Ruby** *into the room and leaves without a word.*

RUPERT [to cabbie]: Back to where we came from, the *Smolny*, please.

The taxi takes **Rupert** *east through London to the ship. He boards it and returns to his cabin, where he climbs into the bunk.*

VOICE: While I was trying to get to sleep, it occurred to me that life itself is not unlike a sleepless night: whichever course you choose, you resemble the invalid who turns over, then turns back on finding the second position no better than the first. Next day, I told my wife that my mind was made up. I intended to go to sea, not to forget by joining a kind of Foreign Legion, but rather to remember and experience. I wanted to watch the sun rise and set in a thousand countries, to be part of wherever my voyages took me.

CUT TO – **Sir Henry's** *London house,* **Rupert** *in one armchair, his father in another, the atmosphere solemn.*

RUPERT [with a sigh]: So that's it, Father. I see no other way. It is not what you intended, or hoped, and it is not the reward your generosity deserved, but it will not be an indulgence.

Sir Henry *leans back in his chair, like a man posing for his portrait. At length, he nods and speaks.*

SIR HENRY [resignedly]: It was an indulgence for you to have been born. Perhaps it will be less so when you have seen more of the world. I suppose you know it will be a jolt. In fairness to your brothers and sisters, I cannot finance you beyond what you get now.

RUPERT: I know, Father, but I need some bitterness.

★ ★ ★ ★ ★

CUT TO – **Rupert** *walking jauntily through London's streets to the premises of the Sailors' and Firemens' Union.*

VOICE: Parting with my wife was the beginning of a lingering farewell that was to last for months. We had loved each other because we were young, she was lovely and we went with the same friends to the same parties in the same places. I had even fought for her, for there had been a charming naval officer on the scene who was already my friend then and was to remain so all my life.

★ ★ ★ ★ ★

CUT TO – Inside the Union's office, **Rupert** *looking dressy amid the shabbiness.*

VOICE: Anyone who thinks that going to sea is just a matter of finding a ship is deceived. Even at the time I did, you had to belong to a union. To that end, I used all the influence I could muster and eventually became the proud holder of a union card. I was signed on as an ordinary seaman on the *Highland Pride*, trading between London and Buenos Aires and whatever other ports the company found opportune.

★ ★ ★ ★ ★

CUT TO – Looking around inside the house at Ennismore Street before departing for the last time. Then gazing at it from the outside, uneasily, with a mixture of feelings.

VOICE: As I turned the key in the door to leave the house in Ennismore Street, it was as though I were unlocking the universe. I must have paused before walking away, for every inch of it had been part of my life – a place of laughter, tears and careless loving, yet never a home. The time I had spent there had been a chapter of wasted words, the house no more than where I had lived too well for too long. The time had come for me to be kicked around. Only that way, I believed, could I marry my experience to reality. At last, I was to taste the great tastes and smell the great smells the world had to offer. And the process began on my own doorstep.

★ ★ ★ ★ ★

CUT TO – The docks, to which **Rupert** *has made his way.*

VOICE: I went straight to the docks to cut myself adrift gradually from the past and surrender myself to the other world into which I was moving.

★ ★ ★ ★ ★

CUT TO – *The Seamen's Mission, against a wall of which leans a man,* **Bill**.

VOICE: I first saw Bill leaning against a wall of the Seamen's Mission, watching everything about him with that casual scrutiny I was to learn was characteristic of the seafarer.

Rupert *approaches* **Bill**.

BILL: Correct me if I'm wrong, sir, but I don't think you belong around here. Are you lost, by any chance?

RUPERT: No, I don't belong around here, but I'm not lost. Not quite, anyway. I'm looking for my new home, the *Highland Pride*.

BILL: Have you bought it?

RUPERT *[with a chuckle]*: No, but there's no telling what I might do with my earnings as an ordinary seaman.

BILL: You're not short of a bit of humour. Signed on, have you?

RUPERT: Yes, I have. Which is it?

BILL *[pointing]*: There, yonder. Dirty old tub, eh? I'm Bill Evans, by the way, and I'll be your shipmate because I'm signed on, too.

RUPERT: So long as it's watertight, I'll overlook the dirt, Bill. I'm Rupert Grayson, and glad to have met you.

They shake hands.

RUPERT: Is there a cheap bed for the night to be had near here?

BILL: For an ordinary seaman, yes, but maybe not for a budding ship owner.

Bill *directs* **Rupert** *to a house in one of the dim streets bordering the East India Docks.* **Rupert** *walks to the house, knocks, and the door is opened by a faded* **Blonde**.

BLONDE: Yeah? Wotcha want?

RUPERT: A bed for the night, if you have one?

BLONDE: Just a bed – empty?

RUPERT: Yes; with no one in it, if that's what you mean. Mattress, but no mistress. Can you oblige?

BLONDE: You're a rum 'un mister and I don't know what your game is with a voice like that, but for three shillings, you can have the third floor back. She'll show yer.

A girl of about twelve **[Mabel]** *climbs the stairs ahead of* **Rupert** *and in the small bare room watches him unpack the hold-all in which are all his possessions.*

RUPERT: What's your name?

GIRL: Mabel Smith.

RUPERT: And do you go to school?

MABEL: Yes, the one in Standing Street.

RUPERT: And what are you going to do when you grow up?

MABEL [*putting fingertips to lips in a gesture of mystery*]: My mother says when I'm old enough I can be a whore.

VOICE: At that moment, from the bowels of the house whence came the reek of boiled cabbage, the mother's voice screamed: "May-bel, May-bel".

Scene: on board the Highland Pride. Bill shows **Rupert** *the sleeping quarters in the fo'c'sle.*

VOICE: This was just what I wanted. I was truly sailing before the mast, even if not in a windjammer. For the first time in my life, I was among men whose lives and those of their families depended on their labour. Without help or influence, they stood on their own feet. I, on the other hand, knew that money was always available to me. I had only to call from any part of the world and help would come. Though I tried to persuade myself I was part of the life about me, I was just an observer. It was a kind of cheating, and only the future would reveal its cost.

Bill *grips* **Rupert's** *arm and pushes him forward.*

BILL: Down there is where we sleep, mate, and eat, mate.

★ ★ ★ ★ ★

CUT TO – The fo'c'sle lined with bunks clamped to the ship's sides. **Bill** *and* **Rupert** *throw their mattresses down in two adjoining bunks that are unoccupied. The old hands are settling in, unpacking and relocking their tin boxes and shifting their gear.*

VOICE: The air reeked with stale tobacco and sweat. I found my way on deck. Under my feet, the ship was already alive. I steadied myself and ran my hand along the smooth teak of the rail, gripping it, seeking to establish that I too was alive and not living a dream.

★ ★ ★ ★ ★

CUT TO – The ship sailing on the evening tide, ploughing through the Thames estuary; the sun setting behind the Kentish hills, gulls circling and sweeping alongside.

VOICE: Bill had twice come for me to go below, but I wanted to savour the departure.

A heavily-built man [Bosun] *grabs* **Rupert's** *shoulder and twists him around.*

BOSUN: Turn in. You'll need all the sleep you can get on my ship.

VOICE: I knew instinctively that this was the bosun and not a man to argue with; though in all my seagoing experience, I was never to meet a bosun who was the bully so often depicted in stories of the sea. I lay awake until far into the night. I had heard that musical people were reputed to snore. If this were so, my shipmates had the makings of a symphony orchestra.

★ ★ ★ ★ ★

CUT TO – Flashback to the same morning, seamen loading boxes and sacks, **Rupert** *standing by, admiring their expertise.*

VOICE: That morning, I had been detailed to help bring aboard boxes of butter and sacks of potatoes. Being unused to lifting and carrying, I burned up energy at twice the rate of my shipmates, who had learned to coordinate their muscles to the exact demands of the job so that no energy was wasted. I soon learned that there was always someone ready to show me how to do a job and even enjoy doing it for me, so long as I was prepared to stand by watching and admiring. I was up to my old tricks.

★ ★ ★ ★ ★

CUT TO – As the voyage continues, the weather worsens. The ship rolls and pitches so much that the deck-boy, known as **Peggy**, *who carries the crew's meals from galley to fo'c'sle at seven and eight bells, performs acrobatics to make the journey to and fro; abused like a thief by the galley staff when he collects the food and by the recipients for its wretchedness when he delivers it. A look at men eating shows a tin of condensed milk encrusted with cockroaches, knives being sharpened to hack through the salted fish, pudding of officers' leftovers covered with thick dough.*

VOICE: The food was indescribable and we truly ate to stay alive, for there was no other reason. Yet it was the beginning of a life I came to love. I had begun to roam the sea's surface, hear its great voice, feel its might and visit strange cities in which to be sad and lonely, wanton and joyful.

★ ★ ★ ★ ★

CUT TO – *Scenes aboard ship:* **Rupert** *and the* **Men** *around him, working, cleaning, mending, moving, and some sitting in groups talking among themselves.*

VOICE: My shipmates accepted me tolerantly. They were by no means the band of brothers I had expected. Each seemed to be living independently of the others. Only rarely did their discussions become acrimonious. When fights took place, they invariably resulted from visits ashore. Mostly they behaved considerately towards each other, though in tropical heat a quarrel could suddenly erupt.

★ ★ ★ ★ ★

CUT TO – *Sitting on their bunks in the fo'c'sle:* **Rupert** *writes,* **Bill** *reads, sweat pouring off them.* **Bill** *sees* **Rupert** *irritably wipe perspiration from his forehead with his arm and look calculatingly at a porthole.*

BILL: Too rough, mate. Open that and when we lean over, the Atlantic'll squirt in like a bleedin' sausage.

RUPERT [*wryly*]: I suppose you're right. And we'd have had our chips, so to speak.

Rupert *writes some more, closes his notebook and climbs from fo'c'sle to deck. He staggers to the rail against the lurching of the ship and, with his hands on it, braving the spray that blows at him, breathes deeply. He moves to the shelter of a corner below the bridge and lies on the deck, soon going to sleep.*

★ ★ ★ ★ ★

FADE TO – *Later. An* **Officer** *patrolling the deck sees* **Rupert** *curled up and shakes him.*

RUPERT [groggy, looking up]: Hello, there. Yes? Can I help, sir?

OFFICER: Seaman Grayson, is it not?

RUPERT: That's right. Should I stand up?

OFFICER: Yes, and go straight back to your quarters and lie on your bunk. One of the craziest things you can do is sleep on deck under a tropical moon. The chances are that if you do it again, we shall be a man short.

Rupert *gets clumsily to his feet, ambles to the companionway and descends to the fo'c'sle.* **Bill** *looks up from a dog-eared book with a lurid cover and grins.*

BILL: Enjoy your holiday?

RUPERT: It was cut short, I'm afraid. An officer flushed me down here again.

Rupert *is silent and thoughtful for a few minutes, and* **Bill** *returns to his book.*

RUPERT: It's odd, you know, but last night and the night before I had the strangest experience: I woke up to find myself on deck, but did not remember getting there.

Bill *puts the book down and brings himself from lying on the bunk to sitting on the edge of it. He looks at* **Rupert** *squarely.*

BILL: You are lucky to be alive. Have you heard of calenture?

RUPERT: Of what?

BILL: Calenture. It's not nice, though it's democratic. Even gentlemen like you can get it, Rupert. It comes of getting too hot in the tropics in a hole like this *[glances around the fo'c'sle]* and turning delirious. The moon shines down, the sea looks like the green grass of home and you want to leap on to it and roll about. And the ship goes marching on.

Rupert *swallows uneasily, which encourages* **Bill** *to continue.*

BILL: If you want to see your loved ones again, we should tie you by the ankle to the bunk post.

VOICE: Bill tied me up as suggested and although I did not get so far as the deck any more, I awoke once or twice to find myself trying to untie his knot. Fortunately, his knotmanship was good – or at least my fingers were no match for it.

★ ★ ★ ★ ★

CUT TO – View from deck as ship approaches a Caribbean port, then ashore, among the dust and dirt, the mix of peoples: Creole negresses, Creole whites, Indo-Japanese, full-blooded Indians, almond-eyed Chinese. Girls lean over the half-doors of their shanties, beckoning, their breasts billowing above and their feet showing below. "Come on, Jack. Come on, sailor," they cry.

VOICE: In the large cities and ports, there were usually Sailors' Missions where we could read and write letters, but even in the great ports, we seldom met female company other than whores. For us, there was only the hospitality of the "love district".

Rupert *and* **Bill** *stop at a bar for a drink. A girl sidles up to* **Bill** *and whispers, but he ignores her and she passes on.*

VOICE: The tepid beer was nectar and the company jovial, but Bill would shake his head when one of the girls muttered in his ear – for though he was free with his dollars, he was mean with his loving. In this and other ways, his life differed from mine. He had learned already; I was still under tuition. He was able to pass without hesitation by doors that for me were all too invitingly open.

★ ★ ★ ★ ★

CUT TO – Buenos Aires' South Dock at night. Mean streets, sinister characters and shadows. Outside a café, a **Beggar** *squats in the dirt. His hand extends as* **Rupert** *approaches.* **Rupert** *puts something into it.*

VOICE: On one voyage, the ship had tied up at South Dock, Buenos Aires, in the centre of the notorious Boca district – a quarter dedicated almost entirely to brothels and sleazy cafés. It was a dangerous district for the average seaman, the natural prey of every dockside thief, pimp and harlot. With nowhere else to go when we left the ship, we were there for the picking.

Rupert *enters a café, sits at a table and is taking a beer, when the same* **Beggar,** *now doing the rounds of the customers, reaches* **Rupert's** *table and is waved away. The* **Beggar** *draws a knife and strikes at* **Rupert.** *Pandemonium breaks out. A shot is fired, knives flash. The lights, which were already dim, go out. Suddenly the police, or vigilantes, arrive and dart among the tables like terriers.* **Rupert** *is grabbed and bundled with a dozen others into a police van. Minutes later, they are emptied roughly into a prison yard.* **Rupert** *recognises a couple of* **Shipmates** *and speaks to them.*

RUPERT: What's this all about?

FIRST SHIPMATE: This is the Boca *calaboose*, mister, if you have not been here before. Easier to get into than Wormwood Scrubs, I tell you.

RUPERT: And as hard to get out?

SECOND SHIPMATE: Depends on the trial, which could be tomorrow or next month.

★ ★ ★ ★ ★

CUT TO – *The courthouse next morning. A clock on the wall says one o'clock. The judge shuts a book and adjourns proceedings until the afternoon. The accused straggle into an open yard adjoining the courthouse. Two vigilantes play pelota against a wall. The ball comes* **Rupert's** *way. Instead of returning it to the players, he hits it with a spin against the wall. The vigilantes beam with surprise and invite* **Rupert** *to play with them.*

FIRST VIGILANTE: Play, play, *gringo*.

SECOND VIGILANTE: How you hit so hard without gloves?

RUPERT: My father taught me to play in England, and my hand got hard.

After several games, in which **Rupert's** *bare-handed expertise excels, the vigilantes go to the guard on the gate and have words with him. They turn to* **Rupert** *and signal for him to disappear. He does so fast, out through the exit and away. When he reaches the wharf, the ship has gone, and in a nearby bar he is told it has sailed for Ensenada, on the River Plate, to load meat. He takes the next train to catch up with it. As he ascends the gangway, he meets the bosun on deck.*

BOSUN: Humph. The late Mr Grayson. We thought we had seen the last of you. Were you, as we heard, locked up?

RUPERT: Yes, but luckily I was able to escape.

BOSUN: You broke out?

RUPERT: Not exactly. The guards let me go.

BOSUN: You don't look pretty enough to have charmed them, but you're here, so just consider yourself to have used up one of your lives and get to work.

CUT TO – A few nights later. The ship stops at a sugar port on the coast of Cuba. **Rupert** *finds all the rooms in the brothel taken, so he makes for the leading hotel. The bed is enormous, but no sooner has he got into it when he is bitten all over. Switching on the light, he sees that the bed teems with bugs and the sheet is polka-dotted with blood where he has squashed them. He dresses, leaves the room and goes downstairs to the front door, whose iron bolts he pulls open with much effort, and lets himself on to the street. He walks to a line of railway trucks opposite, gets into one of them and makes himself as comfortable as he can on sacks of sugar, disturbed now and then when torchlight is flashed on him by a passing vigilante. Next morning, the train clanks into motion and he jumps off. He boards a lighter leaving for the ship, lies on the cargo of sugar and watches the morning light spread from the east. As he climbs the gangway, he realises sugar from the sacks has melted into his lightweight suit, coating it. An officer on deck watches him as he arrives.*

OFFICER *[seeing the stiff, sugar-coated back]*: I think you are the first human *marron glacé* we have had the pleasure of seeing aboard. Maybe you should go straight to the galley and be served at the captain's table.

VOICE: It was nice to know that I was being treated indulgently, even if as something of a buffoon, when my superiors would have been justified in seeing me more as a part-time passenger than a full-time member of the crew.

The officer turns on his heel and goes about his business, while **Rupert** *heads for the fo'c'sle.*

VOICE: On my travels, I often drifted into the shadows of the underworld, – the red-light districts of foreign ports, where every woman was for hire to the passer-by who had the money to pay for her loveless embrace. Yet there was always the proud little artist among them who could dissemble her love-play, so that a seaman, against his judgment, because he wanted to, would half believe her; for a man far from home will forget his loneliness and those he loves in the wanton embrace of a

European moll or the expert service of an Asian doll. An episode from one of my voyages persists in my memory. I had signed on a small ship trading between the islands and carrying deck passengers wherever they could find space to lie. One night, I was roused by a quarrel outside my quarters amidships.

Rupert *emerges from his doorway to investigate the commotion, and as he steps over bodies sprawled on the deck, a young* **Girl** *stands up and points to one of them, at the same time gabbling angrily at him in French patois Rupert strains to understand.*

GIRL *[looking Rupert straight in the eyes, speaking quietly but fiercely]*: Zis man, he vife-handle me.

The moonlight glistens on her body, which is ivory-tinted and naked to the waist. Her dignity contrasts with the state of the man cringing at her feet. She continues to harangue him bitterly in patois, the teeth between her lips flashing white, like those of a young dog. **Rupert** *takes her to his cabin. After telling him where she lives, she curls up in a corner and sleeps.*

★ ★ ★ ★ ★

CUT TO – Next day. Cargo is discharged in shimmering heat. **Rupert** *works mechanically, hardly looking at the work as the derrick lifts and swings its cargo on to the quayside, but glancing from time to time to the little white town on the mountainside. Evening brings relief as the sun declines behind the peak, trailing a skirt of shadow across the harbour.* **Rupert** *knocks off, washes and dresses and emerges from his cabin in white suit and panama hat. On his way through the town, he buys a bouquet of flowers.*

★ ★ ★ ★ ★

CUT TO – **Girl's** *shack in the village on the mountainside, the ship down below.*

Rupert *arrives, somewhat breathless from tramping up the slope, to see her sitting in a rocking chair on the verandah, eyes closed but not asleep. She opens her eyes and he gives her the flowers, at which her face lights up. She goes inside and returns with a glass, which she gives him.*

RUPERT: Thank you. What is it?

GIRL: Taste it and guess. Or perhaps not guess. Just know.

Rupert *sips and rolls his eyes as though for a child.*

RUPERT: One part of it is lime.

GIRL: That is easy. What is the other?

RUPERT: I think it would have to be rum, being here, don't you?

GIRL: Maybe you are guessing, but you are right. Is there not rum in all places?

RUPERT: If you want it, I think there is. But you are in only one place, and all day I have wanted to be with you again. I could see your town from the ship, the houses tinted white, pink and lemon, the streets and the red roofs tumbling down the mountainside. And your directions brought me here.

GIRL: My directions or because you could feel that I wanted you to come.

RUPERT: Both, I think. One could not have worked without the other.

GIRL *[charmingly serious but inconsequential]*: Can you understand me – my speech, I mean, not the sense of what I am saying?

RUPERT: Better than last night on the ship.

GIRL: I was angry then, but not now. I wanted you to see me when I am not angry. I have waited all day to show you. It has been long.

RUPERT: Your voice is almost unnecessary. You speak with your arms, your hands, your shoulders and your eyes. If I stood over by that big palm tree, I would know, I think, what you were saying.

GIRL: Shall I show you my special place?

RUPERT: Please.

She leads him around the house to a space behind it enclosed by dense bushes. A hammock is slung between two trees at either end of the enclosure.

GIRL: Do you know how to get in this? If you go on ships, it should not be difficult.

She gets into the hammock, showing how it is done.

RUPERT: Shall I try?

GIRL: Yes, I want to see you try.

Rupert *gets into the hammock without tipping her out.*

VOICE: I don't know what happened to my honourable resolutions, nor do I know when I first took her in my arms, for it was as though she had been there since we first met. But I surrendered to the enchantment of the moment, particularly when I first heard her laugh as I twice fell out of the hammock. *[Pause]* She did not ask me to return. She must have known that only a ship due to sail and the deep blue sea would keep me away from her. In the days that followed, I hurried from the ship as soon as I could, for I was drawn to her by forces I could not – and would not – resist. We had no common bond of race or culture, but I would have scaled a precipice to reach her.

★ ★ ★ ★ ★

CUT TO – Another day. As **Rupert** *arrives, the* **Girl** *is bent over the washtub. The white suds shine like bubbled cream against the honey of her skin.* **Rupert** *stands holding the curtain aside, watching her. She turns towards him, blue-black hair framing her face as she tries to wipe a soap-sud from her forehead with the back of her hand, only to leave another on her nose. Her dark eyes gleam; her smile is rich and mocking.*

GIRL: It's nice to see you, sailor.

RUPERT: I could say the same to you, though I would not call you "sailor".

She looks thoughtful for a time.

GIRL: Are you a Christian?

RUPERT: Yes. Why? Are you?

GIRL: Of course I am. Otherwise, one day it might be very hot for me.

RUPERT: Even though I am a Christian, it was very hot for me today.

She shakes her head to rid her ears of what she has heard.

GIRL: But you said your name is Rupert and I have not heard of any saint called that, so I am going to call you Juan.

As though to sanctify the christening, she goes to the shabby little wind-up gramophone in the front room of the shanty and puts on a scratchy record of Gounod's "Ave Maria".

VOICE: I did not tell her my name was appropriate because I was more sinner than saint, for I had learned by now that in her own little way she thought things through, and I did not want to leave a shadow over our

169

time together. I spent many hours in her shanty and the hammock in the bower behind it. On the veranda, I would sit in an old rocking chair under a coloured picture of Our Lady and Child. At that time, I was as dark as Othello, and it never ceased to amuse me when she compared her golden skin with mine.

★ ★ ★ ★ ★

CUT TO – Lying awake in his bunk on board, **Rupert** *puts down the book he is trying to read and reflects.*

VOICE: When I thought of the secrecy and strangeness of her life, it was as if she had come to accept a stranger's love and embrace as having no more significance than changing a record on her poor little gramophone. She probably welcomed the money I gave her as an addition to what she earned, but it must never have occurred to her that I was keeping her, and that, at least during my short stay, she owed me the illusion of faithfulness. During the time I was visiting her, I never saw another man enter or leave, though sometimes my eyes would be drawn reluctantly to a cigarette end, and occasionally I caught the faint but unmistakable smell of ship's tobacco. Though no one ever came to the door, I was conscious that someone had been there and left just before my arrival. She spoke always as if today was yesterday and tomorrow would never arrive.

★ ★ ★ ★ ★

CUT TO – The town square by the port. **Rupert** *sits near a dilapidated fountain. The notes of a guitar drift across the small dusty plaza. It is siesta time, with hardly anybody about.*

VOICE: Twice I had a half-day off, and to anticipate the pleasure of visiting her, I sat in the square, drowsy and mesmerised by the quivering heat, the silence broken only by the music of a guitar. I would wait patiently until the track to her house was dusky with shadows.

★ ★ ★ ★ ★

CUT TO – **Rupert** *completing the climb to her house and finding her in her room.*

170

Along one wall of the room are at least twenty pairs of shoes, while hanging up is an assortment of cotton cloth-lengths in various colours, worn, as the one on her shows, Taipai fashion, knotted at the side of her waist, leaving a slit from hip to ankle. Above the waist, she is bare – the breasts accentuating the grace of her movements.

VOICE: After the heat of the afternoon in the town, her little room was as cool as green twilight, sweetened with the faint odour of rose-water. Sometimes, she behaved as if I were not there. As I watched her, lost in her own secret thoughts, there was a delicacy and reserve about her that was in strange contrast to her occasional mood of lasciviousness. She could be completely childlike in her unconsciousness of my presence; at times like these, she made no effort to free herself of her thoughts – nor did I wish her to. There were two sides to her affection: one childishly loving, accompanied by natural and caressing gestures; the other, the uncontrolled sexual hunger of the primitive woman. But at most times, there was a dignity and a gentleness about her that was enchantingly sophisticated. Hers was a charm that defied definition.

GIRL: Juan, go to the verandah and sit down. I am sorting things out but I shall come to you soon. Get yourself a drink to keep you company.

CUT TO – Later, on the verandah, where they sit in their rocking chairs, sipping silently, looking out to sea.

VOICE: She never once asked me a question that could have been thought personal, nor did she ask me when I would be leaving; and when I did leave, she never asked when I would be returning.

★ ★ ★ ★ ★

*CUT TO – Living room of the house, which is spotless. **Rupert** has taken off his shoes as usual. On the table is a small box. He lifts the lid and sees that it is full of banknotes. She casually examines and rearranges ornaments on the mantelpiece.*

VOICE: Early in our friendship, I began slipping *peso* notes in a cedar box

171

on her rickety table. I noticed that none of the money seemed to have been spent, for the box was full.

RUPERT *[lifting the box's lid]*: I think this box has been shrinking. Look!

GIRL: So it has. Maybe we should lighten its load.

She whisks some notes from the box with one hand, takes **Rupert's** *hand with the other and pulls him out of the house and down the track to the town square, which is coming alive in the evening. In a shop she tries on one pair of shoes after another, eventually buying a pair with heels so high that she has to have* **Rupert's** *arm for support on the walk home.*

GIRL: Sometimes, in the town, there is music and dancing. I think it will happen next week.

RUPERT: Will you go?

GIRL: Depends.

RUPERT: On what?

GIRL: Things.

RUPERT: Your tongue is not taking much exercise today. Perhaps it is too tired in the heat.

GIRL: If my legs and feet are exercising, perhaps my tongue may be excused.

Back at the house, she steps out of the shoes. **Rupert** *removes his, too, sighing as his feet feel the cool of the tiles. Hanging from a jacaranda tree behind the house is a canvas water-bucket, in which bottles of beer are cooled by evaporation. Each time* *she passes it, she touches the bucket to keep it swinging and increase the cooling. She does that now, taking out a bottle for each of them and going to the verandah.*

GIRL: Thank you, Juan. Perhaps *[wiggling her toes]* I should call you Santo Juan. *[Wistfully]* The shoes will always be special.

RUPERT: Will you find another arm to go with them?

GIRL: No. But don't say that. I think I want to kiss you again, Santo Juan.

She sits on his knee, puts her arms round his neck and kisses him, her hair enshrouding his head.

GIRL: Please don't ask me anything about my family or my life. I am just a cloud that floated by your ship on its long voyage.

RUPERT: Yes, no questions. We can feel without knowing.

GIRL: Will you dance with me?

RUPERT: Come.

They rest their beers on the verandah ledge and he leads her inside by the hand. She looks among a small pile of records and puts one on the gramophone. It is scratchy, but has melody and rhythm – an old French folk-song. She holds him tightly. The record finishes and they return to the verandah, sit on their rocking chairs and sip in silence.

VOICE: I wondered who were her *clientele*. Who paid for her loveless service? I knew when she had been entertaining someone other than myself from the imprint of the string hammock on her young body. Why did they never come when I was there?

Evening of the ship's last day in port. There is an expression of searching in her eyes and **Rupert's** *own expression indicates his awareness of it. They walk down to the town together.*

RUPERT: This is the first time you have come down here with me.

GIRL: And the last.

Rupert *appears about to say something, but does not. They reach the quayside, where she takes off her shoes.*

VOICE: Flinging her arms around me, she hugged me like a child. It was the last time I was to smell the rosewater in her hair and feel her mouth on mine.

After a last hug into which she puts all her strength, she releases him and scampers away without looking back.

VOICE: She was running out of my life through the violet twilight, leaving a line of little footprints in the dust. Just as the phrase in Vinteuil's sonata and the taste of *madeleines* evoked particular people in Proust's memory, so the distant notes of a guitar and the smell of rosewater always kindle the glowing memory of this little Caribbean girl whose name I have long forgotten.

Rupert *watches until she disappears, seemingly tormented by the urge to run after her, then slowly mounts the gangway.*

VOICE: I was never to return to that small port, but I can never forget her and the air of mystery that enveloped her and masked her thoughts. Nor can I forget the chill of loneliness that ran down my spine as I dragged myself up the gangplank. She had shown that in all human beings, the secret places of the heart and the dark places of the mind are rarely revealed, and I felt a strange sense of gratitude towards her because she had taught me unconsciously a little more about myself. Already I was learning that there are as many shades between right and wrong as there are between black and white, and that no man can exist outside his dreams and his imagination.

Scene: **Rupert** *returns to London after several voyages. He steps from a cab outside the house in Ennismore Street to see wife* **Ruby** *framed in the window. At the door, she appears pleased to greet him, but he feels out of place – though when he had left, the marriage was, in any case, virtually over.* **Rupert** *steps into the drawing room to be drowned in the sound of popping corks, cigarette smoke and Guerlain's l'heure bleue. A* **Stranger** *hails him with a glass of champagne in one hand and a brandy in the other. A cigar is thrust between his teeth.*

STRANGER: Where's your parrot, sailor?

VOICE FROM GRAMOPHONE:
> *Money buys anything but love:*
> *I've been poor and I know which is which,*
> *And I'd sooner be rich…*

VOICE: My return had been the reason for the party, but I did not belong. I knew none of the current jokes. I was no longer interested in social gossip and I was sensitive enough to know I was not good company. Bronzed and slightly barbaric, I was an eccentric and a freak. I remembered a song sung in a bar: *"He was the life and soul of the party, but he's a dumbell when he's at home".* That was me. I realised that our marriage was finished and only the sad farewells remained to be said. We had married just after the war, before young people had become adjusted to the perils of peace. We had all escaped from a world of vast and violent uncertainty, yet it had become a prison out of which I was now breaking. I wondered whether we had ever said anything to each other that mattered. In parting, we were perhaps closer spiritually than we had been in the years of marriage.

CUT TO – The drawing room after the last guests have noisily departed, **Rupert** *and* **Ruby** *sitting in neighbouring chairs amid the debris of the party.*

RUBY *[genial but wary]*: Well?

RUPERT: Thank you for it, but we both know it was not exactly a welcome home, don't we?

RUBY *[nodding slowly]*: When will you go?

RUPERT: Tomorrow. I want nothing. It's all yours. I shall simply shed a skin and walk away from it.

RUBY: It's not all lost, wasted, is it?

RUPERT *[leaning over, taking her hand]*: No. There is a residue we cannot unshare. Do you remember Monte Carlo, when you refused me money from the kitty for that poor devil I was bankrolling?

RUBY: Yes, and the laughter that shamed it out of my purse.

RUPERT: And the night we had a snoring sleeping partner on our honeymoon?

RUBY *[pensively]*: Yes. Gone forever.

RUPERT: No. There forever.

VOICE: We talked quietly through our epilogue in the house that was to me no more than a place I had loved and dreamed in. I was never to return to it. Nor did I see her again, with the sunset in her eyes and the haunting breath of *l'heure bleu* in the air. To stay would have meant drifting back into a life of soft living. I must sign on another ship. It was to be the *London Exchange*, sailing out of London for the USA.

★ ★ ★ ★ ★

CUT TO – The roughest imaginable storm in the Atlantic; seamen fighting their

way about the deck with life-lines and hatches battened down. Huge waves.
Terrifying.

VOICE: We were forced to heave-to for three days in mid-Atlantic. It was the first time I was genuinely frightened at the immensity of the seas, which seemed at every moment about to engulf us. In the fo'c'sle it was whispered that the voyage boded ill for either ship or master, and I wondered which it would be.

★ ★ ★ ★ ★

CUT TO – Entering port and docking at Philadelphia. **Rupert** *leans on the rail watching the activity as hatches are opened and cranes positioned to lift cargo from holds. He is joined briefly by an officer* **[Mac]**, *wearing the uniform of a third engineer. Beyond the wharf lie the port's vast railyards.*

MAC: We leave tomorrow for New York, but there's a saloon over there, the green building on the corner beyond the tracks [points it out], where we could find time for a drink this evening, if you're interested.

RUPERT: That makes sense. When?

MAC: Eight, nine.

RUPERT: I'll be there – if I'm not run down by a train. It looks like an outsized marshalling yard to me.

MAC: Yes, but trains are the least of your worries at night. The yard is unlit and there are armed gangs from Delaware that appear suddenly from behind stationary trucks, kill and strip their victim and dump the body in the river. When you're trying to negotiate a hundred railway lines in the dark, it is hard to deal with an assailant at the same time. The moral is: don't cross the yard alone. Must be off. See you there.

★ ★ ★ ★ ★

CUT TO – **Rupert** *walking along the wharf and beginning to pick his way over*

178

the tracks to the other side of the yard. **Rupert** *warily enters the saloon, mindful of* **Mac's** *warning and looking apprehensive, as though already expecting to see some Delaware murderers. He studies the men who come and go. They look rough but harmless. 11 pm passes with no* **Mac.**

VOICE: I drank in the saloon until midnight, when, weary of waiting, I started back to the ship by myself.

★ ★ ★ ★ ★

CUT TO – The lone figure of **Rupert** *stealthily working his way across the railyard.*

VOICE: I weighed the odds. I had drunk with caution, so was unlikely to stumble, and one man makes less noise than two. There were shadows; some still, others seeming to move. I sensed that I was being stalked. I made my way through the trucks until only one line of them remained between me and the ship. Everything seemed quiet enough except for the night sounds of the river and a sort of breathing movement among the trucks. There were small noises, difficult to identify: the tap of a chain or the tick-tick of metal going to sleep. Or was it footsteps? Someone, I felt, was creeping up on me. At the very moment I realised there was a man beside me: a shot rang out. I rushed for the last line of trucks, then on to the gangplank and safety. It was only then that I knew the shot must have come from on board.

★ ★ ★ ★ ★

CUT TO – **Rupert** *running to the ship's saloon. Lights blaze and the body of the young captain lies on the floor between tables with the top of his head blown off. Blood is everywhere. The first officer appears on the scene and the ship comes to life.*

VOICE: Then followed two of the worst hours in my life. Sirens wailed; police swarmed aboard.

The first officer looks at **Rupert** *and mutters to the* **Police**, *two of whom, taking an arm each, hustle RUPERT to a cabin.*

FIRST COP: What's your name?

RUPERT: Grayson.

SECOND COP: Is that all, limey – are you a lord?

RUPERT: The first part is Rupert.

FIRST COP: So it's "Rupert Grayson"?

RUPERT: That's right.

FIRST COP: Okay, buddy. Tell us everything you did tonight.

RUPERT: All evening, I was in that saloon on the other side of the rail yard, "The Shunter", waiting for a friend who didn't show up. I came back a few minutes ago.

FIRST COP: Alone?

RUPERT: Reluctantly, yes.

SECOND COP: Why "reluctantly"?

RUPERT: My friend warned about thugs in the yard who kill and steal.

FIRST COP: Who and where is your friend?

RUPERT: He is Mac, the third engineer. We arranged to have a drink together but he didn't appear. Where he is, I don't know.

FIRST COP: You realise it looks bad for you, pal? The officer here arrives on the scene and sees you and the deceased and nobody else. Any ideas?

RUPERT: No, officer, except that it's most embarrassing.

FIRST COP: Is that all?

RUPERT: Considering how I dislike embarrassment, it's surely enough.

Ambulance men cover the body and take it away. The **First Officer** *reappears and hands the* **First Cop** *a letter.*

FIRST OFFICER: Earlier this evening, the captain added this to mail for the pilot to take ashore.

FIRST COP *[taking the letter]*: "To whom it may concern". It concerns me.

The **First Cop** *tears the envelope open and reads the letter.*

FIRST COP: I guess this is for the coroner, but *[addressing Rupert]* it probably lets you off, mister. Just the same: if and when we want you, we'll know where to find you.

The police and others depart. **Rupert** *leaves the cabin and walks out on deck to see* **Mac** *come up the gangplank. They are alone.*

RUPERT: Hello, Mac. Do you know what happened?

MAC: Yes. I saw Ted down there. Too bad. Sorry I didn't appear, old man. I'll tell you why later.

RUPERT: Please do me a favour – the reason for which I'll also tell you later. Take a bag ashore for me in New York tomorrow and meet me with it at the Seamen's Mission. I'll hand it to you in the morning.

MAC: Done.

The ship pulls away from the wharf and heads out to sea for New York. **Rupert** *becomes aware of the suspicious glances his shipmates give him as he joins them in the fo'c'sle. He lies in his bunk, staring sleeplessly.*

VOICE: Although they might not have suspected me of murder, I could tell they thought of me as a harbinger of death. I resolved to jump ship when we touched land again and sank into a deep melancholy. Next morning, on the day of Christmas Eve, we steered into New York harbour.

★ ★ ★ ★ ★

CUT TO – New York harbour, approaching lower Manhattan. The sun shines, the sky is blue and the windows of the skyscrapers gleam. The ship berths at a pier on the Hudson River, **Rupert** *descends the gangway, walks off and, after a few inquiries on the way, finds the Seamen's Mission. Inside, he explores the noticeboard and reads a paper. Half an hour later,* **Mac** *appears with his bag.*

Rupert *stands, greets him and takes the bag.*

RUPERT: Thanks, Mac. Is it too early or too late for you to have last night's drink?

MAC *[Scots accent]*: I shouldn't have suggested last night and I'm genuinely sorry, especially as I put your life at risk; and, for all we know now, your freedom. And certainly your reputation.

RUPERT: I'd have liked your company, but never mind. As for what happened on board, it's not the law that bothers me so much as the attitude of the crew. They think I'm a jinx. I'm not going back, Mac.

Rupert *looks* **Mac** *straight in the eye, chin out, as though daring him to doubt his sincerity.*

RUPERT: It fills me with despair that my life at sea is over, but I cannot play the role of Jonah. Just the same, this is Christmas Eve. Will you come exploring with me this evening?

MAC: Thanks, mate, but no. You see – and this is also my excuse for last night – I'm saving to get married and the process is hard. I thought of her. She is saving, too. I couldn't do it.

RUPERT: I understand. *[Brightening]* I found a little money in my pocket, Mac.

MAC: No, that would'na do.

RUPERT: I suppose not. But maybe you would not refuse a wee something now for your wedding day…

Rupert *goes to the counter and returns to the table with two glasses, which they sip thoughtfully.*

VOICE: I have never met a mean Scotsman. Careful, yes, but not one who didn't pay his corner. Mac was not going to spend money he could save; nor was he going to let me pay so long as he had money. That was that.

RUPERT: This where we came in, Mac.

MAC: Aye, that's the way it goes. Take my advice and keep away from here till the heat's off, for it's here they'll be looking for you.

They shake hands and **Mac** *is gone.* **Rupert** *retires to the chair to plot his moves.*

VOICE: Normally I am disinclined to trust a man who gives you a killer handshake, but I have discovered that there are too many exceptions to everything to be tied too closely to convention. I have met the most honest men with close-set eyes and the most brilliant and determined with absent chins. The most reliable man I ever knew and loved had a flabby handgrip. I asked him about it and he said: "The truth is I have hands that perspire and I don't think it's pleasant for people." Changing into evening clothes at the Seamen's Mission somehow lifted my depression and I found that I did not mind being alone. I could now play drifter. In a foreign city, drifting is one of the greatest games to play, because things happen to drifters and they are not always unpleasant.

Rupert *rummages in the pockets of his evening jacket and, like a conjurer pulling a rabbit from a hat, surprises himself, as his face shows, by discovering some money.*

VOICE: Feeling in my pocket, as one does on changing into another suit, to my delight and amazement I unearthed a beautiful twenty-five pound note. When, later, I wrote and told Ruby about this windfall, she replied, illogically: "That's why you never had any money." The important thing was that I now had money not only for my evening, but also five pounds towards Mac's dream house.

Rupert *gets an envelope from the desk, scribbles a note, which, close-up, reads: "Dear Mac, good luck with your plans. Buy a brick in memory of me. Glad to have known you. Yours, Rupert". He puts a fiver in with the note and leaves the envelope for* **Mac** *to pick up. Outside, he takes a cab to the Brevort.*

VOICE: The Brevort in those days was a good old-fashioned New York hotel, run more on English lines than American or Swiss, where I felt safe. No one would search it for a sailor who had jumped ship. It was a refuge for successful artists and America's poor aristocracy.

Rupert *gives his bag to the* **Hall Porter**.

VOICE: I told the hall porter I might be staying with friends and would not yet check in. I preferred to have any discussion about papers, passport and so on with the late-duty porter, having always found it easier to come

184

to terms with creatures of the night than those of the day. After only a few hours in New York, I was in thrall to its breathless vitality. Even the buildings seemed to be alive in the world's greatest jungle.

Rupert *quaffs a large Scotch, lights a cigar and wanders from one place to another, first to Greenwich Village, then by taxi uptown to 42nd Street and Times Square. There, he spots someone [**Sandie** Harvey] he knows scurrying along. He taps him on the shoulder.*

RUPERT: How are you doing, Sandie Harvey?

SANDIE: Not so well, Rupe, but it's just around the corner, boy, just around the corner.

VOICE: Everywhere one felt this wonderful sense of expectation. Besides, I have always enjoyed the American sense of humour, when it is of the dry variety, which can be found in every State of the Union.

Rupert *takes a taxi to the Plaza Hotel on the corner of Fifth Avenue and 59th Street.*

VOICE: On the Park side, I was delighted to see a line of hansom-cabs. I drifted towards it. A hansom-cab was something I could never resist.

Rupert *addresses the driver [**Paddy**] of a cab.*

RUPERT: Take me for a drive, Paddy.

PADDY: In the Park, sor?

RUPERT: Why would I be driving through a park without a girl beside me, Paddy? Drive me through the streets, my splendid man.

VOICE: I saw that we had turned down what I thought was Madison Avenue, so I shouted at him.

RUPERT: Do you pass the Ritz-Carlton?

PADDY: Not if you wish to alight, sor.

The cab draws up outside the Ritz-Carlton. **Rupert** *fishes in his pocket and addresses* **Paddy**.

RUPERT: Take some money to be sure you don't die of thirst, and come back for me in an Irish hour or so.

PADDY: That I'll surely do, sor.

Rupert *enters the Ritz-Carlton, moves through the throng, finds a chair, sits down and lapses into thought.*

VOICE: This was as good a place as any to consider my problem. It was the Ritz, with the unmistakable imprint of the great Cesar – the pink, blue and yellow pattern on the rugs and carpets, the familiar chandeliers, frozen statuary and atmosphere. But it was not the Ritz in London or Paris or Madrid or Barcelona; and suddenly I realised that, however much I might learn to love America, I would always be a European at heart. But now the problem was how to get back to Europe. I had no passport. I could hardly go to our consul-general without confessing I had deserted my ship. I could not leave the USA without a passport. More serious still, I was without any document showing how I had entered the country. After my second scotch, it occurred to me that I was not likely to find the answer to my problems at the Ritz-Carlton. I must seek out a very different world, where things were done outside the law. Tomorrow, the law might be looking for me. In the meantime, it was Christmas Eve and I was alone.

A Young American *gets up from a nearby table and approaches* **Rupert**.

YOUNG AMERICAN: We've decided you look like a lonely Englishman and wonder whether you'd care to join us *[in comic stage English]* if it won't bore you, old boy, and all that.

VOICE: This was an invitation not to be resisted. The importance of accepting any such offer was high in the priorities of the drifter.

RUPERT: If you can put up with a slow-thinking man, I guess I'd like to.

VOICE: The men were friendly, the girls beautiful, the "old-fashioneds" – cold, dry and frequent. I suspected they laughed at me, though not in an unkindly way. At that time, an Englishman was still a curiosity and a bit of a joke. Their questions were friendly. Why was I wearing a dinner jacket? Why did I smoke Turkish tobacco? Was I really alone, all dressed up and nowhere to go? I explained that I had lots of places to go, but could not decide which. This, they did not believe: one of them had already phoned a girl and soon we were a party of even numbers. In the generous American manner, they refused to let me pay for anything, though I was able to organise a little surprise for them.

★ ★ ★ ★ ★

CUT TO – **Rupert** *stepping out from the hotel and speaking to* **Paddy,** *the jarvey.*

RUPERT: Paddy, we need three more jaunting-cars as fine as this one to convey myself and seven friends on a tour of the town and then into the Park, which is only right and proper now that I do have a girl to accompany me. I'd like the four of you to be waiting for us here in half an hour. Can you do that?

PADDY: Of course I can. Consider it done, sor.

Rupert *resumes his place at the table. Choosing the moment when the bill has been paid and they are about to leave, he mutters to the* **Girl,** *stands up and addresses them.*

RUPERT: It is hard for a poor Englishman who smokes Turkish tobacco to find the words to thank you for making this Christmas Eve so surprisingly memorable for me, but I should like you to be my guests in a ride around your wonderful town in the chariots that await us at the door.

At which, his hosts look at each other in surprise; several of them, on whom the wine has not been wasted, breaking into song: "Swing Low, Sweet Chariot". They drift to the front door, expostulating appreciatively when they see the point of **Rupert's** *invitation. They clamber aboard the carts. The procession, with* **Paddy** *leading, clip-clops around Manhattan, before ending up with a dash through Central Park.*

VOICE: My tongue having been loosened by the evening's intake, after we had said goodnight and my hosts had departed, I told Paddy of my predicament on the way to the Brevort and he offered to help.

Next morning, **Rupert** *pays his bill and* **Paddy,** *as arranged, meets him in front of the hotel.* **Rupert** *gets into the cab and is driven to a saloon in a grimy locality and told to wait there for* **Paddy's** *return. When he has not reappeared after three hours,* **Rupert** *begins to wonder whether he will see him again, but at last he arrives, poking his head in through the door of the saloon and expelling a relieved "Ah" when he sees, as though perhaps he did not expect to,* **Rupert.** *Old* **Paddy** *hobbles bow-leggedly to his client.*

RUPERT: I could hug you, man. I thought you'd forgotten where you left me.

PADDY: Yes, the Lord forgive me, but it took longer than I thought. All's well that ends well, though. For eight pounds, a man will get you on a ship with no questions asked. I beat him down. It took an hour, but you can trust him. You've got to sleep at Moore's Hotel tonight. The man will call for you there at six o'clock tomorrow night. You'll pay him the money and he'll see you aboard.

*They clink two jars of Guiness together to seal the deal, shake hands and **Paddy** slips off, popping his face back around the door as he goes to leave a final instruction.*

PADDY: You'll fix your passage money with the captain.

VOICE: I spent the next day waiting, afraid to leave the crummy hotel unless plans were changed and the man came early. But he arrived on time and saw me on to the ship as promised. I arranged to pay the master fifteen pounds on arrival in London. My last voyage as a seaman was over. I learned from a former shipmate that the letter left by the captain of the *London Exchange* proved clearly that he had died by his own hand. My discharge book lay unclaimed in the Customs House, as it would continue to do, bearing the words no seaman ever likes to read: "Voyage not completed".

On his return to London in the New Year, **Rupert** *meets brother* **Tristram** *and they travel together to the family home, Ravenspoint. On the way, he recounts his seagoing experiences to* **Tristram** *and ponders his future.*

VOICE: It was clear that I had to find a job. My efforts to break away from the rich and conventional world into which I was luckily born had failed. Work with regular hours did not appeal. Strap-hanging between home and office would have been spiritual death and a betrayal of the principles on which I was trying to conduct my life. Whatever employment I could get must interest or even amuse me. So far, anything that did that had not the remotest possibility of earning me a living. A doubt kept nagging: was I, perhaps, in my late twenties, unemployable? I considered and dismissed, in turn, a succession of possibilities: mountaineering, whose practitioners I had admired but which was hardly the destiny of one who suffered vertigo on the Snowdon mountain railway; fishing, which held a fascination for me, though as a watcher rather than a participant; head-waiter or *sommelier*, for which I was otherwise suited, but which was not ideal as an occupation for one who, like Wilde, could remember names but not faces. One night at the Savoy, I had grabbed my silk hat from its shelf before the attendant got to it and read on the slip inserted in the band: "guardsman type, sapphire-diamond front stud, tipsy". [Pause]

I remembered I was a director of *The World*, a weekly in which my father was a principal shareholder. But the editor, a journalistic chameleon called West de Wend Fenton, who was otherwise the most generous of hosts, suddenly withdrew his hospitality when it came to finding space for the brilliant pieces with which for a time I had bombarded him. In my dreams, there was one job I'd have liked, if it existed, but who of my friends would recommend me as a courier-cum-tutor to the travelling son of a South-American millionaire with a family of beautiful dark-eyed Chilenas swathed in chinchilla? The truth was that I had dedicated myself wholeheartedly to extracting as much pleasure from life as it had to offer. This included a vast amount of reading, for I found the company of books almost as entertaining as that of women, and in most cases more rewarding. Subconsciously, the well-known finger of fate was pointing me to the great pursuit of writing. It was really for this that I had travelled the world and gone to sea – to learn how the others lived. I had looked into the bright eyes of danger and there were stories in me to be told. The spark was there, but could I fan it into flame? I had gathered the recipes. Now was the time to try them out.

After a few days at Ravenspoint, catching up with the news among his family and those servants to whom such conversation was extended, and meeting a crop of nephews and nieces born during his absence, **Rupert** *returns to London to face the future.*

VOICE: Ruby continued to live at Ennismore street. I telephoned for her to send some clothes to me at the Guards' Club and she asked me to give her a puppy dog, presumably as a substitute for me. Instead, I sent her roses – glorious but short-lived, like our love. The show was over and I was determined not to play the actor who carries on after the curtain has dropped.

Being one of a large family – unassailable within my own herd – I had never become a clubman as my generation knew that figure. Most men used a club when they wanted company; I used mine when I wished to be alone. Staying at the Guards' Club was still a comfortable experience because the valeting was of the highest standard. During a stay of three nights, a member could have twenty or more suits sponged and pressed and as many shoes and top boots cleaned and polished to perfection. I had a second club in St James's whose members came from every level of society: actors, artists, sporting men, financiers and even journalists. It was also whispered that it was the refuge for a coven of struck-off solicitors and

191

a flock of unfrocked clergy. There was one **Member** who seemed as permanent there as the furniture. I never refused his invitation to sit with him because, although I couldn't like him, his knowledge of the bittersweet variety was vast, so I would sit silent and listen even though I realised he was a man without pity. Some secret bitterness was eating into him, so that he was neither a man's man nor a woman's. When he wished to assume a light-hearted manner, it always came out as sarcastic and ill-humoured.

★ ★ ★ ★ ★

FADE TO – **Rupert** *sitting in club chair when* **Member** *enters room, makes for an adjoining chair and grunts at him.*

RUPERT: The usual?

MEMBER: At the risk of establishing a reputation, thank you.

Rupert *beckons a steward and mutters the order.*

MEMBER: I'm glad to see that you enjoy street processions.

RUPERT: On the contrary, I don't like them at all.

MEMBER: That surprises me, because only last week I was watching the Lord Mayor's Show and I saw you lifting up a pretty girl to let her see over the heads of the crowd; and it seemed to me you found the task far from unpleasant.

RUPERT: It was my annual act of chivalry.

VOICE: I wondered whether the word "chivalry" might trigger a reaction, for his face was scarred as if by a duelling sword; though the odds were against it, because, while there were few of us in the war whose flesh had not been outraged by flame, steel or gunshot, it was "not done" to speak about it.

The line of conversation does not develop and they sit silently with their own thoughts until the **Member** *gives* **Rupert** *a piece of his wisdom.*

MEMBER: Ordinary people should always regard every stranger as a potential enemy, whose capacity for harming you has not been measured.

RUPERT: I respect your experience, but does not such suspicion tend to induce in the stranger that which is suspected?

VOICE: He did not answer directly, but surprised me with an unexpected flash of kindness.

MEMBER: The history of man is one of errors and misunderstandings, but don't forget, young man, I'll always be ready to give you advice, however deplorable or squalid your problem might be.

VOICE: Another time, he advised me to avoid the attachment of very attractive girls because it made the inevitable parting more painful, and self-inflicted pain should be avoided at all costs. He was not my idea of a lovable man, but it is possible he would have liked to be. I had already learned that you cannot understand a man until you know the sort of man he'd like to be. I liked him best when he was at his sourest and the invariable undercurrent of anger in his conversation was under control.

The **Member** *is sitting with his back to the window so that his body throws a shadow over the table and even the glasses have lost their gleam.*

★ ★ ★ ★ ★

FADE TO – Another day, when the **Member** *and* **Rupert** *again meet at the club. They greet each other perfunctorily, sip their drinks and stay quiet for some minutes before the older man speaks.*

MEMBER: There's not much point in enclosing ourselves in this place if we also seal ourselves up as individuals. So, let me open a personal shutter.

[Draws breath] I was a student at Heidelberg when I first met my wife. I used to believe in love at first sight. She was standing on the terrace under the castle looking down at the Neckar flowing past the old town. When I spoke to her, my German was sufficiently halting to encourage her to help me out, which she did with enormous charm. She tried to suppress her laughter, but it showed all too plainly in her eyes. After that we used to meet often, and each time I left ever more deeply in love. Of course, I had a rival, a student princeling out of the *Almanach de Gotha* with quarterings on his coat-of-arms like a checkerboard. He must have looked up my humble entry in *Debrett* and decided it was not beneath his dignity to challenge me to a duel, which he did on some trivial pretext: that I'd laughed at him or at the Kaiser, or both. I know only that I had to accept the challenge, as an Englishman and all that.

*A steward hovers. The **Member** glances irritably at him once or twice, not liking to be overheard, and, to get rid of him, orders more drinks sooner than necessary. The steward departs.*

MEMBER: I'd never held a sabre in my life. I persuaded friends to act as my seconds and we set off for the gymnasium where the duel was to be fought. I admit I didn't like it; not at all. He was there with his seconds and a doctor, waiting for me. We put on padded jerkins and head masks that protected the eyes and nose. The cheeks remained exposed. It was some comfort to know there was a limit to how much he could carve me up. It was just before he put on his visor that I first saw his eyes – saw them clearly, I mean. They were ice-blue and the only expression in them was of cold hatred. I knew then for certain that he was out to kill me if he could get away with it.

*The **Member** touches the scars on his cheeks with a swift sweep of the fingers.*

MEMBER: I was on the defensive all the time, fending his blade or hopelessly trying to beat it away from my face, but, as you see, he sliced me at will, cutting me the way he wanted to. But he couldn't reach my eyes. Eventually, the doctor stopped the fight. My adversary won the duel, but I won the girl.

The **Member** *pauses thoughtfully.*

MEMBER: Or did he? We were married a few months later and were supremely happy, and in due course a man-child came along and that was the end of the marriage.

RUPERT: What happened?

The **Member** *looks angrily at* **Rupert,** *as if regretting the disclosure, and speaks acidly.*

MEMBER: Too many words can spoil a story, but if you must know…

The **Member** *gives* **Rupert** *one of his ugliest glances.*

MEMBER [*very slowly*]: … I didn't like the child's ice-blue eyes or the expression of cold hatred in them.

The **Member** *gestures with his hand as though flicking a fly away.*

VOICE: He made the dismissive gesture he used when he wished to end a conversation.

★ ★ ★ ★ ★

FADE TO – Another day at the club, **Rupert,** *relaxed, talking with a genial* **Old Man.**

VOICE: At the same club was a delightful old chap with whom I used to discuss books and topics of the day, but it was a long time before I got any closer to him. I learned that he was the chairman of the food and wine committee. One Easter Sunday I gave him a pair of Georgian silver coasters from Vietche's in St James's, and from then on he did not cease to instruct me in the art of gastronomy.

OLD MAN *[to Rupert]*: Mind you, I am not a cook myself. It is sufficient to know how a dish should taste. No chef worth his salt does the cooking himself. You don't have to work in the plantation to know whether the coffee tastes good.

VOICE: One day, when I returned to London after having been abroad for some months, he was not at the club, so I inquired of the hall porter.

★ ★ ★ ★ ★

CUT TO – **Hall Porter**, *respectful and subdued.*

HALL PORTER: I'm sorry to say, sir, that the gentleman is dead. Of the cause of his death, I remain, however, unaware.

At the bar, **Rupert** *converses with another member,* **Cedric**. *They round off a topic with a laugh, clearing the way for another.*

RUPERT: By the way, that charming old boy who was the resident food and wine buff... is it true that we've lost him?

CEDRIC: I'm sorry to say, yes. All very sad. He was quite big in the City, it seems, but his affairs went wrong and he had been having a thin time. Literally thin, unfortunately. The club waived his subscription and he continued as chairman of the food and wine committee, but he no longer dined or lunched here and spent most of the day in the reading room alone. They found him one night when the club was closing. He was seated in his usual chair, but he was dead, just skin and bone. When his pockets were searched for his address, all they found was a shilling and a kipper rolled in a newspaper.

196

Cedric slaps his thigh with the newspaper he is holding, as though to put a full stop to the story and bring the mood back to normal.

CEDRIC: Must be off. See you around, I hope.

VOICE: I was glad he went. I needed a small interval to remember and mourn alone.

★ ★ ★ ★ ★

CUT TO – The dining room of the Ritz, Piccadilly. **Rupert's** *companion at the table is Bob* **Rankin**.

VOICE: Before leaving to join my brother-in-law in the south of France, I dined with Bob Rankin, who, though older than I, had also served in the Irish Guards. Bob was knowledgeable, a gourmet's gourmet and the best of company. That night, I found him most excitable.

RANKIN *[almost shouting]*: I've nowhere to play snooker.

RUPERT: But did you not present a full-size billiards table to your club?

RANKIN: Yes, less than a month ago; then I had a small bust-up and resigned. But the committee has decided that if I leave the club, I leave the table. It's more depressing than I can say.

RUPERT: Well, it does sound like a tragedy of some kind, but if I were a librarian trying to file it, I should scarcely know where to put it.

RANKIN: What about short stories? Or perhaps, if you see it as the club surely must, humour.

RUPERT: Bob, excuse me for a moment. I told my American brother-in-law I'd ring him in Cannes.

Rupert *leaves the table and walks to the telephone booth outside the dining room and soon returns to his companion.*

RUPERT *[resuming seat]*: Have you got much on at the moment?

RANKIN: Only what you see me in.

RUPERT *[with chuckle]*: I mean: are you busy? Can you throw your diary away for a few weeks?

RANKIN: What had you in mind?

RUPERT: I told Louis we were dining here and he would be delighted if I took you with me tomorrow to the south of France. They have tons of room and I'm sure there will be a billiards table to help you over your loss.

RANKIN: I've run out of protest, Rupert, so, yes, thank you. I'd like to smell the mimosa again.

★ ★ ★ ★ ★

CUT TO – Next day. Dressed in their travelling clothes, **Rupert** *and* **Rankin** *speed south through the French countryside on the Blue Train.*

VOICE: I, too, had run out of protest. I ought to have resisted Louis's invitation and resumed the sterner course on which I had embarked. It was a step backwards from life on the ocean wave as a deckhand, to life on the Côte d'Azur as a non-paying guest. It seemed I was about to take up my playboy existence where I had left it.

RANKIN: Louis is a pillar of Philadelphia, is he not?

RUPERT: You could say so, yes. He is head of the Drexel banking family and is married to my sister Nancy.

RANKIN: You Graysons are so prolific, I can hardly keep up.

RUPERT: Don't try to digest it all at once. Eat us one at a time. Right now, Louis's villa is all you need think about.

A trolley is wheeled along the corridor, dispensing refreshments. They take drinks and it goes on its way.

RUPERT: It is not too complicated there. The linchpin of the place is Eugene, the old French butler, who doubles as *valet*. Then there are Maria, the cook, and her friend Jeanne, who is chambermaid, two *bonnes-a-tout faire*, two greyhounds, and a gardener who has reduced life to picking flowers for the villa in the morning and spending the rest of the day rolling black Algerian tobacco into cigarettes and blowing kisses to the maids.

RANKIN: I think I'm with you so far. Sounds like a smooth-running outfit.

RUPERT: Mostly, it is, though with handfuls of gravel in it here and there. Maria, the cook, you'll fall in love with, especially for her sauces, but, sadly, she and Eugene are like oil and water, or perhaps cat and dog.

★ ★ ★ ★ ★

CUT TO – That evening, at dinner in the villa. **Eugene** *displays a dish to Mrs Drexel [***Nancy***] and, when she has given her approval, announces: "Sole Veronique"; then, to his mistress, but just loudly enough for all to hear, "Dégoutant absolument détestable, ne le mangez pas, chère Madame, je vous en prie."*

VOICE: A few days after our arrival, Bob's life fell into so unusual a routine that we could not but notice it. He began dressing every evening in white tie and tails.

Rankin *arrives in the dining room wearing full evening clothes, including top hat, and behaves unconcernedly, though attracting furtive glances from the guests.*

199

VOICE: He had also unpacked a top hat, which he wore throughout dinner. Punctually at eleven o'clock, a taxi arrived and drove him off to some mysterious destination from which he returned before dawn. Friends dining with us were surprised at his festive appearance and the way he quizzed his old timepiece every few minutes, like a man with a train to catch.

Dinner over, the diners move to the coffee room, and after a time **Eugene** *enters, approaches* **Rankin** *and, excusing himself, tells him the taxi is waiting.* **Rankin** *bids the others goodnight and leaves. In his wake, eyes meet eyes throughout the room.*

NANCY: I must confess to being intrigued. Do you think Bob is playing Cinderella at children's parties?

DREXEL: Or tables at the casino?

RUPERT: I know he's my friend, but I'm as mystified as you are. Perhaps, though, he has hit the jackpot with his heart and is having an affair that comes into bloom only at night – like *Dama de Noche* and jasmine, with their exquisite perfumes.

NANCY: Whatever it is, it takes him all day to recover. It is only when Eugene brings in the evening cocktails that he joins us.

RUPERT: Yes, I must say he times his appearances to the second.

DREXEL *[with a laugh]*: The true pro, surely.

★ ★ ★ ★ ★

CUT TO – Lunch with Louis **Drexel's** *friend Baron de* **Saint-Marc**, *president of the Cercle Nautique, as guest.*

DREXEL *[to* **Saint-Marc***]*: No, Pierre, you have not been misinformed. Rupert brought him from London and he is here right now. Well, he is

200

and he isn't. He's our mystery of the moment: out all night, in all day. I think you'll find that Eugene has taken lunch to him in his bedroom.

Drexel *turns in his chair to see* **Eugene** *and raises his eyebrows.* **Eugene** *nods discreetly.*

SAINT-MARC: Perhaps I can help solve the puzzle.

Faces turn to him expectantly.

SAINT-MARC *[French accent]*: The other night, some friends and I were, as the English say, slumming. We found this sordid little nightclub from which noise was pouring. Curious, we went inside and saw a man on the stage waving a bottle of champagne, which was clearly not the first with which he had associated that evening, and singing "The Man Who Broke the Bank at Monte Carlo", followed by an ungainly dance the audience nevertheless appeared to love. We knew from his accent that he was English, and learned that he had discovered there a nest of fellow Old Etonians and reprobates from Paris. The performance was such a hit that he was persuaded to repeat it on subsequent nights and the little *boîte* is now the smartest in town.

DREXEL: Well, I'll be damned: the sort of things you bring home, Rupert. You're no better than a retriever.

Next evening, when **Rankin** *appears for cocktails, the others gather round him as though he is a celebrity. He looks disconcerted by the attention until* **Rupert** *explains it.*

RUPERT: What's this we hear about you, Bob, becoming a star behind our backs?

RANKIN: Oh, dear. Are you talking about my one-man show? Yes, it

201

started innocently enough, if somewhat alcoholically, but seems to have got out of hand, and, frankly, I don't know how to extricate myself. But before I do, you had better come and see it for yourself because I owe you all an explanation.

NANCY: No time like the present. Let's go tonight while your star is high. When does the act begin?

RANKIN: Midnight, give or take.

Eugene *appears at the door of the salon and ushers the guests into the dining room.*

VOICE: Over dinner, we penetrated the further mystery of how this middle-aged man, who could neither sing nor dance, had so captivated a hard-boiled Riviera audience – if not his Old Etonian cronies. Bob had somehow persuaded the clients that he was not just what he seemed, but was in fact the actual man who had broken the bank at Monte Carlo for two million francs and more.

*Later that evening, after **Rankin's** car has taken him to the nightclub, the others drive off to join him there. They arrive towards the end of his song as he is twirling around in the dance that rounds it off. Above the stage is a gallery, about twenty feet from the floor. Still flouncing theatrically, **Rankin** makes his way up the steps to the gallery and with a final flourish jumps from it to the floor, symbolising, presumably, his flight with the spoils from the casino. **Rupert** and his party gasp at the daring of it and hold their breaths in fear that he might not be able to stand.*

RUPERT *[shocked, to sister Nancy]*: I don't want to see that again and I don't want anyone else to. He's almost fifty, you know, and I'm well aware that one bottle of champagne equals two cushions, but I brought him here and I want to be able to take him away. Please speak to him and tell him to give up this crazy *salto mortale*.

VOICE: Thankfully, she did as I asked, and he did as she asked, though not all that surprisingly, for he was one of the most considerate of men – to others, if not to himself. [Pause] Bob might not have broken the bank, but he did break the cabaret, which lasted only a short time after his departure – the audience having come to love him as did everyone else.

CUT TO – Inside the casino, **Rupert** *not doing well at the roulette wheel and murmuring to the* **Waiter** *who brings his next drink.*

VOICE: In Cannes I was soon recognised as the odd man beloved of society hostesses, so I was soon welcome in many villas and invited to parties from which brilliant and eligible young men were often excluded. I wore a variety of masks. But I also had genuine friends, two of the most important being Fred and Eric, who served the drinks at the casino and acted as bankers when luck was low. Another was Duncan Orr-Lewis, the playboy millionaire baronet and Grenadier. His love affairs, many conducted on his 200-ton yawl *Volente*, were so complicated that it took someone of my romantic-realistic temperament to help him sort them out.

★ ★ ★ ★ ★

CUT TO – **Rupert** *talking to beautiful girl [*Jenny*] at party. An older woman, the hostess, approaches and hands* **Jenny** *a telegram.* **Jenny** *blanches as she reads it.*

RUPERT: Trouble?

JENNY: It's Claud. He's dead.

Jenny *is distraught, eyes darting here and there as though seeking a way out of the cloud that engulfs her.*

RUPERT: My dear, I'm so sorry.

Rupert's *head tilts forward reverently, expressing as much sympathy as he can.*

203

JENNY: I mustn't mislead you, Rupert, dear: if I look shattered, it's not all for poor Claud. I loved him, of course, but his apartment is filled with my jewels, furs and God knows what, and you know the *Code Napoleon* – his wife, the next of kin, is entitled to everything she can lay her hands on. How can I get to Paris before her?

RUPERT *[discarding the intense sorrow and being himself]*: I see what you mean; for a moment, you had me puzzled. If it's a matter of speed, though, I think the only answer is Duncan. Where is the wife?

JENNY: Aix-les-Bains, with her lover, so far as I know.

RUPERT: Then perhaps Duncan and his Bentley have a sporting chance of getting you there first. Come.

Rupert *almost pushes* **Jenny** *to* **Orr-Lewis** *in another part of the room.*

RUPERT: Duncan, I want you to set a new record from Cannes to Paris with Jenny as your passenger. It is more urgent than urgent.

ORR-LEWIS: I know you don't joke where beautiful ladies are concerned, Rupe, so let's go.

They roar off in the long, powerful car, shooting gravel and exhaust fumes behind them.

VOICE: He drove the stricken damsel to Paris in under eight hours, arriving at the apartment twenty minutes before the wife, who had travelled by *rapide* from Aix-les-Bains – and whom she passed on the way out with what she had salvaged. Duncan was not a man to seek favours, but on this occasion I felt he deserved any that came his way.

★ ★ ★ ★ ★

CUT TO – The yacht, Sayonara, *of Louis Drexel's father,* **Tony.**

204

VOICE: My book was coming on well, with Cannes, Monte Carlo and the lonely heights above the Gorge du Loup as a background. Often we would visit Louis Drexel's father, Tony, on his magnificent yacht *Sayonara*. The yacht was furnished throughout with Louis XV pieces standing on Aubusson carpets. So exquisite were the furnishings and decoration that the finest charters were obtained, for Tony knew what refinements women looked for and that it was they who finally decided. One day, we were a party of twenty on board for luncheon. The champagne cocktails had flowed freely.

★ ★ ★ ★ ★

FADE TO – Stewards serving guests at table in the dining saloon. As one set of stewards removes the plates from which caviar and an entrée have been eaten, another hovers with, as a close-up shows, a silver dish of Brussels sprouts. Suddenly, **Tony** *Drexel, at the head of the table, springs to his feet, red in the face, and bellows at the steward.*

TONY: Throw that stuff out the window immediately.

The steward, alarmed, points with the serving spoon first at the sprouts in the dish and then at the port window.

STEWARD: This, *monsieur*, out there?

TONY: Yes, into the sea with it this instant.

The steward goes to the window and heaves the contents of the dish into the sea. Some surprise among the guests at their host's behaviour quickly reverts to well-bred equanimity.

VOICE: Tony's daughter, **Margaretta**, who was married to Lord Winchelsea, was the first to speak.

MARGARETTA: But how do you know some of us don't like Brussels sprouts, Pa?

TONY [*now controlled*]: No one eats Brussels sprouts in any establishment of mine, afloat or ashore…

Tony *points to a bearded guest sitting near him.*

TONY: …not even you, Grand Duke Michael, uncle of Tsar Nicholas though you may be.

VOICE: What was all this about? Tony, healthily bawdy, with a hundred thou' a year (and always grumbling because he couldn't touch the capital), as pleasure-loving and pampered as the grand duke himself… why was this worldly American extrovert paranoid about a few Brussels sprouts? I saw the look of anxious concern on the face of Van Vouris, his friend and secretary, when Tony's angry eyes turned on him; and then he smiled and suddenly everything was back to normal: the Waterford twinkled, the silver shone, conversation flowed. The play had resumed and all were back in their parts. Yet the question nagged. Were the sprouts too plebeian for the guests? Had, perhaps, this homely vegetable played a part in the tragic history of the Romanovs? We drank coffee under an awning on the afterdeck. I was near the grand duke as cigars and liqueurs were being served, when I noticed Sir Hugo de Bathe approaching, limping heavily on his stick.

Suddenly the **Grand Duke**, *angrily drawing in his feet, shouts at* **Sir Hugo**.

GRAND DUKE: Be careful with that stick, Sugy!

Sir Hugo *raises his stick very slowly.*

SIR HUGO: Have no fear, your Imperial Highness; I wouldn't even touch you with the tip of it.

VOICE: Why this hatred? Was the grand duke annoyed because Sugy had wooed and won the Jersey Lily and ex-mistress of Edward VII, Lily Langtry, or was this display of rudeness a form of royal behaviour? Or was it a side-effect from the incident of the Brussels sprouts? Some time later, Tony volunteered an explanation that seemed reasonable for a millionaire. As a boy, he had been sent to school in Brussels, had hated Brussels ever since, and found it impossible to be friendly with anyone who liked anything even vaguely connected with the place. It was beginning to seem that the characters I imagined for my book behaved more like real people than some of the real people I moved among.

★ ★ ★ ★ ★

CUT TO – In the garden at the Drexels' villa Pins Blancs, **Rupert** *writing his book.*

VOICE: I continued to work on my book at the end of the garden under the resin-scented pines. Beyond the white balustrade, I could see Les Lerins lying, like low green clouds, over the blue waters. It was really too lovely a place to work in. Robert Hitchens, author of the bestselling *Garden of Allah*, had a pavilion built in the garden of his villa at Territet with a beautiful view over Lake Geneva – so beautiful, he told me, that he could work only with the curtains drawn. Even without tying myself, Ulysses-style, to the mast, the day came when the book was finished. Never had I held anything so precious in my hands. Yet, as Colonel Putnam, of the American publishing house, told Pat Kirwan, my friend of Berlin days, "Any fool can write a book, but it takes a genius to sell it". I decided to take off for London. My manuscript was too precious to be entrusted to the French and English postal systems.

Rupert *walking on the Croisette with* **Nanny** *and the Drexel children. They meet another nanny with her charge, a little black-eyed Russian girl holding a small dog. While the nannies talk, the little girl lifts the dog, a griffon, into* **Rupert's** *arms and the three make friends.*

RUPERT: I do like your little dog so much. What is its name?

The **Nanny** *confers briefly with the Russian girl and returns her attention to* **Rupert**.

NANNY: She says its name is Luska, which means "lovely one".

RUPERT: She is certainly that.

VOICE: Then I had to leave them, because I had arranged to meet another little girl – one who had not had a nanny for some years.

★ ★ ★ ★ ★

FADE TO – Late morning, next day, in the garden of Pins Blancs. **Nanny** *and the Drexel children come up to* **Rupert**, *one of the children carrying Luska.*

NANNY: The other nanny told her mistress how much you liked Luska, and the mistress insisted that you keep her, sir.

RUPERT: How awfully kind, but Luska belongs to the little girl, so would you please take her back? But wait – I am going to write a note for the little girl's mother.

VOICE: They returned her, but back she came again – this time with a note from the Russian lady explaining that her husband had bought her a blue mink coat, so she had decided to buy a new dog of a colour that would match the coat. Since Ruby had asked me for a puppy, I was determined she should have this one. But how to get her to London? I had no intention of putting Luska into quarantine for six months before she could take up residence in England. I had no qualms about smuggling. Indeed, at that time, I was at the height of my career as a customs-evader, drawing the line at only drugs and white slavery. Smuggling a dog into England would be a new challenge.

★ ★ ★ ★ ★

CUT TO – Veterinary surgery. The **Vet** *withdraws a hypodermic needle from Luska, dabs the site and places a small dressing on it. Then he sits at his desk, writes a certificate and hands it to* **Rupert***.*

VET: There, *monsieur*. I have examined the dog thoroughly and she is in perfect health and has just been inoculated against rabies, as the certificate attests. So, morally, you may hold your head high as you enter England, but how you do so without attracting the interest of officials in your extra piece of luggage *[he smiles, shrugs and gives a French "phtt"]* must be your own enterprise, *non?*

★ ★ ★ ★ ★

CUT TO – On board the train bound for Paris. **Rupert** *opens a penknife, gashes the lining of the heavy fur coat he is wearing and makes a cosy nest inside for Luska, who curls up there and sleeps. By the time they pull into Gare de Lyon, they are the best of friends.* **Rupert** *takes a cab to a hotel where he is not known, the Bristol in the Faubourg St Honoré, and books in for the night. At reception, he asks about trains to Biarritz. Within the bulky coat,* **Rupert** *gets Luska to the room without arousing suspicion. In the room, he frees her and she frolics about. He plays with her, tiring her out, and before long she settles on a cushion he puts in a corner for her, and sleeps. Quietly, he leaves the room, placing a "Please do not disturb" sign on the door. He walks to the rue de la Paix and enters the pharmacy of* **Robert***.*

VOICE: I knew information was exchanged between customs men on

209

both sides of the Channel. A dog seen on the boat train at the Gare du Nord would be immediately reported to the Gare Maritime in Calais, with a description of anyone accompanying it. From there it would be forwarded to Dover, where a reception would await the person. So, I decided to travel by air. I booked with Air France, whose hostess, if the worst came to the worst, would be less concerned than an English one.

ROBERT *[beaming, hand out]*: Ah, *monsieur* Rupert. How nice to see you. It is a long time but you look no older.

RUPERT: Thank you, Etienne. The last time you saw me here, merrymaking had temporarily aged me. You yourself look as well as ever, but, no wonder, with all the antidotes to over-indulgence at your fingertips.

ROBERT: Thank you for your observation, *monsieur* Rupert, but please permit me to say that I am a self-made-man in the sense that during all the years I have been ministering to the indispositions of your father and yourself, I have had no occasion to share with you the balm of my shelves.

RUPERT: Point taken, Etienne, though this time I am here not for myself, but to ask you to recommend a sedative for a small child who is travelling in my care to England and who is inclined to be nervous.

ROBERT: The child is very young? Five, six?

RUPERT: That's right.

ROBERT *[whisking a small bottle from a shelf and holding it up between thumb and forefinger for inspection]*: This should do; not too strong.

Rupert *pays Etienne and hurries back to the hotel with the sedative. Luska rouses herself from the cushion, stretches and licks the trace of sedative* **Rupert** *has shaken on to his fingertip. To his relief, she shows a liking for it by wagging her tail. With his* *manuscript in his pocket and Luska in the lining of his coat, and carrying a travelling rug over his arm to hide the bulge,* **Rupert** *looks bulky as he goes to reception, pays, asks for a cab to take him to the Gare d'Orleans, reroutes it to the Hotel Daunou, where he leaves his luggage, and goes to the rue Scribe, where he boards the coach to Le Bourget. Soon after setting off, an American girl [*Carol*] sitting beside him speaks.*

CAROL: Oh my! You've got a dog with you, sir.

Rupert's *face registers consternation.*

VOICE: Taking the coach instead of a taxi was a mistake, though not too serious, as her next remark suggested.

CAROL: I felt it move. It's only fair to tell you that my aunt was caught trying to smuggle a dog into England last month and she had to pay £500 or go to prison for three months.

At Le Bourget, it is announced that the flight is delayed. Luska is fast asleep. **Carol** *accompanies* **Rupert**.

CAROL: Don't worry. Do what Pa would do: treat yourself to some iced champagne, light up a cigar and watch all the pretty ladies.

Rupert *guides* **Carol** *to a corner table in the restaurant.*

VOICE: She was all-American except for a pleasant hint of Paris in her Schiaparelli coat and skirt, the Hellstern shoes, and a sprinkling of Cartier's diamonds and emeralds to make her glisten. I had noticed that whenever she opened her Hermes handbag, the air filled with the delicious fragrance of Guerlain's Russian Leather. In fact, she was a live advertisement for the Faubourg St Honoré, rue Royale and rue de la Paix. She refused to share my champagne, preferring to drink a *citron pressé*.

211

CAROL: That cigar smells wonderful.

VOICE: This was music to my ears. It confirmed my theory that Havana tobacco is the grandest of all smells, because, uniquely, it evokes yet other and entirely dissimilar smells: Roger *et* Gallet soap, rich cooking and mellow brandy – and even the indescribable aroma of old furniture and royal Bokharas, hanging tapestries and the leather in a Rolls *coupe de ville*. Of all smells, it is the one that most swiftly evokes all that is most seductive in luxurious living and leisure and loving. Which is why women love the smell of a good cigar.

CAROL: What do you do?

RUPERT: Usually the first thing that comes into my head – unfortunately.

CAROL: I don't mean that; I mean, how do you earn your living?

VOICE: That was an awkward one when I thought of the handsome allowance Father made me, but I answered boldly.

RUPERT: I'm a seaman. I go down to the sea and do my business in great waters.

CAROL: Sure, in your fur coat with astrakhan collar and dog hidden in the lining.

RUPERT: I'm sorry if I don't look the part.

VOICE: Going to sea before the mast was the only thing I had to be proud of; the only thing since the war I'd done off my own bat, albeit not too successfully. The interesting thing was not how well I'd done it, but – as Samuel Johnson might have said – that I'd done it at all.

CAROL: Is that all you've done?

RUPERT: Well, I've just finished writing a book.

VOICE: Naturally, it was the first time I had noticed how attractive she was. At an early age, American girls learn to interest and attract men. With her blue eyes assuming an expert expression of seriousness and her lips slightly parted, she was the epitome in colour and form of the top American cover girl.

CAROL: Written a book! That's thrilling.

RUPERT: That's exactly what I hope it is.

CAROL: With lots of murders in it?

RUPERT: It's got a nice contemporary one you'd like and an old-fashioned one to comfort an older generation.

CAROL: You'll promise me a signed copy when it comes out?

RUPERT: Yes, if I ever find a publisher.

CAROL: What is your name?

RUPERT: Rupert Grayson.

CAROL [repeating the name thoughtfully]: It doesn't ring any bells with me.

VOICE: I'd seen her own name on her black kid baggage: Carol Carol-Carol. We walked through the customs shed and Luska did not move. With no luggage, I walked straight through – my heartbeat quickening – hiding the bulge with the rug. I was not stopped by any of the airport police as I walked past.

Rupert *arrives at the exit and waits for the coach. Soon, his American friend comes through.*

CAROL *[breathlessly]*: Don't wait for the coach; flag down a cab.

Her voice is almost drowned by that of a **Customs Officer** *booming over the loudspeaker: "Mr Grayson is wanted in the customs shed".*

VOICE: Someone must have informed on me. As I walked back, my heart sank, knowing I was to be parted from Luska – to say nothing of the £500 fine.

CUSTOMS OFFICER: You're Mr Grayson and you've just travelled on the plane from Paris?

RUPERT: Yes.

CUSTOMS OFFICER: Why didn't you clear customs?

RUPERT: I'd no baggage so I just walked through.

CUSTOMS OFFICER: You just walked through, as simple as that? Well, in future, you just report to customs. We've got you down as travelling on the plane and when you don't check here, you're adrift. Have you anything to declare?

RUPERT: Not a thing.

For sixty seconds, they look each other in the eyes before the **Customs Officer** *relaxes into an expression that is cheerful and friendly.*

CUSTOMS OFFICER *[with a tilt of the head to say "go"]*: Okay.

As **Rupert** *emerges,* **Carol** *is waiting by the bus. She gives him a shining smile and bright-blue wink. This time* **Rupert** *calls a taxi, which takes them into London.*

★ ★ ★ ★ ★

CUT TO – The taxi letting **Rupert** *off near the Hyde Park Hotel. As he shuts the door of the cab, leaving CAROL in it to go on,* **Rupert** *speaks.*

RUPERT: So, Claridges at eight?

CAROL: Yes. Without the dog.

Rupert *takes Luska from the coat and lets her run around in Kensington Gardens. From a hat shop in Sloane Street, he buys an oval box into which he pops her, ties it with a ribbon and large pink bow, and writes on a label: "Luska, fragile, handle with loving care, definitely this side up".*

VOICE: I sent a message to my wife asking her to collect a very important box from the Hyde Park Hotel, just arrived from Paris. Later, I heard from a lady in the cloakroom how delighted Ruby had been. Luska, too, I suspect. I had been only a makeshift mother; now, she had a real one.

★ ★ ★ ★ ★

CUT TO – The lounge in Claridge's, **Rupert** *sitting, waiting.*

VOICE: I had arranged to dine with Carol at Claridge's, so I bought her a flutter of little orchids she could either wear or pin onto her evening handbag. I was looking forward to meeting her again. We had shared a secret and experienced doubt, fear and elation together. Let someone do you a favour and quite possibly you've made a friend. I prayed it might be so with her. In the past I had always betrayed my obvious enchantment with a girl, but with this spoiled, poor little rich girl, I meant to play the part of the cool, cold Englishman. The orchids, I persuaded myself, were

215

no more than a conventional gesture, and, even if I intended ordering an especially good dinner, I'd have done that if she'd come from the back row of the chorus.

Carol *enters the lounge and sees* **Rupert**.

VOICE: She came in, beautiful, glittering and trailing clouds of glory and Chanel.

CAROL: What are you doing here?

RUPERT: I'm engaged, honourably and as arranged, in the task of ordering dinner for two. Is there anything wrong with that?

CAROL: In a way, because we're dining in the suite.

★ ★ ★ ★ ★

CUT TO – Carol's suite and the hubbub of a family occasion.

VOICE: And that is exactly where we did dine, not quite *tête-à-tête*, but with her **Father**, two uncles, a cousin from Devonshire and her old nanny who'd come up from Brighton. None of them had seen her for a long time and it was clear they all loved her, so that even I, annoyed as I was, felt myself drawn into this orbit of adoration.

FATHER: So, you're the man with the dog?

RUPERT: Afraid so, but I know you'll keep it secret, sir.

VOICE: Dinner, at which I was separated from Carol by three aunts and two uncles, was hardly over before the door opened and two more friends from Baltimore and yet another cousin from New York arrived. It was time, I decided, that "the man with the dog" should go.

216

Rupert *slips into the bedroom unnoticed, takes the orchids, now wilted, from his pocket, places them on the dressing table and lets himself out.*

VOICE: Some years later, I went with friends to a very grand party given by the Marchesa Lucia della Romana at her palace in Rome, and saw that my wonderfully gowned and bejewelled hostess, statuesque at the head of the marble staircase, was my accomplice of the airport. As my friends sought to introduce me, she put forth both her hands and cried, "But it's the man with the dog." Carol Carol-Carol had married above me.

★ ★ ★ ★ ★

CUT TO – Winchelsea, tracking to the beach and along it to poet Henry **Savage's** *dilapidated cottage. Half of it has been washed away by rough seas, leaving a living room, two bedrooms and a lean-to privy through which the wind whistles. Pat* **Kirwan** *[last encountered in Berlin] greets* **Rupert** *on arrival. With him is another writer, fellow Irishman Jasper* **Power**. **Savage** *himself is on the seashore, inspecting the long-lines that keep him from starving.*

VOICE: In London, meanwhile, I still had the problem of my own marriage. I handed my manuscript to Eveleigh Nash and, while awaiting his decision, took refuge with the poet Henry Savage in his tumbledown cottage on Winchelsea beach. It was the writer's ideal refuge from publishers and irate females. It had a certain rough comfort, though the sea played more part in its life than a woman could have done. At times, the tide rose so high in the guest chamber that the guest had to push the bed hard against the inland wall to avoid drowning.

RUPERT *[to* **Kirwan***]*: What a long way from the last table I saw you sitting at! Or was it sleeping at? Or singing at?

KIRWAN *[with a sigh, lifting his head from the work untidily scattered about him]*: Hello, Rupert. Yes, you're right. And not just miles. You witnessed the moment of my disenchantment. Oh, there's probably a better word for it because I was not so much enchanted as drugged. Miles, yes, but more importantly, degrees – 180 of them. You will understand if you know I am translating *Women and Monks* by Josef Kallinkov, a writer of genius who was among the first of many to perish at Stalin's hands. But meet Jasper Power, a compatriot whose pen is fuelled with native Irish wit.

Rupert and **Power** *shake hands affably.*

RUPERT: Keep writing, gentlemen; I have shares in a publishing company. I'll pay my respects to Henry, who seems to have an audience of cats down there on the beach.

Rupert *leaves the writers to their work and walks to* **Savage**, *who is surrounded by stray cats gnawing at the carcases of fish.*

SAVAGE: Hello, Rupe. Got your letter only yesterday. The post office takes me less seriously than it should and saves them up. Never mind; it gives me an excuse for not having dancing girls to welcome you.

RUPERT *[nodding to the cats]*: I hope that's not our supper they're cleaning up.

SAVAGE: Not quite, but catering arrangements in this household are upside down: only after they've had their fill do I get what's left over.

★ ★ ★ ★ ★

CUT TO – Inside the shanty that night. Kerosene lanterns, wooden packing cases for tables. **Savage** *officiates at the stove, frying fish for the guests and maintaining the flow of pieces from pan to plate. Each chair is a slab of wood supported by two piles of books.*

POWER *[Irish voice]*: I didn't think the cats would let you get away with all this lot, Henry; do you think they know it's Friday?

KIRWAN: I'm sure they do, but Henry is a God-fearin' man who knows how to feed a multitude when he has to.

RUPERT: These are not Bibles we're sitting on, are they?

POWER: Naw, just unsold volumes of Henry's poems.

KIRWAN: Henry doesn't need books for his literary jewels. Many are pressing up against his teeth, impatient to get out.

SAVAGE: Jasper, I'm sure you've had enough brandy by now to unlock the Scottish balladeer in you. A wee recitation, perhaps…?

Clutching the almost empty brandy bottle by the neck, **Power** *stands up, sending the makeshift seat sprawling in a heap of books, and recites thickly:*

POWER: *Our reverend meenister*
Has turned rather seenister
And taken to wearin' a beard.
While Sandy MacPherson
Exposin' his pairson
And publicly dreein' his weird…

At which, having no further use for it, **Power** *swings the empty bottle and hits* **Kirwan** *over the head with it. The blow is only glancing, but shatters the glass of whisky in* **Kirwan's** *hand. Recovering from the surprise,* **Kirwan** *strikes* **Power,** *who falls to the floor, getting painfully up after a time and rubbing his jaw.*

POWER: What's a blow among friends?

VOICE: And so the night continued, with verse being spouted as cats slunk around our ankles, the moon rode wild over the marshes and the tide crept into my room. In the 1950s, Henry fell ill and was admitted to the Royal Marsden Hospital in the Fulham Road suffering from cancer of the lung. With a group of sorrowing friends, we went to visit him bearing champagne. We had quite a party, saddened only by the whispered intimation of the *medico* that he had but three weeks to live. Next day, stimulated possibly by the wine, Henry leapt from his bed, dressed, and caught a banana boat from the Pool of London to the Canaries, where he lived in joyful debauch for the next fifteen years. He must have been damned near ninety when he died in an old age faithfully portrayed in lines attributed to Dean Swift, but probably written by Alan Herbert or Hilaire Belloc:

Fro Commerce and the Busy World retir'd
Unmoved by Fame; nor by Ambition fir'd,
Calmly I await the Call of Charon's Boat,
Still drinking like a Fish, still fucking like a Goat.

Rupert *lunching with Eveleigh* **Nash** *at the Savoy Grill.*

NASH: Sorry I was vague on the telephone, but I had to call you – Morley Roberts was with me and I somehow hoped to kill two birds with one stone by getting hold of you and giving Morley a sign that I was busy. He's so charming and amusing that one could spend all day with him, but, as you know, everything in its place. Well, we like your book, and here [handing Rupert an envelope] is something to put you a little ahead of the wolf – though, I suppose in your case, Rupert, the racehorse is a more likely predator.

Rupert *opens the envelope and beams at the contents.*

VOICE: It was an advance of fifty pounds on royalties, but it might have been a million. I had gone through thousands in my short life, but this was the first real money, apart from my pittance as a seaman, that I had earned by ache of fingers and agony of soul. I was young and hale, a writer, and could now mix unchallenged with my peers. Somewhat airborne, as we ate and drank in what I could not but regard as a celebration, my mind stayed pinned to the name of the author – the fellow author – Morley Roberts, because Eveleigh's reference to him reminded me that Rudyard Kipling had once mentioned him to me in a letter. He had written: "I like Morley's *Humble Fisherman* because he owns up to a delight in small trout, and that is a mark of sincerity." But I had my own reason for recalling Morley: a tale I had heard about his visit to a gentleman in a grand country house.

★ ★ ★ ★ ★

FADE TO – Morley **Roberts** *arriving by car at a country mansion at the end of*

221

a long driveway. He steps out to be joined, as he approaches the front steps, by a friendly little **Nanny Goat**, *which comes to his side and stays there. He rings at the door and the* **Butler** *opens it.*

BUTLER: Good day, sir; Mr Roberts?

ROBERTS *[tendering card]*: That's right.

BUTLER: Please come in. Sir Ronald expects you.

VOICE: He did not say that he also expected the nanny goat, which accompanied Roberts through the door and into the house.

The **Butler** *looks at the* **Nanny Goat** *briefly as it enters, but not so pointedly as to question its presence, appearing to assume it belongs to* **Roberts**, *whose manner, on the other hand, is that of a man who has accepted that the animal belongs to the house and has the run of it.* **Roberts** *is shown into a beautiful eighteenth century drawing room and almost immediately* **Sir Ronald** *arrives. He greets* **Roberts** *affably, with only the slightest glance at the nanny goat, not wanting to embarrass his guest by implying there is anything unusual about bringing his pet with him.* **Roberts** *cannot hide some surprise when the* **Nanny Goat** *starts butting the furniture and ripping the brocaded chairs with its horns, but quickly wipes it off his face and gives his attention to* **Sir Ronald**, *who is clearly struggling, however, to focus on* **Roberts** *rather than the* **Goat**, *which has begun leaping from one piece of furniture to another.*

ROBERTS*[nervously admiring]*: How beautifully she jumps.

SIR RONALD *[trying not to wince]*: Yes, you must be proud of her. Have you had her trained?

Before **Roberts** *can answer, the* **Nanny Goat's** *hoof slips on the glossy surface of a Chippendale side table, knocking a Sèvres bowl to the floor, where it shatters. As*

Sir Ronald *kneels to pick up the pieces, the* **Nanny Goat** *takes the chance to attack him savagely from, and in, the rear, sending* **Sir Ronald** *forward on to the floor and the shards of the bowl flying from his hand.*

ROBERTS *[embarrassed]*: I don't understand; she is not mine.

SIR RONALD *[angrily]*: But... but... wasn't it with you?

ROBERTS: Not at all. It came in the front door with me, and with such aplomb that I thought it belonged to the house. Are you all right?

SIR RONALD: Frankly, no, but I'll be better when that animal is no longer to be seen – or felt.

VOICE: Sir Ronald was a good-humoured man, and after a time he regained his composure and patched things up, though not, unfortunately, the bowl, which he had to write off to experience.

★ ★ ★ ★ ★

CUT TO – The customs shed at Calais, officers taking a keen interest in **Rupert's** *belongings.*

VOICE: Next day, with a literary future ahead and loaded with large tins of Cow & Gate baby food for little Antonia Drexel, I once more left London for Cannes. It was pleasant to know that this time I was not a smuggler but a *bone fide* traveller, carrying on my passport a request from His Majesty's Secretary of State that I be allowed to pass without let or hindrance, and that anyone concerned should help and protect me. At the Calais customs, with my conscience clear, I declared all I had. It was only then that I realised I was not going to receive the assistance or protection sought on my behalf. I had not until then seen the contents of a tin of Cow & Gate. The product looked harmless to me, but to the French authorities, I now realised, it suggested cocaine.

Rupert, *agitatedly looking at his watch, remonstrates with the customs officers.*

RUPERT: Look here, I don't know what the fuss is about. Try the stuff yourself.

FIRST OFFICER: Bribery will not 'elp you, *monsieur*.

RUPERT: Look, my train is due to go.

Waving his arms, **Rupert** *looks wildly about the shed.*

RUPERT: For heaven's sake, find a young mother and show it to her; she will tell you what it is – for babies; you know, *bebé*.

Rupert *rocks his arms as though cradling a baby and makes a baby sound, which comes out like the baa of a lamb.*

SECOND OFFICER *[French accent]*: The pow-dair must go to the laboratory, *monsieur*, and you must stay 'ere, near the *gare*, until it 'as been examined.

On the scene appears an older and more elaborately attired officer, the **Chief**, *who asks his juniors what is going on, and they explain. The* **Chief** *looks at* **Rupert** *and tilts his head sympathetically, shrugs, utters a French "phtt" and looks philosophical. The Blue Train draws out of the platform nearby.*

RUPERT: Oh, damn; that's my train.

CHIEF: It should not take more than an hour, *monsieur*, and there is anothair train soon after. Meanwhile, perhaps we could 'elp to cement Anglo-French relations by taking lunch together.

VOICE: At this, my mood improved, for no less a *bon vivant* than Edward

VII had described the Calais seaport *restaurant de la gare* as one of the best in Europe.

The customs **Chief** *and* **Rupert** *dine jovially together, near the end of which a junior officer arrives and mutters to his master.*

VOICE: My lunch with the *Chef de Douane* was excellent and I did not care whether his intention was to entertain me or keep an eye on me. Aided by the companionship of a *Chateau Margaux*, he amused me with stories of smuggling until the laboratory had declared the Cow & Gate to be innocuous.

The **Chief** *and his two subordinates wave* **Rupert** *off on the train for Paris. In the compartment, he settles down and reflects.*

VOICE: Wherever I might arrive in the world, there was always a letter from Mother with news of the family or Ravenspoint. We never saw her idle. She would be sewing, embroidering or writing letters, never at a writing table but always on her knees. Sometimes, she would doze off in an armchair after dinner with her writing pad on her lap. Persuading her to go to bed was as difficult as telling a child it was bedtime. Her letters were sincere and brave, but sometimes they contained an echo of melancholy, because secretly she understood more about life's inevitable sadness than she wished us to know. She adored Father, but his frequent absences abroad and his susceptibility to other beautiful women must have hurt her deeply. She took every indiscretion and *peccadillo* of which he, and we, were capable with loving understanding, accepting all except open criticism of us. Then the tigress in her was aroused, because we belonged to her.

The train pulls into the Gare du Nord and **Rupert** *takes a taxi to the Hotel Daunou, his haunt in Paris.*

VOICE: At the Hotel Daunou, I found a letter from Mother telling me that my cousin Freddie Harrington would be calling on me in Paris, whither he was proceeding in a state of spiritual depression and suffering, she said, from a severe attack of unrequited love – which, in my experience, is nothing more than wounded vanity, though no less painful for that. On arrival, he expressed a desire to go to the Eiffel Tower.

Rupert and **Freddie** *taking a drink at Fouquet's.*

RUPERT: You will shame the whole family if you try to solve your problems by jumping off it. It is far too tasteless a structure. The one time I went to the top of it, I was surprised to see an old friend who had gained something of a reputation for his fanatical dislike of every girder and rivet in it. When I told him it was the last place in Paris I'd expected to see him, he replied that he was there because it was the only place in Paris he could not see it from.

Freddie *remains dejected as* **Rupert** *drags him around Paris, trying to shake off the gloom.*

VOICE: I tried quoting Shakespeare and Byron on the futility of love, gave him the well-known antidote of champagne laced with brandy, and showed him the sights of Paris, including the sewers so beloved of Victor Hugo, in an effort to bring him down to earth. Even the enigmatic smile of Mona Lisa seemed wasted as a warning of the folly of loving only one woman at a time. There remained only the radical cure, the shock treatment: sex.

They take a taxi to 25 Porte St Denis, where **Rupert** *pays the admittance charge of a hundred francs. They climb to the first floor and walk past several rooms in each of which a girl lies with a man on a double bed, around which other men stand.* **Freddie** *begins to be curious.*

FREDDIE [*whispering rather hoarsely*]: What on earth is going on? I mean, there's a man with her, so to speak, yet others are present, gawping.

RUPERT: Oh, yes. It is the privilege of any spectator who has paid the entrance fee, should he feel so inclined, to couple with the lady in the manner of his own choosing – but not, of course, before the gentleman *in situ* has abdicated. As you can see, undressing is minimal, so the act itself may be all but concealed in a flurry of petticoats and overcoats. The tension is sometimes relieved when a gentleman's braces break or his hat rolls under the bed or money spills from trouser pockets.

FREDDIE [*brightening markedly*]: May we see other rooms?

RUPERT: Of course, but the hours here are strange: the establishment opens at two in the afternoon and closes at six, so discouraging low-paid office workers. It is about to close.

FREDDIE: But I say, what a lark!

RUPERT: Yes, houses of amusement where the visitor pays for the entertainment he himself provides are not at all commonplace. The average Parisian and even most Anglo-American expatriates have never heard of the place.

FREDDIE [*now wide-eyed*]: How did you learn about it, Uncle Rupert?

RUPERT: I forget, exactly. It was one of the extras we were offered as part of our wider education. It rather powerfully suggests the idea of plurality, don't you think?

FREDDIE: Yes, it does. And of stand-alone sex.

As the sixteenth century house prepares to close, they saunter from it into the late

227

afternoon street and repair to a corner cafe. As they walk, FREDDIE frowns, preoccupied, and glances furtively at his uncle as though wanting to say something and trying to gauge whether the moment is right. At last, he does.

FREDDIE *[bold but quaking]*: Did your wider education inform you of a place where one might enjoy a girl's company in more privacy?

RUPERT: Of course. Let us go there.

VOICE: Freddie was impecunious and could not afford the splendours of the House of All Nations, the Sphinx or the plush luxuries of the rue Caumartin *bordellos*. I took him instead to a *kindergarten* brothel in the rue de la Farriere, where they were unaccustomed to wealthy foreigners and where his money would be more appreciated by the girls serving apprenticeships there.

★ ★ ★ ★ ★

CUT TO – The reception area of another establishment, where **Rupert** *has a word with the middle-aged* **Madame** *before slipping her some money and beckoning* **Freddie** *to join them and be introduced. In the background wait young girls, neatly dressed, each with her hair in a bow.*

VOICE: I arranged to meet him later in the nearby church of Notre Dame de Lorette at the foot of the hill. As I left, I saw the young assistants, intent on amassing a dowry and catching a husband, meekly awaiting the summons to the selection parade. To distinguish one novice from the other – for there were likenesses among them, they being often recruited from the same family – each wore in her hair a beautifully ironed ribbon of distinctive colour, neatly tied in a bow. After the sordid communal activities at Porte St Denis, it was satisfying to leave him in this friendly atmosphere of starched petticoats and freshly laundered sheets. An hour later, in the whispering silence and aromatic twilight of the old church, I suddenly realised that he was kneeling beside me, and in that moment I felt closer to him than I had been all day. Freddie, cured, was offering up his thanks to a kindly and all-forgiving God.

CUT TO – Next day. Rupert sets out from the Hotel Daunou for the Scribe. At the bar.

VOICE: Next morning, fate guided my drifting footsteps into the Scribe to find out whether my old friend Duncan Orr-Lewis, a director of the hotel, was in Paris. He was not, but his brother-in-law, **Sir Albert** Stem, was. He invited me for a drink at the bar.

SIR ALBERT: Well, what are your plans?

VOICE: I have noticed through a long life that people have always been interested in my plans; as though I, of all people, was a man who knew what he would be doing twenty-four hours ahead. I told him, on the spur of the moment, that I had a great longing to visit Bucharest, and was surprised by his answer.

SIR ALBERT: Why not go on one of our tankers as my guest. From Constanza, you can take a train to Bucharest.

RUPERT: Well, now, it's difficult to thank you but impossible to say no. How wonderful.

★ ★ ★ ★ ★

FADE TO – Gare Montparnasse, **Rupert** *boarding the train for Cannes.*

VOICE: To have declined the invitation would have been foolish and ungrateful. The sailing date from the United Kingdom gave me just time to deliver my cargo of Cow & Gate, so my mood was amiable as I boarded the train for Cannes.

A week later, **Rupert** *joins the tanker 'Staua Romana' on the Thames as supercargo.*

VOICE: Once more, I was on a ship's deck. Beyond lay fresh worlds of mystery and adventure. I was in thrall to romantic names. I had already sailed the Spanish Main, rolled down to Rio and the River Plate. I had been through the Panama Canal into the Pacific, sailed north to Yokahama and south to Guayaquil, Callao and Valparaiso – the blessed city where my mother was born. I had been to Canada and the United States, the Gulf ports and the Pacific coast to Long Beach, that brash port for Los Angeles, and on to San Francisco. I knew most of the European capitals and Leningrad and Moscow. But I longed for the golden cities of the Orient, to which the gateways were Istanbul by sea and Bucharest overland. I had been told Bucharest had everything that makes a city agreeable: beautiful women, night-smelling flowers, scented wine and flowing music. Also, I liked the sound of the name. It had the softness and the crispness of a croissant straight from the oven.

★ ★ ★ ★ ★

CUT TO – The Romanian captain, immaculately attired, on the bridge of the shabby 'Staua Romana', overseeing the ship's departure on the evening tide.

VOICE: The captain, like most ships' foreign masters, had a working knowledge of English, and in better French revealed a puckish humour. We lived in a style unheard of in a British tanker.

That evening. Dinner is served with silver on a white tablecloth to **Captain, Officers** *and* **Rupert** *– the only passenger on board.*

CAPTAIN: Well, my English guest, and what do you think of our *aperitif, Suica*, as a means of showing the food the way to the stomach?

RUPERT: I think it is capable of winning my affection, captain, just as *Pisco*, its distant cousin, did in Peru.

The **Captain** *rubs his hands together in satisfaction and leans back as the* **Steward** *serves him with a plate of steaming goulash. On receiving his portion, as outsized as himself, the* **Chief Officer** *flexes his elbows and starts on it without hesitation or grace.*

230

VOICE: Some of the meals I would not have exchanged for dinner at the Tour d'Argent, and my satisfaction with the ship went beyond the captain's table. My own quarters had a bunk as narrow as a monk's, a washbasin and one port. But there was a bathroom, a luxury to which an old deckhand such as I was quite unused. The **Chief Officer** displayed all the good nature associated, often wrongly, with fat people. He caused amusement at meals because he suffered from gannetitis: like the gannet, he tried to put more into his mouth than the orifice allowed. But he was a particularly talented carpenter and it was fascinating to see him making toys for his children.

After dinner. The captain appears in the saloon with a violin case and his audience, with **Rupert** *next to the* **Chief Officer,** *sit around awaiting a recital.*

VOICE: The captain had a talent, too. One evening, when we were clear of the Channel, he produced a violin case, and my heart sank as does that of any Englishman at the appearance of this instrument in other than professional hands. I am ashamed to say that it was in expectation of aural torture that I forced a look of happy anticipation on to my face as he cradled the fiddle in his arms and tucked it fondly beneath his chin. What wonderful surprises life can hold for the young, who believe they know everything: that evening, undeservedly, I was treated to the most exquisite and exciting succession of gipsy melodies I had ever heard. The fiddle was a loved-one that he petted, stroked, coaxed and even, sometimes it seemed, scolded. I had not enough knowledge to judge technique, but the feeling and passion, the laughter and tears he drew from the instrument were overwhelming.

The captain plays the violin. His eyes twinkle as they meet **Rupert's** *on a traverse of the audience. The* **Chief Officer** *leans to* **Rupert's** *ear and whispers.*
CHIEF OFFICER: He thinks his music inspires your writing.

RUPERT *[whispering]*: My writing is nothing compared with his music.

The ship passes through the Straits of Gibraltar and a week after that arrives off Cape

Matapan, the most southerly point of Greece. The ship's whistle blows, the engines stop. A small boat pulls away from the rocky mainland. **Rupert** *leans over the rail with the* **Chief Engineer**, *watching stores being lowered to an old white-bearded man who stacks them carefully on the floorboards of the frail craft.*

CHIEF ENGINEER: We are his lifeline.

RUPERT: Who is he?

CHIEF ENGINEER: He was the master of a small coaster that was wrecked long ago on those rocks. He lost his wife, his crew and all he owned in the world. Since then he has lived like a hermit in a cave on a ledge of rock, existing only on stores left by friendly passing ships.

VOICE: There are certain pictures that stay in the mind's eye. One that remains in mine is that of the old man pulling away from the ship's side, his farewell wave of an arm and his long white beard parted by the wind.

The ship ploughs through the Aegean Sea, escorted by gulls breasting the wind and with the isles of Greece on all sides – their jagged silhouettes rising black in the afterglow of a sunset.

VOICE: As twilight deepened into darkness, the stars came out and the silver web of the Milky Way spread itself above Skyros and Missalonghi, where my fellow Harrovian died bedridden of a fever instead of heroically on the battlefield as he would have wished.

Istanbul seen from the 'Staua Romana' as it approaches the city.

VOICE: Father had warned me that Istanbul looked beautiful only from the deck of a ship. In the sunrise, from our anchorage, the violet-crowned city rested luminously on its seven hills, the mosques and minarets floating in a haze, rosy and golden…

Rupert *goes ashore and into the town.*

VOICE: After descending the gangplank I was swallowed in a squalid maze of rutted streets and alleys deep in filth of the worst kind.

Rupert *explores bazaars, churches and palaces.*

VOICE: I did the rounds of the bazaars and St Sophia, the church of Holy Wisdom, with its fantastic acoustics and superb mosaics, and wandered through the shadows of the gardens of the Topkapi Palace, the old *seraglio* of the sultans – the last of whom, Adbul Hamid, had garrotted 2000 concubines, presumably in defence of what little energies they had left him. The air was charged with the stale smell and bitter taste of cruelty, torture and death. I sensed the same indescribable evil there as had been in the underground cells of the Fortress of Peter and Paul in Leningrad. Returning to the streets, I searched vainly for the romantic, exotic city of Pierre Loti. At every comer, I encountered odours with which I was familiar from an accumulation of centuries of filth and dirt. They came alive and crept forward at my approach as if to salute me as an old friend. The wider streets teemed with ill-humoured crowds, who pushed and nudged from all sides, bashed their way on to overloaded ferry-boats and swarmed down to the Scutari jetty.

A beautiful girl with the figure and face of the Orient catches **Rupert's** *eye as she carries her load of flowers.*

VOICE: Once I saw a flower-laden girl with more of the East than the West in her looks and bearing. She was unveiled and walked like a princess across the Galata Bridge. In the throng, she seemed to tread a solitary path that opened at her approach. It was as pleasing and unexpected as the sight of a rose on a dung heap.

In a squalid waterfront alley, **Rupert** *turns and looks behind him several times.*

VOICE: Once I sensed that I was being stalked by a yellow cur, for there were plenty of dogs with ancestral memories prowling the city and searching the water's edge, as their fathers did in Byron's day, for the headless trunks flung there from the sultan's palace. The horrible animals seemed to be everywhere. I was told they rarely left their own part of the city, for if a dog strayed beyond its patch it was torn to pieces by those whose territory it had entered. I made my way to the Pera Palace Hotel, where the captain and I had arranged to meet.

★ ★ ★ ★ ★

FADE TO – Dining room at the Pera Palace Hotel. **Rupert** *and the* **Captain** *finish their dinner to the accompaniment of Turkish music performed by a small band. The* **Captain** *wipes his chin and pays the bill, leaving enough on the dish to make the baggy-trousered waiter bow forty-five degrees.*

CAPTAIN: If you follow me, I think you will not be sorry.

The **Captain** *leads them through alleyways to a house off the rue de Pera. They sit on large cushions among girls who serve them with small glasses of sarap, before gathering themselves up and dancing to music coaxed by a heavily made-up boy from a strange mediaeval instrument.*

RUPERT: Are they Indian?

CAPTAIN: The girls are Armenian and Circassian. They are dancing a Turkish version of the *nautch*, which, of course, does come from India.

As the performance develops, with hands undulating, hips swaying, bellies rolling and feet motionless as though nailed to the floor, the **Captain** *from his mound of rugs and cushions tosses silver coins among the dancers, who snatch them up and press them to their foreheads, where, to* **Rupert's** *evident surprise, they stick. As the tempo of the music grows, so the movements of the dancers slows until they gently succumb at the feet of the pair.*

VOICE: The dancers, slim, musky and hairless, stilled into a sensual drowsiness; and one little dancer after another fell like petals from a dusky flower on to the foothill of rugs at our feet.

Rupert *becomes part of an orgy of writhing brown bodies.*

VOICE: I lost all contact with my brave captain; nor did I know, in the dream-like confusion of slender arms and budding breasts and kissing tongues, which girl's mouth was breathing jasmine into mine or which was whispering to me in an alien tongue. They disrobed us with cool hands, playing and squabbling over us like children with their dolls, and chattering unintelligible endearments. The music faded away in a dying orgiastic moan. Outside the house, when **Rupert** and the **Captain** emerge, the old *cocher* waits with oriental patience to return them to the ship. Close-ups show contentment on their faces as they clip-clop away.

★ ★ ★ ★ ★

CUT TO – The port of Constanta. **Rupert** *disembarks. The* **Captain** *plays him ashore with a tzigane lament.*

VOICE: The melancholy of the violin's goodbye held me in its thrall until it was replaced by the spell of Bucharest as I neared the destination.

From the outskirts of Bucharest to **Rupert's** *hotel.*

VOICE: Bucharest still had its orchards and every square, its trees. I kept encountering the smell of meadows, the tang of drying hay and the homely stench of the farmyard. The slovenly Turkish influence was dragging the city to the brink of disenchantment, but never quite over it. For me, it had the charm of a superbly beautiful slut.

Inside the hotel. **Rupert** *looks around, checks in.*

VOICE: On arriving in a strange city, I always went straight to the leading

235

hotel, rather as one breaks the crust of a pie before getting down to what is inside. I had, as the French say, "descended" on the Hotel Pallas Athene. It was a sort of Ruritanian Ritz-Carlton with a pleasing Edwardian atmosphere, reflecting in its diamond-studded mirrors the café society of Bucharest at every angle as it strolled and drank and flirted under the glittering crystal chandeliers. It was not without raffish charm of a rather high order, particularly at night, when the women dressed *haute toilette* and the men wore splendid decorations and medals to which they were probably not entitled.

Rupert *saunters to the bar, studying the setting and its occupants on the way and when he gets there.*

VOICE: I soon found that at the Pallas Athene the bar was the favourite *rendezvous* of government officials, whose aversion to uncongenial labours exceeded even mine; the younger secretaries and attaches of the diplomatic corps; the painted, powdered and corseted army officers; the *demi-mondaines*, the foreign correspondents and the inevitable lean and hungry men and women who live by the sale of negotiable information or the cupidity and indiscretions of the wealthy. In this cosmopolitan meeting-place, at 6.30 every evening, the curtain rose on the Balkan scene to the strains of a Hungarian orchestra in pale-blue uniforms playing *"Les Millions d' Harlequin"*, "The Blue Danube" or *"Un Peu d'Amour"*.

Three days later. The clock on the bar wall shows 6.35. **Rupert** *is standing next to* **Four Men** *who are drinking and laughing. After a time, one of them [***Erik***] notices that* **Rupert** *is alone, detaches himself from the others and addresses* **Rupert** *in broken English.*

ERIK: Good evening. You are English?

RUPERT: Yes. Does it show?

ERIK [pleasantly]: Please, I understand not.

RUPERT [slowly, smiling]: I just meant: do I look English to you?

ERIK [catching on]: Yes, yes. I was in England, so I think I have seen you before. Not you yourself, but other English, and you could be one of them. You do not look suspicious. Are you inspecting our city?

RUPERT: Yes, but I wish I could speak to your people in their own language.

ERIK: I think for you it is difficult to learn this language.

RUPERT: Too difficult for me.

ERIK: For anybody who is not Romanian. To others than Romanians, it is a language of barbed wire.

VOICE: Perhaps the reference to barbed wire reminded him of war.

ERIK: So while you are here, it is more important to look than to listen. Tomorrow, there is something that you might like to look at. To remember the victory of the war, we have built near the centre of Bucharest an Arc de Triomphe, just like in Paris, and tomorrow it will be officially opened, or perhaps it is more correct to say unveiled. If you are here at noon tomorrow, I could take you to the ceremony. Yes?

VOICE: Why not, I thought. A staid civic event would help to balance some of the revelry I had seen when I had poked my nose into bars and restaurants over the past few evenings.

RUPERT: I'd like that very much. My name is Rupert. Will you take a drink?

Erik *proffers his hand, which* **Rupert** *shakes.*

ERIK: I am Erik. No, please let me offer you a drink.

RUPERT: Thank you, Erik, but may we leave it until tomorrow? I have an appointment. Here, noon tomorrow, yes?

ERIK: Yes, noon tomorrow, here.

VOICE: I did not want to become involved with a crowd and already I had kept him from his friends – even if it was he, in his kindness, who had kept himself from them. So off I went, as usual, not knowing quite where to, but content to leave that to chance.

Next day. As promised, **Erik** *is at the bar when* **Rupert** *arrives soon after noon.*

ERIK: I can see that you are learning a little of Romania – not to be too punctual. I am joking, of course.

RUPERT: It would be nice to think I was learning, but you cannot make a sponge out of a stone.

They finish their drinks.

ERIK: Come, let us go.

They climb into the drozhki that awaits them outside, with its skapelz in the driving seat.

ERIK: These black horses are from the Imperial Orloff blood. They are athletic, no? The driver not so much.

Rupert *smiles to his companion and nods as the drozhki pulls away from the kerb and heads for their destination.*

VOICE: I had heard about the *skapelz* of Bucharest. They were their own masters, and drove *drozhkis* in summer and sleighs in winter. They were a breed apart, though breed was not perhaps the ideal word to describe them – for they had voluntarily deprived themselves of the ability to reproduce after fathering a couple of children and then submitted to radical castration, which made them large, soft and placid. Even then, I could not but think that their contribution to the world was not so much in driving people around Bucharest, as in showing mankind the way to survival in the shadow of the population explosion that was frighteningly upon us. They had also established themselves as people of discretion, who could be entrusted with the well-being of women and the safety of secrets.

ERIK: The Arc de Triomphe of Bucharest has cost much money – much more than the country can afford. But we do not mind because it reminds us that life and freedom are more important than money. It is sturdy like the country and made of marble, as is its brother in the capital of France.

They arrive at the edge of the crowd and alight. The structure does indeed look solid and majestic, with two lions couchant at the base of the great arch, guarding it with heraldic disdain and looking as though they would do so forever. Soon, voices are raised on the official dais and two figures look like coming to blows.

VOICE: With Erik giving me my own private commentary, I began to feel involved in the proceedings. It was not long before a quarrel broke out between the president of the reception committee and the architect, who announced bitterly to the distinguished gathering, in the hearing of the multitude, that he had not yet been paid for his services.

When the protagonists look as though they can take the dispute no further without using fists, the architect delivers a swift blow with his umbrella to the lion nearest him, decapitating it and sending the shattered head rolling down the ceremonial carpet.

VOICE: At the height of the argument, the architect struck the lion near

239

him a blow on the neck, whereupon the head fell off on the carpet and rolled away from the dignitaries. At first, the crowd, alarmed, sucked in its breath. Then it was realised that the noble marble was nothing more than grade-two plaster, and a roar of Romanian laughter burst from the gathering.

As **Erik** *sees* **Rupert** *laughing with the multitude, he grins sheepishly.*

ERIK: You are learning something this afternoon, my English friend.

RUPERT: And being entertained at the same time. You don't think that was part of the programme, do you – Romanian theatre?

ERIK [*ruefully*]: No, it is the real thing. I recognise it because I have been brought up on it. We are too sincere to act. We even lie sincerely – as the architect has just demonstrated.

The crowd, having enjoyed the entertainment, drifts away to line the street and square. **Rupert** *follows* **Erik** *into a house overlooking the festivities. They climb stairs and emerge on to a balcony overlooking columns of soldiers marching past. On a table in the room behind them are many bottles of wine, to which* **Erik** *draws* **Rupert's** *attention.*

ERIK: It is from every province in the country and there, next door, you will find food, hot or cold. Please help yourself.

RUPERT: This is educational indeed. As a visitor, though, I should like you to show me how.

The two help themselves to the food and drink, and by the time they return to the balcony with their hands full, the parade is in progress below. Military bands predominate. A dislocation of traffic has caused the head of the column to halt at the opening of the square below the balcony and such is the noise that only the leading column can hear any words of command, so the next column, with its band at full

240

blast, marches into the first. A kind of monstrous band contest ensues. Just when it seems the awfulness of the cacophony cannot increase, a third band, blaring away with its colours flying, comes into view and throws itself into the fray. Even **Erik** *cannot pretend any more that it is normal and shakes his head in despair. He gestures to* **Rupert** *for them to depart.*

VOICE *[ironically]*: By now I had worked it out that no matter how formal the occasion was meant to be, it always stopped short of being stuffy.

They enter Capsa, the city's leading restaurant. In the centre of the grandiose entrance, a cleaner has left a bucket of dirty water, around which everyone steps as naturally as though it were a fountain. At the Royal Palace, a bright flower blooms from the barrel of a sentry's rifle.

VOICE: At Mass I heard Viennese waltzes, as though drifting downstream on the distant Danube. Had I not still loved Paris, I might have succumbed to Bucharest: feminine, languorous and deceitful. Twilight drifted in on my last evening.

Drozhkis carry **Rupert**, **Erik** *and* **Friends** *to a gradina on the Sinaia road, where they drink large quantities of chilled wine. A gipsy band appears to entertain them. Now and then, a gipsy, overcome with the festivity's exertions, slides quietly to the ground, and one of the children picks up his fiddle and continues where he left off.*

VOICE: The music grew ever wilder, until shattered glasses surrounded us like a glittering arctic sea. Although there were Conacoznis, Ghykis, Esterhazys, Bratianos and Bibescos in our party, the gipsies, as usual, showed utter disregard for rank or wealth, addressing all by Christian name. They introduced my name into their music and drank my health in song. The entire assembly of gipsy girls and Romanian aristocrats joined in the singing. Not since party games in childhood had I heard my name in song, so now in this little garden restaurant, it was pleasing to hear it pronounced in a dozen different ways.

241

A gipsy girl, slender, dark-eyed and dressed in black except for a scarlet belt entwined with yellow and purple ribbons, approaches **Rupert** *and gives him her hand. He embraces her and listens.*

VOICE: Through the fine cotton of my shirt, I felt the warmth of her body, the pressure of her fingers and the sharp points of her copper bracelets pricking into me. Standing beside me, she sang songs with a voice as pure and melodious as a choirboy's. Later, I was told the songs were extremely rude. It was the first time I had experienced the wild smell of a gipsy girl in my arms.

In the lobby of **Rupert's** *hotel. As he collects the room key,* **Rupert** *is handed a telegram, which he opens and reads.*

VOICE: I had intended to return to England on the *Staua Romana*, but received a cable from Duncan Orr-Lewis asking me to meet him at the Avia Palace in Lisbon. As the trip to Romania had been arranged through his brother-in-law, Bertie Stern, I felt obliged to do so. The rail journey across Europe was not without complications, since I had to change trains at Belgrade, Trieste, Venice and Genoa. I knew Duncan would not have cabled if it had not seemed important at the time, though he usually acted on impulse and always generously. His money was inherited, so wealth did not chafe him as it did some of my friends who had acquired it by work. He asked me to wait in Lisbon until he showed up on his yacht, *Volante.*

★ ★ ★ ★ ★

CUT TO – Arrival at Avia Palace, Lisbon. After checking in at the desk and being handed the key at the elegant ends of the receptionist's finger, **Rupert** *is directed to the* **Manager's** *office nearby. He is greeted with a handshake and invited to sit down.*

MANAGER *[fawning]*: Welcome, Mr Grayson. I hope you will be comfortable here and I do not want to detain you after your journey, but I think you would wish to know that Mr Orr-Lewis has deposited with us for your use the sum in *escudos* corresponding with this figure.

The manager hands **Rupert** *a slip of paper. He looks at it with an appreciative lifting of the eyebrows, folds and puts it in his pocket.*

RUPERT: Thank you for the advice and, yes, I'm sure the comfort here will be fully up to scratch as usual. Do you still have Mr Five-per-cent on his podium?

MANAGER: Yes, sir, this is his home – though we do not call him that here.

With a smile, **Rupert** *departs and makes his way to the suite that has been reserved for him.*

VOICE: The hotel in the long Avenida de Mayo was one of the smallest and most beautiful in Europe. Calouste Gulbenkian, the father of my old Harrow friend, Nubar, lived there, and he was to be seen in the dining room towering at a table placed high on a dais. As the world knows, Gulbenkian as a young man had charmed the oil company for whom he acted as middleman into paying him five per cent in perpetuity for oil concessions he secured for it. Thus the wealth he accumulated was fantastic, and from the eminence it had bought him in the restaurant, he was able to observe everyone – though it was he himself who received the closest scrutiny. I waited for Duncan for more than a week, spending days at Estoril before it became infested with royal refugees, but keeping in touch with the hotel in case he suddenly appeared and wanted to sail on the next tide.

A porter materialises to usher **Rupert** *into his suite, adjust the curtains, tinker with this and that, and, after a trickle of escudos has poured from* **Rupert's** *palm into his, departs.* **Rupert** *goes to the window and muses on the view.*

VOICE: I loved this capital, even though the captains and the kings had long departed. I first met the last king, Don Manuel, in Munich, where I had sat next to him at a cycle of Wagner's "Ring" as he followed each opera from a dog-eared score. For a romantic like myself, to meet the last of the Bourbons against this sonorous background was quite an experience. Later, I used to meet him in Cannes, where he played *chemin de fer* for reasonably high stakes, and in England he often invited me to his house, Fulwell Park. Like the post-Napoleonic Orleans family, he chose to settle in Twickenham. In later exile, Manuel was walking the terrace at Monte Carlo when he noticed a man of considerable girth lifting his hat to him. The king stopped and asked: "Your appearance is familiar, sir; where have we met?" The other answered: "We have never met formally, sir, but I am the publican from Twickenham, where I keep The Crown." Ruefully, the ex-king replied: "That's more than I could do."

CUT TO – **Rupert** *dining alone one evening, with Gulbenkian on his dais dominating the room. The* **Manager** *comes to the table and* **Rupert** *looks up.*

MANAGER: Good evening, sir. You'll be pleased to know that Mr Orr-Lewis arrives tomorrow morning. I have just received a telegram from him asking me to advise you.

RUPERT: Thank you. It's about time, I must say. Is he on his boat?

MANAGER: That I could not say, sir. The telegram was minimal.

Orr-Lewis *appears at the door of the dining room, causing the manager to blink in surprise, and marches to* **Rupert's** *table.*

VOICE: At which, typically, Duncan himself appeared, a day early, and lost no time in pouncing on me.

ORR-LEWIS: Hello, old chap. Sorry to have been so long and to be behaving like a whirlwind now, but we're leaving on the *rapide* tomorrow evening for Madrid, Barcelona and Marseilles. *Volante* has sailed for Southampton. Tomorrow, before leaving here, we have an expedition that I'm sure will set you on fire as a writer.

RUPERT: Hello, Duncan. I'm at your mercy: you move so fast that I can only surrender.

Rupert *leaves the table and they go together to the bar to talk and take a nightcap.*

ORR-LEWIS *[as though giving a lesson]*: A consequence of this country's revolution was that many of the embalmed bodies of the former Portuguese royal family were dumped in the crypt of a small and ancient church outside Lisbon.

RUPERT *[not in the mood for a lesson]*: So they didn't all follow Manuel to Twickenham?

ORR-LEWIS: Don't make light of it, Rupe, or you might feel embarrassed tomorrow.

RUPERT: Tomorrow's going to be a big day. First, I'd like to know what has occupied you while I've been keeping this hotel in business at your expense, and then I'm to mingle with royal ghosts. So when I've finished this, I'm off to bed, if you don't mind, Duncan.

★ ★ ★ ★ ★

FADE TO – Next day. They drive into the hills outside Lisbon and find the small church of San Vicente. The **Sacristan** *emerges to meet them and* **Orr-Lewis** *slips him a wad of escudos, at which the old chap boggles before tucking it into the folds of his cassock, looking around as though to know whether he has been seen receiving it. The* **Sacristan** *leads them down a narrow, musty staircase to the crypt.*

VOICE: As our eyes became used to the light of three guttering candles, we saw around us a clutter of black wooden boxes, each with a glass lid, scattered in disarray as though carelessly discarded by a sodality of drunken undertakers.

Orr-Lewis *leans to* **Rupert's** *ear and whispers, bending over one of the coffins, tilting it for a better view.*

ORR-LEWIS: Take a look at this one.

*As **Rupert** lowers his candle, wax spatters the glass.*

RUPERT: Who is it? I'm afraid some wax has dropped on him, but it has made a pretty lacework pattern.

ORR-LEWIS: It is, or was, Carlos, Manuel's uncle, and, look, his decorations and medals, albeit tarnished, are still pinned to the uniform. God, this is history, Rupe.

From the puffed face Carlos's eyes protrude, seemingly agog.

RUPERT: True, Duncan, but don't you think he seems surprised to see us?

VOICE: I had never seen Carlos alive, but it was not surprising, considering that his body had been filled with several gallons of embalming fluid by injection with a six-inch hollow needle, that his overall expression should be one of startled discontent.

Orr-Lewis *moves on to other coffins, pulling and pushing them about wildly, peering down at them one after another.*

VOICE: Duncan had, as it were, tasted blood and was now widening the search. I sensed, rather than smelt, in a wave of nausea, the aromatic stench of oriental spices and long-forgotten drugs – the enemies of putrefaction.

Soon, **Orr-Lewis** *tires of the investigation and with a grunt indicates that they should leave the tomb. The three walk up and out to the fresh air.*

VOICE: It was beautiful to emerge into the lemon-coloured day with the city spread below, the houses tumbling grey, blue, white and pink down to the distant banks of the Tagus – itself a band of green, glittering in the sunshine.

Rupert *puts his arms round the* **Sacristan,** *who once more looks surprised and scans the vicinity to see whether he is being watched.*

VOICE: Elated, I embraced the old man who had unconsciously guided us through the corridors of death into the reality and glory of life.

The ancient car takes them back to the hotel. They are having a drink at the bar when an **American** *approaches them and peers at* **Rupert.**

AMERICAN: Did you ever live in Paris?

RUPERT: I think so.

Orr-Lewis *is amused by* **Rupert's** *reply, but the* **American** *is not.*

AMERICAN: Damn it, man, you must know.

RUPERT *[innocently]*: Is that the place with the *Mona Lisa* and the big tower like Blackpool?

AMERICAN *[menacingly]*: I've never been to Blackpool, but I had the apartment below yours in the rue des Eaux and I've been trying to catch up on my sleep ever since, you bastard.

Orr-Lewis *consults his watch.*

ORR-LEWIS: Well, unless you want to stay and console this gentleman for keeping him awake, we must move. There is less than an hour to catch our train.

★ ★ ★ ★ ★

CUT TO – The railway station. **Rupert** *and* **Orr-Lewis** *arrive running and board the rapide with minutes to spare. They supervise the disposal of their baggage and install themselves in adjoining compartments.*

VOICE: That night as I lay in my bunk and the train raced on, crashing over points and echoing the last notes of a tunnel as the bogies rattled and swung over steel-laced bridgeways, I could not rid myself of the cadaverous memory of the crypt. It was as though I were still inhaling the stench escaping from the coffins: lavender oil, Venetian turpentine and camomile mixed with the faint sigh of visceral gases. The Egyptians, masters of embalming, had striven to ensure the privacy of the tomb; what we had seen was a monstrous insult to the dignity of Man in death.

★ ★ ★ ★ ★

FADE TO – The train arriving in Marseilles next day. They pick up **Orr-Lewis's** *Bentley and drive to Paris, where they dine, and then on to the Hermitage at Le Touquet. They check in and the receptionist tells them the bags will be taken to their rooms. They face each other.*

RUPERT: Is it sleep?

ORR-LEWIS: It should be, but I'm much too tired.

RUPERT: I, too. Let's see whom we can find.

They stroll to the casino.

RUPERT: I have not been here since 1916, you know, when it was a hospital and I was one of the guests.

ORR-LEWIS: Yes, your wounds. Now it accepts only financial injuries, self-inflicted.

RUPERT [*dreamily, reminiscing*]: Then, of course, it was presided over by the Duchess of Westminster. *[Suddenly brightening, returning to the present]* Good lord, there's Billie Neilson

Neilson *spots* **Rupert**, *smiles broadly and walks to him. They shake hands.* **Rupert** *introduces him to* **Orr-Lewis** *and then turns his attention to* **Neilson**.

RUPERT: How long is it, Billie? Are you still making money faster than you lose it?

NEILSON: Doing my best, Rupe. You don't look bad after all these years – I can't think how many. Perhaps a glass of champagne will tell me. Would you and Duncan come to the table with me and bring some luck with you?

They follow **Neilson** *to the chemin de fer table, where* **Neilson** *puts a bundle of plaques into* **Rupert's** *hands.*

NEILSON: Play these for the party, Rupe. You were lucky here once against odds of another kind, so see what you can do.

Rupert *plays for an hour with* **Neilson's** *money, but over that time his face lengthens as plaque after plaque goes west until he has lost them all.*

VOICE: Alas, my luck was completely out. The cards were running against me and I successfully lost Billie's £500 within the hour. I resolved then never to play with another man's money, unless I had won it from him in the first place.

FADE TO – Next day, at the ferry terminal, where **Rupert** *sees* **Orr-Lewis** *off on the ferry to Boulogne. After it has left, he boards the train to Paris.*

VOICE: On impulse, I caught the train to Paris and then the night train to Rome – where I had carried my first bag as a temporary King's Messenger. I was reminded of that member of Father's staff who could scrawl graffiti in twenty different languages and who, like Henry Miller's fantastic friend, was unable to remember in what language he had first read *Alice in Wonderland*.

As the train speeds to Rome, **Rupert** *reflects on his destination.*

VOICE: This time it was not the Grand Hotel, the Excelsior, the Borghese Gardens or St John Lateran that was drawing me back to Rome. It was the little square into which I had wandered one day earlier that summer, scorched by the noonday sun, the heat-haze quivering over the motionless dust that penetrated every crack and crevice of the baked stones. No eddy disturbed the drowsy air. Unexpectedly I had walked into a pool of blue shadow under a sweetly resinous cypress, beside which was a little flower stall. Next to it, stretched on a rush mat, a girl lay fast asleep, and as I looked at her sleeping eyes, I felt an intruder. In the act of sleep itself, she had created a masterpiece. Without waking her, I slipped into her small brown hand a note sufficient to pay for all her flowers.

The train pulls into Rome station and **Rupert** *alights, works his way through the throng and takes a taxi to his hotel. Next day, he walks to the square. A sharp wind is blowing and the first autumn rains are pelting on to the glistening stones. He looks around and registers disappointment as it becomes clear that the flower stall is no longer there.*

VOICE: In my youthful conceit, I must have believed the universe was created for me alone and that time would stand still at my convenience. I was learning that things that do not happen can be as important in one's life as those that do.

Scene: the gravelled courtyard behind the Drexel villa, Pins Blancs. **Rupert** *is packing a small car to set forth on one of his local expeditions.*

VOICE: Back in the south of France with the Drexel family, I bought myself an Amilcar, which, like most French cars of the period, would submit to every kind of cruelty and neglect. All I needed was a car that would start and stop, climb and descend the cultivated terraced foothills of the *littoral* and the steep mountains of the hinterland.

Having stowed his picnic and writing utensils in the car, **Rupert** *gets into it and drives off. After witnessing his departure, the camera joins him in the car and views the scenery en route.*

VOICE: Every day, I set off – my luncheon basket stocked with *paté*, cheese, fresh rolls, fruit and wine, pens and paper. My journeys took me through the beautiful little villages of Provence and the Saracen towns of the Alpes Maritimes. Usually, I avoided the coastal resorts driving to Grasse, which slept in the sun on its ledge of the foothills, and on to the entrancing blue shadow that marked the Gorge de Loup. It was near here that H G Wells had built a villa, Loubidou, for his charming and talented friend Odette Keun. It was also here that D H Lawrence was later buried. My friend Frank Budgen, painter and author of that wonderful autobiography *Myselves when Young*, was in the neighbourhood at the time and, hearing that an English writer he did not know was about to be buried, went to the funeral out of solidarity. He said it was most depressing: a box dropped in a hole and earth shovelled over it, with not even a newspaperman to report the end of a genius. There were writers of all sorts along the coast. W J Locke lived at Les Acades on the Californie;

Baroness Orczy, whose son was at Harrow with me, in Monte Carlo; as did Phillips Oppenheim, the Ian Fleming of his day. On the Menton road lived Blasco Ibanez, author of *The Four Horsemen of the Apocalypse*. Rudolf Valentino, the ex-waiter film star, was part of the scene; so was Ronald Colman, another object of female adoration, but so short that his leading ladies had to be midgets. Michael Arlen was often in Cannes. One day, he told me he'd kicked around so long with other fellows' wives that he decided he'd like to have one of his own.

The Amilcar enters Sospel, its tall poplars casting so much shade over the town that it seems almost dark in the centre of it.

VOICE: Sometimes, my wanderings took me to the little town of Sospel, where I would stroll through the narrow lanes between tall houses and the people went about their business in everlasting twilight. I was always alone on my expeditions. An agreeable companion can add to the enjoyment, but to be alone sharpens perception and teaches one to examine everything with Proustian eyes.

★ ★ ★ ★ ★

FADE TO – A café table where **Rupert,** *having gestured towards his ears and mouth to indicate handicap, writes on a pad and a waiter stands beside him to receive what he has written.*

VOICE: People over their wine will sometimes clink glasses, because it is a human instinct to add sound where there is already taste and smell. Thus, I sometimes found it comforting to talk aloud to myself.

Rupert *gives the paper to the waiter, who studies it, nods and smiles in understanding and goes off to the kitchen. People who have been guardedly watching from nearby tables break into subdued, speculatory chatter.*

VOICE: But it could also be interesting in a cafe to listen to the comments of those around when I wrote my order down and passed it to the waiter in the manner of a man deaf and dumb. In the discussion that usually followed, I would often hear it said that it would be better to be blind than without speech or hearing.

Pan slowly from the café to the village street drowsing between the poplars, progressing through the town to the edge of it.

VOICE: For me, the real tragedy would be to lose the sense of smell. My memories would be dead if they were without those scents of childhood: fresh rolls and coffee on the morning air, hayfields at harvest time, the tang of manure, new milk and sweating horses, the sickly, stuffy smell of the village shop, the innocent perfume of Mother's gloves, the aroma of Havana tobacco seeping up to our bedrooms after dinner, the fragrance of the first of the mimosa, the cottony atmosphere and the unexpected whiff of machine-oil in the sewing-room, the pungency of the morning papers in the hall, piles of fresh lavender-scented linen, the spicy smells of the kitchen with the Sunday sirloin twisting and roasting on the spit, the linoleum in the servants' hall. These and the countless other smells that return with manhood to remind me of joys and sorrows; and moments of peaceful longing when the aroma of incense rises to the heavens in the dark cathedral; and the scent of the curly head beside me on the pillow creeps into my dreams. Yet nor would I want to forget the evil smells that sting the memory: of rancid mutton fat in a Caribbean port, a bug-ridden bed in Mexico, dirty clothes on dirty bodies in the Moscow Metro on a wet day, the stench of a vulture's entrails bubbling in a tropical sun. It has always seemed strange to me that Degas with his genius should have disliked smells of every description – even the sleepy garden perfumes of a summer's evening.

*Into the sunlight at the edge of the town walks a girl [**Mariette**]. As **Rupert** returns to his car, they meet. She is carrying a shoe in each hand and walks barefoot on the grass.*

VOICE: My solitude was not to last long. She appeared one afternoon out of the twilight streets of Sospel into the sunshine. She was walking between a row of green poplars and the blue shadows cast on the long white wall opposite where I had parked my car. It was as if I had entered a magnetic field. Her vibrations aroused in me an immediate and exquisite response; when I spoke, it seemed I had been waiting for her and she had expected me to be there.

Rupert *gives* **Mariette** *a friendly smile. She returns it and stops to talk to him.*

RUPERT: You live here?

MARIETTE: Yes, with my father and mother. We have not lived here long.

RUPERT: The town is pretty, as, if I may say so, you are yourself.

MARIETTE [*with slight curtsy*]: Thank you, Mister Englishman. Am I right?

RUPERT: Yes, I am English, but friends call me Rupert. And what do they call you, Miss Pretty?

MARIETTE: Usually by my name of Mariette – unless they are angry.

Rupert *laughs and she inspects him.*

MARIETTE: Are you staying here?

RUPERT: Not exactly. I am staying with friends on the coast, but I come up here because the scenery is beautiful and the air is pure. I bring food and wine with me, and a pen and paper with which to write. Will you share my picnic with me today?

MARIETTE: That would give me pleasure, Mr Rupert

RUPERT: Not Mister Rupert; just Rupert.

★ ★ ★ ★ ★

FADE TO – A spot to which they have driven in the woods outside the village, where **Rupert** *unpacks lunch. They sit down close together on the rug he spreads out and dine.*

★ ★ ★ ★ ★

FADE TO – A similar scene in another place (a day or two later). **Rupert** *scribbling on his pad, pausing now and then to think, she embroidering; both wordless.*

VOICE: She worked at home as an *embroideuse* employed by an *haute couturière* in Menton. She seldom visited the coast and knew about the ways of the international set only from what she read in magazines. At every opportunity, she would discard her shoes and walk without them. It was beautiful to watch her walk: she put the weight first on her heels rather than on her toes, so that there was a balance and dignity about her progress that I thought superb.

★ ★ ★ ★ ★

CUT TO – The parlour of **Mariette's** *house in Sostel. She, her parents and* **Rupert** *are taking afternoon tea.*

VOICE: The only cause of friction between us was that as our friendship grew, she became anxious about the money I was spending on her. Several times, she took me to meet her parents and I was conscious of a slight strain in the atmosphere. They were, I realised, anxious about her future.

Excusing himself, **Mariette's Father** *leaves the room and* **Mariette** *does likewise, leaving* **Rupert** *and her* **Mother** *behind. With a glance towards the door through which FATHER and daughter have departed, the* **Mother** *speaks quietly to* **Rupert***.*

MOTHER: I hope you are a good man.

RUPERT [*pausing thoughtfully*]: I try to be a kind man.

Father *and* **Mariette** *return and the tea party, now more subdued, runs its course.*

VOICE: I stopped visiting the parents because their sense of unease seemed to grow in proportion to the gifts I gave, but they never forbade her to meet me. I showed her aspects of life wholly new to her and it gave me the illusion that I, too, was seeing through her eyes. Each day, her awakening to new sights, sounds and smells was like the miraculous opening of a desert flower.

★ ★ ★ ★ ★

CUT TO – A glade where they are packing up after a picnic. They get into the car and drive back to Sostel, enter the Cafe de la Terrasse and take a glass of wine. As the glasses empty, the **Landlady**, *when they might otherwise rise and go, approaches them at just the moment to exert her will and gently leads them upstairs.*

VOICE: The *patronne* was one of those women – France's gift to civilisation: agreeable, understanding and alive with tender memories – who appear like the good fairy in the lives of young lovers when they are most in need of her.

They reach an upstairs room. The **Landlady** *dusts the oval mirror over the fireplace and turns back the counterpane on the bed.*

LANDLADY [*almost to herself*]: Now you can rest after your long drive.

The **Landlady** *leaves the room and soon* **Mariette** *starts to sing a Provençal love song in a voice low and husky, her brown eyes heavy with longing.* **Rupert** *studies her.*

VOICE: Her mouth, even in shadow, was clearly defined and on the

257

last note of the song, her lips remained sleepily parted in the shape of a lover's kiss. Thereafter there were always flowers in the room, the counterpane turned back and the little oval mirror polished. It became our home, where we lived a secret life within our own. She was no peaches-and-cream girl from England or America, but an earthy peasant with the sun and wine and the passionate south in her blood. In her company, the days passed gently, for she had her embroidery and I had my pens and paper. I was persuaded it was to please me that she worked in colours that set off her dark beauty. Our relationship was complete and during the short, sweet time we were together, it was as if we were living within a spell.

★ ★ ★ ★ ★

CUT TO – Cannes, approaching the Carlton hotel, parking and, leaving the car, entering the lobby and then the restaurant, she barefoot.

VOICE: One day, to please me, because she knew she had been a little bitchy the day before, she agreed to lunch at the Carlton in Cannes. Her clothes were charmingly unconventional for that dressy place; I was conscious of the men's admiring stares and the women's censure as they appraised her from the scarlet ribbon in her hair to the sun-bronzed feet on which she walked shoeless into the restaurant.

Mariette *appears oblivious of the stares, both bold and covert, that she attracts, and sits daintily at the table.*

MARIETTE: Didn't I do that beautifully?

RUPERT: You did indeed and I am not the only one who thinks so. I hope you will like the food.

Rupert *explains the menu, but effectively orders for her – an arrangement she graciously accepts.*

VOICE: As I watched her, I realised that here was the delightful embodiment of the phrase "sitting pretty".

Confronted with a variety of knives, forks and spoons, **Mariette** *gives* **Rupert** *secret, inquiring glances and finds her way through the etiquette. A* **Waiter,** *clearly smitten with her looks, hovers close and takes too long to serve them, which causes* **Rupert's** *face to darken.*

RUPERT *[to waiter]:* Why are you so slow? Have you had one too many?

Abashed, the **Waiter** *retreats to a more seemly distance from the table.* **Mariette** *eats tidily under* **Rupert's** *tacit guidance, but with the appetite of a hungry child. The self-possession she has maintained throughout the meal stays with her as they round off the meal with liqueurs and coffee and make their exit from the restaurant. In the car returning to Sospel, she presses close to* **Rupert.**

VOICE: On the way back in the car, she huddled up to me as though she had submitted to an ordeal she would not willingly undergo again. *[Pause]* The days passed, my book progressed and her work continued.

★ ★ ★ ★ ★

CUT TO – One morning, when he calls for her as usual, and with the lunch basket packed, they set off on another outing.

MARIETTE: I am glad you are going this way.

RUPERT: Why so, little gipsy?

MARIETTE: Because not many kilometres away is a place where I lived as a child and I would like to show it to you.

Hardly has she spoken than **Rupert** *slows the car and points to a place beside the road.*

RUPERT: I say, what a perfect spot to rest and lunch.

Rupert *turns the car off the road to a wood through which runs a stream, and where there is a distant view of the sea. But* **Mariette** *looks agitated.*

MARIETTE: No, not here, Rupert. Anywhere but here, please.

RUPERT *[startled but stubborn]*: Why, what's wrong?

MARIETTE *[fearful]*: I said, not here. This is not a place to be.

RUPERT: Oh, let us lunch here or we'll be driving around all day looking for somewhere.

The car stops and they get out, her eyes peering around apprehensively, **Rupert** *busying himself unpacking the basket. Some hours pass,* **Rupert** *writing,* **Mariette** *staying glum, not even doing her usual needlework.*

VOICE: I usually let her have her way, but this time I was adamant. She hardly spoke the whole afternoon. She was like a spoiled child. I became angry and left her to pack the basket while I went for a walk.

Rupert *leaves their site and heads into the wood, which looks beautiful silhouetted against a windy sunset. In the distance, he hears her cry, begging him to return.*

MARIETTE *[from a distance]*: Rupert, come back, please, please.

VOICE: There was anguish in her voice I had not heard before, but, paying no attention to her, I went on into the wood through a leafy passage.

Inside the wood, there is not a sound.

VOICE: I realised that there were no birds in the trees or creatures in the undergrowth.

Ahead of him on the path, **Rupert** *faces what looks like a broken swing, one rope holding the wooden seat just clear of the ground and the other hanging loose, its end frayed, from the branch of a tree. He touches the rope, but it crumbles into dust in his fingers. He stands motionless in the silence. Then he hears a strange sound, subterranean and gurgling, like water trying to escape. His legs squelch in the undergrowth, which becomes a swamp in which he is sinking. He tries to lift his feet, but they are caught in roots. The clearing in which he stood beside the swing expands into a circular space and, as the trees retreat, a cold, glassy surface forms, imprisoning him. When he tries to grasp the wooden seat of the swing, it nudges him like a gipsy begging. The frayed rope hanging loose snakes towards him over the glassy surface and winds around his neck like a noose.*

VOICE: I knew death had me by the throat, but at that moment, I heard my name, – at first whispered like a shiver of leaves through the trees, then louder until suddenly she was beside me, leading me with trembling hands down the tunnel of the path and out of the wood. I felt her brushing leaves off my clothes.

MARIETTE *[pale, shaking]*: You should never have gone into the wood. It is a bad place. You should never have gone into the wood.

VOICE: She took me to the car. I could now see her clearly and the surroundings came into everyday focus.

Rupert *helps her stow the basket and drives them slowly back through the dusk to the Café de la Terrasse. Inside,* **Mariette** *examines his face anxiously, orders a bottle of wine and pours him a glass. After sipping,* **Rupert** *speaks to her.*

RUPERT: You seem to have been right about that place. But what is it? Why?

MARIETTE: I prefer not to speak of it.

RUPERT: You cannot leave me with such questions and no answers.

Mariette *says nothing for a few minutes, then looks at him bleakly.* **Rupert** *is seated beneath the small oval mirror. She kneels beside him.*

MARIETTE *[sighing]*: Then, it is your turn to be right. *[Pause]* That place, long ago, was where two young lovers, a fisherman and his girl, used to meet. One day, the boy was lost at sea and the girl hanged herself with the swing rope at their trysting-place. I heard the story when I was small. The story is known throughout the district. The place is haunted. No one ever goes there.

Mariette *shudders and presses closer to his legs.* **Rupert** *leans over, cups her chin in his hand and tilts her face to look into it.*

RUPERT: Yet you did – for me.

VOICE: When I heard the story, a frigid breath passed through my hair. We never spoke of it again; nor did we drive again on that road. There followed days and nights of languid enchantment, but, at first bluntly, then sharply like pointed teeth, I felt the wolf of restlessness gnawing into me and the great longing to be on my way, warming my body with excitement and chilling my heart with remorse. How was she to know, much less understand, the roving spirit that even in those far-off days consumed me and was one day to destroy me. Sometimes, we would sit silently over our wine in the calm loneliness of each other's company under the cool, patched, faded awning, each dreaming a different dream until the little village street was blurred in smoky shadows.

★ ★ ★ ★ ★

FADE TO – An evening in their room. They are standing side by side, looking out on the deserted street. He turns and gently touches her lips with his. They see each other in the little oval mirror.

VOICE: I had the strange feeling that this might be the last time we were to look into the mirror together. She was gazing at me without surprise or sorrow. Unlike myself, she knew for certain it was the end.

Pins Blancs. As **Rupert** *walks down the hall, he pauses, as usual, to glance at the side table where mail is left. Louis* **Drexel** *passes as* **Rupert** *opens a letter and begins to read.*

DREXEL: In early this evening, Rupe?

RUPERT *[absently]*: Hello, Louis. Er, yes.

Drexel *stops and returns slowly to* **Rupert**.

DREXEL: You all right? You look like I feel when I get a tax demand.

RUPERT *[with half-hearted chuckle]*: Worse than that: I'm invited to London.

DREXEL: Is that so bad?

RUPERT: It's Father. His invitations are commands.

DREXEL: Filial love, I guess.

RUPERT: He thinks I'm wasting my time in bars and brothels instead of sweating over a book.

DREXEL: Then it's filial salvation. But you are sweating over a book, aren't you? – And over goodness knows what else.

Drexel *goes on his way, leaving* **Rupert** *to ponder.*

VOICE: I saw Mariette once more, but she had discerned something in the little oval mirror that I had not: the conflict between our love and my wanderlust. She made no effort to hold me and only smiled sadly when I swore I'd be back within days. She told me she would write to me in London that very night. Autumn had come and the shutters were going up along the coast. The casinos were closing and the leaves of the plane trees were scraping the pavements. I packed my bags, booked on the Blue Train and said farewells. In my heart, I knew a lovely chapter in my life had closed.

★ ★ ★ ★ ★

CUT TO – **Rupert's** *room at the Cavendish Hotel, London.*

VOICE: A few days later in London, at the Cavendish Hotel, I read a letter from Mariette. A marriage had been arranged for her with a prosperous wine merchant and she hoped she would make him a good wife. As I held her letter in my hand, I felt the future confronting me like an enemy. I was realising with bitterness that love has its statute of limitations and that in making one thing you are often destroying another, like the reed that gives forth its music only after it has been torn from the river.

Rupert *pours himself a whisky from the sideboard and swigs it. He sees his reflection in the room's large, oblong Victorian mirror and flings the empty glass at it. In place of his figure in the mirror appears the jagged design of a cross.*

★ ★ ★ ★ ★

CUT TO – *Next day, in the drawing room of the family's London house.* **Sir Henry** *is behind his desk,* **Rupert** *in an armchair.*

SIR HENRY: I know you're writing, Rupert, but, if you'll forgive my saying so, I don't think writing necessarily saves you from being at a loose end. I'm buying Eveleigh Nash and I'd like you to get back into it. Brian would like that, too. I don't think you gave it enough of a go before.

RUPERT [*lamely*]: Perhaps you're right, Father, and of course I'm grateful to you, but…

SIR HENRY: No buts, Rupert. I've given you a good run and it's time you put roots down. Otherwise, you'll keep washing about like driftwood. But there's something else, more immediate, that I'd like you to do – you and the twins.

Rupert becomes attentive, wide-eyed, chin jutting as though determined to understand what he might have to oppose.

SIR HENRY: As I think you know, for some time I've been intrigued by the story of Cecil Rhodes. I'd like you, Ambrose and Godfrey to share my interest in the heroism of his life and work, which, of course, was unfinished. I've booked you a suite on a German ship, the *Ubena*, for Cape Town. It's the last word in comfort, a floating Ritz-Carlton, so you will not experience the rigours of Cecil's first outward voyage at seventeen, but you will be my surrogates and you know I am not one for steerage.

RUPERT: Yes, Father. It's not quite what I had in mind and I don't think it's fair to equate writing with being at a loose end. It's the only end I have in view, so you can hardly call it loose. I prefer to think of it as single-minded and focused. But I admit there may be more than one means to it and following Rhodes' footsteps might well be one of them. So, thank you, Father, and I'll be glad to think it over.

SIR HENRY: The thinking-over has been done, Rupert. It is what you might call a *fait accompli* – a state of affairs to which Rhodes and those he dealt with were no strangers, as I hope you'll see for yourself. Your brothers look forward to your joining them.

Rupert opens his mouth to speak, but closes it wordlessly, realising he is cornered. After a pause, he speaks.

RUPERT: If I may say so, Father, a Ritz-Carlton is hardly the place for the knocks and smells a writer needs. So far, my seagoing career has been less pampered.

SIR HENRY: That was your affair. This time it is mine. You are my ambassador and I am not a banana republic. At Cape Town, I want you coming down the gangplank empty-handed, not going up it carrying your possessions in a rag on the end of a stick.

RUPERT [*mischievous*]: If all the arrangements have been made, Father, might I ask whether they include mink-lined sleeping bags for the *veldt*?

Sir Henry's *brow darkens and his eyes flash. Thinking he might have gone too far,* **Rupert** *seeks to placate his father by offering him a cigar.* **Sir Henry** *waves it away and takes one of his own.*
★ ★ ★ ★ ★

CUT TO – Cape Town, a month or so later: the suite in which **Rupert** *and his twin brothers,* **Godfrey** *and* **Ambrose**, *are staying at the Mount Nelson hotel. Garbed in lightweight tropical suits and pith helmets already on their heads, they recline with coffee after breakfast before going out.*

GODFREY [*drains the cup, puts it down, wipes his lips*]: Not bad; excellent, in fact.

AMBROSE: It's coffee country, so it should be.

RUPERT: They grow coffee to the north of here, chaps, by more than a thousand miles, but not in South Africa. If you make such blunders, I'll tell Father you don't know about Cecil Rhodes' roads.

AMBROSE: Don't be a pedant, Rupe. You know very well what I mean. If it is not a coffee country, it is a coffee continent, which is the same in principle. We are on the coffee side of the equator.

RUPERT: Well, let's agree that breakfast was good and the Mount Nelson buys its coffee at the right shop.

GODFREY: And why not? Father knows his ships and he knows his hotels. And his families. This hotel belongs to a hotel family that embraces the Galle-Face in Colombo, Raffles in Singapore, the Taj Mahal in Bombay and Shepheard's in Cairo.

RUPERT [*musingly*]: Father's stepping-stones.

AMBROSE: On his world treks.

RUPERT: I should not use the word "trek" too freely around here. It is a South African term and rather sacred.

GODFREY: Now that you mention it, words do seem to change meaning here, don't they? In the dining room last night, I called "waiter", you may remember, and although there were two or three blacks hanging about in white jackets, none of them took the slightest notice.

AMBROSE: They hopped to it, though, when that head-waiter fellow bellowed "boy".

GODFREY: Exactly.

RUPERT: It's a matter of practice, I suppose, but I find it hard to shout "boy" at a man old enough to be my father.

Rupert *stands and stretches, signalling that they are on their way, and the twins rise from their chairs. There is a knock on the door and when* **Godfrey***, who is nearest, opens it, they see a tall, thin black man [***Deuteronomy***] dressed in a robe and with a fez on his head.*

DEUTERONOMY: Good morning, genelmen. Ah's yo' guide, hired by Sir Henry to show you the what, the where and the how of Cape Town. Mah name is Deuteronomy, but you can call me Deut.

GODFREY: Good morning, Deuteronomy. These are my brothers, Mr Rupert and Mr Ambrose. Did Sir Henry pay you?

DEUTERONOMY: Yeah, he did, sah, thank you sah.

GODFREY: How much?

DEUTERONOMY: Twenty pounds, sah, English money.

GODFREY [*drawing notes from his wallet*]: Well, here's another twenty pounds. Our plans have changed, you see, Deuteronomy, and we're not staying in Cape Town long enough to enjoy your services, but thank you very much all the same. We shall tell Sir Henry you were punctual and helpful.

Deuteronomy *takes and pockets the money, looking rather surprised, bows deeply and retreats before there is a change of mind, muttering "thank-you genelmen" as he goes.* **Godfrey** *closes the door and faces the other two questioningly.*

RUPERT: Well done. Our schedule is too tight for a tour with Deuteronomy or anyone else from the Old Testament. As it is, we'll have to cut quite a few corners to complete Father's itinerary.

GODFREY: Do you think Father put Deuteronomy on it as an obstacle to test us, like a bunker on a golf course?

AMBROSE: He's quite up to it. Perhaps we'd have lost points in Father's game by keeping him on. What do you think, Rupe?

RUPERT: I'd say Deuteronomy was just another bubble, long since burst, in Father's enthusiasm for the project. Forget about him. Let us be guided instead by our old friend Rudyard Kipling. Ambrose, see whether you can raise the desk on the telephone and order a car to take us to Muizenburg. It is one of the places Rudyard loved most.

Hardly has **Ambrose** *put the phone down, than it rings with advice that the car is waiting for them.*

AMBROSE: Let's go, brethren.

★ ★ ★ ★ ★

CUT TO – In the car, headed for Muizenburg. Arrived at the beach, they get out and watch the Indian Ocean's long rolling combers unfurl, like a huge blue and white flag.

RUPERT: I'd like to try the surf, as Rudyard recommended, but I think it would make a fool of me.

GODFREY: That's no doubt what he intended. The poor man has not had much to laugh about for years.

They get back in the car and go on, telling the driver to pause on the Simonstown Road at a small cottage.

RUPERT: According to my information, this is where Rhodes completed the process of drinking himself into the grave. It is also the southernmost point of Africa, where God brought the Atlantic and Indian Oceans together – though not peacefully, since tides and winds fight here forever.

Together they build a cairn of stones, wedge a tree branch into it and look at each other to see who will donate a flag.

RUPERT: As your leader, I suppose I must make the sacrifice.

Rupert *strips off his shirt and ties it by the sleeves to the top of the tree-branch pole.*

GODFREY: I'm sure Turnbull and Asser would be proud to know their merchandise had brought a touch of civilisation to this extremity of the globe, pitting its silken tails against the fire of the sunset and the anger of the wind.

RUPERT: Well said, brother, but have we not paid enough tribute to Father's hero today? I vote we slink back to Cape Town and explore the work of urban pioneers. Ambrose, do your duty and get us home.

AMBROSE *[to the driver]*: About turn, driver: back to the Mount Nelson.

GODFREY: Where we can find our leader another shirt.

RUPERT: Just so.

★ ★ ★ ★ ★

CUT TO – **Rupert** *emerging from the hotel in his evening attire. Streetlamps throw lurid fans of light at each intersection of the narrow alleys, in which the darkness is speared now and then as doors open and music and voices escape into the night. Figures move silently here and there among the shadow and occasionally the whisper of women whose eyes gleam like cats' is heard.*

VOICE: That night, I trod the lower section of Cape Town amid pungent odours of stew and chilli. Magnificent African smells blew all about – the fumes of ship's tobacco, the reek of cheap perfume. Excitements from my seagoing days assailed me.

★ ★ ★ ★ ★

CUT TO – The respectability and elegance of the Mount Nelson, where whites sit over their after-dinner coffee playing bridge, discussing Rugby football and politics, comfortably insulated from the pulsing sensuality of Black Africa.

★ ★ ★ ★ ★

FADE TO – Later that night at the hotel, when the guests have retired to bedrooms or homes, leaving behind discarded newspapers and overflowing ashtrays. The old, black **Night Porter** *is the only person about as* **Rupert** *returns.*

VOICE: Hours later, I went back to the hotel – now empty but for stale cigar smoke, hothouse scents, spent newspapers and filled ashtrays. The old African night porter brewed me a pot of tea, which I drank to please him. I have always enjoyed the fellowship of those who work by night in the hushed halls and lounges of great hotels. The night porter is kindly, moves quietly and treads softly. He welcomes company, but knows discretion and performs works of mercy. At the Gloria in Rio, there was a night porter who on one occasion not only put me to bed and changed my cufflinks into a clean shirt, but thoughtfully laid a bottle of Alka Seltzer on my bedside table with one glass of pure water and another of its stronger brother.

★ ★ ★ ★ ★

CUT TO – A downtown street in Cape Town on another evening. **Rupert** *sauntering along it, slows, his nose quivers and he sniffs the air.*

RUPERT *[under his breath]*: Whether it's gin and freshly cut cucumber, I can't be entirely sure, but I can surely find out.

Rupert *turns into the doorway and goes to the bar. Drinking by himself nearby is a young man [***Tom***], who gives a friendly smile to* **Rupert** *and addresses him.*

TOM: You don't look like anyone I've ever seen before.

RUPERT *[laughing]*: I don't know whether that means I'm a stranger to you or a freak.

TOM: Please pardon me for my clumsiness. I don't think you're a regular, that's all, and if I may say so, you don't look much like a South African, but that's not against you. In fact, there are so many things wrong here that I'm sure you are better off being a foreigner.

RUPERT: For better or worse, that's what I am: English, but with an Irish mother. Nothing exotic, I'm afraid.

TOM: Your first time here?

RUPERT: Yes, and it's all rather breathtaking.

TOM: Been to the top of Table Mountain?

RUPERT: Not yet, but I've thought about it.

TOM: What holds you back? I'm Tom, by the way.

RUPERT: And I'm Rupert. Well, I don't like cable cars, and the alternative of hoofing it up there is pretty daunting. I'm rather an armchair adventurer, you see.

Tom *looks eager.*

TOM: I'll take you there in my private armchair, if you like. It has wings and a propeller.

RUPERT: Are you saying you're an aviator?

TOM *[looking at watch]*: Yes, with a Tiger Moth. And it's not too late to take a spin in it up there now, if you like.

RUPERT *[face lights up]*: I would very much. It would solve my twin fears of cable cars and exercise. And give me something to boast about.

They finish their drinks, go to his car outside and drive to his private airfield. **Rupert** *is strapped in and they taxi out and take off. After climbing up the side of the mountain and flying along within a few feet of the summit,* **Tom** *does a sharp turn that throws*

273

Rupert *heavily against the side of the cockpit, after which* **Tom** *flies out to sea. Below, one of the Union Castle ships, heading ocean-wards, drifts into* **Rupert's** *lens as he is trying to take a photograph. The plane nosedives and twists into a spiral.*

VOICE: Was I flying with a slightly drunk madman or a slightly mad drunk? Thoughts of death possessed me and I felt a kind of elation, because, I suppose, I am a death-snob. What matters to me is how and where it happens. I do not want to die in a ratepayers' office behind the Wigan town hall. Or shot dead in a sleazy joint in Panama City or killed by a bicycle on the Promenade des Anglais. A dear friend of mine, an exquisite of his generation, was killed by a runaway bus in Notting Hill Gate, where he was waiting for a number 31. Nothing could have been more wounding to his dignity: killed on the wrong side of the park, waiting for a bus on its devious route to some deplorable destination. Not much majesty in death for him.

The plane spirals down towards the ship, whose size grows at a rate that widens **Rupert's** *eyes with alarm. He nevertheless continues to reflect.*

VOICE: As we plunged down, I thought of Borodin dropping dead at a fancy dress ball – an end that would not have appealed to me. Another whose exit I did not envy was Herr Adlon, the kindly owner of Berlin's former leading hotel and the gentlest of men, killed by a drunken soldier who hit him on the head with a bottle from his own cellars. The friends of Gerard de Nerval, the eccentric French poet, were surprised when he hanged himself with his top hat on – until they realised it was his last gesture of contempt for a life and a society he had found little to his liking. My elation left me as I became giddily aware that we were no longer heading for our Mother, the sea, but for the deck of the vessel below. I had no wish to be spattered among the deckchairs. But he pulled out of the dive just before we hit and began to circle her at mast level.

Tom *gropes in the cockpit and pulls forth a bunch of flowers, large and costly. He* *throws it and in a flash of cellophane, it disappears down a funnel. Passengers on the deck look up in agitation, pointing, some women covering mouths with hands as they gasp.* **Tom** *leans out of the cockpit, waving, and motions* **Rupert** *to do the same. He keeps circling the ship dangerously until a long, huge blast from the ship's horn hints that captain and crew have had enough.*

★ ★ ★ ★ ★

CUT TO – Landing twenty minutes later on a tiny airfield in the Constantia district. **Tom** *gets out, helps* **Rupert** *out and opens a bottle of Nederburg wine.*

RUPERT *[Indignation fading]*: What on earth was all that about?

TOM: That's how I make my living. I wanted you to come particularly. You didn't know, but you were impersonating someone else – you were a sort of stand-in. No one can recognise who's who in a flying helmet. It's smart in these parts for people to say to their friends, "We'll fly over the ship, bunch you with flowers and wish you God-speed." I'm hired to do that but I've got to have someone else with me. The people who hire me are usually too frightened to come themselves. *[Laughing]* So everyone's happy. You've climbed your mountain without exertion, my client's friends have been farewelled and I've got my cheque.

They sing in unison.

TOM and RUPERT: So everyone's happy.

★ ★ ★ ★ ★

CUT TO – Night on the veldt. **Rupert** *lies awake in his sleeping bag under the stars, surrounded by sounds of life in the dark.*

VOICE: As darkness fell, the *veldt* came to life. Animals were on the move. The life-and-death struggle for existence had begun. A low wind had risen, carrying the smell of rotting wood. I was aware of a shape darker than the night, near and moving, and for a second I saw a pair of glittering emerald eyes. My ears detected the slither of reptiles going about their scaly business. A breathing silence, a scuffle, a short cough and an angry growl, the heavy breathing of animals locked in a death struggle. I smelled the stench of fear and heard the crunch and crack of bone and the rip of living flesh, followed by a lapping of tongues. Above in the trees was a rustling, a flapping, and against the white of the African moon, I saw the death-grey outline of vultures drowsily patient in their upper branches. I pulled the cape over my head because I had been warned that hyenas would take a running bite at a man's head, or anything that moves. Suddenly, with a chill that raced through my body from head to foot, I heard the roar of a distant lion and knew this at last was Africa. I was listening to the very heartbeat of the continent.

As dawn breaks, the silhouettes of animal heads appear through a veil of low-lying mist. From all directions, they cautiously approach the pan to drink: antelope, zebra, giraffe. Wild dogs splash in the water, scuffling and fighting.

VOICE: It was as though the animals silhouetted in the dawn were shrouded in white tulle. Each herd had a leader moving forward or waiting until he decided it was safe for all to advance. The wild dogs were the most vicious and formidable of the vermin; even lions would wait their turn at the waterholes until the brutes had moved on. By the time our camp was awake, I was ready to sleep, but the civilised smell of morning coffee was on the air, the sun had risen and the game had vanished.

★ ★ ★ ★ ★

FADE TO – Bright morning, the white **Hunter** *delivering coffee to* **Rupert**.

HUNTER: This will get you going, Mr Grayson. I see you had a visitor during the night.

RUPERT: I thought something was staring at me, but it didn't stay.

HUNTER: I doubt that you'd have noticed the visitor, I mean.

276

The HUNTER picks up a stick and points with it to marks on the ground.

HUNTER: You see this?

Rupert *looks to the ground near the end of the stick.*

RUPERT: Yes. A kind of ripple. Looks like my signature.

HUNTER: It goes right around you. Do you know what it is?

RUPERT: No.

HUNTER: The track of a homed viper, one of Africa's deadliest snakes. It was probably looking for a way into your sleeping bag to share the warmth, but I'm sure you would not have wanted it all for yourself.

Rupert's *hand trembles as he gives the empty cup to the* **Hunter.**

★ ★ ★ ★ ★

CUT TO – A day's walking and driving across the veldt, birds scattering in alarm whenever a gun is fired.

VOICE: The death bag numbered ten duck for the pot. Vermin for the sad human pleasure of killing tallied six hyena, three jackal and eight wild dogs. Later, at the Bulawayo Club, I gazed with respect at the old faded photographs of the bearded giants who had opened up Rhodesia. Had I been around then, I would have waited in Cape Town until they had built the railway.

★ ★ ★ ★ ★

CUT TO – Rhodes' grave in the wilderness of rock.

RUPERT [*to* **Hunter**]: I wonder why he chose this isolated place in which to be buried.

HUNTER: He is reputed to have said, Mr Grayson: "From here, a man has a view of the world."

RUPERT: Such a narrow world now. I suppose he knew instinctively that it was as far north as his dream would take him.

Rupert *reads the epitaph aloud.*

RUPERT: So these are Kipling's words:
"His immense and brooding spirit still
Shall quicken and control.
Living he was the land, and dead
His soul shall be her soul."

[Resignedly] Well, I can tell Father I made it.

VOICE: Thirty feet of African rock and earth had protected his body from the circling vultures and the prowling hyena. Only the worms had taken their toll. In the late afternoon, we set out for the Victoria Falls.
★ ★ ★ ★ ★
CUT TO – Approaching Victoria Falls.

RUPERT *[cocking head]*: What's that? The Falls. Are we so close?

HUNTER: Still twenty miles off; the wind is carrying the sound.
★ ★ ★ ★ ★
CUT TO – The Falls themselves, bursting on to the scene with their thunder.

VOICE: It is a spectacle I recommend to all who are not hydrophobic: a river the width of Oxford Circus to Marble Arch, a flood of molten silver moving inexorably to hurl itself over a sheer precipice into an unfathomed cauldron 400 feet below, its spray reaching a thousand feet into the African sky in a galaxy of rainbows and stars.

★ ★ ★ ★ ★

CUT TO – The bar at the Falls hotel. RUPERT, GODFREY and AMBROSE raise their glasses and drink to Livingstone and Rhodes – and Father.

St James's Street, London. **Rupert** *strolls towards the Carlton Club on a sunny but chilly day to meet his father,* **Sir Henry***. Nearing St James's Palace, he removes the pipe from his mouth and stuffs it in his overcoat pocket. Ahead is a sentry box, and no officer of the Brigade is supposed to smoke a pipe in the street. From the overcoat pocket, a trail of smoke begins to leak.* **Rupert** *falters at hearing an urgent Irish whisper [from* **Sentry***].*

SENTRY: You're on fire, sor.

Rupert *looks around, sees no one and realises the voice has come from a guardsman inside the sentry box.* **Rupert** *approaches him and the guardsman hisses like a ventriloquist from the corner of his mouth.*

SENTRY: Saw the smoke a way off, sor.

Rupert's *nose wrinkles and sniffs, and quickly he removes his overcoat, the smoke from which has by now caught up with and enveloped him. He sees how badly burnt it is and drops it in a nearby dustbin, where it continues to smoulder as he walks away.*

VOICE: Oddly enough, because of the chill in the air, I had been debating, while walking along, whether to get myself a heavier overcoat. Now, the question was decided for me.

★ ★ ★ ★ ★

CUT TO – *The Carlton Club, where* **Rupert** *joins his father,* **Sir Henry***.*

SIR HENRY: Where's your coat?

RUPERT: As a matter of fact, Father…

Sir Henry *interrupts.*

SIR HENRY: I know, playing the Spartan. Well, it's madness to go without a good overcoat in England at this time of year. You're not in Cannes now. You'd better call at Leslie & Roberts and order yourself a coat on my account. But, first things first: it's time for lunch.

★ ★ ★ ★ ★

FADE TO – The dining room, where **Rupert** *and* **Sir Henry** *face each other across a table for two.*

SIR HENRY [*ebullient*]: Had an odd experience recently. While you were spoiling yourself in France, I was selflessly serving the majesty of English law.

Sir Henry *breaks off a piece of bread roll and nibbles it, giving* **Rupert** *a chance to coax the story from him.*

RUPERT: How, Father?

SIR HENRY: For the first time in my life, and I shall not be sorry if it was the last, I was summoned on to a jury.

RUPERT [*turning up his nose*]: Hmph. Thankfully, it hasn't happened to me.

SIR HENRY: It was doubly bad because they appointed me foreman.

RUPERT: Do you mean doubly bad or half as bad, Father?

SIR HENRY: Doubly, because I made rather a fool of myself. Larceny was the charge and I was sure the prisoner was innocent, though all the other jurors thought otherwise. It took me more than an hour to win them over and hardly had I done so, than the clerk of the court appeared and told them their services were no longer required because the man had changed his plea to guilty and asked for ten other charges to be taken into consideration.

Rupert *thrusts out his long chin and drops his jaw to denote sympathy and gloom. Food and wine come, plates go.*

RUPERT: Perhaps, after that, Father, they won't trouble you for jury service again. I found in the army that ineptitude was as useful a defence against unwelcome duties as a gun was against the enemy.

Sir Henry *gives his son a look of disapproval and remains quiet.*

★ ★ ★ ★ ★

FADE TO – The smoking room, where **Rupert** *and* **Sir Henry** *are served with Cockburns '97 and Larranana Corona cigars.*

SIR HENRY: As you know, I have bought Eveleigh Nash, and it will continue under the imprint of Grayson & Grayson. Brian and I want you to be a talent scout. It will be a roving commission, almost a playboy's life, with ample expenses and time to do your own writing.

Rupert's *face brightens as* **Sir Henry** *talks.*

RUPERT: It's hard to say no to that, Father.

SIR HENRY: Quite so. Yet the setup is less than I should have liked.

RUPERT: Oh?

SIR HENRY: I had found just the place for us in the City, almost alongside St Paul's, but only the leasehold was for sale; which, of course, precluded alterations. So, I have settled for premises in Curzon Street. Not a bad position, given that it's the West End rather than the City, but some vandal had renovated it and I have called in Sir Albert Richardson, who is tops on Georgian, to restore it to original condition.

★ ★ ★ ★ ★

FADE TO – Grayson & Grayson's new premises in Curzon Street, with authentic porticoed front door and fanlight, the door itself old, black and glossy, with a brass knocker. A bow window, delicately carved and jewelled with Georgian glass, bulges into the street. Inside, paint and varnish have been stripped away to reveal pine panelling.

VOICE: Five friends were co-opted into the firm. I could not call it a business because publishing was then an occupation for gentlemen. Although my associates were diverse, two things they had in common: great charm and almost total ignorance of printing and selling books for profit. There was carefree Albert Monico, whose father owned a famous restaurant in Piccadilly when it was the hub of fashion rather than the haunt of hippies; Richard Hogg, descended from a companion of Shelley's youth; handsome Martin Wilson, son of the Edwardian *flaneur* Sir Matthew (Scatters) Wilson; David Tennant, known as "White" David to distinguish him from his cousin "Black" David; and Gerald Kearley, later Lord Devenport, who alone had acumen and took the business seriously. The unfortunate Mr Taylor, Father's secretary, acted as financial watchdog.

*PAN TO – **Rupert's** room in the new premises and his workplace; a Georgian table, which **Rupert** thumps lightly with his fist and tries to shake, testing it for sturdiness.*

VOICE: As soon as I had taken over my delightful Georgian table, so friendly and un-desk-like, I went in search of my old friend from Berlin days, Pat Kirwan.

*Flashback to **Kirwan** sitting at his table in the bleak Berlin bar, head down on arms.*

VOICE: This was no easy quest, since he might be in London, Berlin or Dublin. Someone had seen him here, someone there. As I walked in one door, it seemed he had just left by another. Pat had a remarkable flair for knowing what was going on in the underworld of talent striving for attention. I, myself, of course, had been away from London and the literary scene.

★ ★ ★ ★ ★

CUT TO – Cameos of **Rupert** on missions to the likeliest parts of London to find **Kirwan**: St John's Wood, Swiss Cottage, Camden Town, Kilburn. He is contemplating the heights of Primrose Hill when he is spotted by a **Man** he knows well enough to accept an invitation to lunch.

MAN: Rupert Grayson, isn't it? What are you doing here?

RUPERT: I mustn't tell you in case you have become a newspaper reporter.

MAN [with a snort]: Please let me give you lunch to show that I am not. I've a table permanently booked at the London Zoological Society.

RUPERT: Of course. I remember you're the animal man. That is to say, zoological authority. I have been out of town some time and my mode of expression has roughened. Please forgive me.

★ ★ ★ ★ ★

FADE TO – Outside the RZS's premises, where the two emerge after their lunch.

MAN: Since we've just fed ourselves, let me show you another species at luncheon: it is feeding time for the lions.

★ ★ ★ ★ ★

CUT TO – The pair standing outside a bleak cage watching the performance as the keeper throws what looks like the contents of a butcher's shop to the lions.

VOICE: The lunch had been so splendid that it would have been churlish

284

to refuse to visit the lions in what served as their den, though nothing depressed me more than the sight of such noble creatures pacing up and down in lifelong captivity within their horrible cages.

★ ★ ★ ★ ★

CUT TO – The monkey house, whose inmates of the commodious enclosures are jumping, skipping and swinging in ecstasy amid a cacophony of chattering and screeching.

VOICE: At the first chance, I slipped away and entered the more congenial atmosphere of the monkey house. Here, at least, was the sort of enjoyment seen in a school playground.

PAN TO – Far side of the monkey cage, zooming to the figure of a man who catches **Rupert's** *eye. He is large and stern, clad legally in black Homburg, black coat, striped trousers, carrying neatly rolled umbrella and The Times under one arm.*

VOICE: My eyes met those of a man on the far side of the bars. I recognised him as an eminent magistrate in whose house I had wined and dined. His whole bearing reflected a most sober approach to life, yet I was moved by the expression of happy concentration in his shrewd blue eyes as he watched the monkeys.

★ ★ ★ ★ ★

CUT TO – A monkey performing a double somersault in the line between them, causing the two men to look at each other.

VOICE: As the monkey landed between us, once more our eyes met and were transfixed. There was something unbecoming about our encounter, so I looked away. Yet, even with our eyes disengaged, our ears still shared the pandemonium and chattering from the little animals as they sprang about. It seemed that this ludicrous situation, staring at each other through the bars, would never end. It was as if one of us was in prison and the other visiting.

An ape comes between them to break the spell and **Rupert** *looks away, but when it scampers off, their eyes once more meet and are locked.* **Rupert** *summons all his will to drag his gaze away and hasten to the exit. Walking away, from a distance he looks back and sees the magistrate wipe his forehead with a handkerchief, like someone who has had an ordeal.*

VOICE: As I broke away and escaped into the London crowds, I wondered what this man with his vast knowledge of the law was up to, studying in such an uninhibited department of life. I could find no answer and hurried off to continue my search. I had heard a rumour that Pat had been seen in Earls Court.

FADE TO – Saloon bar of a pub in Earls Court Road. Wicker chairs, potted palms.

VOICE: It was said, in the years before it became part of the Australian outback, that if you went into any pub in the Earls Court Road and asked the barmaid whether the Major had been in yet, she would say, "Not yet, sir, but he's bound to be in later if you care to wait."

The **Barmaid** *approaches* **Rupert**, *who leans towards her and whispers.*

RUPERT: Has Mr Patrick Kirwan been in yet?

The **Barmaid** *smiles and softly replies.*

BARMAID: I don't think I know a gentleman of that name, sir.

Rupert *becomes aware of the* **Customer** *next to him at the bar, a ponderous man whose every movement seems the result of long deliberation. He wears a bowler hat and guards a briefcase before him on the bar. He raises his whisky glass and levels his eyes at* **Rupert** *over the rim. After some contemplation, he addresses* **Rupert**.

CUSTOMER: Excuse me, but I could not help overhearing your question.

RUPERT [*somewhat defiantly*]: I tried to make it discreet.

CUSTOMER: Even so, sir, don't you think it's best left to us?

VOICE: He didn't sound like the Russian secret service, but what was he – a bailiff, a writ-server? From what I had known of such people, they drank ale in the public bar, not whisky in the potted-palm department.

CUSTOMER: A false move now, just when I'm getting a lead, and he'll be off to God knows where. We don't want that, now, do we, sir?

VOICE: His boots were large. Was he a policeman?

RUPERT: We certainly don't.

CUSTOMER: He's what you'd call elusive.

RUPERT: You can say that again.

VOICE: I was beginning to feel like a partner in a cross-talk act devised by some Kafka of the music halls. What the devil was it all about?

CUSTOMER: You've no need to tell me who you are, sir. Your question over the bar told me at once. It's my job to put two and two together.

Rupert *nods agreement.*

CUSTOMER: I'm waiting here for my contact. He's another Mick – very cagey. I wouldn't like him to see you – might carry information back – so if you wouldn't mind…

RUPERT: You want me to go?

CUSTOMER [*nodding*]: Yes, it's best to leave it entirely to us. Most injured parties do.

Rupert makes a hasty and conspiratorial exit, stifling a laugh on his way to the public bar.

VOICE: Pat was in close hiding, sure enough, but not from the Russians. He was evading a private eye enlisted by a posse of cuckolded husbands, for one of whom I had been mistaken.

Through a hatch from the public bar, **Rupert** *is able to keep the private detective under surveillance. Soon, the "contact"* [**Mick**] *appears.*

VOICE: He was a "Mick", all right; all six feet of him: grey-haired, square-shouldered and unmistakably ex-guardsman.

Customer *entertains* **Mick** *lavishly, speaking earnestly to him, and, as he* [**Customer**] *leaves, presses money into* **Mick's** *palm. From the public bar,* **Rupert** *watches the sleuth walk down the street and vanish into the Underground.* **Rupert** *hurries to the saloon bar to confront* **Mick***.*

RUPERT: I think we might have met. Irish Guards?

MICK: Spot on. And perhaps we've met, but let me be lazy: remind me.

RUPERT: Grayson. My brother Tristram is Colonel of the Regiment.

Mick *grasps* **Rupert's** *hand and shakes it enthusiastically, at the same time roaring with laughter that causes heads to turn their way.*

MICK: Of course. Of course. The Grayson trademark is all over your face. But what a strange place to find you.

RUPERT: Yes, but we could both say that.

MICK: So what brings you here?

RUPERT: Perhaps you can help me. You must know Pat Kirwan. I am looking for him.

MICK: Indeed I do. My wife and I are caretakers of a house where for the time being Pat is lodging. Small world?

Rupert *looks* **Mick** *in the eye and laughs in wonderment.*

RUPERT: What on earth is he up to?

MICK: You should know better than to ask. The price of knowing Pat is not knowing him, if you know what I mean. At the moment, he is amusing himself with that clod who was here a few minutes ago. I am keeping an eye on the fellow for him. I am under orders to betray Mr Kirwan's whereabouts to him at our next meeting, but Pat has not yet decided whether the man should be given the address of a whorehouse in Paris or a dry-out for drunks in Tipperary.

They finish their drinks and **Mick** *puts his glass on the bar with a finality that says they should be on their way.*

MICK *[with a nod towards the door]*: Come.

★ ★ ★ ★ ★

CUT TO – Walking to the house through streets off Earls Court Road.

MICK: Pat's presence here is both the cause and the result of some confusion. The house is owned by the widow of an Anglo-Irish general, and the old lady, a little weak in the head, is engrossed in the affairs of an Irish loyalists' association founded to give comfort to the landlords of the

Ascendancy who left Ireland and their estates when the Irish gained independence. When Pat presented himself at the house looking for a bed, the old lady, on hearing his name, had deemed him to be one of the Kirwans of Castle Hackett, fleeing from Connaught revolutionaries – his horses and cattle maimed, his crops destroyed and his ancestral home in flames. She had insisted he be given refugee status, three pairs of bedsocks and the largest room in the house. I was thrown in as batman.

Rupert *considers* **Mick's** *tale as they complete the walk to the house.*

RUPERT: Pat is some gymnast, the way he keeps landing on his feet.

MICK *[ascending the stairs]*: I think you might find that this time he has landed on his back in bed.

They trudge up the stairs. **Mick** *knocks on and opens the door to the large room to see* **Kirwan,** *as predicted, in bed, though sitting up working on the book he is writing.* **Kirwan** *stares at* **Rupert,** *speechless.*

RUPERT: I must say I have never known anyone to spend so much time between the sheets, whether at work or at play, as you do, comrade. I am glad to see that on this occasion it is work.

KIRWAN: I must say that my retriever does bring home some strange odds and ends.

RUPERT: At least he didn't have to drag me to Dublin or Berlin. [Pause] How do you fare, anyway?

Kirwan *breaks into his favourite lament, "The Famine Song".*

KIRWAN: *Oh the praties they are small*
Over here, over here

Oh, the praties they are small
And we dug them in the fall
And we ate them coats and all
Full of fear, full of fear.

VOICE: His baritone must have surely reached and brought comfort to a thousand bed-sitter occupants bending over their gas rings. Even the ticket collectors under the great glacier of Earls Court Station, which I saw through the window, must have pricked up their ears with pleasure, for it was in the days before the onslaught of ghetto-blasters and jaded ears.

RUPERT: Pat's evocation of the starving fills me with inspiration: let us unto the Ritz, dear friends, where there is business to be done.

MICK: Please count me out, gentlemen. I'm on duty here.

CUT TO – **Kirwan** *and* **Rupert** *boarding a taxi and driving to the Ritz.*

VOICE: Wherever Pat put his lips to the glass, he also had his ear to the ground. I was soon moving in a world of poets and pimps, writers and publicans.

The Grayson & Grayson office as a going concern, shelves filled with books, filing cabinets, manuscripts piled up, typewriters clacking, secretaries taking letters.

VOICE: Despite our rather amateur status in publishing, under our logo, the Tudor Rose, we soon had a list of authors worth more than a second glance. It included Francois Mauriac, Algernon Blackwood, Liam O'Flaherty, Percy Wyndham Lewis, Ilya Ehrenbourg and Colette. Pat and I persuaded Frank Budgen, painter and friend of James Joyce, to write an account of their friendship in Switzerland. He did so under the title *James Joyce and the Making of Ulysses*. It was the first intimate report of the great Irish writer and his work at a time when *Ulysses* was still banned in England, America and, of course, Ireland.

★ ★ ★ ★ ★

FADE TO – **Joyce** *and* **Budgen** *in* **Rupert's** *office, the Irishman perusing* **Budgen's** *galley proofs. As* **Joyce** *leafs through them, the pile that has accumulated on his knees falls to the floor and* **Budgen** *obligingly bends and picks them up.*

JOYCE: Galley proofs remind one of the persons of the Trinity – get a good hold of one and you lose your grip on the others.

BUDGEN: An extravagant metaphor, but…

JOYCE: It's the Irish, Frank; we're an extravagant lot. And before I use up today's quota of hyperbole, let me say that I did not know you could write so well – it must be your association with me.

BUDGEN: You're beyond your quota now, James.

★ ★ ★ ★ ★

292

FADE TO – **Rupert** *in a reverie at his desk as the sun slopes in through the window, suggesting drowsiness and reflection. He gazes at the shelf opposite, on which are some of the titles that come to his mind.*

VOICE: We published *The Long Journey* by Johannes V Jensen, followed by his beautifully written historical novel *The Fall of the King*, which Pat Kirwan translated. Jensen later received the Nobel Prize for literature.

★ ★ ★ ★ ★

CUT TO – A mélange of scenes in bars, clubs and salons frequented by characters disreputable, clever and witty.

VOICE: Our plan was to drift about those bohemian circles where one was most likely to meet writers in search of a publisher, or one that was more sympathetic. It was in keeping with my way of life and pleasanter than standing on literary agents' doorsteps waiting for scraps from rich publishers' tables. The dog that runs around finds the bone, we believed. But it was as if we were in shadowy undergrowth of woods, shot with the occasional ray of sunshine and from which some paths led to fame and others to death. There were bestseller novelists who lived on the hilltops high above the dark forest. Many of them had staked territorial claims that they jealously guarded. Hugh Walpole was hugely popular, with the ambition to be the Grand Old Man of English letters, which he might have become had not Somerset Maugham ridiculed him in *Cakes and Ale.* They were old enemies, having quarrelled over a good-looking waiter in Florence. Then, there were the critics – some unofficially reading for publishers and officially being most helpful to them. They could be seen creeping to clandestine conferences with their masters. There were the men of letters, uncompromised but lean, lugging their review copies to the second-hand booksellers. Arnold Bennett in the *Evening Standard* could overnight create a bestseller once a week. *[Pause]*

There was little room for me in the galaxy, but in the space allocated to my writing, I had conceived a secret-service character called Gun Cotton, who was not without a faithful following. Yet Gun Cotton took his share of knocks. "There's one thing that puzzled me," said an acquaintance who had crossed the street to say he had read my latest book. "Please tell me," I asked him eagerly. "I can't understand why you ever wrote it," he replied. *[Pause]*

Brian had chosen a small team to read manuscripts. Its members were literate and alive. Only the occasional manuscript was sent to the retired university don or impoverished vicar in Cornwall. Percy Wyndham Lewis, author of that superb satirical work *The Apes of God*, was a difficult fish to play.

FADE TO – **Rupert's** *office. Brother* **Brian** *enters and sits in the armchair opposite* **Rupert's** *desk.* **Rupert** *looks up from the papers he is working on. His expression is uneasy.*

BRIAN: Well?

Rupert *looks at Brian, then away, gets up and walks to the window.*

RUPERT: I think we have hooked, but by no means landed, the man. I can't even classify him yet.

BRIAN: Do you need to?

RUPERT: I know his name is Percy Wyndham Lewis, that he is tall and dresses heavily in black both winter and summer, but whether he's highbrow, lowbrow or elsewhere on the American scale of intellectual value, I'm still damned if I know. He's so original that I have to start at the beginning to learn what he's made of. He has the mind of a machine and I'm sure he is as uncertain about me as I am about him.

BRIAN: But you don't know whether we get the book?

RUPERT: I hope we shall. But it's like asking whether I'm going to get past the friendly customs officer when my pockets are stuffed with diamonds. Not that you could call Lewis friendly. [Pause] Do you know how he described *Ulysses*?

BRIAN: Not until you tell me.

RUPERT: He called it "monumental diarrhoea". And he's Joyce's friend.
BRIAN: Yet you rate him super-intelligent?

RUPERT: He is certainly that. I'm not in his class at all, which is one of the problems.

BRIAN: Is he sick?

RUPERT: There's no laughter; just ice-cold brain – which nevertheless produced some heat with his piece on Hemingway entitled *The Dumb Ox*.

BRIAN: And gives him no hope for the human race.

RUPERT: Quite so. I went to his house, by the way.

Brian *looks expectantly at* **Rupert**.

RUPERT: The place was sealed, locked, padlocked, bolted and chained. There were packing cases for furniture and only an easel to represent civilisation. He left the room we were in and went to another. The sound I heard from it was of a man peeing into a tin can.

BRIAN: Perhaps he really is conventionally sick and his doctor wanted a specimen.

RUPERT: I noticed a peephole and squinted through.

BRIAN: And saw?

RUPERT: An eye peering through from the other side – the only time we have seen eye to eye.

BRIAN: He seems to keep his body wrapped as tightly as his thoughts.

RUPERT: His expression is not always easy to see beneath that great hat and behind the horn-rimmed glasses, but I think I detected a smile the other day.

BRIAN: There must be one somewhere. I understand Pound, Joyce, Eliot and Ford Madox Ford all credit him with an acute sense of humour.

RUPERT: Well, he's not granted me a glimpse of it yet.

★ ★ ★ ★ ★

FADE TO – New York's skyline, closing to a cellar-bar in that city.

VOICE: One evening, years later, I ran into Percy in New York. His hat was pulled down over his eyes even more than usual and with his voluminous garb, he resembled a Russian anarchist. We did the rounds together, for we seemed to belong to each other like the two sides of a coin. At one bar, we encountered an uncomfortably inquisitive clutch of young intellectuals.

*A **Young Man** sidles up to **Rupert**.*

YOUNG MAN: Who's your impressive-looking friend?

RUPERT: "Impressive" is right. He has edited and largely written a number of literary periodicals, and is the author, among other things, of *The Apes of God*, which I am proud to say my company in London published.

The **Young Man** *instantly turns from* **Rupert** *and confronts* **Lewis**.

YOUNG MAN [*in awe*]: *The Apes of God*. Then you must be Osbert Sitwell.

While **Lewis** *treats the youth to a look of disdain,* **Rupert** *slinks away.*

VOICE: I left the party in a hurry, hoping Percy would forget I had been there. In fact, I never saw him again. At the end, blindness imprisoned him in its darkness. "Pushed into an unlighted room," he wrote, "the door banged and locked forever, I shall have to light a lamp of aggressive voltage in my mind to keep at bay the night." [*Pause*] Yet it was not the only occasion in my publishing career when I had to retreat in shame.

★ ★ ★ ★ ★

CUT TO – Café Royal, London, the stylish coming and going.

VOICE: Bertie Hollander, a friend of my Riviera days, was a regular at the Café Royal. Although he bore the external signs of what the French tax collector would consider affluence, in fact Bertie was often hard up. During one of his lean periods, he rashly took a bet for £500 to walk from Paris to Nice. On the night of the 28th day, with only a few hours to go, he staggered, wrecked, into the Hotel Ruhl. Maurice Ruhl put him to bed and called the doctor, who, after examining him, recommended that he drink more red wine and take some exercise. Bertie was too weak to throw the *medico* into the street. [*Pause*] Bertie spoke perfect French, and I once saw him borrow a taxi-driver's cap and go into Maxim's, where he accosted an unsuspecting stranger, demanding, in the latest *argot*, an unpaid fare. Paul, the head waiter, was in on the joke and we were soon seated at the bewildered man's table with a magnum of champagne to placate him.

★ ★ ★ ★ ★

CUT TO – **Rupert's** *party in the Café Royal, drunk and noisy.*

VOICE: It might have been the memory of Bertie's prank that infected me one evening in the Café Royal. I had gone to the men's room…

★ ★ ★ ★ ★

CUT TO – The men's room, where **Rupert***, after stumbling about, half-tipsy, washing and drying his hands, rearranges his clothes, reversing his shirt collar and turning the waistcoat around so that its black satin lining comes to the fore.*

VOICE: …and suddenly decided, in a jaded and stupid moment, that it might quieten down the party I had just left if I returned in the guise of a clergyman. With the clerical-grey suit I was wearing, the transformation was complete.

Rupert *weaves his way back to the party, attracting stares that quickly become furtive glances.*

VOICE: On my way back to the *brasserie*, I became aware of eyes turning away from me and embarrassment displacing conviviality. Only when it was impossible to avoid my presence were glances, a mixture of guilt and respect, directed towards me – behaviour to which I was quite unused.

Rupert *proceeds from the awkwardness of other guests to the exuberance of his own circle, which, on spotting him, steps up its hilarity and drinks to his health with shouts of "Bung-ho, Bishop! Cheers, Curate! Prosit, Pope!" From beyond the immediate rowdy party come glances of all kinds, ranging from the sympathetic and pitying to the censorious and hostile.*

VOICE: It was my turn to be feel embarrassed. I no longer belonged to the world of my own group and was certainly disgracing some good man's calling. What was to have been a harmless joke, conceived on the spur of the moment amid the sterile porcelain of the men's room, had gone sour.

★ ★ ★ ★ ★

CUT TO – **Rupert** *slinking from the Café Royal into the street, hailing a taxi and boarding it.*

VOICE: Desperately ashamed, I slunk away like a scolded cur. I called a taxi and even the driver didn't fail to rub in my ignominy as he boomed in his most reverential tone: "Careful of the step, sir." *[Pause]* Despite the fascination of publishing, I had a dread of doing the same thing daily, meeting the same people and exchanging similar ideas on similar subjects. I was determined never to lose my interest in the inhuman daredevilry of life.

★ ★ ★ ★ ★

FADE TO – Paris, with a medley of scenes and accordion music as background to reminiscences.

VOICE: My escape hatch was beloved Paris, with its river, *quais* and thirty bridges. I spent most weekends there. Somehow or other, I had persuaded myself that I would never fall in love again. This must have been a sign of self-disgust, for I have always believed an intelligent man during a lifetime falls continuously in love, while realising that, but for variations in colour, race and creed, it is always with the same woman. I had loved Mariette so recently that now she was no more than a cat in my mind – a magical cat, of course – crouched in security, basking in the Provençal sun and warming herself at her husband's *grand bourgeois* fireside. She would be the best of all French wives, womanly and wise, offering tenderness and understanding, one foot in the *cuisine* and the other in the *chambre et coucher*. But remembrance is only another word for regret.

★ ★ ★ ★ ★

CUT TO – **Rupert** *walking from the Hotel Daunou to the rue Faubourg St Honore, where he enters a florist's shop divided by a transparent screen. Waiting to be served, he sees behind the screen a girl* [**Princess**] *arranging flowers into little posies. Unnoticed, he is able to watch her like an expert examining a canvas. The table lamp casts a glow on her face as she bends over the task. Her eyes are dark and almond-shaped, her nose is short and a little tilted, her cheekbones Slavonic. She wears a scarlet peasant blouse with full white sleeves and little red embroidered bands at her wrists. Her head bears the sort of black cap girls wear in Georgia; it is pushed back and almost falling off.*

VOICE: When you send flowers to a girl who works in a flower shop, it does not take long to get to know her or her family. I have always respected flowers as a means of establishing one's identity. Soon, she took me to her home.

★ ★ ★ ★ ★

CUT TO – **Rupert** *helping* **Princess** *from a carriage and up the steps of a rather splendid house, where he is introduced to her brothers, sisters and parents.*

VOICE: There were several of her family in the house, all princes and princesses. They ran a nightclub in Montmartre and, to do that successfully then, Russians, unless they were grand dukes, had at least to be princes. I was enchanted. I threw my garlands of affection and admiration at her feet. I took her riding in the Bois, we lunched at La Perouse, dined at the Tour d'Argent and did the simple ordinary things – a day on a *bateau mouche* on the Seine or an evening at the Bal Moulier, where James Joyce celebrated after he'd arranged for *Ulysses* to be privately printed by Sylvia Beach.

★ ★ ★ ★ ★

CUT TO – Moulin de la Galette, where **Rupert** *places her on the ballroom floor; to Notre Dame, where Henry of Navarre stood.*

VOICE: One day, I took her to the Moulin de la Galette, where Manet painted his famous picture, and made her sit where the girl in the centre of the canvas sat on the edge of the ballroom floor in her striped blue and white dress, with her little straw hat shading her laughing eyes. At Notre Dame, she stood with me before the altar where Henry IV as Henry of Navarre must have stood beside Marguerite de Valois, when, on the eve of the Massacre of Saint Bartholomew, they were married.

★ ★ ★ ★ ★

FADE TO – Small restaurant ("off Place de Terne") where impressionists used to meet. They walk streets Renoir had trod, sat where the drunken genius Utrillo and his mother had sat. On returning to the restaurant for lunch, they are greeted effusively by the **Patron**, *who puts on their table the bottle of chilled Montrachet that has been waiting.*

300

VOICE: Sitting there, her dark head outlined against the off-white wall, she looked at first like an unfinished portrait, but gradually the picture became complete. There was the colour of the light, and of the eyes and lips; a glint of teeth and steel cutlery, green salad, shining rolls, crisp and crusty; a golden wine and white table-cloth. I was no artist, though, and in the Valhalla where walk Renoir and Toulouse-Lautrec, both must have envied my luck. She was that wonderful character part invented by French women, *une petite amie* – a combination of love and companionship; perfection of person and perception of mind. Alas, though utterly irresistible, she was utterly unattainable.

★ ★ ★ ★ ★

CUT TO – **Patron** *as he approaches them.*

RUPERT *[to patron]*: I say, how do you keep your cheeses so perfect?

PATRON: I keep them under my mattress, *monsieur.*

Rupert *and guest laugh; she amused, he admiring.*

RUPERT *[leaning to her confidentially]*: This man should be commended.

PRINCESS: Of course, yes. You are right about the cheeses.

RUPERT: But not only for his cheeses or even for the entertaining way in which he guards their quality. Above all, such candour shows his respect for the truth.

VOICE: As an historic instance of honest purpose and uncomplicated simplicity, I told her the story about Ivan the Terrible ordering the Dutch Ambassador's hat to be nailed to his head because, although many yards distant, he had failed to remove it in Ivan's presence, and of another occasion at the theatre when the performance of the villain was so convincing that His Imperial Majesty had him beheaded when the curtain fell.

301

Princess *shakes her head, incredulous at such atrocities.*

VOICE: Although frustrated, I was living for my weekends in Paris. In fact, life started when Badger, the Pullman steward, brought me my first drink on Friday evening as the train slid out of Victoria Station. I was infatuated by this Russian girl, this creature of my own invention, linked in a relationship like that of an ill-starred brother and sister, each afraid of his love for the other. We wandered through the great salons of the Louvre and I held her hands for the first time when we read the love-words, steel-engraved, dedicated to an unknown Egyptian queen in 700 BC.

Princess *touches* **Rupert** *on the arm to gain his attention and make her words more compelling.*

PRINCESS: History must be filled with such wickedness, but do you think it is happening now, tonight, here, in Paris?

RUPERT: Of a sort, yes, but less cruel.

PRINCESS *[eagerly]*: Tell me about it.

RUPERT: Well, the champagne does not have far to travel, the brothels and streets are teeming with girls, wealthy old British and American men pay fortunes to finance orgies…

PRINCESS: Have you been to such an orgy?

RUPERT: Once or twice, but only as a spectator.

PRINCESS: Will you take me to one?

RUPERT: I'm sure you would not like it.

PRINCESS: But please let me find out. Please.

Princess's *face strains with pleading.* **Rupert's** *half-hearted shake of the head is of assent rather than denial. They leave the restaurant and take a carriage to a street where* **Rupert** *leads them down steps to a cellar. They take a table in a section for viewing rather than participating.*

VOICE: The party was comparatively mild. Unless you are prepared to enjoy yourself in a kind of team-spirit, it can be unappetising to eat a complete dinner, caviar to strawberries, laid out on the nether region of a recumbent girl without the aid of cutlery and only the curly locks of a little Arab boy through which to wipe greasy fingers. Silent, she never moved from my side. We remained spectators.

When he moves to leave, **Rupert** *has to break a spell into which* **Princess** *has fallen to coax her away. They climb the steps to the street and he hails a cab. Before* **Rupert** *can give the driver directions, to his surprise she instructs him to take them not to her home beyond the Place de la Concorde but to her flower shop in the Faubourg. No sooner has the cab stopped than she hurries from it, while* **Rupert** *pays the driver.*

VOICE: In the perfumed darkness of the shop, I sensed rather than saw a great impatience in all her movements.

★ ★ ★ ★ ★

CUT TO – Inside the shop, where **Princess**, *having thrown off her clothes in a frenzy of undressing, tears at* **Rupert's** *and strips him bare, all the while whispering lewdly in his ear, caressing, scratching, biting.*

VOICE: On the rough fur rug, I felt her nails tearing my flesh as though she were taking revenge by tooth and nail on all her father's Bolshevik enemies, heaving herself over the bounds of lust into a half-world beyond my understanding to depths where I could no longer follow.

Princess's *laughter is wild and mad as she attacks him with hands and mouth.*

VOICE: Her laughter was maniacal as we flailed around among the flowers, and her tears ran over my face and stung my throat where she had torn it. Though closer to me than ever before, she had never been further away.

Eventually, like an animal, **Princess** *licks* **Rupert's** *wounds with kisses and lies spent in his arms.* **Rupert** *lights a cigarette and forces it between her bloodstained teeth.*

VOICE: For a moment, she was still, like someone listening to the wind, then slowly her eyes came back to mine and I knew she had returned from wherever in that turmoil of the flesh she had been lost.

PRINCESS *[whispering]*: Take me home, my love.

Princess *scans the wreckage of glass and flowers as they leave the shop, her face mirroring its desolation, and shrugs.*

VOICE: I was like a man in a rudderless boat. I had no illusions about what had happened. As I walked down the hill under a starless sky, my thoughts passed uneasily over the evening. I had learned more about her than she ever intended me to know. I could not put the memory of her lovely eyes, dark and unseeing, out of my mind. Clouds covered Paris. There had been nothing to warn me of the full moon riding in the sky, white as her unsheathed teeth.

★ ★ ★ ★ ★

CUT TO – Next day, the shop of **Roberts**, *pharmacist, in the rue de la Paix.*

Roberts *cleans and dabs at* **Rupert's** *wounds, stands back and looks curiously at him.*

ROBERTS: You must keep a young wolf as a pet.

Rupert *does not reply.*

VOICE: For the rest of the weekend, she was quiet and pensive, attending only languidly to anything I said. I wondered what dark thoughts were going through her lovely head and I was afraid. We were like strangers in a hotel, together yet distant. During the time I had known her, she had been *gamine*, woman, sister, slut and *religieuse*. Her moods had been wild and wayward as gossamer – one moment joyous, the next tearful. On the weekends that followed, my thoughts were confused and uneasy. Was what had happened inevitable? Had she sensed its approach as a shepherd reads the moon and stars? Was she waiting, minute by minute, hour by hour, and night by night for the darkness to beckon her again? We could no longer talk about nothing and enjoy it. Now, I arranged to be with her only in company. To her dark eyes had come a shadow of disquiet and to her lovely face a slightly off-balance expression I had not noticed before. The slow-burning candle of my love was flickering. Once I missed seeing her for a fortnight, then a month, until all light had gone from our companionship. We met no more and so the shadow passed.

★ ★ ★ ★ ★

CUT TO – Paris in wartime some years later. **Rupert** *is walking in the Bois de Boulogne at night when the figure of a woman approaching the other way materialises into the* **Princess***. He pulls his hat down and collar up and passes her without being recognised.*

VOICE: I last saw her during the war in Paris, when my duties took me there. She was walking at nightfall, lingering and inviting the attention of strangers in uniform who haunted the Grande Lac in search of adventure. There must always be some magic spark remaining in the heart for anyone you have loved. There was in mine. But there was also a deadly fear when I saw that there was a full white moon reflected on the waters of the lake.

Sutton Park House, Surrey, **Lady Grayson's** *country home. Tour house and gardens.*

VOICE: The Edwardian world of my boyhood was gone, consumed by the fevers of the twenties, its death rattle only faintly heard as Hitler shrieked and ranted. But at Sutton Park House, my mother's country home, the remaining footmen still wore livery and the butler still ruled over the remnants of his staff.

★ ★ ★ ★ ★

CUT TO – Ravenspoint, where renovations are going on, with their clutter of bricks, sand, ladders and workmen. Patios, where elegant, happy family gatherings were held, have been torn into rubble for filling elsewhere.

VOICE: Our old family home, Ravenspoint, in Anglesey, once swarming with children, dependants and retainers, now too big and full of memories for an old and often lonely woman, was being turned into a hotel by some great consortium. Mother's marriage had broken up late in life when one would have thought any difficulties it contained had long since been surmounted. Mother, wise as she was, had been fairly tolerant of Father's amatory detours. When a friend of hers confided that she was praying to the Almighty to put an end to Father's infidelities, Mother told her she should pray not to God but to the Madonna, adding: "You know how these men stick together." Mother's way of dealing with a rival was to befriend her, especially when the interloper was occupying one of the many cottages on the estate. In this way, she defused, as it were, critical situations.

★ ★ ★ ★ ★

CUT TO – **Sir Henry's** *luxurious villa at San Remo: marble floors, lofty ceilings,*

306

tapestries, chandeliers, curtains of imperial purple framing windows looking across a splendid garden to the sea.

VOICE: In the end, though, defeat came from the most unexpected quarter. One of her greatest friends, whose greatest friend in turn was Princess Beatrice, second daughter of Queen Victoria, that supreme respecter of marital ties, vacated her cottage on the estate for a more commodious life in Father's villa at San Remo. Father, stout Protestant though he was, was always proud to present fronds from his palm trees to St Peter's in Rome for the papal blessing on Palm Sunday. He used to board the Blue Train at Victoria and arrive next morning in San Remo – the end of the run, where he could take his time; and where Turner would valet him, not forgetting to change at the frontier the scarlet rosette of the *Legion d'Honneur* for the scarlet and white of the Crown of Italy, of which order he was a *Commendatore*. But already the square, syphilitic figure of Mussolini was rising to hasten the end of Father's world.

★ ★ ★ ★ ★

CUT TO – Sutton Park House

VOICE: Mother, meanwhile, inhabited Sutton Park House, the dower house to Sutton Place, then owned by the Duke of Sutherland and later the home of Paul Getty. The house had been extended at intervals. The oldest wing dated from Henry VII's reign. A hundred yards away was the little Catholic Church where Henry VIII married Anne Boleyn. The vestments of the priest at the royal nuptials were worn by Mother's own chaplain at the Mass, where she prayed for the salvation of us all.

★ ★ ★ ★ ★

CUT TO – Views of the estate: pasture, cows, stream, bridge, water-meadows.

VOICE: The estate was split by a river curving like a sickle through smooth green pasture on which cattle grazed. Where the drive crossed the little bridge, the water overflowed the banks on to land growing rush and sedge and starred with forget-me-not. Plovers cried above the reeds and the evening sky was filled with pigeons flapping home to copses dotting the park.

★ ★ ★ ★ ★

CUT TO – The house, moving from outside to inside.

VOICE: It was a sprawling mansion of winding corridors on different levels and many rooms, all occupied at weekends when the family arrived with children, dogs, friends and friends of friends. Over it, Mother reigned supreme – restless and all-absorbed. On occasion, when argument ran high, she intervened, declaring forthrightly, "If anyone's going to decide the dispute, it is I, because I'm top dog in this house." Ernest Laing was still with us as her private secretary, trying to keep her finances in order, but no more successfully than his own.

★ ★ ★ ★ ★

CUT TO – **Lady Grayson's** *large London flat in Albert Hall Mansions.*

VOICE: Once a year, around Christmas, the whole family, young and old, would meet in Mother's huge London flat, whence, after much champagne and ginger beer, it would proceed in a hired London Transport bus on a tour of the metropolis.

CUT TO – **Brian** *as the bus tour's master of ceremonies, pointing out the highlights. The excursion ends at Olympia Fun Fair in Bertram Mills' Circus, whose swings and roundabouts, coconut shies and fortune-telling booths are soon swarming with* **Graysons**. *Tired out, the younger are later whisked home by their nannies, while the elders mumble about nightclubs.* **Brian** *and* **Rupert** *confer.*

RUPERT: Has the censor done the rounds?

BRIAN: Yes. The old gent is as dependable as night itself.

RUPERT: Good. It would be a shame to strike a discord at this stage. Mother's not all that happy, you know.

308

★ ★ ★ ★ ★

CUT TO – The pavement outside a club in Soho, where two cars disgorge the adult **Graysons**. *An ornately-clad negro rushes up to* **Lady Grayson** *and embraces her heartily.*

VOICE: Frisco, the celebrated coloured gentleman whose night-spots in London and Paris were not, in their unexpurgated state, for the delicately nurtured, always gave Mother a tremendous welcome and saw to it that no "ruderies" transpired in her presence. It was perhaps from such occasions that Father had taken flight, surveying all family proceedings contentedly from afar. Old lions don't mind a gambol with their progeny when they are adorable cubs, but keep well away once they are grown.

★ ★ ★ ★ ★

CUT TO – Sutton Park, in the grounds of which **Rupert's** *twin brothers,* **Godfrey** *and* **Ambrose**, *stand by a half-built aviary, conferring and pointing to aspects of the structure on which workmen are busy.*

VOICE: At Sutton Park, only the twins were now left with Mother. They spent their time designing and building a huge aviary that might have inspired Lord Snowdon's later effort.

★ ★ ★ ★ ★

CUT TO – Littlehampton harbour and its boats, zooming to one of them which belongs to **Rupert**.

VOICE: At this time, I had a sixty-foot motor yacht that I kept in a yard at Littlehampton, manned in my absence by my pet parrot. News reached me that he had died. He was found sprawled in the sand of the cage like the bright body of a stricken matador. This saddened me, because he was a good friend. I had nursed him from a tropical Brazilian port into an English winter; a transition made possible only by doping him with whisky at all hours of day and night, so that for most of the voyage home we both swayed and lurched, irrespective of the movements of the ship. We had become close friends, united in our drinking bouts. He had lived with me

309

and talked to me in drunken sailor language with perfect understanding. I would miss him. Alas, I had even less luck with peacocks.

★ ★ ★ ★ ★

CUT TO – **Rupert's** *arrival by sea at Tangier. Wearily, he makes his way from the turmoil of the dock to a hotel, and without unpacking goes straight to bed – though, not to sleep. Next to his bedroom a newly-installed lift keeps rattling and clunking, making sleep impossible. He gets up disgustedly and goes to the bar, where he sees an* **American Woman** *writer he once met and tells her of his plight. She hands him the key to her apartment.*

AMERICAN WOMAN: It so happens, Rupert dear, that I leave this very night for Paris and shall be away some time. This is the key to my apartment. Please use it as though it were yours. Here's the address.

The **American Woman** *delves in her bag and pulls out a pad on which she scribbles, tears off the sheet and hands it to* **Rupert**.

RUPERT *[ordering drinks]*: Thank you so much. I came here to escape trouble that was developing at home, but did not expect to run straight into the arms of an angel. Please accept, upfront, some liquid rent.

★ ★ ★ ★ ★

CUT TO – **Rupert's** *room, where he packs and leaves the hotel, pausing at reception to complain at having been put next to the noisy lift. He takes a cab to the American's apartment, with its tiled floor, yellow walls, shelves of paperbacks, record player and stacks of discs, clean sheets, gaily-striped Moroccan blankets.*

RUPERT *[murmuring to himself]*: Ah! Haven for the weary in a Vassar gal's authentic pad.

Rupert *unrolls the Bokhara prayer rug that is among his accoutrements, turns back the bed covers and sighs in anticipation. Naked, and with toothbrush in hand, he opens the door of the bathroom, to be greeted by a maniacal shriek.*

310

VOICE: My blood froze. The apartment was already occupied – by a couple of peacocks, man and wife. The cock and I immediately hated each other. His wife seemed indifferent.

As its fantail spreads, the male bird advances on **Rupert**, *whose left hand instinctively moves to shield his vulnerability, while his right fences with the toothbrush as he retreats back into the bedroom, the peacock following before he can close the door.*

VOICE: My adversary's tail spread enormously, scintillating and aquiver. Again he shrieked before advancing on me, neck outstretched and beak poised for the peck. Frontal nudity has its advantages in certain situations, but this was not one of them. It made me feel shrunken, while my predator seemed to have doubled in size. I was reminded of being caught by shellfire while squatting in latrines at the Front.

Rupert *hastily builds a barricade around the bed with boxes, suitcases, the sofa, books, and lies down, besieged until the charlady appears in the morning.*

VOICE: When the *Fatima*, or charlady, arrived to end the siege, I gathered, from my scraps of Arabic and her almost incomprehensible French, that the *mustapha*, or *concierge*, reared peacocks to sell to tourists. Knowing that *Madame* was off to Paris, and as he himself had business in Agadir, he had installed the peacocks in the empty flat. He would be gone several days and without his consent and help, it was impossible to evict them.

The charlady corrals the birds in the bathroom and shuts the door, while **Rupert** *dresses, packs, leaves the apartment and catches a cab back to the hotel. After words at reception, a porter takes him to a room away from the lift.*

VOICE: I slunk back to the hotel out of which I had flounced, begging to be reinstated. I had no strength left to look elsewhere. Absence seemed to have changed my luck, for I was given a room far from the lift. I fell on the bed and was almost asleep, when what sounded like distant thunder jerked me awake. Focusing on the sound, I identified it as the conversation of turtle doves. Angrily, I phoned for an explanation. The rooms about me, I was told, were occupied by a dove-act under *Signor* and *Signora* Columba, whose feathered accomplices billed and cooed through the days until in the evenings they fluttered to their cabaret appointment. Wearily, I accepted fate's verdict and caught a ship back to Europe and the domestic strife from which I had sought respite.

★ ★ ★ ★ ★

CUT TO – Sutton Park House, where **Rupert** *is greeted in the hall by* **Lady Grayson**. *They move into the drawing room and sit.*

RUPERT: Are the ornithologists still toiling on their avian folly, Mother?

LADY GRAYSON: Their interest in it seems to be waning in favour of another enthusiasm, the cinema. They've been dragging me from one movie to the next until I don't know whether I'm seeing *Beau Hur* or *Ben Geste*. Your brother-in-law, Dick Rawlinson, has also caught the bug; he's writing film scripts instead of plays.

RUPERT: More money, I imagine.

LADY GRAYSON: I don't know about that, but between them, all they seem to lure here are a stream of film directors and suchlike with Hungarian names, though they're actually all from Hollywood.

RUPERT: Well, Mother, it's the age of technological make-believe, so perhaps it's the same with the personalities.

LADY GRAYSON: One of them, Lothar Mendes, is charming enough to be a Hungarian, but he's from Hollywood just like the rest. I mention him because he seems to have become addicted to, of all things, English beer, and spends most of his time in the local pub. He pays a price, though: some of the yokels pester him like flies.

★ ★ ★ ★ ★

CUT TO – The local, the Cock Robin. **Rupert** *enters it after having been walked there from Sutton Park House by his twin brothers,* **Ambrose** *and* **Godfrey**. *The bar is an island. As* **Ambrose** *orders beers for the three,* **Godfrey** *nudges* **Rupert** *and mutters to him.*

GODFREY: Over there, opposite, is the quasi-Hungarian Mother mentioned, and attacking him is one of the flies, a garrulous gossip named Harry Mather, for which there is no known spray.

The three raise their glasses.

GODFREY, AMBROSE, RUPERT: Cheers.

They overhear the conversation opposite between Harry **Mather** *and Lother* **Mendes**.

MATHER: If it isn't a rude question to ask, sir, I hear you make these here cinnymattygraf pictures we sees.

MENDES: Why, yes, I do.

MATHER: I suppose you're married, sir, if it isn't a rude question.

MENDES: I am.

MATHER: Like them others, I suppose you've been married pretty arften.

MENDES: No, only once.

MATHER: Reckon there's a lot of money in this 'ere fillum business.

MENDES: Lots, and more every day.

MATHER: If it isn't a rude question, sir, you've made a bit in your time, eh?

MENDES: Just a bit.

MATHER: I'd like to ask, if it isn't a rude question, how much d'you reckon you make a week?

Mather *drinks his beer in his own time, places the tankard on the counter, rises to his feet and eyes* **Mather** *steadily.*

MENDES *[gently]*: And I'd like to ask, if it isn't a rude question, why you don't mind your own bloody business.

A roar of laughter goes up from the company and shouts of "Good for you, Yank"; after which, **Mather** *remains silent and thoughtful.*

★ ★ ★ ★ ★

CUT TO – Exterior of Claridges, panning to an office opposite it and following Pat **Kirwan** *inside. An imposing man [***Korda***], with thick mane of hair and heavy central-European accent, gestures* **Kirwan** *to take an armchair opposite his large desk and rolls a huge cigar towards him, pushing a lighter after it.*

VOICE: Pat Kirwan also contracted the cinema bug, but, as was usual with him, by mistake. He had received a mysterious message asking him to call on a Mr Alexander Korda, of whom he had never heard, at an office across the street from Claridges. He was received by a man with a lion's mane and a heavy mid-European accent

KORDA *[growling into the phone]*: Please get me Hollywood. I wish to speak to Marlene.

Korda *replaces the receiver and addresses* **Kirwan***.*

KORDA: Sorry for that; it don't stop.

Kirwan *exhales a cloud of smoke from the cigar.*

KORDA *[eagerly]*: You like it?

KIRWAN: Very much, thanks.

KORDA: My own leaf, grown on my own island in the Caribbean, you know. *[Pause]* I wish you to write a feelm about ze Indian Army for ze leetle boy Sabu.

KIRWAN: But I know nothing about films, Mr Korda.

KORDA: I know about feelms. You know about soldiers.

KIRWAN: Why do you think I know about soldiers?

KORDA: Because you have written about Mr Kipling and you know Mr Kipling. If you know Mr Kipling, then you know about soldiers.

★ ★ ★ ★ ★

FADE TO – **Rupert** *in his club. He receives a letter at the desk and retires to an armchair in the lounge to read it, frowning now and then and pausing, with a look around the room as though to confirm reality.*

VOICE: Despite the logic, Korda was right. Pat had been a youthful but serving soldier when the First World War broke out. Now, within days, he found himself on troopships to India, seaplanes to Egypt and participating in the "little wars" of the British Raj with hundreds of Lascar extras and "ze leetle boy Sabu" on the North-West Frontier. Under these and other influences, the twins also decided to write, direct and produce films. I myself was calmly going about my business as writer and literary scout, aloof from that frenetic world, when I received a message from Father,

315

who, despite having gone off with "that woman", was still by remote control running our various lives. Film studios in London were to be bought and equipped, and I was to take the twins to Hollywood to study the tricks of the film business. The infection was spreading.

★ ★ ★ ★ ★

CUT TO – On board the Maur. **Rupert** *and the* **Twins** *are taking cocktails in the first-class lounge and not looking thrilled about it.*

RUPERT: I do not want to seem ungrateful to Father, but do you not think first-class is a trifle less than exciting?

GODFREY: It does make for a deeper sleep.

Rupert *surveys the lounge and the twins do likewise. They are easily its youngest occupants.*

RUPERT *[glumly]*: That's more or less what I mean.

AMBROSE: Worse than the Athenaeum. Do you think they're waiting for the taxidermist?

RUPERT: If you ask me, he's been and gone.

GODFREY: I found myself straying into tourist-class last night and, by comparison, they might all have been sniffing oxygen. No one there looked more than thirty.

RUPERT: You mean years, I presume; for this lot, it's degrees Fahrenheit.

AMBROSE: And millions of pounds stroke dollars.

GODFREY: If you insist, which I think you are, why don't we take a look. I probably remember the way.

316

They get up and leave the lounge.

★ ★ ★ ★ ★

CUT TO – Tourist-class lounge. Many young people are laughing and drinking. As the three brothers sit at a table, a **Girl** *at the one next to them looks at* **Ambrose** *and smiles.*

GIRL: Slumming again?

AMBROSE: You don't look like a slum-dweller to me.

GIRL: But we don't get caviar.

AMBROSE: Then sue the shipping line. Surely no one sails without caviar?

A **Young Man** *with the* **Girl** *joins in.*

YOUNG MAN: I was told a curious thing recently about caviar: that it makes a lady fonder of a man than she would otherwise be. I wonder whether there's any truth in it.

RUPERT: Why not experiment? We'll try to help.

★ ★ ★ ★ ★

CUT TO – The **Graysons** *in their spacious first-class suite;* **Rupert** *conferring with the steward,* **Harris**. *The weather is wild, and* **Harris** *dances this way and that trying to keep upright. The others are sitting.*

RUPERT: We are picnicking with friends tomorrow, Harris, and shall need a supply of caviar.

HARRIS [*amused*]: I hope you won't be venturing too far into the country, sir; it's very damp hereabouts.

RUPERT: I'm sure you're right, but just bring the caviar – about mid-morning.

Harris *gives a little bow and, with a smile to match, withdraws awkwardly, thrown this way and that from the suite. The three relax, with difficulty pouring drinks before dressing for dinner.*

VOICE: Normally, the availability of caviar on transatlantic liners was not publicised. It was produced for only the few – not the moneyed few, but the devout, among whom I was quickly accorded a place. Happily, caviar was in abundance, since, strangely, few of the first-class passengers liked it.

★ ★ ★ ★ ★

CUT TO – Tourist-class lounge next day before lunch.

VOICE: In the morning, Harris brought us two large pots of caviar and we smuggled them to our tourist-class friends when they were taking late-morning drinks. The young man with the theory about caviar looked particularly pleased, even a trifle breathless, as he peeped at the caviar in the bag we had put it in so as not to advertise it. I thought he looked at the girl with an appetite for more than just food.

YOUNG MAN *[eyes raised to the deck above]*: How good to have friends in high places.

RUPERT: We hope you'll report well on it tomorrow.

★ ★ ★ ★ ★

CUT TO – New York skyline slowly enlarging as the ship approaches.

VOICE: We paused briefly in New York and in the company of old friends, who had acquired shady associations, were warmed by the breath of gangland without being burnt. We went on to California, where in Hollywood we rented a bungalow on the corner of La Cienega and Sunset

Boulevard. Had I possessed then the money the agent asked for its purchase, I would now own one of the most valuable sites in the world.

★ ★ ★ ★ ★

FADE TO – Los Angeles and Hollywood, corner of La Cienaga and Sunset Boulevard.

VOICE: Strangely, at that time in Hollywood, whose scandals had shocked the world, no marriage or divorce had taken place, for the good reason that there were no law courts there. And there was only one studio within its limits. Greta Garbo surprised me by saying: "I have never made a picture in Hollywood, nor have I ever lived in Hollywood. I have made all my pictures in Culver City and have always lived in Beverly Hills."

★ ★ ★ ★ ★

CUT TO – The 20th Century Fox lot, and roam its assortment of make-believe.

VOICE: On the 20th Century Fox lot, I stood in Piccadilly Circus, fed crumbs to the pigeons in Venice's Piazza del Marco, drank a coffee on the terrace of the old Shepherd's Hotel in Cairo, picked my way through the jungle to an African village and rode a rickshaw in Colombo. It was like living in a giant nursery of spoilt children, who were beautiful and eager and always dressing up. On a mountainside, there was a sign, HOLLYWOOD, in letters seventy-five feet high – and why not? – children like to read big letters. I dined with friends who poured vintage French wine into rabbit stew, ate melons and oranges that were cheaper than potatoes in London, and a film star next to me at a party remarked: "Not only has he broken my heart and wrecked my life, but he's ruined my entire evening!"

★ ★ ★ ★ ★

CUT TO – Glimpses of Hollywood's recreations and opulence: tennis, swimming, deep-sea fishing, luxury mansions and the security devices surrounding them, yachts, sports cars on super-highways…

San Pedro, the port for Los Angeles. A British destroyer, HMS Bounty, goes through

319

the routine of docking, eventually tying up and lowering a gangplank, down which walks David Niven.

VOICE: Soon, I ran into David Niven. I had first met him when he was a youth at Bembridge on the Isle of Wight. There, he already exercised the charm and amiability that were to make him an instant success in Hollywood. He arrived now not on the smart Chicago-Los Angeles express known as The Chief, but in a more Nivenesque manner down the gangplank of a British destroyer, *HMS Bounty*, on which he had hitched a lift to San Pedro.

Niven *is greeted by studio bigwigs and driven away in a Cadillac.*

VOICE: For Niven, it was a happy landing. There were at that time a number of British actors in Hollywood, including Aubrey Smith, the perfect army type with rank never below that of colonel; little Ronnie Coleman, who was perhaps too polished and perfect to be accepted with American enthusiasm into the extrovert film fold; Nigel Bruce, likeable and bumbling both on and off the set, but unfortunately "typed" by too much Dr Watson of Baker Street fame – though, without whom Basil Rathbone as Sherlock Holmes would have been as Hamlet without the ghost. Famous actors like George Arliss, Paul Muni and Charles Laughton formed an elite, surrounded by butlers who knew when to wear alpaca jackets and white ties. There were those who could tell the director which way the port decanter should circle the table, when to say "Your Ladyship" and when "My Lady", and other pompous customs from those more "gracious days". Michael Arlen once told me he enjoyed seeing one of his books on film because it usually gave him an idea for another.

In no time David was mixing his film directors and his girls as artfully as his drinks. The film producers were quick to realise this was what they had been waiting for: the personification, to the American mind, of the English Gentleman, who could bring champagne bubbles to the most insipid of stories and give them that almost indescribable thing known as quality. The producers soon learned that if the contract was right, so, as a matter of *noblesse oblige*, would be his performance. The scribes began to write-in parts for him.

★ ★ ★ ★ ★

CUT TO – The Hollywood Tennis Club. Under a striped umbrella at a table on a lawn beside the courts, which are busy, **Niven** *and* **Rupert** *are in conversation when another man [***Flynn***] joins them.*

NIVEN *[introducing them to each other]*: Errol Flynn, Rupert Grayson. That was timely, Errol, because I'm just going to make a fool of myself on the court. Rupert has been here long enough to know what the world is like inside out. You can tell him what it's like upside down.

RUPERT: Australian?

FLYNN: Yeah, but the upside-down joke is wearing thin. David can do better than that. He warms up in the evening.

NIVEN: No, evening is Errol's time, Rupert. Ask the ladies.

Niven *smiles and leaves the two together.*

RUPERT: Tell me, Errol, I'm still feeling my way around here: is there much work about for a writer?

FLYNN *[sour, blunt]*: I never talk business on Sundays, sport!

A close-up shows **Rupert's** *face drop as he is taken aback by the boorishness.*

★ ★ ★ ★ ★

FADE TO – A pier at Malibu, where a fishing boat is being prepared for sea. Provisions and tackle are loaded aboard and the crew seems composed entirely of pretty girls. **Niven** *is in charge.*

VOICE: At weekends we met David at Malibu, where he would be moored ready to set off for the day's fishing.

Niven *emerges from the cabin and gives a tankard of champagne to* **Rupert***.*

NIVEN: Take this, Rupert, before all the bubbles escape. You look a Dom Perignon man to me.

RUPERT: If not, it's nice to be mistaken for one. But how about your hard-working crew?

NIVEN: More hard-working than hard-bitten, I'd say. They're known as the Ship's Belles. Merle selects them.

Merle Oberon *with captain's cap on is farther along the deck.*

NIVEN: That's Merle over there doing nothing. She doesn't want to be known as Ship's Mate because it sounds too intimate, so we call her Number One. She comes to life when the fish start biting.

Rupert *downs the champagne and looks on approvingly as the loading is completed and the crew lolls on deck in the sun. The boat takes off and furrows its way out to sea.* **Niven** *disappears into the cabin and returns with more champagne for* **Rupert***.*

★ ★ ★ ★ ★

CUT TO – A few miles off the coast, which, seen from the deck, is almost below the horizon. The boat has stopped and is tossing about in the swell. Niven straps **Rupert** *into a chair and hands him a rod and line. Hardly is he installed than he and the rod start wrestling with each other.* **Niven** *returns to the cabin, but the rest of the crew watch* **Rupert's** *first encounter with deep-sea fishing.*

VOICE: The next thirty minutes were hell, because I realised from the time David left me, there was a fish on the end of my line.

★ ★ ★ ★ ★

CUT TO – **Rupert's** *reel whirring as the line runs fully out because he has forgotten to put on the drag. He and chair are pulled into the scuppers, at which some of the female crew put hands to mouths in alarm, thinking he might bounce from the scuppers over the gunwale into the sea.*

RUPERT *[looking alarmed himself]*: Help, David, help!

Through his confusion, **Rupert** *catches sight of the crew's faces peering at him amusedly. From the cabin comes* **Niven's** *voice. Farther along the deck, Merle calmly and expertly hoists another fish from sea to deck with a faint oriental smile. Niven shouts to* **Rupert.**

NIVEN: Carry on, old boy.

Rupert, *on his back, winds frantically at the spool, but too much line has gone out for him to haul the catch back alone, so several of the crew come to his help, and he soon sees, through the jumble of bronzed legs and arms, a large bonito arrives on the hook at the end of the line.* **Niven** *appears, a bottle of Dom Perignon in one hand and tankard in the other. With a twinkle in his eye,* **Niven** *looks down at the catch.*

NIVEN *[to* **Rupert***]*: I don't know what you think, old man, but I believe *bonito* make good live bait.

Niven *hands* **Rupert** *another tankard of champagne.*

NIVEN: One day you'll make a real catch, Rupert, but meanwhile there's nothing like keeping your hand in with the old Dom.

VOICE: Only then did I realise he'd extracted the largest of the live bait from the tank and hooked it on to my line. *[Pause]* David was unique in being able to arouse admiration without stirring up envy. He was always the strolling player *par excellence,* who played the music he liked at the time he liked for the money he liked. He little guessed that one day I would return to Los Angeles with more serious things on my mind and a consul at hand to sign for my diplomatic despatches.

Recede from the fishing scene to the shore for a visual review of **Rupert's** *Los Angeles activities.*

VOICE: So we played tennis at the Westside Club and danced at the Trocadero; fished off Malibu with Merle Oberon and David Niven, and lunched with the Temples. I played noughts and crosses with Shirley Temple, the little girl who earned £1000 a week even then. I shot pigeons with Clark Gable; and on one occasion, Ginger Rogers tapped out "Rupert" in Morse code with the smallest and loveliest feet in Hollywood. During dinner at Marion Davies' beach house in Santa Monica, William Randolph Hearst – the millionaire newspaper proprietor and Marion's protector, sponsor, lover and the original Citizen Kane – turned to Arthur Brisbane, one of his senior writers, who had been ribbing me about the un-funniness of *Punch*, and said: "Do you think, Arthur, that *the New Yorker* will still be amusing when it's as old as *Punch*? There were the occasional liquid evenings with Scott Fitzgerald, who in his slide towards the grave was being tended by Sheila Graham. After nine months in Hollywood, I had become friends with most of these fantastic creatures whom the world idolised while knowing nothing of them except for the "scandals" and "romances" concocted for publicity. I had seen them as human beings – children, it is true, but as children acting out their private fantasies and not the commercial celluloid dreams their masters and fans paid them for. I decided to make a film of them as I knew them, with their hair down. Without realising it, I was on my way to becoming the first candid cameraman. Some occasions, however, were amenable to only the camera of the mind.

★ ★ ★ ★ ★

CUT TO – **Rupert** *driving his car at night in a Hollywood canyon. It is dark and rainy. In the beam of the headlights, a girl (***Maria***) stands on the road, erect as a guardsman and saluting like one.*

324

VOICE: At that time, all roads for lovely girls led to Hollywood, unaware that they were venturing into the greatest rip-off of all time. Between visits to couch-upholstered agencies, the would-be stars ranged the drug stores by day and the bars by night, hoping to be spotted by a casting director, agent, scout or anyone, just anyone, with a studio contact. Gradually, they learned that Hollywood was no more than a concrete jungle of wolves. Most of the girls were beautiful and still young enough to believe in miracles. Disillusionment came with the dawn. Too ashamed to go home, desperate for dollars, they settled for jobs porno-soft, then porno-hard, until they came to walking the streets and finally haunting the canyons where the rich lived.

Rupert *stops the car and opens the door.* **Maria** *gets in.*

VOICE: This little one slips into the seat beside me like a small-town girl whose date is on time.

MARIA: Ciggie.

Rupert *flicks his lighter for her cigarette and it momentarily illuminates her face.*

VOICE: In the flash of the lighter, I saw her the way painters and writers see people for the first time. I noticed that her skin was porcelain, like a child's, and a crescent of lowered lashes. She smelled of the open, clean and fresh, if a bit rainy.

Maria *sheds her dripping raincoat. She is wearing jeans, a brown-and-white-check shirt and scarlet scarf. She turns suddenly to* **Rupert** *and speaks in the phoniest vaudeville English.*

MARIA: Drive on, James, and don't spare the horses.

Rupert *looks surprised.*

VOICE: I was at a loss for words, like the actor at rehearsal who does not know his lines.

RUPERT: Very good, m'lady.

MARIA [amused]: That's better, my man. Go straight! Bear left! Turn right at the intersection! Now, stop! I said STOP!

Rupert brakes as hard as he dare on the wet surface, outside a sleazy hotel in downtown L.A. Without a word, **Maria** gets out and goes in while **Rupert** parks the car and returns to the hotel.

VOICE: I was still young enough or foolish enough to be unable to resist the unknown. But she was known here all right – as the look on the night porter's face told me.

The **Night Porter** leads **Rupert** to the interior of the hotel and flings open the door of a jet-black room.

VOICE: I sensed her presence; she was in that room.

RUPERT: What about a little light on the scene.

MARIA [voice low, husky]: I prefer the dark. It's warm and friendly, and you're a big boy now.

Rupert switches the light quickly on and off.

VOICE: I've never been smart enough to cheat anyone, but I had to know what I was letting myself in for, and now she knew I knew she was blind. She felt for my hand and whispered words of endearment. I felt the nearness of bedclothes. She undressed me with all the tenderness of a mother putting her little child to bed.

In the blackness of the room are heard her sounds of undressing.

VOICE: As I lay back looking into the darkness, naked, defenceless and a little uneasy, I listened to her undressing. She was unknotting that scarlet scarf, untying the bow in her hair and shaking out her ponytail, kicking off her *espadrilles* and lowering her jeans.

★ ★ ★ ★ ★

*CUT TO – A street scene in a poor Mexican town, kids playing in the dust. From an adobe house comes a young girl of about fourteen [**Maria**] tapping with a white stick. She is accompanied by a younger boy, her **Brother**, whose arm she touches now and then.*

★ ★ ★ ★ ★

*CUT TO – **Maria's** arrival at and progress through the border point, where she seems known and is allowed through without hindrance. Her lone progress on US soil, helped by the stick, is followed until a truck picks her up and shrinks into the distance.*

VOICE: There was the snap of elastic and something slithery and silken was thrown on the bed-rail. She knew where everything was. A door opened and closed. There was the unmistakable swirl of water in a *bidet*. A moment later, she was beside me, skin cool, with gentle fingertips and lips that traced the shape of my face. Loving and exploring, she was like a musician stroking a cherished instrument. There followed what even the American major writers were running short of words to describe, but because of her butterfly movements, there was a tenderness and a whispering closeness. Her loving was akin to the petals of a flower opening on its stem. Then came that exquisite pool of silence sweeter than a sigh and described by the Romans' *homo post coitus est* – surely not unlike the grieving platform after the train has left, or the deserted runway after the aircraft has taken off. There is only a void in the eye of a hurricane.

★ ★ ★ ★ ★

*CUT TO – Dawn as **Maria** approaches the border going south, and again crossing*

327

it unchallenged. Dissolve to her arrival home and giving her mother, who kisses her, a small handful of dollars.

VOICE: We talked deep into the night as strangers will when their bodies and their lives have met. The curtains of the confessional were drawn; there was a baring of the soul. I had christened her Maria, because her lips on mine from the first had shaped the name, and I had learned that half the art of writing is the art of listening. Here was not the old whore's story learned from her mother. There was no unhappy childhood or drunken father, no seduction or betrayal. Nor did she rant about her merciless God. She had been born blind and lived the way God had decreed, with her body flexible rather than on her knees in prayer. The rest of the family lived south of the Rio Grande, where she had first learned the ancient trade at one of the Gulf ports. Her parents feared for her, but she never failed to return safe in the slate-grey dawn and with a roll of foreign currency.

MARIA: I'll tell you something, mister, to make you laugh. Men are suspicious, but they rarely cheat blind whores.

VOICE: Soon, she asks me the question: whom do I know in the studios? Someone who knows someone. Anyone will do. I hear things I would sooner forget. This little dropout really believes that one day she could be the world's sweetheart. Secrets whispered into my ear fill my heart with pity and despair, for I know she is drawing me into the dark net of her life, a relationship too close for a casual encounter, and because I know that those who live by the sword of youth and beauty will die by it. I am with someone I love and someone who loves me. My heart is filled with despair. As I hold her in the darkness, I wonder how she can deaden her sensitivity to summon the courage to live the life she is leading, accepting in her own darkness and loneliness the stranger's embrace – rich man, poor man, beggar-man, thief, brutal, drunken, or merely willing, like me, to pay for her services.

★ ★ ★ ★ ★

CUT TO – The adobe house of her family, where **Maria** *undresses and gets into bed to sleep, her mother at the back grappling with the washing she takes in.*

VOICE: My day was roughly divided, like that of most mankind, between daybreak, noon and night, with meals that intervene, but hers was all night-time without the dawn ahead, and nothing but darkness daggered with dangerous encounters. No one listened for the sound of her footsteps or her key in the lock. If this little expendable was unafraid of eternal darkness, I should never be afraid of death. Life, I have long realised, is only the overture to death, the rehearsal of a vast orchestra. When I no longer hear the little melody on the flute I have learned to love, persistently threading its way through the cacophony, I will know I am in the presence of the dark stranger I no longer fear, garbed in black and standing on the threshold of the tomb beside the dying lilac trees, graceful, ingratiating and beckoning. As I drift through my dreams into the half-world between waking and sleeping, I am conscious of caressing hands and a perfumed head lying beside me on the pillow.

★ ★ ★ ★ ★

CUT TO – The hotel bedroom dimly illuminated by the first light of dawn filtering through the shutters. **Rupert** *steals quietly from bed and stuffs a wad of bills into an old envelope with his name on it. Sun-stripes through the Venetian blinds criss-cross the bed as he bends to kiss her.*

VOICE: As I kissed her nun-like eyes, I saw small beads of perspiration making diamonds on her upper lip. She raised the hands that were her eyes and for the last time I felt her fluttering fingers trace my face. Sensing my thoughts, she whispered.

MARIA: Don't worry about me. My footsteps will always make their own path.

VOICE: As I looked back into the shabby little room, she was lying with one knee raised in a gesture of childish innocence.

329

★ ★ ★ ★ ★

CUT TO – The Trocadero Bar, that evening. **Rupert** *talks to bartender* **Joe**.

RUPERT: Joe, you know Hollywood and everyone in it, and most times what they're up to…

★ ★ ★ ★ ★

CUT TO – **Joe**, *cutting* **Rupert** *short*.

JOE: Sure I know Hollywood and everyone in it; and maybe I even know a little tramp called Maria. But before you ask any favours, mister… sir… in all this crazy dump, there's no director that dumb he'd cast a blind girl to play a blind girl.

VOICE: That was that, so I pushed my glass for Joe to do the necessary. After all, it was only one more drink for the lonely sad road.

★ ★ ★ ★ ★

CUT TO – **Rupert's** *office in his Hollywood bungalow. He is behind the desk and in an armchair is a Swedish cameraman, Niels* **Larssen**.

LARSSEN: From what you said on the phone, Mr Grayson, you're proposing something quite daring. Cameras around Hollywood can make people more nervous than guns. Point one at the wrong person and you're in trouble.

RUPERT: I know, and at first I thought it could not be done, since all the contracts forbid actors to be seen by a lens not owned by the studio. But I did the rounds and, rather to my surprise, I have secured the dispensations I need. Fox is even letting me film during shooting.

LARSSEN: You must thank the Heavenly Father for having been born English. The English are a protected species here. Look how many of them do nothing but collect a thousand bucks a week for supposedly conferring tone on a cultural slum? Don't tell your chums back home or there'll be another gold rush.

330

RUPERT: Be that as it may, Niels; you're available?

LARSSEN: I am. Say when.

★ ★ ★ ★ ★

CUT TO – **Larssen** *under* **Rupert's** *direction moving from set to party to drawing room, training the camera on top-priced stars, trying to suppress their glee when they capture moments of embarrassment or ill-temper.* **Krock,** *a scriptwriter, sidles up to* **Rupert** *by a swimming pool as he and* **Larssen,** *alert as usual for material, take a drink.*

KROCK: Live and let live is my motto, Rupe, and I might say that's a pretty rare sentiment in this paradise that looks so cute until you poke about in it. But a dicky bird tells me vipers might be stirring.

RUPERT: Was your dicky bird any more explicit than that?

KROCK: It seems that some of the studios held a secret meeting the other day and you were on the agenda. Not just on it, but heading it.

RUPERT: Did your dicky bird read the minutes of the meeting?

KROCK: Enough to know you will not be allowed to leave California with your negative. Watch it, Rupe.

With which, smiling ruefully, **Krock** *drifts away and* **Rupert,** *with a lift of his eyebrows, catches* **Larssen's** *attention as he speaks to someone nearby.* **Larssen** *unhurriedly joins* **Rupert.**

LARSSEN: You been talking your way into the scriptwriting business?

RUPERT: Listening, mainly, and I didn't much like what I heard.

LARSSEN: How come?

RUPERT: Krock thinks there's a move to block our material. The studios have decided they don't, after all, want us to do what we're doing.

LARSSEN: I thought they'd agreed.

RUPERT: So did I. But Krock says they'll stop our negative from going commercial.

LARSSEN: Then we might as well give up. Hiding the negative in your bungalow is no good. If they want it, they'll break in and take it. You couldn't even trust it in a bank that's got anything to do with a studio. We need influence. Think, Rupe.

Rupert's *chin goes down on his chest as he stares at the poolside tiles and ponders. He looks up at* **Larssen** *after a time with a shake of the head.*

RUPERT: Letters of introduction seem all very fine when you consider the names: Sir Phillip Sassoon to Mary Pickford; the Duke of Sutherland to Charlie Chaplin. And so on. But what are they worth against the monsters that run this industry? I don't think even God could beat them.

LARSSEN: Do you have a letter from God?

RUPERT: Not quite, but I've got one from his representative in our parish at home, Father Breen, to his brother Joe, whoever he is.

While **Rupert** *continues to look gloomy,* **Larssen's** *face lights up.*

LARSSEN: Breen, did you say?

RUPERT: Yes. B-r-e-e-n. Does it mean anything to you?

LARSSEN: It sure does. Joe Breen means more around here than the Pope. Do you know the Hays Office?

RUPERT: Something to do with censorship?

LARSSEN: Everything to do with censorship. If a film doesn't get the Hays Office say-so, it might as well go into the trashcan. And Joe Breen is the Hays Office, the boss. Let's hope you have that letter.

Rupert *and* **Larssen** *leave the poolside and make for* **Rupert's** *bungalow, where he finds the letter and kisses it.*

RUPERT: God does move in mysterious ways.

VOICE: Once the word went out that I was not to be inconvenienced, I had what might have been called the "freedom of California", which at that time, where films were concerned, meant freedom of the world. No one dared question it. For the first time, I felt like an insider.

★ ★ ★ ★ ★

CUT TO – Hammersmith Studio exterior, closing to interior with **Sir Henry** *showing* **Rupert** *around and explaining the renovations.*

VOICE: We returned to London, where Father had bought Hammersmith Studios. We cut and put a soundtrack to the film and obtained the best possible distribution rights as an independent producer. The film was unique, a peep behind the scenes at lives hitherto taboo; the first intimate sneak glimpses of the stars as themselves. I found time to thank Father Breen and tell him how much his letter had been worth to me, though not in actual dollars. Had I told him that, he might well have wanted a new church. *[Pause]* Grayson & Grayson was also doing as well as a small publisher could expect. One evening, out of the blue, came a bonus.

★ ★ ★ ★ ★

CUT TO – The dining room at Richard **Hogg's** *home in Draycott Gardens, South Kensington.*

VOICE: I was dining at Richard Hogg's in Draycott Gardens with his mother and father. The decanter of port was on its third voyage around the table when Hogg senior spoke to me. Though his words were quiet, they hit me like a bomb.

★ ★ ★ ★ ★

CUT TO – **Hogg Senior,** *seated beside* **Rupert,** *whom he nudges.*

HOGG SENIOR *[softly]*: We have in our possession more than 150 unpublished letters between Percy Bysshe Shelley, Mary Godwin Shelley and my ancestor Thomas Jefferson Hogg. Subject to certain conditions, you may have the rights to publish them.

VOICE: In one fortunate evening, I had struck gold of the highest quality. It was arranged for Professor George Gordon, president of Magdalen College, Oxford, vice-president of the university and, incidentally, Pat Kirwan's company commander in the war, to edit the letters. Manscripts of them were made and Random House in New York was to undertake simultaneous publication. Alas, it all came to nought, eclipsed by war clouds from across the Channel.

★ ★ ★ ★ ★

CUT TO – **Rupert's** *office, where he is in conclave with brother* **Brian.**

BRIAN: No. It's smart in only the most negative of ways, but publishing, like so much else that thrives on peace, is doomed for the time being, so those who cut their losses soonest might live to thrive another day. You must know better than I that Shelley's letters would be among the first casualties of war, along with whatever money and effort we put into them. We must close and the sooner, the better.

★ ★ ★ ★ ★

FADE TO – **Rupert** *some days later, shutting the heavy black Georgian door of*

Grayson & Grayson's premises. He descends the steps to Curzon Street, takes a long look back, turns and walks away.

VOICE: And so it was that the firm wound up its affairs and closed its door for the last time. We ceased to exist as a publishing house. I walked up Curzon Street and along Half Moon Street, crossed Piccadilly, went through Green Park, past the front of the palace with a thought for their Majesties at this point in history and reached the destination pre-determined by my first-war service in the Irish Guards.

★ ★ ★ ★ ★

CUT TO – The regimental orderly room of the Irish Guards at Buckingham Gate. **Rupert** *sits across a desk from a* **Major** *with glasses and a paunch, who consults a file before speaking. He raises his eyebrows and looks owlish. His manner is brusque.*

MAJOR: Sorry to have kept you, Grayson. We've had rather a rush. I'm surprised you're on the doorstep so soon, considering the knocks you took first time round. Are you mended?

RUPERT: Thank you, sir, yes.

MAJOR: I'll come right out with it: you're not front-line material any more. Age is against you, I'm afraid, so fitness is irrelevant, but I'd like to suggest we put you with a reserve battalion. Chaps with your sort of experience can make an invaluable contribution, particularly on the training side.

VOICE: Yes, I thought; giving lectures in tactics I couldn't compose and lessons in killing I couldn't impart, with port and biscuits in the anteroom to break the monotony. The prospect was dismal and not improved by seeing the man before me.

RUPERT *[rising]*: Thank you, major; I suspected as much. Might I have some thinking time?

MAJOR: Of course. They say it might fizzle out in a few months, anyway. Goodbye, Grayson, and good luck.

RUPERT: Goodbye, major.

★ ★ ★ ★ ★

CUT TO – **Rupert's** *yacht at Littlehampton.*

VOICE: Not even Sydney Fitzgerald, that most charming and humane of men, the Lieutenant-Colonel of the Regiment, would rate me as cannon fodder, so I retired to my boat at Littlehampton, rigged an awning over the afterdeck and settled down to sulk.

★ ★ ★ ★ ★

CUT TO – **Rupert** *snoozing under the awning, a book having slipped from his grasp on to the deck, when a voice awakens him and he sits up, blinking. It is Jasper* **Power,** *whom* **Rupert** *last saw at Henry* **Savage's** *tumbledown cottage on Winchelsea beach.*

POWER: Permission to come aboard, sir?

RUPERT: Only if you sing an Irish lament appropriate to the occasion.

POWER *[removing shoes and stepping on to the deck]*: And what sort of occasion might that be, Captain Grayson?

RUPERT: This is not a mosque, Jasper, and I think I'd prefer your feet to be covered.

POWER: Ay, ay, sir. But why the lament?

RUPERT: For the Guards, Jasper. They don't want me to help them win the war.

POWER: Yes, I heard. Pat sent me here with a bottle of consolation.

336

Behold! *[Jasper holds a bottle aloft]* But you already won one war for them; you must not be greedy. Besides, I've got an alternative for you.

Rupert *looks calculatingly at the visitor.*

RUPERT: What?

POWER: I work for a group of men, without uniform, badges or ties, who are carrier pigeons for the Admiralty, taking important messages from place to place. With your qualifications, all you would need to join us is someone to vouch for you as a responsible person. Do you think anyone would go that far?

Rupert's *suspicion melts, as* **Power** *talks, into an expression of interest and gratitude. Then, his face clouds.*

RUPERT: Thank you, Jasper, and my answer is an enthusiastic yes, but there is one proviso. On the rebound from the Guards, I contacted the Foreign Office; for my first love has long been, to give it its full and formal name, the Corps of King's Foreign Service Messengers, into which I was once temporarily inducted to carry a confidential bag from London to Rome. As might have been expected, the Corps is at full strength, for it's a job second to none. But I have been promised the first vacancy that turns up.

POWER: Fair enough, but meanwhile it can't hurt to do an apprenticeship with the Admiralty. They're a fine lot, and the job's the nearest a scarred and grizzled forty-year-old is going to get to the action.

★ ★ ★ ★ ★

CUT TO – The office of Captain Ivan **Colvin**, *R.N., chief of the Admiralty's M Branch or Courier Section.* **Colvin** *has been perusing papers* **Rupert** *put before him on the desk.*

337

COLVIN: Good, Grayson. References OK: cabinet minister, permanent civil servant, and [smiles] the clincher, the owner of a grouse moor and a mile of fishing on both banks of the Spey – who happens to be the Duke of Sutherland. Please call again same time tomorrow

★ ★ ★ ★ ★

CUT TO – Next day's appointment, same setting. **Colvin** *gives* **Rupert** *a paper to sign.*

VOICE: At the end of the second appointment, Captain Colvin, who would already, of course, have delved so exhaustively into my credentials as to make the references mere embroidery, produced a copy of the Official Secrets Act and pointed to where I must sign. As I left, he said casually: "By the way, you'll travel under the name of Johnson until you hear otherwise."

★ ★ ★ ★ ★

CUT TO – **Rupert** *shaking hands with* **Colvin** *and walking away, meditating.*

VOICE: In the First World War, Edward Guelph, a man of many names who became Edward Prince of Wales, then the King of England, and finally the Duke of Windsor, had without his knowledge been known secretly by Intelligence as Black Diamond. So who was I to complain when my own name was to be changed and by one syllable only? And yet a slight foreboding persisted. If change my name I must, then I'd sooner have made the choice myself. It was too much like borrowing a stranger's overcoat to be comfortable. I suppose I'd have chosen a grand name like that of my friend at Harrow, the Marques San Carlos de Pedroso, who, in spite of having killed a man in a duel during his summer holiday, never made it into the school fencing four.

Paris, June 1941, a city braced for and resigned to German occupation, whose precursors are already strutting the streets and helping to polarise the inhabitants into attitudes for and against the invaders.

VOICE: The Hun was at the gate of Paris. The Fifth Column was ready for the most sinister clowns in history to goose-step through it with their weapons of death. But luck had not deserted me. I had landed myself a job I liked with people I liked. Someone once said: "If Rupert ever threw himself in the Thames, he'd be washed up into the Savoy Grill."

★ ★ ★ ★ ★

CUT TO – An underground loading-room at the Admiralty in London. Bags are being lifted on to a van with a round roof.

VOICE: The job consisted of delivering Admiralty bags containing secret books and ciphers to navy ships or their land bases, mostly within the British Isles. Foreign journeys seemed to fall mainly to me. Colvin knew I'd lived abroad before the war, but I could not help wondering whether it might not have involved the connivance of colleagues who had no wish to be separated from wives, sweethearts and golf clubs, or who perhaps just hated abroad. Presumably because I'd lived in Paris, I found myself constantly in charge of consignments of confidential documents without which ships could not put to sea. Those I delivered to the Paris Embassy went on to the British Mediterranean Fleet based in Marseilles, but soon the cross-country route would have to be abandoned, and I expected each mission to be my last. In the underground loading-room, I was checking my bags on to the Covered Wagon – so-called because its rounded steel roof, which protected the cargo against fallout from the blitz, gave it a Wild-West appearance.

Colvin *appears as the loading is finishing.*

RUPERT: Hello, Ivan; 242 items. Is it a record?

COLVIN: As a matter of fact, it is – the largest consignment ever to leave here. *[Confidentially]* You know what that means: France is doomed. I came to wish you a comfortable journey.

Colvin *looks away.*

COLVIN: I thought you would want to say farewell to your beloved Paris.

RUPERT: Duty mixed with beauty. You know your cocktails, Ivan. Thank you.

★ ★ ★ ★ ★

CUT TO – The Covered Wagon setting off and making its way to Waterloo.

VOICE: The Paris run seemed subject to influences from some shadowy underground world. Unusual incidents would occur, expected delays, strange encounters, sometimes merely annoying but sinister because they were unexplained. One had a feeling of being under observation, as though watchful eyes were waiting for the unguarded moment when a miscalculation might make the difference between life and death and threaten the security of the bags. They kept the courier in a state of tension.

★ ★ ★ ★ ★

CUT TO – Loading the bags on to the Southampton train at Waterloo, six or so porters and **Rupert** *supervising. On board the train,* **Rupert** *is locked into a compartment filled with bags. At Southampton, the compartment is unlocked and porters transfer the bags on to the ship for France.* **Rupert** *follows them to the hold, padlocks them in and zips the big key into his inner pocket. He sighs as the key is tucked away and, relaxed at last, goes up to the bar, where* **Fred** *the barman is in charge.*

RUPERT: Evening, Fred. No need to ask how you are because you're a picture of health, and not surprising with this medicine all around you.

Fred *places a drink on the bar for* **Rupert**.

FRED: Good evening, sir, but I wonder whether my doctor would agree. Have I anticipated your preference correctly?

RUPERT: As usual, Fred, thank you – and my arrival as well, it seems. I'm sure you were mixing it as I stepped off the train.

Rupert *nods one by one to a group of men he joins at one end of the bar and they murmur welcomingly back at him.*

VOICE: When I surveyed Fred's other customers, I was not disappointed. They were my usual cross-Channel friends. We had drifted together like logs in a river. We were all in plain clothes, met only *en voyage* and never addressed each other by name. We discussed little more than the weather; never our jobs or destinations. All we had in common was that we were fellow travellers. I had no idea whether they were there individually or collectively, from Scotland Yard, attached to the shipping company or involved in some sort of undercover game, but we were all moving in a world where it was wiser not to ask.

*The bar on the cross-Channel ferry to France. A **Stranger** joins the group, which falls silent as he strides confidently into its presence. On approaching, he addresses **Rupert** in a voice that is cultured and poised, but stammers.*

STRANGER: Well, well, Mr Johnson, I presume – or should I say *Monsieur* Johnson, or even Mr Grayson?

*Rupert turns abruptly and frowns at him without recognition. The **Stranger** throws his coat aside as though settling in to do big business with **Fred**. He makes a lordly gesture of the hand that embraces the group.*

STRANGER: Drinks for everybody, if you please, barman.

*Rupert continues to look coldly at the **Stranger**, who, unperturbed by the anger in **Rupert's** eyes, addresses him.*

STRANGER: I know your brother, Tristram, and your voice betrayed you. No two voices could be so alike. May I butt in?

VOICE: It wasn't that he was the sort of man I didn't care for. It was the man himself I didn't like.

*The **Stranger** moves closer to **Rupert**, who draws back, to find that the man was only reaching for his glass. Noticing **Rupert's** reaction, the others also shrink away.*

VOICE: I had no intention of asking his name, but it was as though he read my thoughts.

STRANGER *[stammering, to the group]*: Just call me Harold; I'm a man of no importance. I'm *The Times* correspondent on my way to GHQ.

VOICE: This did nothing to endear him to me. His editor, Douglas Dawson, a man who was well-informed, obstinately used the columns of the *Old Thunderer* to preach appeasement. It was clear that we were meant to infer that he was *The Times* Special Correspondent on his way to see Lord Gort, the Commander-in-Chief.

The group, having flinched from the **Stranger's** *brashness, closes ranks and is no longer at ease. The* **Stranger** *hardly draws breath, discoursing authoritatively on what is going on behind the scenes and holding the group in thrall. As the* **Stranger** *reaches out with his arm,* **Rupert** *stiffens, but it is only to steady himself at the bar. He faces* **Rupert**.

STRANGER: I hope I did nothing to discomfit you.

RUPERT: In no way; it's just that I dislike coming under the close scrutiny of a stranger.

STRANGER: I'm sorry, but I like to memorise people. Besides, I am no stranger. I'm on my way to see your brother and also interview Fighter, our C-in-C.

The **Stranger** *calls on* **Fred** *for another round of drinks and the group, as much in thrall to his hospitality as to his oratory, meekly accepts.*

VOICE: This man of thirty or so performed like a charmer ripe in experience and oozed vanity. He was entertaining without being anecdotal, witty without being funny, and somehow he contrived to tincture his monologue with originality. He dispensed hospitality generously, though I had a feeling he might have wanted to say he had drunk a courier under the table. But my head was the harder and my secrets remained inviolate

– something for which I have since given thanks to providence and my hard-drinking ancestors. I had been twice pv-d, or personally vetted, and when I had in my turn questioned my inquisitors about what quality they considered to be the most security risk in a man, each had plumped for vanity.

The scene of **Stranger** *regaling the group recedes, so that he is seen to be talking away but not heard as other than a mumble, while the present* **Rupert** *pursues his own reflections.*

VOICE: As I listened to him stuttering on, my mind was carried back to a night on the African *veldt* with Ambrose and Godfrey and our white hunter. We were seated beside a dying campfire when we were assailed by a smell so atrocious as to have stayed dormant in my mind – until now, when for the first time since so long ago I was reminded of it by this man's presence. It conjured up the vision of that night when a dying hyena, dragging its hindquarters in a globule of entrails, slunk out of the shadows into the failing light of the fire. Was the intruder visiting the enemy camp for comfort or consolation? It was a strange encounter, like so many in one's travels. In the light of what we know today about this animal of the shades, who was to end his traitor's career in Moscow as Kim Philby in 1988, it seemed not without interest that he was on his way to interview Lord Gort, Commander-in-Chief of the British Armed Forces.

★ ★ ★ ★ ★

CUT TO – Le Havre, as the ship berths. **Rupert** *looks about but sees no sailors to help him assemble the bags for disembarkment. There are, however, some soldiers peering at France emerging from the morning mist. He addresses them.*

RUPERT: I say, chaps, could you lend a hand, please?

Rupert's *manner is so charming that they jump to without hesitation. A colonel who has just appeared grows red-faced with consternation and explodes at* **Rupert**.

344

COLONEL: And who the hell do you think you are, giving orders on my ship?

RUPERT [*composed, haughty*]: My identity is not for you to know, Colonel, but I can tell you I'm a damned sight more important than you are.

VOICE: I could see trouble ahead with this man so I decided to contact the authorities. Luckily, the officer commanding in Le Havre was Brigadier-General Cary Evans, a son-in-law of Lloyd George and a friend of my family. I soon forgot the Colonel.

★ ★ ★ ★ ★

CUT TO: The quayside, where a van and armed escort are standing by to take the bags to the Rapide. A British **Sergeant** *appears and introduces himself to* **Rupert**.

SERGEANT: Mr Johnson?

RUPERT: Yes, Sergeant. Are you in charge?

SERGEANT: Yes, sir. A van and armed coach are reserved for you. Brigadier Evans presents his compliments and a packed lunch, and bids you "*bon appétit*".

CUT TO: The train, where **Rupert** *installs himself in his compartment with his bags and explores the basket containing a bottle of iced Chablis and food as the train pulls out.*

★ ★ ★ ★ ★

CUT TO: Arrival at Gare Saint Lazare, Paris, two hours later. An embassy car drives up to the train and unloads the bags, **Rupert** *squeezing in among them. They drive off.*

By car through the streets of Paris to the embassy in Faubourg St Honoré.

VOICE: My arrival at St Lazare lit a fuse of reflection. I have always loved the living warmth of even the draughtiest railway stations and quaysides, just as I hate the inhumanity of the concrete and clinical international airports. And no station sparked off more golden memories than St Lazare.

★ ★ ★ ★ ★

FADE TO – A montage *of scenes corresponding with the thoughts that follow.*

VOICE: It was from dear grimy Saint Lazare, immortalised by Degas on canvas and on whose steps Renoir first met Matisse in the station's early days, that I had so often set off for August in Deauville or a Normandy *manoir* with criss-cross beams and china cats chasing china pigeons across the roof; or sometimes to join a wealthy friend on his yacht. Was it not from this beloved station that Marcel Proust in his great work set out to meet the experience of seeing, hearing, tasting, feeling, smelling, understanding and speaking, in that miraculous train, the 1.10 pm? And was it not outside this station that J Beachcomber Morton was heard to make the immortal remark as he stepped from the train and fell headlong into the darkness of the goods yard: *"C'est magnifique mais ce n'est pas la gare".*

★ ★ ★ ★ ★

CUT TO – Car driving through Paris to British Embassy.

VOICE: I was driven to the British Embassy, which occupied the gracious house in the Faubourg St Honoré that had once belonged to Napoleon's sister. Again I breathed the floating smells, so dear to me, of Paris: that glorious mixture of French bread, spilled *vin ordinaire*, garlic, Algerian tobacco, roasting chestnuts and the less pleasant odour of male cats.

346

★ ★ ★ ★ ★

CUT TO – Arrival at the embassy, **Rupert** *being greeted and receiving the signature of the ambassador's secretary for receipt of the bags.*

VOICE: Having handed the bags over, I was free to go about my own business or pleasure, and, not being a businessman, I knew which it would be.

★ ★ ★ ★ ★

CUT TO – An elevated view of Paris showing the Opera and streets around it, and narrowing to rue Daunou, in which **Rupert** *alights from a taxi to enter the Hotel Daunou.*

VOICE: In Paris, Admiralty couriers usually stayed at the Bristol because it was close to the embassy, but, just as an old dog likes his own kennel best, I preferred the little Hotel Daunou, a *garçonnière* in the street of the same name.

★ ★ ★ ★ ★

CUT TO – The desk of the Hotel Daunou's tiny hall. **Rupert** *hands his passport to a bored clerk.*

VOICE: I was conscious of a cathedral hush, as if Madame Tussaud herself were lying dead upstairs with black candles flickering at her head and feet. From the clerk, who spoke in a whisper, I learned that my old friend Pierre, the night porter, had left for parts unknown, anticipating the Bosche. No longer, alas, would he be there to annoy me by remarking, as he had so often done when I emerged from my room at midday trying to put a bold front on it, "I trust *Monsieur* is in good health; he was looking a little pale when he returned at six this morning."

★ ★ ★ ★ ★

CUT TO – Ascending to his floor in the little old iron-cage lift and the few steps along the passage to his room.

VOICE: In my old quarters, I was no longer assailed by the smell of cigars

347

and wine and flowers or the sound of voices in the corridor. Already, the German presence was throwing its shadow across the city.

Rupert *showers and dresses, walks downstairs, out the front door, across the street and into Harry's New York Bar.*

VOICE: I put on a suit as dark as the blackout and instinctively went to my old haunt, the New York Bar, directly across the little street. Harry McLehone, the proprietor, was at home packing to take the road south. The *embusque* were on the move. In the semi-darkness, I stood alone at the bar with my scotch-and-soda and my memories, which included the evening long ago when Scott Fitzgerald and I had concocted a new recipe for a book of cocktails Harry was preparing. Now, a battery of suspicious eyes appraised me as I stood where Scott had stood. I swallowed my drink and left. Minutes later, I lit a cigar in the unmoving darkness of the rue de la Paix. The years rolled back, and once more I was standing with Scott and Zelda in front of Cartier's window.

★ ★ ★ ★ ★

CUT TO – The rue de la Paix, closing on Cartier's window, with **Zelda** *and Scott* **Fitzgerald** *and* **Rupert** *standing outside it.*

ZELDA *[moaning]*: No one ever buys me lovely emeralds like that.

FITZGERALD *[shouting, pushing in through the door]*: No one would be that crazy; no man, not with eyes like yours.

★ ★ ★ ★ ★

CUT TO – Pera Carva, a mountain village in the Alpes Maritime, in the twenties. Drinking wine after an afternoon's skiing are the **Fitzgeralds, Hemingway** *and* **Rupert***.*

Zelda *leaves the table to go outside, scoop up snow with her hands and plaster it on the car.*

VOICE: On their first visit to France from America, Scott Fitzgerald and his wife Zelda seemed determined to become known as high-calibre eccentrics, but they never understood the European scene and it was not long before the European sophisticates, with whom they liked to mix, regarded them as no more than exhibitionists in a double-act. While Hemingway, helped by Scott in his literary career, had learned the *a la carte* and wine list backwards, Scott was still unable to read the *table d'hôte*. Thus he suffered the fate of most benefactors, because neither man, both dedicated writers, forgave the other – one for what he'd given, the other for what he'd received. But it was Scott who carried the chips on both shoulders. Behind the veneer of the would-be cosmopolite, there always peered the wonder eyes of the little show-off from the Middle West. When I first met these expatriate American writers in Antibes, I was regarded as no more than an amiable Englishman about whom they knew little and probably cared less, until they realised I too was in search of the raw material of life. Perhaps they saw in my eyes a glimmer of the strange things I had already seen and experienced, even though I was so much younger. [Pause] One day, we skied at the mountain village of Pera Carva and afterwards drank litres of the local wine. Zelda insisted on piling snow on top of the car, heaping it anywhere it would lodge; everyone must know where we had been.

★ ★ ★ ★ ★

CUT TO – *The drive down the icy road to Nice, parking in the promenade des Anglais and entering the Negresco for drinks. Hemingway is quiet for a while, brooding.*

HEMINGWAY: Time we left. More wine and the truth will start flowing.

FITZGERALD: Isn't that what we want? You needn't thank me, if that's what you're afraid of.

HEMINGWAY: Too late for that now. Pupils don't thank their teachers. They perform.

FITZGERALD: You're a single-action pump, Ernie. While you're taking in, you don't give out. It's either one phase or the other with you. I, on the other hand, am what the salesman would call a double-action pump. In one end and out the other at the same time.

HEMINGWAY: Perhaps I save my discharges until I'm sure.

FITZGERALD: Like an outdoor man taking aim? Do you think of yourself as a hick?

HEMINGWAY: And yourself as a lapdog?

ZELDA: You both talk shit.

Having rallied to expostulate, **Zelda** *slumps back to how she was.*

RUPERT: Do you all think we should descend to a more normal altitude? Rare air removes veils and shows us too plainly.

FITZGERALD: A week ago, I would not have taken any notice of you, Rupert, because you're an Englishman that has been stamped out like a gold sovereign – all glitter and no feeling.

HEMINGWAY [*challengingly*]: But?

FITZGERALD: I have seen what's in his eyes. He's cracked a few eggs and soon the omelette will be served.

★ ★ ★ ★ ★

CUT TO – Two hours late, as they are emptied into the promenade des Anglais, staggering around trying to remember where they have parked the car.

RUPERT – There it is, but someone's cleaned it. Or maybe it's our car's twin.

350

Going up to the car and realising her snow has melted, **Zelda** *starts crying noisily. A small crowd gathers and looks menacing, believing the others are ill-treating her. The four board the car and drive off hastily. Soon, swaying along the route d'Antibes, their voices rise in song. They turn inland to wine country where the men, women and children work late in the vineyards until darkness falls, and find a small auberge on the terrace of which they dine. As the light fades, so do their voices. Zelda folds her arms on the table and rests her head on them, her hair mingling with the wine stains on the wood.*

VOICE: Perhaps our voices were silenced by the stillness of the evening, the perfume of the *Dama de Noche* and the eucalyptus trees, the magic of the stars, like white flowers in the dark meadows of the Mediterranean sky, or because we were all too tired to laugh or too tipsy to talk. So we sat before our wine glasses until the welcome jingle of preparation from the kitchen interrupted our dreams and Scott lifted his glass and drunkenly whispered, so as not to wake Zelda.

SCOTT: I taste the *vino* and, methinks, I smell the food, but *ou sont les neiges d'antan, mon ami, ou sont les neiges d'antan.*

VOICE: Poor Scott and Zelda little knew what dark clouds were gathering over their golden heads. That happened a million years ago in a period known as the Roaring twenties; careless days and carefree nights, and with them, Scott and Zelda and my youth.

351

The American Bar at the Ritz, Paris. **Rupert** *enters, looks around, buys a drink and ruminates.*

VOICE: The American Bar at the Ritz had always been a meeting-place for expatriates. Here, as at Harry's, there was the strained atmosphere one associates with a first-night party after an obvious flop. Frank, the head barman and everyone's friend, was an Austrian, and a worried one, as well he might be.

Rupert *beckons* **Louis** *Bretau, a young waiter, who responds promptly and cheerfully.*

LOUIS *[proudly]*: How may I help you, Mr Grayson?

RUPERT: Champagne cocktail, Louis, with a dash of sunshine.

LOUIS: I see what you mean, sir. The customers have shed their petals.

RUPERT: And such a pretty gardenful they were.

LOUIS *[wryly]*: Now, they have the blight.

Depression among the **Gays***, who are a feature of the bar, turns into bickering.*

FIRST GAY: Believe it or not, he's packing up his things to leave.

SECOND GAY: He's like a snowball; when the heat's on, he melts out of sight.

THIRD GAY: Is this a private conversation? Unless it is, I'm not interested.

FOURTH GAY: I burnt my fingers on the Bourse yesterday.

FIFTH GAY: That'll teach you not to pick up lighted cigar-ends.

RUPERT: Dear, oh, dear; our ladies are tense today! Talking of ladies, Louis, do you still remember the measurement?

LOUIS: Seventy-two centimetres, Mr Grayson.

At which, **Rupert** *claps silently.* **Louis** *moves back to his glasses and takes them one by one from the shelf to polish.* **Rupert's** *eyes follow the motion of the towel, which lulls him into a reverie.*

VOICE: One evening, a sweepstake was organised among *habitués* of the American Bar to decide the exact circumference of the Venus de Milo's waist. Young Louis had been sent in a taxi to the Louvre. How he obtained the information remained a mystery – presumably with ladder, tape measure and the connivance of the attendant. The sweep was won by Alan Inverclyde, naturally, because his income was reputed to be £100,000 a year and his father, the first Lord Inverclyde, was a shipping magnate. "To him who hath…" etcetera, or "ect", as Scott Fitzgerald used to abbreviate it. Alan had a fund of knowledge for which there seemed no immediate use – a sample of which he would pull out unexpectedly like one of Little Jack Horner's plums: Prince Rupert's dog Boy followed the prince's horse into battle and was killed at Marston Moor; Charles VIII of Sweden had twelve toes; Cervantes died on April 23, 1616, in Madrid, on the same day as Shakespeare died in Stratford-upon-Avon. One of Alan's less agreeable traits was never to order a second magnum of champagne until the first had been drunk, but I had learned to hold my empty glass in the right hand and lift it across to my left shoulder like the second movement of the

353

"present arms", and in those days the observant *sommelier* knew what it meant. As I sat in the gloom of the Ritz, I remembered the stranger who stood beside me at the bar long ago.

★ ★ ★ ★ ★

FADE TO – The same bar, different barman. Beside a younger **Rupert** *is a middle-aged* **Stranger**, *his face lean and sallow, sombrely dressed.* **Rupert** *sneaks sideways glances at him and soon cannot contain his curiosity.*

RUPERT: I say, would you care for a drink? You are English?

STRANGER *[aloofly]*: Naturally.

RUPERT: Of course. My name's Grayson.

The **Stranger** *bows graciously and draws from his pocket a visiting card, which he gives Rupert.*

STRANGER: I accept your invitation to a glass of brandy gladly, but first, my card.

A close-up of it shows the card to be engraved: Mr Sherlock Holmes, 22A, Baker Street, London, W.

RUPERT *[politely, impressed]*: Not THE Mr Holmes?

STRANGER *[smiling sweetly but scrutinising Rupert]*: None other.

RUPERT: And your friend?

STRANGER: I suppose you are referring to poor old Watson, with all the tiresome wounds he acquired God knows where and the mystery of his marriages. Alas, my only unsolved case, as a matter of fact. I gave him the slip at Charing Cross.

*The **Stranger** leans confidentially to **Rupert**, who sways away as brandy fumes sear his nostrils.*

STRANGER: I'm afraid Watson rather neglects his practice and, what's more, he never stops that "amazing, Holmes" routine except when he's saying "but, my dear Holmes, what on earth?"

RUPERT: Are you here for long, Mr Holmes?

STRANGER *[polishing off his brandy like a flame-swallower]*: I leave tomorrow. *[In a whisper]* I'm here on the strange case of the missing signet ring *[burps discreetly]* which involves a certain royal personage. *[Pauses to listen]* And now, if I'm not mistaken, I hear my cab drawing up in the rue Cambon.

*Pulling a deer-stalker from his pocket, the **Stranger** sways delicately on his way.*

VOICE: He looked more like a tightrope walker on the wire than a great sleuth on the trail. I was learning that most men of intelligence contrive some form of escape from the world of reality.

★ ★ ★ ★ ★

*TRACK TO – A salon opposite the men's bar, where materialise in ghostly form a young couple, chatting and explaining to an earlier **Rupert.***

VOICE: I remembered with a pang an American couple I used to meet frequently in a salon across the corridor – whose marriage, while it lasted, had a simplicity that was quite enchanting. Apart from their love for each other, each was absorbed in different interests. She was crazy about exquisite clothes, which she wore like a *Parisienne*, while he was madly in love with his baby-grand piano, which he played remarkably well. In time, terrible scenes of jealousy took place. She would use a hatchet to smash his piano, while he would tear her clothes from their hangers and burn them. Thus, they lived in amity until the slump on Wall Street destroyed the basis for their marriage. She no longer had money for new and beautiful clothes, while he no longer had money for new and beautiful pianos. As they no longer had an acceptable reason to quarrel, the marriage broke up, confirming what I've always suspected: that it isn't money that's the root of unhappiness, but its absence.

★ ★ ★ ★ ★

FADE TO – **Rupert** *leaving the Ritz and making his way thoughtfully to the rue Charbonais and about to enter the House of All Nations; a brothel with luxurious furnishings, international clientele and jovial ambience. Tour the premises and close on a sumptuous room housing a lavatory splendid enough to be a throne.*

VOICE: In certain moods, there had never been a better place in which to relax than the House of All Nations in the rue Charbonais, where champagne and cigars of the finest quality were served. Certain favoured clients were even permitted to occupy, for the same purpose, the chair especially constructed to support the portly King Edward VII when he wished to play, what Rabelais affectionately termed, the "close buttock game". There was another chair, less tilted, which had been designed to accommodate the monarch after he had undergone his annual dietary cure at Marienbad. To the anger of regular clients, this second chair had been sold for 10,000 francs to a collector of interesting antiques in Hamburg, and who, it was rumoured, had the vulgarity to display it in one of the houses of the Reeperbahn. But I was in no mood to watch the brothel preparing its welcome for the field-grey troops from across the Rhine, while realising that a successful *madame*, like the eagle, recognises no frontiers.

★ ★ ★ ★ ★

CUT TO – **Rupert** *hesitating and turning away from the House of All Nations, sauntering to the Place Vendôme and hailing a taxi, which takes him across the Seine to Les Deux Magots.*

VOICE: It was my custom, when in doubt, to signal a taxi, hail a gondola, summon a rickshaw or catch a train. So, I took a cab in the Place Vendôme and drove to Les Deux Magots. The last time I had been there I'd split a bottle of "the widow" with Horace de Vere Cole. In his youth, the practical joke had been a form of social behaviour among the *jeunesse dorée* – those perpetrated by Edward VII being justly famous for their tastelessness. His favourite prank was to pour a bottle of Veuve Clicquot over the head of a guest. This he considered excruciatingly funny, especially as it was *les majesté* for the victim not to laugh heartily during the process. When the royal *bon vivant* proposed…

★ ★ ★ ★ ★

FADE TO – *A meeting of the committee of the Marlborough Club. The* **Chairman** *looks over his spectacles gravely and addresses the* **Other Members**.

CHAIRMAN: And now, gentlemen, we come to an item of some delicacy. Our sovereign has forwarded for membership the name of a certain maharajah, and we know what our policy and that of our founders is in regard to orientals. How do we observe it without offending the king?

Gloomy rumblings among the committee members, but no suggestions until one of them half-raises a hand.

CHAIRMAN: Smithers?

SMITHERS: If you consult the Constitution, Mr Chairman, I think you'll find that Rule XI states: "two black balls categorically debar a candidate from membership".

Uneasy laughter around the table. The **Chairman** *turns to the secretary taking minutes.*

CHAIRMAN: Can you confirm that, Potter?

POTTER: Yes, Mr Chairman, it is indeed so, but seldom invoked.

CHAIRMAN: So I should hope. But dare we use it? Even though the king is his own jester, might it not be going a little far?

SMITHERS: Normally, yes, but the proposer is reputed to owe the maharajah vast sums of money and could thus have been under pressure.

CHAIRMAN [*feigning anger*]: Duress, you mean?

SMITHERS: Just so, chairman.

CHAIRMAN: Then, let us rescue His Majesty. Send him a letter, Potter, drawing his attention to Rule XI, and let us hope the royal sense of humour is in order when he receives it.

Growls of assent and a few smiles around the table.

VOICE: The sovereign was so delighted with the tact displayed by the committee that he forthwith retracted the proposal form, leaving his friend and benefactor to face the ridicule.

★ ★ ★ ★ ★

CUT TO – Platform 12, *Victoria Station, where a boat train stands ready to leave; the* **Driver** *looking back from his cab for the* **Conductor** *to blow his whistle and wave him away.*

VOICE: A joke I liked was staged on Platform 12 at Victoria Station.

★ ★ ★ ★ ★

CUT TO – **Horace De Verb Cole** *standing beside the engine, which hoots and begins to move off, with slow puffing and clouds of steam billowing from it. An* **Accomplice** *of* **Horace's**, *standing elsewhere on the platform, fills his lungs and emits high-pitched cries of distress.*

ACCOMPLICE [*at the top of his voice*]: Help, help, help!

★ ★ ★ ★ ★

CUT TO – *Inquisitive heads popping out of every window and* **Horace** *removing their hats one by one as the carriages pass along the platform, placing the hats in a large laundry basket he has acquired for the purpose. Cries of anger and shaking of fists as the deprived are carried inexorably away.*

★ ★ ★ ★ ★

CUT TO – *Outside lost property office, its identity printed boldly above the door. A van arrives and the* **Driver** *carries the laundry basket to an* **Attendant** *at the counter inside.*

ATTENDANT: Cor, posh lids! Sure you got the right address, Charlie?

DRIVER *[laconically]*: I have at that. Don't stow'em too far away, though. They'll not be lost for long.

★ ★ ★ ★ ★

CUT TO – *Outside The Ritz, Piccadilly.*

VOICE: The famous "picking up" of Piccadilly, often credited to Horace, was in fact carried out by Crawley de Crespigny of the Grenadiers. Hearing a fellow member of White's boasting that he would be driving up to the Ritz the following evening for dinner with his brand new mistress in his brand new Napier, Crawley wagered him twenty guineas it would never happen.

★ ★ ★ ★ ★

CUT TO – *White's, where, as they arrive for lunch, four friends of* **Crawley** *de Crespigny are button-holed by him one after another, breaking into laughter and nodding assent as he whispers his plan and requests their co-operation.*

★ ★ ★ ★ ★

CUT TO – *Next evening, outside the Ritz.* **Crawley's** *four friends, disguised as roughly-clothed workmen, have roped up half the street along the front of the hotel and hung red lamps. The* **Driver** *of the Napier is forced to park the car beside the Green Park railings and walk his lady past the cheering working party to the hotel entrance.*

★ ★ ★ ★ ★

CUT TO – Inside the hotel, where **Crawley** *collects his winnings.*

VOICE: Horace frequently visited Augustus John's Chelsea studio, and one day, on some pretext, borrowed three of John's pictures.

★ ★ ★ ★ ★

CUT TO – Horace with the three pictures on display in King's Road and an upturned hat beside them. Passers-by look and sniff, but few coins enter the hat. At the end of the day, **Horace** *packs up and returns to* **John's** *studio in Mallord Street. Handing back the paintings,* **Horace** *looks contemptuously at* **John**.

HORACE: Call yourself a painter? I've been the whole afternoon exhibiting your work and all I've earned is fourpence and a thirty-shilling offer for the lot.

★ ★ ★ ★ ★

CUT TO – The Cafe Royal, where sit **Rupert**, **Horace**, *Pat* **Kirwan** *and Augustus* **John**.

VOICE: Later that evening, John had his revenge – the only time I saw the laugh turned on Horace. John would pretend to be deaf if he was saddled with a bore, while Horace, for his part, would put on a mad act when he wanted to clear a room of a railway compartment.

A stranger comes up and sits at their table. **Rupert** *nudges* **Kirwan**, *who turns expectantly to* **Rupert**.

RUPERT *[whispering to* **Kirwan***]*: Watch this.

Horace *puts his hands together and closes his eyes before launching into what seems like a prayer or incantation, some of which sounds Latin and some gibberish. He pauses, rolls his eyes so that the whites show, and begins to foam at the mouth. The stranger, alarmed, gets up and steps hastily away, looking back only once. Whereupon,* **Horace** *returns to normal.*

360

HORACE [*smugly*]: You see, I knew how to get rid of that bugger.

JOHN [*more smugly*]: Yes, but you didn't tell us he'd be taking your new umbrella with him.

★ ★ ★ ★ ★

FADE TO – Les Deux Magots.

VOICE: My memories continued to be driven to the past by the grimness of the present as I stood among the empty chairs and tables of Les Deux Magots. It was here that James Joyce had made his momentous agreement with Sylvia Beach for the private publication of *Ulysses*. It was outside this writers' and artists' haunt that passers-by were surprised one day to see an empty hearse standing – until they learned that an old Russian *habitué* known to most of us had died, and his last request had been that on the way to Père Lachaise his coffin might be allowed to rest for a few minutes in the cafe where he had spent so many enjoyable hours.

★ ★ ★ ★ ★

CUT TO – **Rupert** *slowly and sadly walking from Les Deux Magots, filled with thoughts. He hails a taxi.*

VOICE: I called another taxi. I might as well do the rounds. Paris in the darkness of her fear was, that night, like a dark beautiful slut – bewildered, yet still bewitching.

RUPERT [*to driver*]: rue Daunou, please.

DRIVER: Which part, *monsieur*?

RUPERT: Hotel Daunou.

DRIVER: Yes, *monsieur*? It is almost too small for me to know it. You have been there before?

RUPERT: Many times. It is big enough for me. You need not hurry in this blackout.

The taxi meanders across the river to the Hotel Daunou.

VOICE: I was alone with my ghost in a sad city of dreams, where the poor, if they were artists, had always been richer than the rich, but within our small circle the rich without talent were a thousand times poorer than the poor. In my beloved family, there had been no distinction between rich and poor, race and creed. Security and comfort we regarded as both normal and proper, and this must have implanted in us an inherent confidence in our relationship with life. So when I went to sea as an ordinary seaman and first encountered what for many were real and usual – poverty and squalor and their attendant discomforts and temptations – I was filled with a mixture of amazement, anger and compassion. Mother had always subscribed generously to charities, but, what was more, she had given herself, her heart and her time to not only her family but also those less fortunate. Father's life was too full for him to become involved personally, but he knew the poor and lonely were always with us, so at regular intervals he distributed lead-lined chests of tea from Trincomalee and oranges packed in pine crates from Jaffa to less fortunate friends and acquaintances. He also signed monthly cheques and distributed other monies for servants on pensions and to local charities. None of his gifts were made as a feudal gesture or to ensure himself a ringside seat at an English heaven. It was done because he was essentially a kind man with all the instincts of a generous one, and because it was a time when the words *noblesse oblige* still had meaning. My own charitable efforts had, alas, been confined mostly to assisting friends, acquaintances and sometimes strangers out of their temporary difficulties, usually while we were bellied up at bars constructed of mahogany, oak, teak, cane, zinc or even empty packing cases, according to the part of the world into which I'd drifted. I seldom earned what I gave away and there was little virtue in being generous with Father's money. Most of my friends had been older and wiser, so I sought their company

362

because I must still have been in search of the holy grail, pressing on undeterred by those drafts of experience I had already imbibed from the poisoned chalice.

★ ★ ★ ★ ★

CUT TO – **Rupert** *alighting from the taxi and disappearing into the Hotel Daunou.*

VOICE: For the first time in my life, I was pleased to leave the beloved, sad, waiting city, simmering uneasily while the scum rose to the surface.

★ ★ ★ ★ ★

CUT TO – *Gare Saint Lazare next morning. A man shabbily dressed [****Jewish Writer****] fights through the crowd towards* **Rupert**, *who, as the newcomer taps him on the arm, embraces him.*

RUPERT: I expected nobody, Leon. How come…? But the train is leaving. Please get on it. England is safe.

JEWISH WRITER: I cannot go running away all my life.

VOICE: I could have replied: "It's better to run away and live to write another day"; but he was one of the many continental writers who displayed that useless, lonely courage so characteristic of the Jewish people.

★ ★ ★ ★ ★

CUT TO – **Rupert** *squeezing a place for himself at the door of the carriage to wave to his friend as the friend waves.* **Rupert** *swallows to contain that which it is too late to utter.*

Rupert *and his friend and colleague Alec Robertson [**Robbie**] sit in armchairs adjoining each other in a secluded corner of* **Rupert's** *club.*

RUPERT: It's not just for the pleasure of having you as my guest that I asked you here, Robbie. I've received the call – THE call, at last, and, although I might try to pretend otherwise, the excitement is a bit much for one person, so I'd like you to share it with me.

ROBBIE: A vacancy for a King's Messenger?

RUPERT: Yes, but on the grapevine I hear there might be two. Would you consider it?

Robbie *reaches for his drink, takes a sip, says nothing, looks thoughtful.*

VOICE: When the summons to transfer to the Foreign Office came, I felt that irresistible call of the out trail, the best of the offshore wind and the thrash of deep-sea rain. As a King's Foreign Service Messenger, I would revisit the golden cities I had known across the great wide oceans, the green islands and the busy ports I had seen as a young seaman. I was to have the opportunity given to few men of replaying the dreams of their youth. In my heart I knew that this longing to be on my way was like a fatal disease, stronger than even my love for the girl I was determined to marry. Was I fool or knave?

Robbie *looks straight at* **Rupert**, *smiling.*

ROBBIE: I don't need to hesitate; for me to do so would be pretending, too. It's been in my mind for some time.

RUPERT: So it's yes?

ROBBIE: I'd feel irresponsible, letting you go off on your own just when you are beginning to respond to my training. Or am I pretending again?

VOICE: Robbie was amusing, down-to-earth and shrewd. Bad eyesight had kept him from active service, but he had been too restless for a chair-borne job. He was a faithful friend and a canny companion, with dry humour and the sort of wisdom I lacked. He had attached himself to me at the Admiralty as a kind man adopts a stray. He was neat and tidy where I was not. Letters must be answered instantly, appointments punctually kept, conventions respected.

RUPERT: Shall we visit the Foreign Office together tomorrow?

ROBBIE: I think not. First, let's write. Besides, we have to disengage ourselves from the Admiralty.

Rupert *frowns exaggeratedly.*

RUPERT: I don't like that word; couldn't you say "detach ourselves from the Admiralty"?

ROBBIE: If it makes you feel less of a cad.

★ ★ ★ ★ ★

CUT TO – Pall Mall, ten days later. **Rupert** *and* **Robbie** *alight from a cab and walk through the entrance of the Royal Automobile Club and into the hall, where* **Rupert** *goes to the counter and speaks to a* **Receptionist**.

RUPERT: Mr Roy Kinneard, please. My name is Grayson.

RECEPTIONIST: Would you and Mr Robinson care to take a seat while I call him?

GRAYSON: Thank you.

They do not sit, but stand. The **Receptionist** *speaks to an assistant, who scurries off, and seconds later a man,* **Kinneard**, *emerges from the interior of the club and makes for them. He is tall, slim, silver-haired and has no difficulty in recognising his guests. He smiles at them anti-pompously.*

KINNEARD: Delighted to meet you, and welcome to the club, though you have no doubt been here before. As a senior KM, I have been asked to tell you something about the Service and what it gets up to. I'm sure you will be more receptive if we sit over in that corner and take an *aperitif.* It is possible that you know more about the Service than I know myself, so please stop me if I send you to sleep – though, of course, by then it would be too late. Call me Roy.

RUPERT: My friend here is Robbie and I am **Rupert**, so between us we are three Rs – as at school.

ROBBIE: We'll have to remember our own names again after having been sailing under flags of convenience.

KINNEARD: I hope what I say does not smack too much of the schoolroom, and names of convenience might rear their heads for you again now and then.

At **Kinneard's** *suggestion, they sit at a table in an alcove. A steward appears and leaves with their order.*

KINNEARD: Forgive me if I dive straight into this, but my time is rationed by my superiors. As I say, gentlemen, and as you will already know, you have not left secrecy behind; you are exchanging one brand of it for another. King Charles the Second founded the Corps, of course, to, quote, carry out its sacred duties to preserve, secure and inviolate, to the utmost of its power, under every circumstance and every emergency, the dispatches entrusted to its care, unquote. Whatever you might say about the postal service today, it was worse then, and Charles had to institute his own postal service to carry letters between England and the Continent when he was exiled in Holland. Like Alice in the Looking Glass, the king needed one messenger to bring and another to take.

RUPERT: I don't know about my friend here, who can be startlingly erudite, but I think that in an examination on the Origins of the Corps, your mood would have to be extremely good to give me a pass. I had not imagined the Corps' headquarters could be traced quite so precisely to that particular monarch, though I imagine he had more secrets – political, military, amorous, even medical, no doubt –than one man could safely handle.

ROBBIE: Steady, Rupe. You'll have us kicked out for smearing the founder before we're even in.

KINNEARD: Don't worry, gentlemen. We are less concerned about yesterday than today. As I was saying, even now, with all our modern communications and methods of concealment, the Corps is unlikely to be supplanted by any other means of communication where confidences are concerned. The air can be tapped too freely, messages unscrambled, ciphers broken. The King's Messenger is never parted from the bags or pouch in which he carries letters and documents unless they are in safe custody. Thus, there is…

★ ★ ★ ★ ★

FADE TO – increasingly distant view of **Kinneard** talking on as they dine and wine, **Rupert** and **Robbie** putting questions here and there to express interest, real or feigned.

★ ★ ★ ★ ★

CUT TO – The front of the club as they leave, **Kinneard** *having a last word as they shake hands and part.*

KINNEARD: Oh, and prepare to leave at a moment's notice.

★ ★ ★ ★ ★

CUT TO – The Grayson house, where **Lady Grayson** *and* **Vari,** *Rupert's fiancée, help* **Rupert** *pack, he supervising. (Rupert's second marriage was to Vari Colette)*

RUPERT *[coming and going excitedly]:* Don't forget that I shall be visiting every kind of climate, so my suits should range from the lightest to the heaviest.

LADY GRAYSON: We're way ahead of you, Rupert. You should know by now that women have brains as well as hands.

Vari *does not join in the banter and* **Rupert** *also becomes quiet.*

VOICE: As I watched Mother and Vari pack my bags, the elation evaporated and I was anything but happy. A month ago, I had been so deeply in love that the idea of being parted from Vari would have been unthinkable. Was it the model with whom I was in love or the portrait? Was I even capable of love or was it no more than the reflection of myself in someone's eyes? Could I bridge the wide river that flows between youth and middle age? Only time would tell. I had set out to experience life in as many forms, in as many parts of the world, as my health and sanity would allow. I had, I hoped, a lively inquisitive mind, yet, with more opportunities than most to absorb wisdom, I knew I was no wiser than the countryman or the commuter who raises a family and leads a humdrum life within a few miles of his home. I no longer had hopes of high attainment and had shed any illusions about myself, for it seemed I was destined to be always a day late and a dollar short. Yet I was determined there must be as few mysteries outside my experience as possible before fate administered the final heave-ho.

★ ★ ★ ★ ★

CUT TO – Next day. Through the window the taxi can be seen waiting, the cloth-capped driver coming and going with **Rupert's** *suitcases.* **Rupert** *and* **Vari** *engage in a prolonged embrace, which they conclude with a sustained gaze into each other's eyes.*

RUPERT: I can tell you it's not all fun.

VARI: What's not?

RUPERT: Being, well… a romantic, I suppose.

At which, **Vari** *gives a wintry smile and dabs an eye with her handkerchief.*

★ ★ ★ ★ ★

CUT TO – *The taxi,* **Rupert** *getting in.*

RUPERT *[to driver, as he waves* **Vari** *and* **Lady Grayson** *goodbye]*: Euston, please.

★ ★ ★ ★ ★

CUT TO – Greenock-on-Clyde, Scotland, closing on the huge 'Mauretania', whose name, though painted out, can be discerned close-up on the bow. **Rupert** *turns to* **Robbie**, *who is following him up the gangway.*

RUPERT: I can't deny being elated at what this means, but never has one embarked so dismally. Just us and this great ship, no one to say goodbye, damned seagulls squawking as they try to bomb us…

ROBBIE: Is it true we're the only passengers?

They resume the trudge up the gangway and along a corridor to their accommodation.

369

RUPERT: So far as I know, yes – apart from two others, both celebrities like us: the chief bandmaster of the Royal Air Force and Karsh of Ottawa, the photographer.

VOICE: Karsh was considered the greatest photographer of his time. He had been to England photographing the brightest lights in the Allied constellation, including the king and queen. He had immortalised Churchill in a picture that became famous overnight. Churchill had taken up the pose in which he wished to be depicted, but at the last moment Karsh had snatched the cigar from his mouth. This unprecedented impertinence sparked off a mighty flash of anger in the great man's eyes. The result, as millions know, was a photograph of Winston in his most ferocious bulldog mood as the man of blood, tears, toil and sweat. It gave history the only photograph Churchill ever approved for publication that did not include his trademark: the cigar. It took a foreigner to drum up such cheek and a genius to apply it.

The pair follow corridors, looking this way and that, checking numbers and muttering to each other about where they are going.

RUPERT: If virgins are your cup of tea, Robbie, this ship should suit you. It completed its sea trials a month ago and we are on the maiden voyage, and a highly inauspicious one at that.

ROBBIE: Why so?

RUPERT: Because I have just discovered that the ship is as dry as a bone. Not a bottle or keg in the length and breadth of her. They told me ashore. It is to conform to the American naval regulation that no ship should carry intoxicating liquor. They are keeping it pristine for the Yanks, more than a thousand of whom, I understand, will board her for the return voyage.

ROBBIE: A thousand Yanks should put paid to her virginity. But if you are joking about the liquor, please don't.

RUPERT: Sorry, old chap, but I'm not. The Americans are going to win the war for us and there is a terrible price to pay, starting now.

ROBBIE: But we are not American. Nor is the ship, and it can't have been handed over yet. And we so few. You mean utterly, completely dry?

RUPERT: As dry as a camel's bones that have lain for a thousand years beneath the sun of the Sahara. Well *[lowering his voice to a whisper too soft for Robbie to pick up]*, almost.

They stop outside a door and **Robbie**, *without putting his luggage down, nods at it.*

ROBBIE: Yours. Mine's next door if the numbering's right. I'll visit you when I have turned on the air-conditioning and hung up the tuxedo.

★ ★ ★ ★ ★

CUT TO – **Rupert** *entering his cabin, which is sumptuous enough to be first-class. He dumps his small suitcase and rummages in an overnight bag from which he takes toilet items, and keeps burrowing until from the womb of a rolled-up towel he draws a bottle of Scotch. He exultantly holds it up to the cabin light so that the label shows, looks at the doorway to ensure he is alone, and kisses the bottle. The door opens suddenly and* **Robbie** *enters. With a look of alarm,* **Rupert** *impulsively starts to hide the bottle, but then relaxes before his friend, brandishing the prize and grinning.*

ROBBIE: Good Lord! Johnnie Walker Black Label. Where did you get that? *[His voice drops secretively]* Do you have more?

RUPERT *[wistfully]*: Tragically, no. I wonder what good soul had the compassion and forethought to plant such a gift in our midst. If we try to match that kindness, we are going to have to share it with our fellow passengers, don't you think?

ROBBIE: You haven't even offered to share it with me, yet.

RUPERT: No, but I can't avoid doing so, can I. It is not that I mind so much drinking alone. We all do from time to time. But to have you knowing that I was doing so…

ROBBIE: Why on earth one bottle? It's neither dog nor wolf, Rupert. Most unlike you…

RUPERT: And if you don't mind my saying so, it's not like you to look a gift horse… But, as I've said, it was nothing to do with me. A well-wisher slipped it into my bag at the last moment. I saw something furtive going on and afterwards it felt heavier; and I do know something about the weight of bags. But it poses a moral dilemma, don't you think?

ROBBIE: Whether to share?

RUPERT: Of course. I caught sight of the other two on the dock and they looked so miserable. Their faces were like… like… *[gropes for a word dire enough]* mayonnaise. Could we have them on our conscience right across the Atlantic?

ROBBIE: It's up to you.

RUPERT: No, I want your opinion. It's too serious a matter for a man to bear on his own. If we are going into partnership as consumers, we must also share responsibility as suppliers. For my own part, I don't think I could look in the mirror if we hoarded it and drank on the sly. That would mean growing a beard and I have been given too many razors for that. Come to think of it, why have I been given so many? Is there some fear that I might become a rabbi?

372

ROBBIE: No, the donors probably hope you will shave in a storm. But I agree it would be like starting off on the wrong foot in our new career, which behoves us above all to be gentlemen.

RUPERT: For me to become a rabbi?

ROBBIE: No, to be mean. I'm afraid we must suppress our baser instincts and share your windfall.

RUPERT: So, it's decided. But there are other responsibilities. We must ascertain how long the voyage will take and at what rate to consume our stock.

ROBBIE: Before we get too virtuous, ought we not find out whether our fellow passengers might also have had a windfall? You never know: the bandmaster must be a jolly fellow with lots of friends – one of whom could have stuffed some contraband into his trombone.

RUPERT: A "contrabandmaster". But you may be right, so we must not show our hand prematurely.

ROBBIE: Perhaps we should call a meeting with the other two and sound them out.

RUPERT: You do it; you're more of a convener than I.

★ ★ ★ ★ ★

CUT TO – **Rupert's** *stateroom, the four passengers in conclave.*

KARSH [*showing palms of hands*]: The answer, I'm afraid, is 'Nothing to Declare'. We were as dumbfounded as you must have been to find the ship dry. As a matter of fact, when I heard there were only four of us on board, I thought, hell, what an onus we're under to do more than our bit at the bar. Funny, huh! [*Shakes head incredulously*].

Rupert *eyes the bandmaster inquiringly.*

BANDMASTER: The same goes for me. I never dreamed there could be drought in mid-ocean. But as a musician, I appreciate the God-given opportunity to wet my whistle – though "moisten" would seem a better word.

RUPERT: So much for stocktaking. Our concern now, if I may take the chair of the One Bottle Club, to which I assume you have appointed me, is how most enjoyably and prudently to consume the bounty, in all its modesty, with which providence and an unknown benefactor have endowed us. It is a responsibility I would not have chosen for myself, since our way ahead is far from clear – to us, that is; I hope the captain thinks otherwise. You see our options: we could liquidate the stock at one stroke, throw the evidence overboard and grow haloes the size of lifebuoys for the rest of the voyage. In that way, we would insure against the irony of being torpedoed with the bottle unfinished and having to polish it off, perhaps not equally shared, in a lifeboat, or even trying to pass it around while treading water. Or – and I think this is to be preferred –we can make certain assumptions and ration it, so that its benefit is maximised during what we estimate to be our time aboard. Robbie thinks the trip will take about six days, but not even the Master can know for sure, since he receives his orders as we go along according to factors like weather, submarines and icebergs. To help me in my frailty, gentlemen, I suggest we mark the bottle into six parts, one for each of Robbie's days, and share it equally among us when we meet for the purpose each evening, which I propose be at the hour of six. At each meeting, we must decide the venue for the next. We do not want to establish a pattern that would be conspicuous to those charged with upholding the ship's discipline.

ROBBIE: That is one of the finest speeches I have heard you make, Rupert. It shows what a man can rise to if the cause is worthy.

KARSH: Quite Churchillian.

BANDMASTER: 'ere, 'ere. My cheeks burst to blow you a fanfare, sir, but my brass is in the hold.

RUPERT: Secrecy, mind. The crew's eyes are on us. Let's start in my cabin this evening and take it from there, a sip at a time. Now, I don't mind if you leave me to have a nap.

★ ★ ★ ★ ★

FADE TO – **Rupert's** *cabin that evening. The ship is pitching and rolling as* **Rupert** *dispenses the quotas with as much precision as he can achieve against the tossing. He squints and holds the bottle up, trying to make the surface of the whisky horizontal.*

VOICE: Thus began the ritual. So anxious were the participants to convey the Black Label safely to their mouths that for stability they sat down to drink, holding their tumblers with both hands as we used to bear birds' eggs gingerly home after a day raiding nests as children.

BANDMASTER: On sojourns in the United States, I have been impressed by the speed with which Americans down their drinks – their shorts, that is. It is reminiscent of a martial art. The elbow shoots up, the head snaps back, the rim of the glass hits the nose, the gullet twitches, the pharynx exudes a victory sigh and the deed is done – the equivalent of a whole week's ration gulped in the time a lizard takes to snap a fly.

RUPERT: You bring the phenomenon vividly to life, Bandmaster, if I may call you that. But it does nothing to strengthen my restraint. Our radio operators, you know, have a concept called fine-tuning. The Americans do not apply it to their drinking and I must say that so far I have had few occasions to apply it to mine. But now, we must all become fine-tuners.

★ ★ ★ ★ ★

CUT TO: The ship's lounge a week later. **Rupert** *and* **Robbie,** *the only*

375

occupants in its vastness, sit together at a bare table, silent and gloomy, rocking from side to side with the ship's roll. Robbie looks at his watch and speaks.

ROBBIE: Time, gentlemen, please. We must leave for our last appointment. D'you know, Rupe, it is the only series of meetings I have ever attended for which no one is ever late. The punctuality record has been 100 per cent. Do you think the world would keep its appointments better if they were all lubricated so sparingly?

RUPERT: Scarcity is a powerful force.

ROBBIE: I think you're right. *[Pause]* The past few nights I got the impression that Karsh was dragged here by the bandmaster, as though his heart was not in and he was turning up to pay his respects rather than claim his quota.

RUPERT: In that case, he could have sent a note of apology and let us deal with his. Perhaps there has been too much honesty in this enterprise. A bottle to ourselves would have made a lot of difference to our morale, don't you think?

ROBBIE: I'd like to agree, but to do so would be like saying you ought to have left me out of it and swigged it by yourself.

RUPERT: There is a difference between my coming clean with you, whom I have known for much of my life, and doing so with two people who only a week ago were strangers to us. Besides, no officer worth his pips would hide the last bottle from his servant.

ROBBIE: Especially if the servant was really the officer's brains and would be all too aware, anyway, that his master had been drinking.

They rise together from the table and stroll along the deck to their last drink meeting of the voyage. Beyond them is the expanse of deck intended for fun and games, romance and the excitement of travel, but now bleakly empty.

ROBBIE: Eerie, isn't it?

RUPERT: It cannot be what the designers had in mind.

*As they round the bend to **Rupert's** stateroom, they see a **Steward** standing at the door with an envelope in his hand.*

STEWARD: For you, Mr Grayson, from the bridge.

Rupert *takes the envelope and the steward moves off, hesitating only slightly in case there might be a tip. Inside the cabin,* **Rupert** *opens the envelope and reads the contents before handing it to* **Robbie,** *who reads and returns it to* **Rupert.**

ROBBIE: Rather changes things, doesn't it?

RUPERT: Halifax! Have you been there?

ROBBIE: No. They said New York was the destination and I believed it.

RUPERT: What sort of Man Friday are you, letting them do this behind your back?

ROBBIE: Have you been there?

RUPERT: Not that I remember. I heard about it at school. It consists entirely of fish and winter.

★ ★ ★ ★ ★

CUT TO – **Rupert's** *stateroom with the four passengers present.*

KARSH: You two look glum. I had expected you to be rejoicing, perhaps throwing your final ration over each other to celebrate our New York arrival.

BANDMASTER: Or daring to invite the Master for a farewell sip.

Rupert *hands the note to Karsh, who grins as he reads.*

RUPERT: I don't know whether you're responsible for this, but Halifax is one of your country's appendages, is it not?

KARSH: This is new to me, but I should have thought you undercover chaps would have been in the know.

ROBBIE: I doubt whether even the captain knew until yesterday. I believe we changed course during the night. Do you have any Canadian money up your sleeve, Rupert? I haven't a bean.

RUPERT: Afraid not. I was relying on New York for funds and made no provision for getting lost.

ROBBIE: I suggest, then, that we be nice to Mr Karsh, on whom we might have to rely for introductions.

KARSH: Mr Karsh has no influence in Nova Scotia, of which he has barely heard, and which he is sure contains nobody worth introducing to men of your calibre.

Rupert *pours the last of the whisky into their glasses, which are arranged in a line along a towel on the dressing table. He bends down like a surveyor, trying to make sure the surfaces are level, but because of the ship's motion has to thrust his spare hand behind or beside himself now and then to avoid toppling over. After holding the bottle upside down over the last glass for half a minute, smacking its bottom when he can spare a hand, he straightens up.*

RUPERT: Whatever predicament might await us, let us drink to triumph over adversity and thankfulness that we have arrived, or are about to, albeit in a part of the world that has barely been discovered.

KARSH: This Canadian will not be provoked, but he might just lose interest in bringing his nationality to the aid of certain imperialists who find themselves stranded in one of their most primitive former colonies, with nothing in their pockets but monogrammed handkerchiefs.

ROBBIE: Come, Karsh, don't be barbaric. You have mingled with the great and are, of course, great in your own right. Besides, with any luck, we'll find a telephone in Halifax and might not need your help, generously though I believe you would offer it.

RUPERT: I think Robbie's on to a possibility there, even two possibilities. Or a possibility in the case of the telephone and, judging from Karsh's enjoyment of our selflessly shared bottle, a probability in the case of the help. Or even a certainty in the latter case, since if we found a telephone in Halifax, it would be certain that Karsh would have interceded for us even if we now no longer need him to.

KARSH: You are talking Foreign Office crap, Grayson, and I am no match for that even though I have contacts that go way over your head. Is this mine?

Karsh *takes the glass containing his final portion, downs it at once and replaces the glass on the towel.*

KARSH: Thanks. Good luck. Sleep well. See you tomorrow. I'm going to pack.

BANDMASTER: See, you've sent the poor chap packing.

GRAYSON: Don't worry about Karsh. His hide is tougher than a buffalo's. It has to be.

★ ★ ★ ★ ★

*CUT TO – Next day. The dock at Halifax as they straggle ashore to a couple of old taxis that take them to the nearby Canadian Pacific Railroad Hotel, where they dump their stuff in the lounge and sit at a table with two bottles of Canadian Rye and larger glasses than those they have been using for the past six days. **Rupert** takes a mouthful and gasps with satisfaction.*

RUPERT: I feel like a pony out to grass after having been stabled for a week.

They all take another swig.

ROBBIE: Not too much grass at the moment for us, Rupe.

RUPERT: Quite so. Stay here while I visit the railroad station yonder and see whether we must spend the rest of the war here fighting alcohol, or can return to our original agenda.

***Karsh** begins to rise, but sits again as **Rupert** puts a hand on his shoulder and presses him into the chair.*

RUPERT: Too many people heading for the station in a place like this might be thought a stampede. We don't want to be lassooed or thrown into the sea as too small to fry.

ROBBIE: If you're not back by sundown, I'll send the Mounties.

*With a circling of arm and hand above his head in imitation of a cowboy winding up and throwing a noose, **Rupert** utters a refined "yippee" and leaves the lounge.*

BANDMASTER: Now that we're in what you might call frontier territory,

380

it should not be out of place to succumb to a little gambling fever, so if you critters are willing to take me on, I'll wager Rupert succeeds in his mission.

KARSH: I'm tempted to take you on, but I get the impression that none of you Limies has any stake money.

ROBBIE: All his life, since he roamed the world as a child wherever he could persuade his father to take him, Rupert has enjoyed what for want of a better word we might call "travel-charm". It is a magic oil with which he anoints the paths he treads, smoothing them for himself and all who tread with him. Where travel is concerned, he is a kind of souped-up St Christopher. Underestimate him at your peril.

★ ★ ★ ★ ★

CUT TO – The station across the square from the hotel, with **Rupert** *saying an effusive thank you at the ticket window as he turns, smiling, and walks away. He returns to the lounge grinning and waving two tickets, one of which he peels off and gives to* **Robbie.**

BANDMASTER – I had been on the point of telling you, Karsh, that I'm not quite so broke as our two friends here, but in view of what I now see and hear you should be thankful I am slow.

RUPERT: I think it's worth another slug, as Karsh might call it. We are on the night express to Montreal, Robbie, thanks to what seems to be a system of rolling credit. When I explained our predicament and uttered a few magic words, the booking clerk issued the tickets against recovering the money from the sleeping-car attendant, who will be reimbursed in Montreal by the porter who takes our luggage, who will be paid by the taxi driver who delivers us to the Ritz-Carlton, whose hall porter will pay the taxi driver and who will in turn be recompensed by the hotel cashier, who will, after making a telephone call, see us on our way to New York and a final reckoning with His Majesty's representative. When such a concatenation of deals can be arranged by someone as innocent as I, it is not hard to understand how the world becomes pot bound with dubious financial entanglements.

★ ★ ★ ★ ★

CUT TO – The sleeping compartment of the express, where **Rupert** *and* **Robbie** *are trying to retire to their bunks in the confined space.* **Rupert** *has been given the top one, but is having to be helped there by* **Robbie,** *who puts his hands under the other's foot and heaves him, wobbly from the Canadian Rye, up.*

RUPERT: You make a dreadful stirrup, Robbie.

ROBBIE: Most travellers of your age make it to their bunks unaided.

Clothes come over the side of **Rupert's** *bunk as he undresses. A shoe lands in the washbasin.*

RUPERT: Lock the door and admit no blondes. I'm off duty until morning.

★ ★ ★ ★ ★

CUT TO – The train pulling into Montreal. **Robbie** *and* **Rupert** *take a taxi to the Ritz-Carlton. Inside,* **Rupert** *has a word with the hall porter, who sends a boy to the taxi with money.* **Rupert** *saunters around the lobby and pauses to gaze at the carpet with its red, blue, pink and yellow flowers.* **Robbie** *joins him.*

RUPERT: Yes, we'll go up now. I was just savouring the place. It has memories for me, you know. Childhood memories. Or perhaps the very end of childhood. Father brought me here with my sisters in 1912 and I enjoyed, unbeknown to Father, my first taste of love.

ROBBIE: Not on this carpet, surely?

Rupert *laughs tolerantly.*

RUPERT: No, no. My interest in the carpet comes from a fascination with textiles. The carpet, if you didn't know, was woven in Hong Kong especially for Cesar Ritz. As to the other matter, my initiation into the garden of desire happened not between, but on, another textile – the sheet, up there, *arriba, [rolls his eyes to the ceiling]* – in a room whose number I remember to this day, 513.

Rupert *reflects.*

RUPERT: I wonder what became of her – prosperous *madame*, gangster's moll, society hostess, or perhaps under a gaudy tombstone in a Mexican cemetery.

ROBBIE: Can we take your dreams upstairs? I'd like to unpack and shower.

RUPERT: Of course, but you must be understanding with us middle-aged romantics. Our memories are fragile.

ROBBIE: Come on.

They step into a nearby lift and the door closes on them.

★ ★ ★ ★ ★

CUT TO – That evening, emerging from the same lift, shiny and dressed. Nothing much is doing in the lobby and when they wait for a few minutes at the front door, no taxi appears.

RUPERT: Let's walk. I don't think the snow's too deep yet and the exercise will do us good. Head for the glare. I know it's a French city or with French separatist tendencies, but there used to be a part of it called the French Quarter that was lit up more than the rest.

ROBBIE: Lead on.

They walk in single file, **Rupert** *in front, and after a few twists and turns come to a street of bright lights and neon signs.* **Rupert** *leads them into a restaurant.*

RUPERT: It's a pig in a poke, but let's pretend we know it's all right.

ROBBIE: Why not?

They pass a dance floor and sit at a table behind it in the restaurant. They pick up the menus that are put in front of them.

RUPERT: Perhaps we ought to have walked farther. Beaujolais is the only wine on the menu, but two fugitives from wineless, fruitless, meatless, blacked-out Britain must be grateful for anything out of a barrel, especially if the steak is of peacetime quality.

★ ★ ★ ★ ★

CUT TO – A view from across the dance floor, where couples gyrate, to the rear where **Rupert** *and* **Robbie** *are tucking in.*

ROBBIE: I suppose we risk being misunderstood, two grown men gorging like pigs while priorities elsewhere in the place are quite different.

RUPERT: I'm happy to be vulgar for the moment. Let us be impressed while it doesn't matter. Soon enough, we'll have ambassadors' tables at which to be *blasé.*

ROBBIE: We owe it to the Service to practise enjoying the unenjoyable – with its policy of pretending to do everything on a shoestring.

Rupert *ingests a particularly large mouthful, which causes a spasm of his Adam's apple and subsequent reddening of the face as he swallows it prematurely to reply.*

RUPERT: Pretending, yes. How could it actually do things on a shoestring with servants like us?

384

ROBBIE: Thanks to the Admiralty for its training. But the Service is creative as well as functional. What use would have been our classical education if we took everything literally and overlooked the metaphor, hyperbole and even casuistry that spiced our academic diet?

RUPERT: You're outwitting me, Robbie. Let's change the subject. Or, rather, stick to it.

ROBBIE: Which?

RUPERT: Beaujolais, of course. Wash your mouth out with it. Forget what you said about defrauding the Service. And let's have another plate of chocolate mousse. Spooning up that stuff almost makes me forgive the French.

★ ★ ★ ★ ★

CUT TO – *The dance floor, where lovelies with French mannerisms catch* **Robbie's** *eye.*

ROBBIE: I think *mousse* is not the only French invention here tonight that can please the British appetite.

RUPERT: I have eyes, old man, but from them, at the moment, I am composed largely of indifference.

ROBBIE: Your stomach does not seem to have thrown in the sponge.

Rupert's *mouth is too full to reply. The two sip quietly and ruminatively for some minutes, a pool of calm within the ferment of the premises.*

RUPERT *[eventually]*: I agree that we must stand out like sore thumbs here and I know sleep is about to replace hunger in my priorities. So this sore thumb would like to bandage itself in bedclothes.

ROBBIE: Yes, and tomorrow we hit the trail to our masters in New York, where we must present brave but needy faces.

★ ★ ★ ★ ★

*CUT TO – Settling the bill and walking clumsily out of the restaurant into the snow, which now blankets everything. As they stumble along, **Robbie** pauses now and then to take bearings. They reach the Ritz-Carlton to find the front door locked. **Rupert** tries to peer in through the spy-hole and raises his fist as though to pound on the door, but **Robbie** grabs his arm and points to beside the door where there is a flap, which, when lifted, reveals a button.*

ROBBIE: No need to behave like bailiffs when there are these electrical aids.

*No sooner has **Robbie** pressed the button than a **Porter** opens the door and looks them up and down as though deciding whether to let them in. As he gives them the benefit of the doubt and turns aloofly away to lock the door, **Rupert** slaps his pockets with a look of concern.*

RUPERT: I say, did you see my Viennese cigarette case? I'm sure I had it in that restaurant. It was gold and this is not where I should prefer to have lost it.

ROBBIE: Yes, you must have had it. I remember trying to dodge your filthy smoke.

RUPERT: Is your geography good enough to get us back there?

ROBBIE: Now?

RUPERT: Of course. You don't expect it to wait there indefinitely, do you?

ROBBIE: You were so proprietorial about the French Quarter that I dared not stick my nose in.

386

RUPERT *[eyes narrowing shrewdly]*: Perhaps geography is not that necessary. Let us make haste, dear Watson. Where has that damned fellow gone?

★ ★ ★ ★ ★

*CUT TO – The **Porter** emerging from behind a pillar.*

PORTER *[Irish accent]*: Is this the damned fellow you're wanting, sor?

RUPERT *[flustered]*: Oh, there you are. No, at least, I did not mean you were a damned fellow. Damned fine fellow is what I meant. In the small hours, I tend to make my sentences smaller and left out a word. Please forgive me and *[fumbling in his pocket for a fiver]* take this note as a token of my regret and a sign of our gratitude for opening the front door to let us in again. We have another little excursion to make.

*Mollified, the **Porter** turns the key in the door and opens it.*

PORTER: Thank you, sor, but are you sure you want to go out again on such a night, and if you do, sor, will you not let me try calling a cab?

Rupert *is already out the door and on his way.*

RUPERT: Thank you, Shamus. That is your name, is it not?

PORTER: Not exactly, sor, but near enough.

RUPERT: No, Shamus, we do not want a cab because the whole point of our going out is to search for something in the snow. Perhaps, if you want to be useful and have kept up relations with the Almighty, you might pray that we find it.

*The **Porter** cocks his head on one side, grins and murmurs.*

PORTER: He could be a Catholic at that.

Robbie *is quiet, as befits a man who has been dragged out into the cold when he has been looking forward to a whisky and bed. He follows behind* **Rupert,** *somewhat more steadily though with not quite the precision of a Guardsman. Snow falls lightly. Their homeward footprints have begun to fill, but still show as dents.* **Rupert** *doggedly follows them, now and then leaning over and peering down like an expert, veering away from their course and lurching back to it again. Once when he turns round to look for* **Robbie,** *his legs become mixed up and he falls. Realising he is not hurt, he laughs, and* **Robbie** *joins in, laughing at, rather than with,* **Rupert.**

RUPERT *[struggling to his feet, still giggling]*: That's what you get when an Irishman prays for you. I hope the Scots are better at it.

With snow still patching **Rupert's** *back and bottom, they round a corner into the bright street they were in before and the footprints lose themselves in slush through which people come and go.*

ROBBIE: Without the help of prayer, I believe the doorway we are now approaching is the one we want. Why not stumble through and make inquiries?

Rupert *goes in and a minute later, while* **Robbie** *waits outside rubbing his hands, emerges triumphantly brandishing the cigarette case.*

ROBBIE *[dourly]*: Sure it's yours?

RUPERT: Saint Christopher has permitted me one of his lesser miracles.

ROBBIE: Let us hope he does not squander them. I suspect miracles are what we'll need when the going gets serious.

The two retrace what is left of their footsteps back to the Ritz-Carlton. The night scene dissolves to be replaced by next morning in the hotel lobby, the two in conclave with the **Cashier,** *who is issuing money and rail tickets to them, explaining as he goes.*

388

CASHIER: My instructions, sirs, are to make available to you 500 US dollars each, train tickets to take you from Montreal to Washington and sealed letters to be opened once you are on your way. And there is a telegram for you, Mr Grayson.

The two go to a far corner of the lobby, sit at a desk and open their envelopes, and, in **Rupert's** *case, the telegram.*

RUPERT: The telegram is from my sister Nancy and her husband Louis, who are the kindest of people. No wonder Philadelphia is their home. They will meet us at the railway station there as the train passes through.

ROBBIE: Kind indeed. Let us hope it stops. These letters, though. I had thought New York was the next port of call, but it seems our destination is Washington.

RUPERT: I had thought so, too, but I suppose Washington will do as well for our purposes. It is curious, though, that our masters keep putting New York out of reach. *[Thoughtful pause]* It might seem far-fetched, but I wonder whether those clever dicks at the Ministry have it on record that I once jumped ship in New York and are keeping it and me apart.

ROBBIE: As you say, far-fetched, but not impossible. Many little mouths at the Ministry have to be fed and they sing all sorts of tunes for their supper. I believe they are linked up now, the various arms of the Civil Service, into one happy family that swaps information as in a village. I should be surprised if your little episode was not safely under your name on every official file in the country.

RUPERT: Perhaps, but if the net is so widespread, it is surely as effective in Washington as in New York.

ROBBIE: Yes, but New York is anarchy, and with little but contempt for

British representation in this country. If you needed rescue from the consequences of a past indiscretion, Washington would be the best – perhaps the only – place in the US to find it.

Rupert *ponders this, opens his mouth as though to speak, shuts it and looks at his watch.*

RUPERT: Time we thought of leaving. I don't know about you, but there is a restlessness in me, and now that I know St Christopher is on our side, I am eager to throw myself into the business of travel – if only to give him something to do.

On the train, through the windows of which can be seen speeding past the countryside approaching Philadelphia. A sign beside the track, saying Ph 10m.

Rupert *glances at* **Robbie** *to confirm that he has seen it.*

RUPERT: Does it mean minutes or miles?

ROBBIE: Much the same, I should think, at this stage, slowing down for America's friendliest city.

RUPERT: It will be friendly if the Drexels are meeting us.

Rupert *sits straighter in the seat, adjusts his tie, smoothes his jacket, pulls a comb from his pocket and runs it back through his hair.* **Robbie** *stands up and leaves the compartment. The outskirts of the city thicken as* **Rupert** *looks vacantly out at them with his own thoughts. The train slows and is soon creeping into Philadelphia's 69th Street Station to the donging of a bell and messages over loudspeakers. The brakes squeal as the wheels grind to a stop and the platform is full of bustle and colour, as if the curtain has lifted from the stage at a theatre – though the thickness of the windows muffles the activity.*

RUPERT *[excited, beaming]*: There they are, Robbie. Good lord, what have they got? Come. No, stay and guard our things.

Rupert *leaves the compartment, hurries along the corridor and down the steps on to the platform. He dodges between people and waves an arm to catch the attention of his sister and brother-in-law, who see him as he arrives at the luggage trolley they have rigged up with tablecloth, silverware and napkin-covered mounds. The outfit* *draws glances of curiosity and amusement from travellers.* **Rupert** *embraces his relatives, first* **Nancy**, *then* **Louis**. **Rupert** *tilts his head towards the trolley and its cargo.*

RUPERT: Don't tell me you've swapped banking for catering, Louis.

LOUIS *[with a nod towards Nancy]*: I delegate, Rupert. Lovely to see you.

Nancy *lifts the cloth away from the top of the trolley.*

NANCY: Dig in, Rupert. Trains don't linger here. The engine is panting to go.

RUPERT: Wait, Robbie's inside. I'll fetch him.

Rupert *disappears into the carriage and returns with* **Robbie**, *who is introduced while wine, sandwiches and savouries are thrust into their hands.*

RUPERT: The trouble with kindness on this scale, dear sister and brother-in-law, is that it makes one-way streets of our mouths and we cannot say all the things that should be said.

NANCY: You could at least give a quick *resumé* of things at home.

LOUIS: Dig in, though. Let's move down near your compartment. Where is it?

The trio and the vehicle move up the platform, **Rupert** *leading, both hands full, eyeing the compartments as they progress.*

RUPERT: Stop, we're here.

NANCY: Where to after Washington?

RUPERT: We really are the most miserable of guests, for we can't tell you a thing about our destination, which we don't know ourselves until the embassy has seen our faces. While France was rolling over on its back to the Hun, we were busy turning ours on the spectacle. The bags might have been filled with toilet paper.

NANCY: Don't be coarse, Rupert. What about Mother and Father?

Rupert, *who has taken a large bite, starts trying to speak with his mouth full and then swallows hard to clear it, his eyes watering with the effort.*

RUPERT: They're still apart. Father is still climbing all over the girders at the seaside, at least mentally, but his international ramblings have stopped. He might now have returned to London, which changes many things. He doesn't know what I am up to. Mother does not understand what the phony war is about and has stepped up her good works. They send their love, of course, and when I communicate with them we shall give them yours. Along with, of course, the nicest description I can of your mobile catering. It is really so kind, and… oh, blast [as whistles start blowing and a voice shouts to board the train], the picnic is over.

*At their hosts' urgings, they fill the goblets with more wine and the paper plates with food, and, so laden, do their best to say thank you and farewell while leaning forward and holding their spoils to either side like gulls spreading wings for takeoff. The travellers turn and climb into the carriage, **Robbie** first and then **Rupert**, while **Nancy** and **Louis** pass refreshments up to them. As the train pulls out, they wave through the window of the compartment to the two below, who reciprocate from beside the plundered trolley. Then, they are gone. The travellers lounge back in their seats to complete the repast.*

ROBBIE: Yours is the kind of influence I like, Rupert. Delightful.

RUPERT: She did not want to come here to live, but America seems to have done her no harm. Louis' money can't have hurt, of course.

ROBBIE: It often doesn't.

They sit silently for a minute as the train gathers speed.

RUPERT: I seem to have grown casual about the calendar. Do you know what day it is?

ROBBIE: Good question, but I'd go for Sunday.

RUPERT: I'd suspected that, but do you think the embassy, on which we are depending for financial salvation, will be open when we get there? No one said anything about meeting us and embassies don't meet our kind of wayfarer, anyway. We report to them, don't we?

ROBBIE: But if the tickets came from the embassy, they must know when we would arrive and in what condition.

RUPERT: Broke?

ROBBIE: Not exactly. But needing the usual official nursing. Where to stay, orders from London – everything, in fact, to avoid being lost and strayed.

RUPERT: We can hardly plead poverty. They gave us 500 dollars each. It would take many bourbons to flatten us so soon. But if the embassy is closed, where do we camp tonight? Our sealed letters did not cover that. I could grope my way around New York, but not Washington. It has always been outside my territory.

They look out of the window, but it is dark, with only a light here and there.

ROBBIE: There should be an emergency number even if the place is shut. I mean, ordinary British people must need the embassy's services on

Sunday. But why do we need it today, anyway? We still have enough for a drink and a meal, I'd say, and if we strike out on our own and find a hotel for the night, one of us can always stay there as a hostage in the morning until funds have been found.

RUPERT: Yes, I dare say they're less trusting in Washington than in Canada. But I think we'll find that Washington is stiff with brass and braid. It would be sad if two of His Majesty's finest had to spend their first night in the American capital on a park bench. Maybe taken by the police as hoboes or even taken by hoboes.

ROBBIE: Not a pretty picture, but might you not be over-imagining? You were a thriller writer.

RUPERT: The trouble is that our Philadelphia stop was so short and I no sooner got the feel of being with those people than we were torn away, and there is bound to be a reaction. As an antidote, why not open that bottle of whisky I saw you wrapping in your underwear in Montreal?

★ ★ ★ ★ ★

CUT TO – Washington station, which is busier than the last, with uniforms galore and many black faces – one of which, belonging to a **Cabbie** *who looms up at them expectantly, they address.*

ROBBIE: Could you take us to the British Embassy, please?

CABBIE: Yessir, folla me.

The **Cabbie** *begins to walk away.*

ROBBIE: Hold on, we've got things with us.

The **Cabbie** *pauses, twirling car keys around on a finger. A* **Porter** *brings the bags and they set off again. The* **Porter** *opens the boot and stacks the luggage inside. The*

395

two travellers wait to make sure it is all aboard before paying the **Porter** *and getting in. The taxi weaves through the lights and gleam of early evening traffic, until they turn into a driveway and pull up outside a building with the nameplate of the British Embassy by the entrance. A light shines dimly from within.*

RUPERT *[to cab driver]*: You'd better wait while I see what's going on, if anything.

Rupert *gets out, mounts the steps to the front door and presses a button. A light on the porch above his head comes on and the door opens to reveal a seedy fellow [***Smithers***] with rimless glasses and a waistcoat and gold chain.*

SMITHERS *[with as much hauteur as his appearance allows]*: Good evening. How might I help you?

RUPERT: My name is Grayson, King's Messenger. I am with a colleague, another KM named Robertson. Are we expected?

SMITHERS: No, but then I would not know, sir, unless specially informed. There is nobody here but me and I am by way of being a clerk, grade two. Do you have credentials, sir?

RUPERT *[irritably, pulling letter from pocket and thrusting it at clerk]*: Of course. This was delivered to me in Montreal, with a similar one for Robertson. Do you not think it strange that we are unexpected?

SMITHERS: One might say that, sir; perhaps an oversight, which would not be unusual nowadays.

RUPERT: Where is the ambassador?

SMITHERS: Away for the weekend, sir, and today is leave – or stand-down, as we are expected to call it during the war – for all staff.

RUPERT: Extraordinary. What happens if there is an emergency that demands the ambassador's attention?

Smithers *looks almost French as he shows the palms of his hands and shrugs.*

SMITHERS: His Excellency is away today but will be here tomorrow. Do you have an emergency?

RUPERT: In a manner of speaking, yes. In your arm of the civil service, you would probably rate it as an emergency grade three. We had rather fancied someone here might be awaiting us and our feelings are hurt to find that it is otherwise. But of more practical importance at the moment is the question of accommodation. We need a bed. Indeed [thinking suddenly distastefully of Robbie], two beds.

SMITHERS: Accommodation has become quite impossible, what with politicians crowding the capital and military people coming and going and businessmen swarming like flies after defence contracts. But we have a friend who might be able to help: Mr Arnold Cunningham, an archivist. Please come in and take a seat in the hall.

Rupert *follows* **Smithers** *inside and does not sit, but studies pictures on the wall.* **Smithers** *reappears.*

SMITHERS: We are lucky. You are both booked at the Mayflower Hotel and your names must mean something to Mr Cunningham, if not, begging your pardon, to me, because he has got you a room each. He's quite a magician where this sort of thing is concerned. And, come to that, I suppose in other ways, too. Books and papers, for example. I've no doubt that…

RUPERT [*with impatient flutter of hand*]: Most interesting. Do you mean that if we go to the Mayflower and give our names, we shall get rooms?

SMITHERS: That's right, sir. Ring me if you have difficulty.

RUPERT: And your name?

SMITHERS: Smithers.

RUPERT: Thank you, Smithers. One other thing. You don't have authority to issue cash, do you? We shall have to turn our pockets out to pay for the hotel.

SMITHERS: Don't worry about that, sir.

Smithers *draws a card from his pocket.*

SMITHERS: Give that to the hotel's cashier and tell him to charge it to the British Embassy. They know us at the Mayflower.

RUPERT: So they should with a name like that. But I hope it is more comfortable than the original.

Smithers *is unsure how to respond.*

SMITHERS: I understand it is popular with the navy, sir, though I am sure they will make you and Mr Robertson feel welcome and at home.

RUPERT: We hope so. If it is not up to standard, you will find us back here on the doorstep. And I'm sure your master would not like to return to find such high-class vagrants hanging about.

SMITHERS: Quite so, sir. Is it to be presumed we shall see you here tomorrow?

RUPERT: Of course. Thank you, Smithers, and good night.

Rupert *goes down the steps and enters the taxi. The* **Driver** *turns round inquiringly.*

RUPERT: Mayflower Hotel, please. *[And then to Robbie]* There was no-one there except a clerk, but through some friend of the embassy we seem to have been booked in at the place we are going to.

Robbie *grunts. In a few minutes, the cab draws up at an old-fashioned mansion. Above the entrance, around which curl wisteria vines, is the name in gothic lettering: The Mayflower Hotel.*

ROBBIE: The definite article and all.

RUPERT: Let's hope the booking is, too.

They get out, **Rupert** *paying the* **Driver**, *and carry their bags up the steps. It is busy in the foyer, with much navy braid. At the desk,* **Rupert** *consults a* **Receptionist**, *who nods, asks for passports, writes in a book and summons a* **Bellboy** *to take the baggage to the rooms. They all get into the elevator, the door closes on them and the scene cuts, to resume briefly in the corridor leading to their rooms. The doors adjoin each other and the* **Bellboy** *puts the bags down outside them, receives a tip from* **Robbie** *and goes.*

RUPERT *[nodding to the bedroom doors in turn]*: You take that one and I'll take this. When you've unloaded, come to my room and join me in a consultative drink. It might help us guess where our careers are going.

★ ★ ★ ★ ★

*CUT TO – Next morning. As the taxi drives off, they ascend the steps to the embassy and the door is opened by a man [***Jones***] somewhat more imposing than* **Smithers**.

JONES: I trust that I have the pleasure of greeting our two King's Messengers, Mr Grayson and Mr Robertson.

RUPERT: We are they, to keep our appointment with the ambassador, if he is in.

Jones *loses most of his smile.*

JONES: Please follow me, gentlemen, and let me have your passports for a few moments if you please.

*After handing the passports over, they enter a large room and are greeted by a thin man [**Ambassador**], who rises from behind a desk that makes up for his slightness, walks round it, shakes each by the hand and motions them to be seated in two armchairs on the other side of the desk. He walks back to his own chair and sits.*

AMBASSADOR: So, you're in the Mayflower. Not quite the Ritz, but a roof over the head. And, of course, with a name to gladden a patriot's heart. We've extended your stay there for a couple of days, during which we'll decorate your passports with visas and your bottoms with injections. Do you know Washington?

RUPERT: For myself, a little. I don't think Robbie has discovered it yet.

AMBASSADOR: Never mind, Robertson. It's chaotic at present. A bad time to start your education. And you, Grayson, does Washington enjoy your esteem?

RUPERT: My first impression of Washington as a city of great beauty, particularly in the residential district of Georgetown in early spring at cherry-blossom time, has endured over the years. Yet, I have found that in other ways, it is a city without charm. So unfortunate: beautiful, yet charmless. How does it stand with you, sir?

AMBASSADOR *[with a laugh]*: You should not ask a diplomat such a question because the answer would be unreliable. Tact beyond the bounds of truth is the path we follow to see good where there is bad. Our calling is a near-miss both ways: one degree to the left and we would be in prison; one to the right and in the pulpit.

RUPERT [grinning]: You have wriggled out of that elegantly, sir. But if you loved Washington, you could have admitted it, could you not? Without sinning, I mean.

AMBASSADOR [having taken their measure and begun to relax]: Yes, and I do quite like it, but for consistency's sake one becomes accustomed not to give answers that could be sensitive. We might be talking about people rather than places. It would be all right for me to say I disliked this or that monster, because everybody dislikes monsters – except perhaps [a sly glance at Robbie] the Scots – and an opinion to the contrary would be unbelievable. Yet when the time came for an opinion on someone who was not a monster, but was liked by some and disliked by others, I could not give any sort of answer without offending. Or, turning the proposition another way, one's feelings would become pretty clear if one were to heap praise on two people and not on a third. So you see, as a dogmatist, I am unworthy because I have been trained to bend with the breeze or behave as though becalmed. By the way, do you have any inkling of what your playgrounds are to be?

ROBBIE: Not really, sir. A pencilling, you might say, but not an inkling.

AMBASSADOR: See what you make of these.

At which, the ambassador pulls open a drawer and takes from it two passports, which he flicks deftly in turn to their respective owners, who as deftly catch them. They open and examine them.

AMBASSADOR: When you gave me these on your way in, the pages were pretty blank. Look at them now.

401

As they do so, slowly turning the pages, the two murmur from time to time as though impressed.

ROBBIE: I'd say, sir, that not much of South America has been left out.

RUPERT: Or central America. You know the difference, Robbie?

ROBBIE: As it happens, yes, even more than that between Scotland and the country to the south of it whose name I cannot recall.

Rupert *opens his mouth to speak but the* **Ambassador** *beats him.*

AMBASSADOR: I see there is a fine *esprit de corps* between you.

RUPERT: I suppose, sir, we do have our respective spirits, which makes for a British cocktail of sorts, but I'm sure it will not blow our heads off.

AMBASSADOR: So far you have been together, but soon you will go your separate ways, weaned of each other's protection and meeting only as your paths cross. I hope you are ready for the solitude of the King's Messenger.

The three smile at each other without speaking – the **Ambassador** *serenely,* **Robbie** *politely,* **Rupert** *somewhat anxiously, at the same time scratching his thigh.*

★ ★ ★ ★ ★

CUT TO – Evening at Washington train station. The Florida Limited is waiting to leave for Miami. **Rupert** *and* **Robbie** *board it and stow their bags. The compartment is sumptuous. A black* **Steward** *puts his head in the door.*

STEWARD: Evenin' folks. Redda for yoh bedsa be made up yet?

RUPERT: Thank you, but no. Leave us for an hour to have a little drink. Then we'll visit the dining car and you could sneak in here and make it comfortable for us to pass the night. [*To* **Robbie**] You agree?

402

ROBBIE: Of course.

Robbie *tips the* **Steward**, *who leaves. Through the window, the platform slides away, people waving and mouthing messages of farewell. The picture speeds up and vanishes as the platform ends. The train spears through the miscellany of night: lights of building and traffic, mixtures of shade and dark, now and then the ding-dong, which penetrates even the sound-proofing, of a level crossing. Soon, enclosed by the padded armrests of their seats, each holds a glass of whisky.*

RUPERT: Do you know this part of the world?

Robbie *drops into Scottish dialect as though to emphasise his lack of travel.*

ROBBIE: Nae, I cannae say I doo, mon.

RUPERT: Then I'm sorry for you in a patronising sort of way. It is a pity you are missing it. Let me paint a picture of the scene through which we shall soon be passing while you are still under Foreign Office anaesthetic. To right and left of us will be small homesteads dwarfed here and there by the porticoed mansions of large plantations. Looking at them by day, you would feel the breath of dense crops and dark-green citrus trees, and go back to what you can remember of William Faulkner and Tennessee Williams and others who drew on it for their sweltering atmospheres, swamps and tobacco plantations, tragi-comic negro life, dilapidated splendour, uneasy happiness, a here and now that is at the same time strange and distant. Train travel is hard to beat.

Robbie *eyes monitor* **Rupert's** *face from under eyebrows that seem to thicken.* **Rupert** *sips absent-mindedly and peers through the window, trying to make out what is there. Instead of seeing, he has a dream sequence in which famous trains on which he has travelled drift past his inner vision: the Orient Express traversing the flats of the Danube Basin on its way to Istanbul, the Red Arrow from Leningrad to Moscow through clouds of snow, the Johannesburg night train twining to the Great*

Karoo, the express from Bergen skirting fjords, the 20th Century from Chicago to New York, The Chief via Santa Fe to Los Angeles, the Flying Scotsman, the Brighton Belle to lunch at the Metropole on a Sunday, the White Train between Port Said and Cairo, the Bullet from Osaka to Tokyo and the Lisbon Express hooting its way between Alicante and Denia in Spain.

ROBBIE: Your *reverie* is respected, Rupert, but this train will not be one of your favourites if we do not make it to the restaurant soon.

RUPERT *[snapping to]*: You're right. Lead the way.

★ ★ ★ ★ ★

CUT TO – The restaurant car. They are eating with forks in the American way, having cut up the food with knives.

ROBBIE: So far our travels have been empty of drama, if we leave out your cigarette case.

RUPERT: We are having our first taste of secrecy, but I don't think it's deliberate. Our masters are not withholding anything. It's just that they don't know. We are receiving tuition for the blind without being given it, if you understand me. It is occurring spontaneously. That garrulous ambassador just about knocked all the questions out of me.

ROBBIE: He could have been a schoolteacher

RUPERT: Yes.

They prong, chew and sip wordlessly for some minutes.

ROBBIE: Do you think Miami is our destination or just a pickup point for instructions?

RUPERT: No idea. Just drift with the system, if that's what it is.

404

Washington had a purpose. We got visas in our passports, money in our pockets and punctures in our bums. Miami must have one, too, even if it's only escape from London's privations.

★ ★ ★ ★ ★

CUT TO – Next day, Miami rail station. Harry **Bond** *scans the train as it pulls in. He sees what can only be them stepping down from the car they are in. While* **Porters** *in the background get their bags from the carriage,* **Bond**, *who limps, approaches the pair with hand extended.*

BOND: Grayson and Robertson, I presume? Harry Bond, British Consulate, with my own greetings and those of Michael Robb, our consul, who would like you to join him for lunch when we've checked you in. My job is to look after King's Messengers here.

The three shake hands with diplomatic smiles, leave the platform exchanging small talk and make for two cars – one for themselves, the other for the bags.

★ ★ ★ ★ ★

CUT TO – Inside the car that has collected them from the station.

BOND: The car will take you to a hotel where you are booked in for a few days, during which you can find yourselves an apartment. It will pick you up again at one o'clock to join us for lunch.

★ ★ ★ ★ ★

CUT TO – The dining room at the consulate. **Rupert** *and* **Robbie** *are the guests of the young consul, Michael* **Robb**, **Mrs Robb** *and Harry* **Bond**. **Robb** *speaks while the others continue to sip their soup.*

ROBB: So, although Washington is officially the centre from which you work and take instructions, our employers have decided that in the case of you two gentlemen, whose foreseeable assignments will largely concern central and South America, it makes more sense to work for a time out of Miami, which is on the doorstep of that territory. The FO's instincts sharpen when it comes to saving money.

RUPERT: Do you have instructions for us yet?

ROBB: I think Harry has something up his sleeve.

Bond *bends and lifts a briefcase from beside his chair, opens it and takes out an envelope, which he hands to* **Rupert**.

BOND: For you, Rupert. They're keeping you in suspense, Robbie, but not, I think, for long.

★ ★ ★ ★ ★

CUT TO – That evening, on a patio of their hotel with a view across Miami, **Rupert** *and* **Robbie** *are finalising their evening round of drinks.*

RUPERT: I glanced at my envelope. From what I can make out, we alternate between the South American eastern and western routes, meeting and crossing over about every fortnight or so in Buenos Aires. But let's make more sense of it when you've picked up your secrets tomorrow.

Robbie *polishes off the last of his whisky and puts the glass on the table.*

ROBBIE: I'm off to bed.

RUPERT: Very wise.

ROBBIE: While you study your plans in the morning, I'm going to see what I can find in the way of accommodation.

Robbie *disappears into the hotel while* **Rupert** *lingers on the patio, looking out across the town and its lights, musing.*

VOICE: I had no preconceptions about Miami. It materialised as a bumptious, bouncing, blazing burg populated by working Floridans, mid-Westerners on business and wealthy wintering visitors who were prey to the con-men and gangsters infesting the jungle of hotels, gambling clubs, nightspots and racetracks. The other side of the picture were the residential areas peopled with mild-mannered, kindly old folk rocking away their last years on porches, stirring the occasional mint-julep and totally removed from the wealthy beaches with their glass, concrete and steel hotels, each with its swimming pool. Robbie quickly found a suitable apartment for us close to the consulate and set in a garden of shady trees. We were looked after and cosseted by a black man Robbie had lassoed from a corral of coloureds across the tracks. His name was Leroy and he was to play an important part in our lives, as a manservant should.

★ ★ ★ ★ ★

CUT TO – The new apartment, evening. **Rupert** *and* **Robbie** *are sitting in armchairs reading newspapers.* **Robbie** *puts his down and addresses* **Rupert***.*

ROBBIE: Did you notice anything about Leroy this evening?

RUPERT: Such as?

ROBBIE: He seems to have changed. I noticed it this afternoon when you were out. Instead of creeping almost apologetically about, he was striding around like a general. He looked taller, as though transformed from batman to officer. I heard him humming the *"Marseillaise"*. Have you raised his wages?

Rupert *puzzles for an instant until an explanation dawns. He laughs.*

RUPERT: It's the name, I think.

★ ★ ★ ★ ★

FADE TO – The day before, **Rupert** *and* **Leroy** *in conversation, getting to know each other.* **Rupert** *lowers the newspaper he has been reading and* **Leroy** *pauses in tidying the apartment.*

RUPERT: Of course, Leroy, you know where your name comes from?

LEROY: From mah daddy, ah guess – his gift to me.

RUPERT: That's right, but the name existed before your father did and is a streamlined version of the "*le roi*" – the French word for "king". The pronunciation has just been changed a little to make it easier to say in English.

Leroy's *eyes widen. He looks first at* **Rupert** *and then out the window.*

LEROY *[awed, slowly]*: So I'm a king, I'm a king.

RUPERT: Your ancestors once belonged to France under *le roi soleil*, the "sun king", Louis the Fourteenth, who sold to America the entire territory from the Gulf of Mexico to the Rockies in the west, and up to the Canadian border in the far north, for fifteen million dollars.

Rupert *pauses as* **Leroy** *nods slowly in wonderment.*

LEROY: Some deal, man.

RUPERT: It sure was, Leroy. They called it The Louisiana Purchase.

LEROY: Yeah, I heard about this Louisana Purchase. *[Shaking head]* But ah thought it was jess a fillum. That ancestor of mine must sure have been a rich king.

Leroy *walks about the premises more upright than before, shoulders back, head erect, hardly lowering it for dusting, humming to himself.*

★ ★ ★ ★ ★

CUT TO – The present.

ROBBIE: Apart from turning him into a king, though, you almost choked him to death.

408

Rupert *looks questioningly at* **Robbie** *with eyebrows raised and mouth open.*

RUPERT: How?

ROBBIE: At lunchtime, he was serving me soup and I thought he would burst. His face was not purple, of course, but it was kind of bulging, and so were his eyes. I asked him whether he was feeling all right, and he replied that he was not: he was gasping for air because you told him the best servants in England held their breath when they were serving at table.

VOICE: Leroy's first loyalty should have been to Robbie, who had engaged him, but it was I who had put him on the throne and placed the crown on his head, addressing him always as "*Le Roi*". His outlook had become so British that I was afraid his allegiance might switch from Old Glory to the Union Jack.

Views of Havana, Cuba, 1941, with crumbling white buildings of medium height, many in Spanish style; leafy streets, plazas with broken fountains, storm-drains, narrow alleys.

VOICE: Before the tourists discovered it, a favourite meeting place in Havana was Sloppy Joe's. Here the King's Messenger would meet new arrivals to Cuba, those about to leave and those who stayed on. It was here that Ernest Hemingway lined up the *daquiris* and threw his weight around. It was a long bar, as every bar should be, allowing a man to avoid his enemies and find his friends. It had two entrances, as every bar should, so that if you were thrown out one door, you could return by the other. Despite the singing and the laughter, I was always conscious of an atmosphere as taut as the strings of the guitars that accompanied me as I wandered back to my hotel in the dusk. The flashpoint of tempers was low. I remember listening to an argument between two men who had been taking it in turns to push a bicycle up a hill. One claimed he had pushed it farther than the other. The disagreement became a quarrel, knives flashed, followed by a scream. Then, silence; the triviality of the squabble exceeded only by its finality. But nature, there, was volatile, too.

★ ★ ★ ★ ★

CUT TO – The bar of The Floredila, where **Rupert** *is taking a drink with Arthur* **Floyd***, an elderly British expatriate and keen gardener.*

FLOYD: I don't mind telling you, Grayson, I am not the happiest of men this evening.

Rupert *says nothing, but looks at his companion quizzically and then away at his drink, awaiting explanation.*

410

FLOYD: Most people scorn the idea that language and emotion exist between trees, but you ought not to fall for that.

RUPERT: They say plants listen for the voice of the gardener who feeds and waters them.

FLOYD: Yes, and it goes deeper.

Rupert *stays quiet for the sequel.*

FLOYD: I had two palm trees in my garden. One died recently and I'm afraid the other has started to wilt. It is not only people who can grieve unto death.

Rupert *shakes his head sorrowfully. Then, face brightening, tries to lift the mood.*

RUPERT: Only recently, there was a well-authenticated case, of which you are no doubt aware, of the tree that emitted distinct vibrations when the head gardener of an estate was having it off with his girlfriend in a potting shed a mile away.

Before **Floyd** *can react, and with* **Rupert's** *expression suggesting he is a little anxious about how he will do so, an* **Announcer** *breaks urgently into the music from the radio – first in Spanish and then English.*

ANNOUNCER: Attention, please: a hurricane centred on Cuba is approaching at a hundred miles an hour.

There is a clatter of feet and shrilling of voices as the bar empties. **Floyd**, *with the dignity of one already sorrowing and who, anyway, does not have many years to lose, unhurriedly takes his leave.*

FLOYD: I suppose this is as good a moment as any to go.

With a shadow of anxiety on his face, **Rupert** *seeks the correct interpretation of what* **Floyd** *has said.*

RUPERT: Home, you mean?

FLOYD: Yes, there's nowhere else I'd be going just yet, I hope.

RUPERT: Of course not. Good luck with the palm.

★ ★ ★ ★ ★

CUT TO – The lounge of the hotel to which **Rupert** *has walked from the bar. Staff of all kinds – receptionists, cashiers, porters, bartenders, chefs, waiters, pastry cooks, chambermaids – rush out through the front doors for home.*

VOICE: On every West Indian island, a hurricane warning is the signal for public places, *bordellos* excepted, to close. Shutters go up, buildings are hastily reinforced, small craft are hauled from the water, large ships put out to sea and even priests intoning vespers take to their heels.

A group of **Guests** *drift together in the lounge. The inevitable organiser emerges from among them, convenes a meeting, appoints himself* **Chairman** *and addresses the others.*

CHAIRMAN: The hotel has abandoned us, but we certainly won't abandon the hotel.

Nervous but eager applause as guests crane curiously to know what is going on.

CHAIRMAN: There is no reason why we should not continue to live in that luxurious manner to which we are all so unaccustomed.

Laughter from guests as they grow bolder.

CHAIRMAN: No one must be allowed to die of either hunger or thirst.

The **Chairman** *sits down to rounds of cheers. As he does, a group of anxious-faced guests returns from a reconnoitre of the hotel. One of the* **Guests** *reports to the* **Chairman**.

GUEST *[gloomily]*: Everything locked, barred and bolted: bars, kitchens, stores, fridges.

The **Chairman** *receives the news grimly.*

CHAIRMAN: We'll just have to think around it.

★ ★ ★ ★ ★

CUT TO – Three little **Cuban Girls** *in another corner of the lounge.*

VOICE: Quite unconcerned by this, however, were three beautiful little Cubans who were also attached to the hotel, though quite unofficially. They roamed it by day, disporting their amber bodies at the pool and haunting the bars and lobbies by night as artlessly as children. Now, they had retired to the far end of the lounge, awaiting events; their sleek dark heads forming themselves into a whispering posy.

★ ★ ★ ★ ★

CUT TO – Another part of the lounge where the respectable **American Women** *guests have gathered. They are discussing how to penetrate the barred and locked doors that confront them. Now and then, bleakly but with sure feminine instinct, they glance towards the three putas, recognising that only these Cuban girls, who know the hotel's secrets, can show them where the keys are hidden. Yet they hesitate to approach the girls outright because of sneers and slights they have dealt them in the past.*

VOICE: The little Cubans were accustomed to a certain ingrained prejudice to their way of life from their more secure sisters-in-sex, and had to accept it as something to be borne in the interests of human endeavour and the gaiety of mankind. However detached these American women had formerly been within their own social status, this major crisis called for a degree of unity. If there was any hesitation on their part, it concerned which

413

of them was to approach the Cubans. Eventually, three of the matrons were persuaded to sink their pride and plead with the girls – though whether on the basis of woman to woman or *puta* to *puta* was not clear.

Three of the **American Women** *leave their group and walk over to the* **Cubans**, *who are friendly and smiling. One of the American women remaining in the group speaks to another of their number.*

AMERICAN WOMAN 1: It's better that they volunteered; drawing lots is too much like compulsion, even though it might be perfectly fair.

AMERICAN WOMAN 2: You're right, and they know their way around this place better than the rest of us.

AMERICAN WOMAN 1: Though that doesn't mean they have anything in common with those girls.

AMERICAN WOMAN 2: Of course not. At least *[nipping a giggle in the bud]*, I don't think so.

★ ★ ★ ★ ★

CUT TO – The **Cubans** *and the* **American Volunteers**.

VOLUNTEER 1: You girls may be able to help. It seems the doors of everything in this place are locked and, of course, the staff, who seem to have taken off, would not want us to face a hurricane without refreshment.

VOLUNTEER 2: So if you could get the keys to open the kitchen, the storeroom and the bars, we would say the nicest possible things about you to the management when everything is back to normal. You would probably be written up in the newspaper as heroines of the hurricane.

VOLUNTEER 3: And we would, of course, expect you to join us in sharing whatever goodies you helped to make available.

The **Cubans** *need little persuading. Uttering cries of "Sure, sure", they scamper away and soon return with a bunch of keys, which they brandish for all to see as they dance back into the lounge, sparkling like children at a party. The keys are handed over to the* **American Volunteers,** *who, with other guests, go off to find locks for them. The camera moves from bar to refrigerator to kitchen to larder as each is opened and raided, the spoils being conveyed to the lounge as though by chain-gang. It also picks up the faces of the womenfolk, whose eyes, so recently ingratiating, resume their usual hard glaze. Cubalibras and daquiris start lining up three deep on the bar of the lounge. Strangers greet each other as long-lost friends. Though the musicians have gone, the piano remains, and someone unearths a few old guitars. The women dispense roast joints, spare ribs, hams, turkeys, chickens and game. Lobsters and oysters emerge from the recesses of the refrigerator.*

VOICE: Hung with ribbons and garlanded with roses, the restaurant took on the appearance of the Hotel Alfonso XI in Seville at fiesta time. Caviar was being ladled out of vast tureens and joints were rolled on to serving tables, along with the juiciest of steaks – some crowned, Rossini-style, with *paté de foie gras.* Corks popped and volleyed. The smoke of cigars, the glory of Havana, dusted the air and mixed with the spicy aroma of Brazilian coffee, while brandies from France and liqueurs from the four corners of the earth sweetened the atmosphere.

The twang of badly-played guitars clashes with the crash and crunch of broken glass and crockery. With everyone serving himself, there are the inevitable calamitous collisions, yet no one is anything but good-humoured about them. Eventually, the guests start singing "The Star-spangled Banner" and "Swannee", and Rupert, who has been watching the proceedings from a quiet corner, drifts over to the three **Cubans,** *who by now have returned to their corner.*

VOICE: Although I was enjoying the wine and the company, I was faced with an early departure next morning and decided it was Rupert's bedtime. In the quiet corner they had resumed, I paid my respects to the three little sisters of mercy. Ominously, I realised that the American equivalent of *Boule de Suif et Cie* was back in business.

415

★ ★ ★ ★ ★

CUT TO – Corridor along which, seen from behind, walks **Rupert** *and one of the* **Cubans,** *he holding a magnum of champagne by the neck as they walk to his bedroom.*

VOICE: How often had I made duty my pleasure! I invited her to enjoy a glass of champagne and laid my hands on a magnum. We had hardly entered my room when the radio suddenly blared the news: the hurricane had changed course and would bypass Cuba. From below rose the sounds of revelry unabated. We decided it was no business of ours to interrupt their enjoyment with such embarrassing news. Next morning, as I left the hotel to be driven by an embassy official to the airport, the building seemed lifeless. The occupants were sleeping it off, having the ecstasy without the agony.

Willemstad, capital of Curaçao, clean and Dutch, with its fretwork fronts and pastel colours – pink, brown, blue. Scan the harbour and move to the hotels, converging on the Inter-Continental.

VOICE: I had first briefly visited the island of Curaçao, off Venezuela, as a seafarer. Now, I had returned as a King's Messenger. The capital, Willemstad, retained the atmosphere of the Dutch settlement it originally was. The old pontoon bridge, which I had first seen from the fo'c's'le head, still opened and closed like a fan across the harbour entrance. Many of the original houses remained, with their Dutch facades in pastel shades of pink, brown and blue, adorned with white filigree-ornamental design, the entire scene burning under a fierce sun. Tourists flocked to see the new hotels and holiday inns where they could feel at home in little America, air-conditioned and uncontaminated by the sweetly-sick odours that pervaded many other islands in the region.

★ ★ ★ ★ ★

CUT TO – A bar at the Inter-Continental. When **Rupert** *enters it, only one other man is seated at it on a stool, a drink before him. He is a rangy,* **Texan** *type.* **Rupert** *orders a rum and coke. The* **Texan** *studies* **Rupert** *and addresses him in a drawl.*

TEXAN: Good-day, friend. You look well enough dressed to be a Limey, or should I say Englishman?

Rupert *smiles and swigs the rest of his drink.*

RUPERT: You're right, and either will do. And might I guess that even with no clothes on at all you'd be a Texan?

TEXAN: Right in one, pal. Not a policeman, are you?

RUPERT: No, but you're only a few letters out: I'm a postman.

TEXAN: But not on your usual round. Or are you saying you're a man of letters!

RUPERT: If I tell you everything, I'll have no secrets.

TEXAN: Let me get you a tongue-loosener. The same?

RUPERT: The first tasted all right, so, yes, thank you.

The **Texan** *lifts a finger for the barman to see, waggles it to indicate them both, and two drinks are put before them.*

TEXAN: If you're at a loose end, postman, what do you say we look in on The Happy Valley?

VOICE: I had visions of a Caribbean jazz festival, a beach discotheque, even a *pierrot* party imported from Llandudno or Bognor Regis.

RUPERT: Not tonight, if you don't mind.

TEXAN: Aw, come awn.

VOICE: He used that tone of American persuasiveness I have always found irresistible.

RUPERT *[weakening]*: What exactly is The Happy Valley?

TEXAN: Why, you don't know the Campo Elegre?

VOICE: He spoke delightedly because he knew he had his fish on the line. He dismounted from the stool and when I heard him call the hall porter for a hire car, I knew I'd had it.

★ ★ ★ ★ ★

CUT TO – In the car, leaving Willemstad and heading inland.

RUPERT: Where are we headed, Texas?

TEXAN: I give you my solemn word that if you ask no questions, you'll be told no lies.

*The **Texan** produces a bottle of rum and gives **Rupert** a drink.*

VOICE: I've never had an American friend who could not produce a bottle of something alcoholic out of, it seemed, thin air, or from some secret cellar on his person. Even after we'd swigged three-quarters of the bottle, he managed to speak without a stutter.

TEXAN: You know sumthin, Limey? Tonight, I'll learn you longitudinal legality and latitudinal logic – sum'n you won't read about in a guidebook.

The car slows as they enter what looks like a large carpark.

TEXAN: Yessir, this is quite a burg.

*They get out of the car and the **Texan** leads them through a sort of guard-house and into an open square.*

TEXAN *[tapping the pocket of his bush-jacket]*: They usually frisk you for knives, guns and cameras. We were lucky. Money-changing, of any make so long as it's money, is kind of important here. They just love it in this whorehouse and it's the largest in the world, and one that's open night and day.

The **Texan** *breaks into song.*

TEXAN: "Night and day, you are the one". It is known to sailors the world over as The Happy Valley.

CUT TO – Four rows of bungalows converging on the square where the pair stand. The **Texan** *leads the way to a large canteen and bar, which they enter. It is air-conditioned and well-stocked with women and wine.*

TEXAN: You see: wine, women and, from the juke box when you want it, song.

RUPERT: You have shares in this, Texas?

TEXAN: A share of the goods now and then maybe, but no shares. It's owned and run by the government.

VOICE: Wandering in and out were girls of every description: Creole negresses, Creole whites, Indo-Japanese, pure-blooded Indians from Peru, almond-eyed Chinese from Trinidad and women from the islands and the mainland of Venezuela and Colombia – the last renowned for the regularity of their features, their dark eyes, small wrists and ankles, firm young bodies and strong, even teeth polished white by sugar-cane.

The **Texan** *and* **Rupert** *sit at a table and survey the scene.*

TEXAN: You notice, Limey, they don't come to our table or to any other table. Hustling is against the rules. A girl must be invited.

★ ★ ★ ★ ★

CUT TO – The **Girls***, whose deportment, though they are dressed to kill, is prim and proper.*

★ ★ ★ ★ ★

CUT TO – **Rupert** *scrutinising the inmates.*

RUPERT: You know them, Texas. I leave it to you to choose our guests.

VOICE: They all had one thing in common, whether they were bold or sly, sulky or laughing, resigned or angry: a desire expressed in the universal language of the eyes.

TEXAN: I guess there's safety in numbers, right.

Texan *beckons four of them over. They choose to drink cola.*

VOICE: They were all charmingly dressed as if each wished to be the most attractive at the party, but I noticed one little beauty during the evening who kept leaving the bar and returning wearing something different.

Rupert *beckons one* **Little Beauty** *to the table and speaks to her.*

RUPERT *[amused]*: Tell me, why do you keep changing?

LITTLE BEAUTY *[with a big black wink, whispering]*: Like that, I sometimes get the same boy twice.

RUPERT: That's favouritism, isn't it?

LITTLE BEAUTY: For him or for me?

RUPERT: For him, of course.

LITTLE BEAUTY: You are kind, sir. I think you must be English.

RUPERT: That's right. You're a bright girl. But I think your lucky boy might be waiting for you.

LITTLE BEAUTY: Goodbye for now, sir.

RUPERT: Goodbye and good luck.

Now and then, a girl approaches a table discreetly and, on the way past, without stopping, swiftly lifts her cotton dress above her naked body, bobbing a convent curtsy, to entice a visitor to her quarters.

VOICE: The girls understood all too well the language of men's eyes, the yeas and nays, and knew when to flash a smile of understanding and move elsewhere in search of loot and laughter and even love.

*One of the girls snuggles close to the **Texan** after he has whispered in her ear.*

TEXAN [*to **Rupert***]: This little lady is taking me for a walk, so maybe we could meet up here later at about the time Cinderella's slippers gave out.

RUPERT: Yes. I see you are a smoothie with both women and words. Are you in the oil business?

TEXAN: I'll think that over while I'm away, friend.

RUPERT: But not to the exclusion of other thoughts, I hope.

*The **Texan** and his girl get up and leave. The other girls linger briefly at the table, but now that their sponsor has gone, and **Rupert** seems not yet ready to be detained, gracefully take their departure. **Rupert's** eyes wander to a girl [**Blue Eyes**] standing near the doorway. With a tilt of the head, as though bidding at an auction, he calls her over. Unlike the others, she is wearing a cowboy shirt and beautifully-cut blue jeans with patch pockets above the knee. As a gentleman, **Rupert** stands as she arrives holding a glass of soft-drink and sits.*

VOICE: It was only when she was seated that I noticed her eyes, which were as startlingly blue as her Nordic father's must have been.

RUPERT: Thank you for visiting me. Do you speak English?

BLUE EYES: Yes. My mother taught me.

RUPERT: She is English?

BLUE EYES: No, Colombian. You are English?

RUPERT: Yes.

BLUE EYES: So far from home!

RUPERT: Yes, but not for the first time. And you are from Colombia?

BLUE EYES: Yes, Cartagena.

RUPERT: Are you busy tonight?

BLUE EYES: Not so much. There is a *fiesta* in Willemstad, so there are fewer visitors. You were with a friend?

RUPERT: Yes, a very new friend. Do you know him?

BLUE EYES: No, but I think I have seen him before.

RUPERT: He has gone with a girl, to see her house.

BLUE EYES: Would you like to see my house?

RUPERT: I'd love to.

BLUE EYES: Then come.

Blue Eyes *takes* **Rupert's** *hand and together, he a little self-consciously, they leave the canteen. It is a short walk to her house, which is no more than a bed-sitter with kitchen adjoining. It is clean but spartan, like a nun's cell, with no flowers, pictures or other intimacies to soften it or reflect her identity. They sit on hard chairs facing each other across a wooden table. She pours him a glass of rum and herself a cola. They talk, while through the window the summer evening turns to darkness and lights come on around the Campo.* **Rupert** *looks about and his eyes pause at the bath and bidet in a corner.*

RUPERT: You seem self-sufficient here.

BLUE EYES [*proudly*]: Yes; constant hot and cold water.

VOICE: For her amenities, she paid five dollars a day. They included the services of a cleaning woman and a compulsory weekly visit to the doctor. From her earnings, she had to repay her travelling expenses from Cartagena to the Campo in accordance with a contract drawn up between the Campo agent and her mother. No girl could stay at the Campo longer than three months consecutively, but if she behaved well, she could return for a further term. I limited my involvement with her to research. I paid her, but did not take my due. Perhaps it was because the place was so spotless and I did not want to stain it, or maybe it was to do with seeing her missal and rosary entwined among the dollar bills when she opened her bag, or just that by then I had drunk more than enough, but I told her to think of me that night as an uncle paying her a visit. She laughed, but quickly her blue eyes clouded and she blinked faster than before. Soon, I took her back to the canteen and we said goodbye, with all my questions unsaid.

FADE TO – **Texas** *rapping the window of the car to wake the* **Driver**. *They get in and head for Willemstad, the* **Driver** *stifling a yawn.*

TEXAN: I don't know what you're tired for, boy. You ain't done nothin' but sleep in this jalopy and I hope for everyone's sake you're not hungover.

DRIVER: No, sah. But a yawn when you've woken from a little nap surely is the most natural thing in the world.

TEXAN: Maybe you're right.

*The **Driver** turns on the radio.*

TEXAN: Turn it off.

*The **Driver** turns the radio off.*

TEXAN: That's better. Now we can enjoy the scenery.

VOICE: There was, of course, no scenery, because the night was pitch black. As we thumped along over the potholes, I wondered whether the authorities had not shown worldly wisdom in promoting an establishment where men separated from those they loved could forget their loneliness and appease their bodies' hunger. The Texan read my thoughts.

TEXAN: I know what you're thinking, *amigo*. Sure we all travel the rough road. Most of us do it mile by mile… the difference is that those girls do it male by male. A hard-working kid can earn as much as 3,000 bucks a month. That'll make a fine independent woman of her back home; she'll even be able to choose her man.

VOICE: Within the rather strict rules and regulations – as necessary there as in a girls' kindergarten – the Camp Elegré was more civilised, gentle and hygienic than the brute sensuality of Saint Pauli, the animal jungle of the USA, the sordid sex life of London, the furtive prostitution of the *grandes boulevards*, the mama-sadism of the orient or the erotic byways of the jet-set.

Aboard a DC-3 in flight. **Rupert** *occupies four seats for himself and his bags, which sit upright like dummies. Through the windows are seen dramatic clouds and, in breaks between them, peaks of the Andes.*

VOICE: In the average man's lifetime, it must be seldom that he has to overnight in Arequipa, but it happened to me, flying from Santiago de Chile to Peru with diplomatic bags. The King's Messenger came to prefer certain flights to others, just as he had his favourite capitals and most dreaded airports. That between Santiago and Lima was the flight to which I most looked forward. I was contemplating the pleasures ahead, comfortably ensconced in my reserved section of the plane. At the end of the day, I would be enjoying the company of my friends Sir Courteney Forbes and his wife and the delicious *cuisine* from their embassy cellar, which was the envy of the French diplomatic *corps*. Courteney was unconventional, which might explain why he had befriended me from the time I joined the Foreign Service. He had studied Peruvian history since the Incas, and his wife, whom the *Limenos* adored, had compiled a cookery book containing all her favourite dishes. I suspected Courteney was more popular with the Peruvians than with his fellow diplomats, for whom he was perhaps too independent. He showed me many aspects of Lima I would otherwise never have seen.

★ ★ ★ ★ ★

FADE TO – **Courteney** *escorting* **Rupert** *around a palace.*

COURTENEY: Archetypal wedding-cake architecture, don't you think? Built by the viceroy Manoel de Anat for his mistress, the actress known as La Perrocholi.

RUPERT: It could have been designed by the pastry chef at Gunter's.

Courteney *and* **Rupert** *enter the palace and ascend a stairway leading gently upwards from an ornate chamber to what were* **La Perrocholi's** *private rooms.*

COURTENEY: Old Manoel, you see, need not have been a mountaineer to pay his respects.

RUPERT: Indeed: a most considerate gradient for the optimistic septuagenarian.

BACK TO the DC-3 in flight.

VOICE: Courteney showed me the Torre-Tagle Palace, a superb example of Spanish colonial architecture like the Alhambra in Granada, clearly owing its beauty to the Moors. Sometimes we dined at the old Hotel Maury and later, as if to take the curse out of our excursions, we might visit, sandwiched between the hotel and less wholesome places, the cathedral with its twin towers in the Plaza Mayor. [Pause] We had been flying for about two hours in a cloudless sky when I heard it: a sound only an experienced traveller would notice, a slight hesitation in the rhythm of the DC-3's starboard engine, no more than a mother might discern in the breathing of a sleeping child.

★ ★ ★ ★ ★

CUT TO – View through a window at the starboard engine, from which a wisp of black oil streaks.

★ ★ ★ ★ ★

CUT TO – The cabin indicator flashing a seat-belt sign.

★ ★ ★ ★ ★

CUT TO – **Rupert** *pressing a button to summon the air-***Hostess***, Maria, who ignores it to visit the cockpit, from which she emerges to check passengers' safety-belts. When she reaches* **Rupert's** *seat, she bends down and whispers.*

HOSTESS: We've got to make Arequipa, Mr Grayson. There is no alternative.

VOICE: Poor Maria, with whom I had flown often. But I too had my problems. Assuming we made a safe landing, I would have to sleep on my bags and pouch. There would be no British Consul to provide security. I would be alone and friendless in the beautiful mountain town the *Limenos* knew as El Pueblo Blanco.

★ ★ ★ ★ ★

CUT TO – View through a window. As the plane breaks cloud, the evening lights of the town twinkle below. A mountain looms behind it in the twilight.

VOICE: Our pilot made a perfect single-engined landing. Every bump on the runway was a kiss of welcome.

★ ★ ★ ★ ★

CUT TO – The plane trundling to a halt. A hush in the cabin gives way to clapping and cheering. The captain emerges from the cockpit and smiles like a father on the passengers he has brought safely down.

VOICE: As a King's Messenger, I was flying about 30,000 miles a month. Had I been killed I would have died reasonably in credit, because I never failed to insure myself for vast sums at every airport on every flight just for the pleasure of confounding friends. "Rupert died a millionaire," they'd have said, astonished, adding, no doubt, "he must have been too absent-minded to spend it."

While the other passengers gather up their belongings, **Rupert** *is first off the plane. Maria signals a taxi to take him and his bags to the quinta, or country house, she has recommended.*

VOICE: The *quinta* was owned by an American widow named Bates, known to all as Tia and acknowledged as Queen of Arequipa.

The taxi **Driver** *turns to* **Rupert** *as they drive through the grandeur of the western Andes and approach the town huddling below the dormant volcano El Misti.*

DRIVER: La Senora Tia expects you, sir. She likes English and American visitors to practise the language.

RUPERT: I look forward to meeting her, but how did she know the plane would make an emergency landing here?

The taxi **Driver** *takes both hands off the wheel, raises them in surrender and shrugs to show he hasn't the faintest idea. The taxi arrives at the quinta, a little out of town, and as the* **Driver** *opens the door for* **Rupert,** *a fine-looking middle-aged woman* [**Mrs Bates**] *appears at the top of the steps, well-groomed and smiling.*

DRIVER: La Senora Tia herself, sir.

With one eye on the bags, which the taxi **Driver** *is carrying to the front porch,* **Rupert** *approaches* **Mrs Bates**.

RUPERT: You must be Mrs Bates.

MRS BATES *[Southern accent]*: Right. And you cannot be other than Mr Grayson, making an unscheduled stop. It gives me much pleasure to meet you.

RUPERT: I likewise, but your intelligence is first-class. If I might ask, how did you know I was coming?

MRS BATES: Oh, there's no mystery. The airline simply telephoned and said your arrival was likely.

RUPERT *[laughing to lighten the moment]*: I'm glad to hear that. It can be unsettling to be expected unexpectedly.

Mrs Bates *beams at the effect of her reassurance and turns to the* **Driver,** *who politely waves away* **Rupert's** *offer to pay.*

MRS BATES: Please put Mr Grayson's things in the hall, Manolo.

Mrs Bates *escorts* **Rupert** *up the steps and into the hallway, where she opens a large visitors' book for him to sign.*

MRS BATES: I'd just love you to read the kind things one of your countrymen said about me and my little hotel.

Rupert *reads with interest, the camera noting that the rather long unsigned entry is only two pages back in the book.*

VOICE: As I read the lines to which she pointed, I realised I had happened upon the trail of an itinerant versifier of some talent. As my eyes perused the lilting lines, the words "capricious whim of fates" rang a bell in my memory. There was something about this unknown traveller's style, concise and flamboyant, that stirred the memory and then drifted beyond recall.

Her name is plainly Mrs Bates,
A strange capricious whim of fates
To crown with such banality
So strange a personality.

In the back of my mind, something signalled. The someone who had written in that book was someone I knew. I sensed panache and flourish. For an instant, his name might have been on my lips; then, it faded.

★ ★ ★ ★ ★

CUT TO – The bar, where **Rupert** *is drinking and talking with an elderly* **American** *man.*

AMERICAN: No. We've been here five or six times, I guess. It's a habit we find hard to break.

RUPERT: How did it start?

AMERICAN: By accident; a pleasant one, of course. Someone I met knew the family of the lady who runs it, Mrs Bates, or Tia, as she is called here, and told a little of her story. She was born and raised in upstate New York. The fellow she married was something of a wanderer who brought her this far and got the place running, before going on his way. It was many years before he returned, and then only because he wished to die in congenial surroundings. As you see, they are surely that.

RUPERT: Indeed. It's hard to stop looking.

AMERICAN: It's remarkable how she's grafted herself on to this place. Or maybe it has grafted itself on to her.

When **Rupert** *says nothing but looks thoughtful, the other resumes.*

AMERICAN: Well, she makes it a guesthouse in fact as well as name. Everyone who comes here ends up feeling like her favourite. Not only has she acquired the language, but actually looks like a South American woman, don't you think? The gestures, the language of body and hands. Sometimes, her conversation could be set to music like a Peruvian love-song.

★ ★ ★ ★ ★

CUT TO – A tour of the guesthouse, followed by a view of the mountain through a window.

VOICE: She had furnished the *quinta* lovingly over the years, each piece, and framed in most of the windows was El Misti, its peak capped with perpetual snow. By day, its cone was encircled in drifting cloud that made

431

a wreath of white flowers through which we'd miraculously found our way on one engine. But at sunset, when the stars came out, it hung in the sky – a diadem aglitter with jewels.

★ ★ ★ ★ ★

CUT TO – The dining room.

VOICE: That night, I dined off avocado pear "à *la Tía*", anointed with her secret dressing patiently mixed drip by drip, followed by lobster from the cold Humboldt Current that winds through the warm waters of the South Pacific from southern Chile to Ecuador.

★ ★ ★ ★ ★

CUT TO – A Peruvian army officer at a neighbouring table, gorgeously attired as though for comic opera.

VOICE: At the next table, a Peruvian army officer had taken his place. He was clearly of the highest rank, garbed, or perhaps upholstered, in a sky-blue uniform ablaze with gold braid, medals and decorations. What delighted me was that he had assumed a posture of nonchalance, more suited to a man posing for his portrait in oils than waiting for his *hors d'oeuvres*.

★ ★ ★ ★ ★

*CUT TO – Alternating shots of **Rupert** sneaking glances at the officer, his expression combining amusement and contempt, and the officer sneaking glances at **Rupert** and registering disapproval of the dowdy Englishman being served no less assiduously than he in all his glory.*

VOICE: I almost regretted I was not in our court uniform, which we were expected to wear at *levees* and state occasions. It was dark-blue, cut like a frock-coat and discreetly edged with gold lace, though the trousers had a rather bold red braid from hip to toe. Not unnaturally, the *pièce de résistance* was the silver greyhound pendant worn from the blue ribbon of the Garter hung around the neck. Had I been sporting this I might have competed with him, but the effect that evening would have been ruined by the fact that, for security

reasons, I was still accompanied by my white-and-green-striped canvas bag –
one of thousands stitched together by resident guests of His Majesty's prisons
and rather resembling a traveller's laundry receptacle. And I was in nothing
more resplendent than my old Johns & Peggs travelling suit.

★ ★ ★ ★ ★

CUT TO – The lounge, where **Mrs Bates** *has joined* **Rupert** *for coffee.*

MRS BATES: … so, originally, it was the physical side of the place that
beguiled me. Your eyes will tell you what I mean. But it also has a spiritual
side that unfolds more gently.

RUPERT: It cannot be easy here to think all architects are human.

MRS BATES: True, but the Great Architect shakes His finger now and
then to frighten us. I refer to the *terremotos*, or earthquakes, that regularly
remind us we are not yet in heaven.

RUPERT *[grinning ruefully]*: Or soon could be?

MRS BATES: Yes. And that Providence must be appeased. A traveller like
yourself, Rupert, would do well to take with you some of Arequipa's
superstitions.

RUPERT: Such as?

MRS BATES: I don't know how often you pick an eyelash off a girl's
cheek, but when you do you must put it in a box and make the sign of the
cross over it, so that any letter you are expecting will overtake you. If you
buy pieces of iron or steel needles, do so on any day but Good Friday. And
on no account step out of a hotel except with your left foot leading.

RUPERT: Thank you, Tia. We people on the move need all the protection
we can get.

VOICE: That night, anyone might have fallen in love with the rambling old guesthouse with its roses and magenta bougainvillea clinging and climbing over the balustrades and staining the white walls like *vino tinto*, but I must have fallen slightly in love with the idea of Tia herself because she belonged to her *quinta* as much as I belonged to it that night.

★ ★ ★ ★ ★

CUT TO – **Mrs Bates** *seeing* **Rupert** *to the bottom of the stairs as he makes for bed.*

MRS BATES: Good-night, Rupert. You will always be welcome here.

★ ★ ★ ★ ★

CUT TO – **Rupert** *climbing the stairs, walking to and entering his room, undressing and taking a sip now and then from the glass he has carried upstairs with him.*

VOICE: In my room, the smell of eucalyptus seeped from the giant trees and penetrated from the little salon hung with Inca tapestries. The hotel was pungent with the aroma from branches and leaves burning in braziers. I drank my *pisco* sours with a sense of contentment that was rather alien to me. Then, I slept under chinchilla rugs and was reminded of my beloved mother who arrived in England from Chile as a young girl with a bundle of these skins – so many, indeed, that eventually they were given to the servants to trim their petticoats.

★ ★ ★ ★ ★

CUT TO – **Rupert** *sitting up in bed, smiling a little, eyes glazed, as he finishes his drink and meditates.*

VOICE: Vicuna, I learned, is the product of the charming animals that roam the upper sierras of Peru, often in the company of llamas, which are like woollen-haired, humpless camels. I was rather endeared to them when I learned that they were the only beasts of burden with the sense to lie down when they decide they have been overloaded. Though I have not confirmed it with a lawyer, I was also given to understand that a law

434

forbade a *peon* to drive them more than a day's journey unless he was accompanied by wife or girlfriend, because the females of the species customarily lie down at night on their backs.

★ ★ ★ ★ ★

CUT TO — A view of the alley below the window, lit dimly by streetlamps and moonlight. Faintly on the air comes a woman's cry: 'Ama de leche, ama de leche.'

VOICE: My bedroom overlooked a crooked alley. I slept dreamlessly until something must have stirred me, something distant and elusive. It might have been no more than the wind shifting on the *pampas* a hundred miles away, but I was sad, because I knew I'd never return to Tia's *quinta*. It was then for the last time that I heard faintly that strangest of all street cries, sad and pleading, from the woman with her breast milk to sell — the age-old cry of the wet nurse.

★ ★ ★ ★ ★

CUT TO — Next morning in the hallway as **Mrs Bates** *sees* **Rupert** *off. She stands beside the visitors' book and turns to the page with the lines that puzzled* **Rupert** *the evening before.*

VOICE: The sun was climbing the side of El Misti. The heat of the long day would soon be upon us. I guessed I must read the rest of her poet friend's valediction. As I did, we were no longer alone. A figure was beside me. It was the Master himself, reciting the words in his own inimitable style, high-pitched, clipped and plummy:

The spirit of the place conserves
An anodyne for jangled nerves.
The water's hot, the beds are soft,
The meals are many times and oft.
The flowers are sweet, the grass is green,
The toilet is austerely clean,
Which in this ancient continent
Occasions vast astonishment.

Of every place I've been to yet,
This I shall leave with most regret.

My plane left for Lima at 9.30 am and I was never to return, except in fondest memory.

An aerial view of Rio de Janeiro and its symbol, the sugarloaf mountain topped by the Cristos statue, closing to airport runway with a DC-3 breaking down through the cloud, landing, taxiing to a stop. **Rupert** *disembarks and is met by a van that takes him and his bags to the terminal for diplomatic clearance.*

VOICE: Rio was one of those airports that frightened the living daylights out of most travellers because of the blanket of cloud that often hung over it, which made landings seem like the ultimate gamble; hence my practice of taking out maximum life insurance on every flight.

★ ★ ★ ★ ★

CUT TO — The taxi completing its journey to the city and delivering **Rupert** *and bags to the Gloria Hotel, Rio.*

VOICE: Wherever I went, I preferred to stay at the smaller and older hotels rather than the Holiday Inns, the Hiltons and the Sheratons. In Rio, I loved the old Gloria. It had the Edwardian atmosphere you would expect to find in Bath, Aix-les Bains, Menton or Vichy.

★ ★ ★ ★ ★

CUT TO — The old-world serenity of the Gloria's lobby and lounge: brocaded sofas and chairs, drowsy drawing-room gossip, an old lady knitting, a string quartet playing sedately at the entrance to the restaurant.

VOICE: Everywhere was the faint aroma of Havana tobacco, fresh-ground Brazilian coffee and an atmosphere of good living and a rosy past, as if Cesar Ritz had been that way, checked the cellars, inspected the kitchens and ordered the flowers in all rooms to be changed daily.

★ ★ ★ ★ ★

CUT TO — Behind the hotel, a terrace with white tables on which striped umbrellas bloom and, beyond it, gardens with palms and shrubberies.

VOICE: One day, sitting on the terrace, I conceived the idea of creating a secret English garden, which I would plant behind the palms, enclosed within the bushes in a patch of its own. Since I was visiting Rio from Washington twice a month, it was not difficult to obtain seed to sow surreptitiously. Phlox, hollyhocks, fragrant stocks, wallflowers and roses soon bloomed in splendid confusion. I am no gardener and must thank nature for allowing beauty to triumph over disorder. The old *jardineiro*, whom I would see pottering among his exotic plants, must have wondered what strange wind had swept such alien and uninvited seed into his tropical beds, but, magic or not, he kept my little enchanted "corner of a foreign field" well watered.

★ ★ ★ ★ ★

CUT TO — The Copacabana. **Rupert** *finishes his meal and moves to the gambling room, where he sits at a roulette table.*

VOICE: One night, having inspected my English garden, I decided to leave my fellow guests to their *table d'hote* at the Gloria and dine on my own. My old father used to quote: "a man should eat well but wisely and talk well but not too wisely". At the Copacabana, I knew I could eat well and I had not yet reached that stage of loneliness when a man must address himself. After my meal, solitary but for the companionship of a bottle of wine and the usual uninvited shadow at my feet, I went into the vast gambling room and sat at one of the roulette tables.

★ ★ ★ ★ ★

CUT TO — **Rupert's** *table, where the ball repeatedly favours his bets and the tokens pile up beside him.*

★ ★ ★ ★ ★

CUT TO — The face of a girl opposite, studying **Rupert's** *play closely.*

VOICE: My luck was in and I was soon conscious of a girl's vivid green eyes watching every move I made on the table. In the age-old tradition of casinos, I pushed a small pile of plaques across to her. Judging by the jewellery she was wearing, she might have ignored my gesture, but I knew all gamblers were superstitious and she took the *jetons* with a faint smile. She continued to follow my game until luck began to desert me.

★ ★ ★ ★ ★

CUT TO − **Rupert** *and* **Green Eyes**, *without a word, or even a glance of understanding, leaving the table together and changing their plaques into cruzeros.*

GREEN EYES: *Venez* crack *une bouteille ensemble, vieux* chap.

VOICE: This was the sort of Franglais I rather enjoyed. As we wandered towards the bar through the grill-room, where the tables were unoccupied except by orchids, in the most friendly way she slipped her arm through mine.

★ ★ ★ ★ ★

CUT TO − A wing of the casino where the tables are not busy and the walls and pillars are lined with mirrors of all shapes and sizes. In them **Rupert** *sees the image of* **Green Eyes** *replicated, her face and hair flecked with stars dancing off the chandeliers.*

VOICE: It was not unlike visiting the exhibition of an artist who has fallen in love with the model and painted her in a hundred different poses.

★ ★ ★ ★ ★

CUT TO − A corner of the long bar into which they have strolled. **Green Eyes** *sits in a corner.*

VOICE: I observed her as closely as any artist would have done. Unconsciously or otherwise, because beautiful women know what it's about, she presented a study in green, even to the *crème de menthe* in a glass whose stem she now encircled with emerald-encrusted fingers. About her was a green radiance. As with many beautiful Brazilians, there was the faintest suggestion of a shadow, no more than a whiff of smoke, over her full-lipped mouth.

439

★ ★ ★ ★ ★

CUT TO — The **Barman** *serving* **Rupert** *and* **Green Eyes** *with drinks, but afterwards hovering around, which, as his expression shows, annoys* **Rupert,** *who sends him away.*

VOICE: When the barman hung about more than I considered necessary, I told him in my best Brazilian to take a walk.

GREEN EYES: Baccy, please, baccy.

Rupert *hands* **Green Eyes** *his cigarette case.*

GREEN EYES: You notice I speak very good English, like you.

RUPERT: Of course.

GREEN EYES: I also speak French with strangers. This is an opportunity... *bien trouvé*, to speak English. Before you arrive at the *chemin de fer* table, I was nearly... *[she measures an infinitesimal space between finger and thumb]*... *déplume*.

★ ★ ★ ★ ★

CUT TO — **Green Eyes** *seen from some distance away, her expression animated and her lips busy as she enchants* **Rupert** *with her story [as per the following].*

VOICE: She was like a child at her first grown-up party, with no one to tell her "do this, don't do that". It seemed that her father was a wealthy coffee king whose *fachada* was so vast that he had to use a private plane to manage the estate. Was she not the favourite of his children? Of course, for the very human reason that she was the only one in the family who had inherited his green eyes. I was completely enchanted not only by her story, but also by the manner of expressing herself in the language I loved of the hand and the body – the circular gesture of the first finger and thumb as she threw a *nada* into the air, the slow raising of the chin, the

440

hardly perceptible lift of her shoulder and the swiftly-changing expression in those go-go eyes; one moment cuddling her body in her arms in ecstasy, then making a point by bringing her thumb and forefinger together, shutting her eyes in resignation, lifting hand to eyes in a masking gesture conveying darkness and whispering of love *avec le bouche ouvert.*

★ ★ ★ ★ ★

CUT TO — The couple close-up

RUPERT: Where did you learn to speak French so perfectly?

GREEN EYES: In Paris, where else.

RUPERT: Is that where you learned to speak with your hands, too?

Green Eyes' *finger travels to her eye.*

GREEN EYES: No, I learned that from my father's polo ponies.

RUPERT: And what did you learn from your mother?

VOICE: For a moment she hesitated and I knew she was inventing.

GREEN EYES: I learned to love emeralds.

Green Eyes *looks challengingly at* **Rupert**.

GREEN EYES: Anything else you want to know, *monsieur*?

RUPERT: Of course.

VOICE: I had the sense to know a story will out. When she began with "once upon a time… ", her smile was irresistible.

GREEN EYES: My grandfather was at the court of the last empress of Brazil, so my mother was brought up in Petropolis, and she instructed me in the manners of the court.

*Green Eyes slides off her bar stool and backs away to the nearby door of the little girl's room; before entering, she sweeps **Rupert** a graceful curtsy.*

VOICE: I cannot remember her name or the one she was using that night. It was offbeat, like Grisela or Shelmerdine, but certainly not Brazilian. I do, however, remember the wide-eyed curiosity on her face when she returned.

GREEN EYES [*anxiously*]: Should I have asked permission to *faire pee-pee*?

*Before **Rupert** can reply, **Green Eyes**, remounting the stool, fires another question at him.*

GREEN EYES: What do you do for a living?

RUPERT: I am a postman.

Green Eyes *shows surprise.*

RUPERT: But I carry only royal mail.

Rupert's *qualification means nothing to her.*

VOICE: Since she apparently had hosts of loving friends, it puzzled me that she should be wasting her time and talents on a lonely impecunious Englishman when she could clearly have wealthy lovers wherever she chose to cast her eyes. Apart from beauty, she had the charm to keep a man's senses and curiosity aroused, for there was a certain strangeness about her that might have been beautifully dissected by Proust.

RUPERT: Your mother gave you the emeralds?

GREEN EYES: She gave me enough to keep me quiet. One day, I will inherit the rest.

Rupert *looks her straight in the eyes.*

RUPERT: The most beautiful are those you inherited from your father.

VOICE: I don't think she was listening, for her expression was shadowed. She had gone on some journey a long way from this Copacabana bar. When she spoke again, her eyes were relaxed, and as she talked slowly through the smoke of her cigarette, it was as though she were remembering and recounting a dream.

GREEN EYES: I have learned there are only three things in life that matter: love, hunger and the sharp edge of the machete. The day I inherit the *fachada,* I will destroy every *bidonville* with fire and water and the people on my land will build their own houses because people love most the homes they have built with their own hands. There will be rivers and lakes and music and the children will have kind teachers. There will be work for everyone on my *fachada* and the coffee beans will shine brighter than gold, and I will walk and laugh and share their sorrows. *[Pause]* I will be alone when I wish to be alone.

VOICE: As she talked thus through the smoke of her cigarette, her eyes were challenging and full of courage, and I wondered whether she was purging her mind of the government's rape of Amazonia.

RUPERT: Until the handsome prince in shining armour comes riding by on his white charger.

GREEN EYES *[looking down at her emeralds]*: There will be no princes riding into my life. Only traders whose currency is death.

443

There is silence between them for a minute.

RUPERT: You have shared some of your secrets with me. Please share one of mine.

GREEN EYES: I am waiting.

RUPERT: At my hotel, I have created an English garden that nobody knows about but I.

Green Eyes *speaks emphatically.*

GREEN EYES: That's something I must see. I'm tired of inspecting Japanese prints.

They leave, **Rupert** *settling the bill as they pass the bar. In the street, they catch a cab to the Gloria and walk to the rear of the hotel where* **Rupert** *shows* **Green Eyes** *his garden.* **Green Eyes** *tells the cab driver to wait.*

VOICE: Dawn was breaking, and the swallows were swooping and scrawling lines on the slate-grey sky. She looked wonderingly at the stocks, mignonette, forget-me-nots and London Pride, while I looked wonderingly at the toenails peeping through her sandals and twinkling like rubies in the emerald grass. She was certainly a lady of jewels, with all the dark affinities of the *Carioca* fused within her. Yet, there was also a bright saneness in her eyes – a little alarming because it seemed she was forever on guard.

*A uniformed embassy driver [***Gaston***] comes down the path towards them and signals* **Rupert**, *who waves to acknowledge the signal, whereupon the driver retraces his steps.*

VOICE: Gaston, the embassy driver, with his discreet eyes, arrived ahead of time as usual; and her taxi was waiting.

Green Eyes *takes* **Rupert** *hands in hers and lifts her mouth to be kissed with the grace of a Brazilian aristocrat.*

VOICE: Most women, I thought, are born actresses. They write their own parts in which to cast themselves. How sweetly this one played her role that night, even to the final empty kiss.

Green Eyes *trips away, blowing a kiss behind her, and* **Rupert** *goes to his room to collect his belongings.*

VOICE: I picked up the diplomatic bags at the embassy and Gaston drove me to the airport. In a few hours, the scene would change to Buenos Aires. But I could not get the little casino tramp out of my mind. How could I be expected to reconcile the splendour of her dreams with that all-revealing glance I'd intercepted between her and that bloody barman? Besides, listening to all that crap about her parents, her grandmother and the imperial court hardly made up for losing my Viennese cigarette case of plaited coloured golds and its clasp of one small emerald.

Rupert *arrives by taxi at the City Hotel, Buenos Aires, and goes to reception, where he is known and expected. The* **Clerk** *reaches for the room key as* **Rupert** *enters. With the key there is a note, which* **Rupert** *opens and reads aloud as he strolls away from the desk.*

RUPERT *[to himself]*: "See you in the dining room at eight". Good; so we've managed to intersect.

★ ★ ★ ★ ★

CUT TO – *The dining room later,* **Rupert** *and* **Robbie** *sharing a table.*

ROBBIE: Flight down okay, thanks, except for the usual bumps, but I'm afraid the pilot said there was a storm chasing us. I hope it doesn't ambush you in the morning.

RUPERT: Well, let's eat, drink and be merry, and double the flight insurance. That's the one item the accountants don't seem to argue about.

ROBBIE: Because they know you'll never get your money's worth.

VOICE: Speaking of our masters back home reminded me of the austerities we had left behind and made the food we ate that night all the tastier, including baby-beef as tender as mushrooms and luscious as peaches. Yet Buenos Aires, like Washington, came high on my list of the world's most magnificent but charmless cities. As a shopping centre in 1940, it was unsurpassed, with every kind of Scotch available in two litre bottles and Cooper's Oxford Marmalade in stock throughout the years when it had vanished from English shelves. The Argentinian prided himself on his Latin origins and southern-European outlook, displaying, it seemed to me, all the vanity of the Italian without the Italian's *panache*. Although he was a mixture of Spanish, German, Japanese, Greek, Italian and English, unlike the products of other South American countries that were equally polyglot, in the Argentinian those ingredients had somehow failed to meld. [Pause] For now, though, I was less interested in anthropology than meteorology.

★ ★ ★ ★ ★

FADE TO − Inside a DC-3 descending bumpily to land at Mendoza. The **Hostess** *points to the seatbelt sign and recites it in English and Spanish, before bending down and speaking in* **Rupert's** *ear.*

HOSTESS: You might not be sleeping in Santiago tonight, Mr Grayson.

Rupert *looks anxious.*

RUPERT: The weather?

The **Hostess** *nods to save shouting above the roar of the engines. Through the window behind her, the bulk of the Andes' eastern ramparts towers over Mendoza.*

VOICE: Cordoba had been our first touchdown since B.A., but it was at Mendoza that we refuelled and sought clearance for the fearsome flight through the High Andes. Though one of the finest aircraft ever designed, the DC-3 was small compared with today's and could not get high enough to fly over the mountains, so it had, as it were, to fly through them. The course it followed was that of the Mendoza Santiago railway, passing over the lonely weather-station on the accuracy of whose reports our lives largely depended. There was a particularly narrow section of the pass where a down-draught might force the plane into the purple depths in breathtaking air pockets – on such occasions, I prayed that the pilot was wide awake, for he must bank sharply to avoid smashing into the perpendicular walls of the mighty Aconcagua, rising almost 23,000 feet into the icy green sky. As well, there was always the risk of colliding with

447

one of the rusty-brown condor eagles that haunted the valley and could snap a propeller blade like a twig.

The plane lands and taxis to the airport building. As the propellers come to a stop, a close-up of the **Pilot's** *face shows an expression of inquiry as he looks towards the building, from which emerges an* **Official** *who looks towards the* **Pilot** *and slowly shakes his head.* **Rupert**, *as usual leaving the aircraft first, with his bags, also sees the gesture and returns a few paces to speak to the* **Hostess**, *who is helping passengers on to the tarmac.*

RUPERT: It looks as though I'll need your hotel tonight and a taxi to take me.

HOSTESS: I'll arrange it for you. Five minutes, please, Mr Grayson.

★ ★ ★ ★ ★

CUT TO — **Rupert** *in the taxi heading for the hotel in Mendoza. On arrival, he locks the bags into the safe and goes to his room, the familiarity of the routine suggesting he has done it before. He lies on the bed and tries to read, but his eyes keep wandering from the page. Particles of dust drift in the last of the afternoon light filtering through the Venetian blinds as the sun sets behind the foothills of the Andes.*

VOICE: The corridor through the High Andes followed the original mule track, which also became the route of the railway, through the mountains and was first plotted by Antoine Saint Exupery. The great Frenchman had many facets: air pilot, writer, visionary. He had conceived a postal air service between Toulouse in France and Santiago in Chile, and he must have been one of the first to foresee the future of air travel as it is known today. In 1918, with two of his co-pilots of the First World War, Mermoz and Guillaumet, he formed the first commercial company in the history of civil aviation. At the same time, this strange man was able to write such masterpieces as *Vol de Nuit* and *Vol de Sable*. He was the first exponent of desert flying, which inspired him to pen that incomparable fairy story and adult allegory *Le Petit Prince*. *[Pause]* As I lay on the bed that afternoon, I became aware of a second presence in the room and drifted back to a spring morning in Paris many years before, when my old friend and fellow-scribe Bagot Gray suggested, to my delight, that I should meet the remarkable Frenchman.

★ ★ ★ ★ ★

FADE TO − **St Ex***upery's apartment in the place Vauban overlooking Les Invalides. The door is opened by Count Antoine de Saint Exupery himself: ponderous, dark-eyed, heavy-featured. He seems curious rather than friendly, though promptly invites them in. The room is enormous and starkly naked because its only furniture is a double bed on a vast, rug-less parquet floor. It is lit by high curtain-less windows. In the centre of the area stands* **Madame Ex***upery, small and dark-eyed, of Latin extraction. She looks the visitors up and down defiantly.*

GRAY *[addressing them both]*: Saint Antoine and Madame Exupery, please meet my friend Rupert Grayson, a leftover from the war.

MADAME EX *[bitterly]*: Welcome to our *cochonière*, where we live like pigs. I expect Tonio has told you he insisted on putting every *sou* into Airpostale.

VOICE: Was this the famous double act I had seen performed before guests by many husbands and wives? It was the voice of frustration. Coming from humbler stock, she perhaps yearned to be La Comtesse, but Saint Ex, as his friends called him, and Tonio, as she did, refused to use his title, and until his death she had to be content with *"Madame"*.

Madame Ex *spreads her arms to embrace the room.*

MADAME EX: *La Voilà!*

VOICE: Although she used the accents Spanish-speaking people give to the beautiful French language, I was surprised at how deep and strident her voice was.

449

With a sweep of the hand, **St Ex** *indicates the bed for them to sit on.*

ST EX *[phlegmatically]*: Suppose you produce the whisky for my friends, Consuela.

St Ex *speaks in French.*

ST EX: I have no English; only sentences I consider essential: "serve me a whisky"… "what is the time"… "call me a taxi"… "where is the boot jack, *valet?*".

Madame Ex *fetches glasses and a bottle of Scotch.*

MADAME EX: Mermoz has been killed; Guillaumet has gone. The best friends and husbands die. Next, it will be Tonio's turn.

VOICE: Hating flying as she did, it ruled her life and thoughts. I should have liked to know her background because, although she had met and married Saint Ex in Buenos Aires, and I knew she had been born in San Salvador, she spoke only of Guatemala. I had been told it was love at first sight and if that was so, they seemed to have learned to live unhappily ever after. As she continued to purvey her gloom, St Ex lifted his eyes to the ceiling with an expression of patient fortitude, which, considering he and I were meeting for the first time, showed a certain indelicacy, though I had read his books and knew he was a man of sensitivity.

★ ★ ★ ★ ★

CUT TO − *The group seated at a table in another room.*

VOICE: It seemed ages before luncheon was served, when for the first time we sat facing each other. It was delicious and served with excellent Bordeaux. Chairs had been borrowed from the *salon* and a manservant had clearly been hired for the occasion.

★ ★ ★ ★ ★

450

CUT TO — *An hour or so later. The manservant places sweets and champagne before the guests.* **St Ex** *eyes his wife dolefully.*

ST EX: Another course and perhaps another subject for conversation?

MADAME EX *[now thoroughly worked up]*: No, no, no, not until you promise me never to fly again. If you do not promise me, I am going to elope with Bagot.

★ ★ ★ ★ ★

CUT TO — **Bagot,** *who is so electrified by her words that he splutters into the champagne he is sipping, has to turn away from the table, doubly embarrassed.*

VOICE: But I was less astonished than my old friend, for it was clear that Bagot with his good looks and wit had charmed *Madame* and it seemed she was bored with the world of flying even to the extent of being unable to discuss anything else.

★ ★ ★ ★ ★

CUT TO — **Rupert** *and* **Gray** *leaving the apartment and saying goodbyes. They walk east away from the square.*

RUPERT: It's a privilege to have met him. Thank you.

GRAY *[wryly]*: And her?

RUPERT: She does have a bee in her bonnet. *[Mischievously]* Perhaps the B stands for Bagot.

GRAY: A pity he saddled himself with a wife, when all he wanted was a mother to look after him.

RUPERT: And a pity she constricts him so. Every time he started to talk the language another writer would wish to hear, he suddenly turned to other matters.

GRAY: I know what you mean. Consuela, I'm afraid, is the lid that holds down his personality.

★ ★ ★ ★ ★

FADE TO — The hotel room in Mendoza. The sun's rays gone, evening is setting in. **Rupert** *gets up from the bed and pours a drink.*

VOICE: Alas, poor Consuela's pleas and threats were of no avail. Saint Exupery's name was already listed for death. His turn came when he disappeared flying with the Free French during the Second World War, thought to have been swallowed by the blue Mediterranean and never heard of again. I don't know whether he actually flew the southern pass, but if so he probably stayed at the same charming hotel in Mendoza where accommodation was always available for travellers in an emergency.

The characterless hotel in Recife where the KM customarily stayed.

VOICE: Recife, once known as Pernambuco, liked to be called the Venice of Brazil, though there were no *vaporettos* churning up a grand canal and across a busy lagoon, or a Harry's Bar, or the ghost of poor Byron on his balcony beckoning the *gondolieri* to bring him their wives and daughters, or even sons, to share his couch.

Rupert *drifts into the bar, presided over by* **Manoel**. *An American* [**Masterman**] *is the only other customer as* **Rupert** *walks in.* **Manoel** *signals* **Rupert** *by elevating the eyes until only the whites show.*

VOICE: Invariably, there was a middle-aged American keeping Manoel company, supporting himself with his elbows on the bar, of which he had become as much a part as the stool on which he managed somehow to remain seated. Although I had on occasions met him when he was sober, that evening he was in what I have heard described as an advanced state of intoxication, drinking with the urgency of someone who has only a few hours to live. He was holding forth in a mixture: two parts Portuguese, three parts American and five parts gin. Although trying to please, he laboured under the disadvantage of his business calling. However tolerant one may be, it is difficult to take kindly to someone whose aim, by hook or by crook, is to sell you a billiards table.

CUT TO – **Masterman** *focusing with difficulty on* **Rupert**.

MASTERMAN: Where you from, Limey?

RUPERT: Washington.

MASTERMAN: That's a long way. You must be thirsty. What's your poison?

RUPERT: That's very civil of you, Masterman. I'll have a martini.

Masterman *turns jerkily to the barman.*

MASTERMAN: Manoel, you old black bastard, give my friend a martini; very large, cold, and dry as an ash-heap on a Sunday afternoon.

VOICE: Though a heavy drinker, he was not a disagreeable man. Something had upset him.

RUPERT: What's your trouble, Masterman? You're among friends. Tell everything.

VOICE: Masterman's face turned red with anger, then purple, like a colour television on the blink.

MASTERMAN: Two years and this bugger has owed me for the table I sold him.

Masterman *turns bleary eyes on* **Rupert**.

MASTERMAN: This time he's not getting away with it.

Cunning creeps across **Masterman's** *face. He leans towards* **Rupert**, *as though about to be confidential, and* **Rupert** *leans towards* **Masterman** *to receive the confidence. Suddenly,* **Masterman** *shouts at the top of his voice.*

MASTERMAN: Do you know what this is?

★ ★ ★ ★ ★

CUT TO — **Manoel** *behind the bar, showing alarm by putting down the glass he is polishing.* **Masterman,** *clutching a gun, speaks gently and slyly.*

MASTERMAN: I think you know what this is.

RUPERT: It looks remarkably like a lethal weapon.

Masterman's *eyes blaze.*

MASTERMAN: When he sees this, friend, he'll pay up… or else.

Masterman *slides off his stool and sways to the door with his drink in one hand and the gun in the other, supporting himself against the wall.* **Manoel** *looks scared and helpless, his eyes beseeching* **Rupert** *to do something.*

RUPERT *[whispering to himself grimly]:* Keep him talking. *[Audibly, but still quietly]* Let's have a look at it.

Rupert *reaches slowly for the gun.* **Masterman** *instantly draws back and starts twirling the gun in a circular motion around his trigger finger as they do in Westerns, but makes what looks like a dangerous mess of it.*

MASTERMAN *[truculently]:* Oh, no, you don't.

RUPERT: That's rather a neat trick you're doing.

Masterman *leans back, a little off balance and swaying, his arm outstretched and the barrel of the gun describing irregular circles in the air.* **Rupert** *embarks on another approach.*

RUPERT *[pleasantly]:* What's the make of that gun?

MASTERMAN [*angrily*]: It's a friendly persuader, that's what.

RUPERT [*with nervous laugh*]: Doesn't look very friendly to me.

Masterman *leans forward.*

MASTERMAN [*in a half-whisper*]: I'll tell you why it's a friendly persuader.

Masterman's *mood changes.*

MASTERMAN: I guess you can keep a secret, Limey.

Masterman *burps as a newcomer, unaware of what has happened, pushes past him into the bar.* **Masterman** *fumbles the gun back into his pocket. He turns to* **Rupert** *before leaving, looking back with a smile of infinite patience, and speaks in a stage whisper.*

MASTERMAN: I call it a friendly persuader because it's twenty years since I've had a bullet that would fit it.

VOICE: He'd certainly had the laugh on us and I hoped the new arrival, unaware of the farce that had just been enacted, did not notice that the hand holding my glass was less steady than I'd have liked.

New York City, 1943. **Rupert** *is waiting at the Knickerbocker Club for Louis* **Drexel** *and fellow KM* **Robbie**. *The servants go about their duties quietly, straightening chairs, refolding newspapers, emptying ashtrays and supplying members' needs.*

VOICE: In the thirties, New York City still possessed a certain European elegance. Each side of fashionable Fifth Avenue was bejewelled with eighteen-carat boutiques and fashion-houses, and at twilight, when the stores and offices closed, the sidewalks sparkled with girls who were incredibly lovely because of their mixture of origins. The luxurious apartments of Fifth and Park Avenues spilled their white and blue-striped awnings on to the pavement. The city offered something of the chic of Paris and the majesty of London. It was becoming famous for its hotels, because of either their luxurious accommodation or their character. There was still a Ritz-Carlton on Madison, there were the Plaza and the Biltmore, the old Waldorf, the Carlyle and the Pierre. There was the Sherry Netherland, and famous for its round table in the restaurant was the Algonquin. Here the staff writers of the *New Yorker* used to live, and it was to this address that the wit Robert Benchley cabled from Venice: "Streets flooded, advise". I was once invited to join them at a rather dreary luncheon, but could think of nothing witty to say so I was not invited again. Book stores were scattered about the city and most of them prospering, which was surprising because one rarely saw anything being read but periodicals, newspapers and comics. For me, the island of Manhattan was a narrow carpet of dreams at least three times a year. It was my last night in New York. In sunset sadness, I came to the portals of the Knickerbocker Club, where I had been made an honorary member by Willie Rhinelander Stewart so many years ago. Here I used to meet the "golden youth" of the US, who might have been described as the governing class had they sold their polo ponies, resigned from the golf clubs and vacated their cocktail stools – a class of which I have always been in favour unless it tried to govern me. At the Knickerbocker, I awaited my brother-in-law Louis and fellow messenger Robbie, who were travelling from Philadelphia to see me off. Here I found all the peacefulness of a London club, where the servants knew the proper order of things and went about their duties quietly, straightening chairs, refolding newspapers, emptying ashtrays and serving members with European wines and South American coffee.

As six o'clock approaches, the stream of commuters outside on Fifth Avenue swells.

VOICE: Seated beside the windows overlooking Central Park, I watched the six o'clock commmuters on Fifth Avenue hailing taxis or climbing into buses, returning to their breeding-grounds like salmon to their headwaters.

★ ★ ★ ★ ★

CUT TO – The bar on the floor below, its walls hung with prints appropriate to enjoyment.

VOICE: The bar below was where the serious drinking was done. Its walls were hung with Hogarth-Wildeian prints depicting the ill-effects of drink on the working classes and the alarming effects of work on the drinking classes.

★ ★ ★ ★ ★

*CUT TO – The Country Aviation Club on Long Island, where **Rupert** is shown **Miles Vernon's** red and gold private aeroplane. They take off in it and perform the events described below.*

VOICE: To a degree, I was able, like a chameleon, to be absorbed into the atmosphere in which I was moving, and I had learned that it was possible to hit the target if you didn't aim your arrows too high. I convinced myself that all things were possible in New York. On meeting Miles Vernon, an imaginative Knickerbocker playboy, I was invited to the Country Aviation Club on Long Island. From there, after a sufficiency of drinks, he flew me from one end of the State to the other, showing me more in a few hours than I could normally have seen in a month. After diving down among the skyscrapers of Manhattan, we swooped on to his friends' country houses at the Hamptons, surprised country clubs in wooded estates, golfers at play and workers on railroad repairs – amusing here and alarming there. Once, we zoomed down on to a polo field where a game was in progress, causing merry hell with ponies and riders engaged in an international match. We hovered over the glories of Bear Mountain, the great grey buildings of West Point and Hyde Park, the Hudson home of the Roosevelt family. In this panoramic triangle, I had seen the wonders of Scott Fitzgerald's Gatsbyland.

★ ★ ★ ★ ★

CUT TO – *Manhattan's Colony Restaurant,* **Rupert** *dining with* **Jessica Brown**.

VOICE: In those careless, rapturous days of the twenties and thirties, it was as if I were married to London and enjoying Paris as my mistress, but New York always had a special place in my heart. It was in this magic city that I used to take Jessica Brown to the Colony Restaurant – at that time financed by Sir William Wiseman, who had run our secret service in America during the First World War. The cuisine was superb, for he was a pleasure-loving man, well-informed in the art of living. He was also a great collector, though of young mistresses rather than Old Masters. Jessica was surely the most beautiful of the Ziegfeld girls.

JESSICA: As an Englishman, don't you find New York astounding, astonishing and amazing?

RUPERT: Not exactly. I merely find it fabulous, fascinating and fantastic.

VOICE: But she knew I was referring to her. Later, in London, she was trapped into marriage by Lord Northesk – a wild and lovable man with his own way of doing things. He invariably took in one the steep flight of stairs at the Kit Kat Club in London – on one occasion to the accompaniment of a drum roll played by the Prince of Wales. It was said that King George V's language when he heard about it would have made a sailor blush. It was typical of him that he employed a totally inefficient soldier-servant, confessing that he liked him around because, although they were the same age, the servant looked at least two years older than his master. The same servant also performed a magnificent mime of a drunken pawnbroker lifting a grandfather clock over a country stile.

★ ★ ★ ★ ★

CUT TO – The England of **Rupert's** *youth, as described below.*

VOICE: But now it was 1943 and I was seated at the Knickerbocker, awaiting with my usual impatience the arrival of my friends. That night, I was sailing for England. If I was longing to go home, it was not so much to Blitz-scarred London as to an England of my youth, with a countryside of old trees and coaching roads, low stone bridges and lazy streams with banks of sedge wandering through willow-studded meadows…

REFERENCES:

Noel Coward verse:
Day, Barry (2011) *The Complete Verse of Noel Coward* – Methuen, UK

The Praties:
Sharpe, Caroline (1969) *Come Listen* – Ginn & Co. Ltd. UK

Lightning Source UK Ltd.
Milton Keynes UK
UKOW04f1301150514

231733UK00001B/15/P